THE PROMOTION OF SOCIAL AWARENESS

THE PROMOTION OF SOCIAL AWARENESS

Powerful Lessons from the Partnership of Developmental Theory and Classroom Practice

Robert L. Selman

Russell Sage Foundation • New York

The Russell Sage Foundation

The Russell Sage Foundation, one of the oldest of America's general purpose foundations, was established in 1907 by Mrs. Margaret Olivia Sage for "the improvement of social and living conditions in the United States." The Foundation seeks to fulfill this mandate by fostering the development and dissemination of knowledge about the country's political, social, and economic problems. While the Foundation endeavors to assure the accuracy and objectivity of each book it publishes, the conclusions and interpretations in Russell Sage Foundation publications are those of the authors and not of the Foundation, its Trustees, or its staff. Publication by Russell Sage, therefore, does not imply Foundation endorsement.

Library of Congress Cataloging-in-Publication Data

Selman, Robert L.
The promotion of social awareness : powerful lessons from the partnership of developmental theory and classroom practice / Robert L. Selman.
p. cm.
Includes bibliographical references and index.
ISBN-13: 978-0-87154-757-6 (cloth) ISBN-13: 978-0-87154-756-9 (paper)
ISBN-10: 0-87154-757-0 (cloth) ISBN-10: 0-87154-756-2 (paper)
1. Educational sociology. 2. Socialization. 3. Social skills—Study and teaching—United States. 4. Interpersonal relations—Study and teaching—United States. I. Title.

LC192.4 .S42 2003
306.43—dc21

2002036742

The paper used in this publication meets the minimum requirements of American National Standard for Information Sciences—Permanence of Paper for Printed Library Materials. ANSI Z39.48-1992.

Text design by Suzanne Nichols

RUSSELL SAGE FOUNDATION
112 East 64th Street, New York, New York 10021
10 9 8 7 6 5 4 3 2 1

Contents

About the Authors

Robert L. Selman is the Roy E. Larsen Professor of Education and Human Development at the Harvard Graduate School of Education and professor of psychology in the Department of Psychiatry at the Harvard Medical School.

Sigrun Adalbjarnardottir is professor of education in the Department of Social Sciences at the University of Iceland.

Carolina Buitrago is a staff member of the Early Learning Services at the Massachusetts State Department of Education.

Amy J. Dray is a doctoral candidate in the Human Development and Psychology Area at the Harvard Graduate School of Education.

Preface

EACH SEPTEMBER for the past decade, I have said a few words at the orientation meeting for the fifty or so incoming students who will take part in the one-year Risk and Prevention Program at the Harvard Graduate School of Education. They have come from all over the country—and beyond—to a university that is heavily oriented toward research. However, they have chosen a program focused on practice with and service to children and adolescents who face adversities that put their health and welfare, not to mention their education, at risk. The aim of the Risk and Prevention program is to discover, refine, and teach ways of helping children, especially those living in low-income communities, to develop resilience in coping with the societal and personal adversities they face even as they strive for academic success in school.

To explain my connection to the program, I talk about the events that led me to make a transition from my initial interest in the practice of psychological treatment with individual children into theory and research in developmental psychology, and then back into a very different kind of practice from what I had envisioned as a graduate student:

> What seems like not so many years ago, I was sitting in your place. At the time, I had no thoughts about becoming a researcher, let alone a theorist, which seemed like an imposing job to have in life. I started out to be a clinician, a psychotherapist. I wanted to help people, mainly children, get along in life, one person at a time. I wanted to listen to people and ask them questions about their problems—to help them solve those problems, not to profess my own ideas. Many of you may feel as I did then, that your primary mission is to provide service, to children, their families, or the institutions in which they grow up. You may be skeptical about too much theorizing. But as you do your training you may find that for you to achieve these goals you need to under-

> stand, if not embrace, one or more theoretical frameworks. You may learn, as I did, that one needs a theory to listen to people, or maybe more than one theory.

I go on to give some examples of how theory and practice relate to one another in the risk and prevention work they will do. For instance, I tell them about Kesia Constantine (whom we meet in chapter 4). Through her practice with two boys, Kesia, a student in the Risk and Prevention Program, helped us to better understand theoretically the way they, and other children like them, construct their social reality. I emphasize to this group of students that whether one ends up doing practice or theory or research in the area of psychosocial prevention and development, one cannot work alone. The very essence of work in the prevention of poor life outcomes and the promotion of healthy ways to relate to adults and peers is forming, by necessity, a partnership with others dedicated to this task. No one discipline or profession alone can provide the solution. To emphasize the partnerships between theory and practice, I describe for entering students some of the collaborations and partnerships I have been involved in over the course of thirty years working in this field.

Similarly, throughout this book the work I describe has largely been undertaken in the form of partnerships, both institutional and individual. For much of the first two decades of our work, as described in the early chapters, the institutional theory-practice partnership was between the Judge Baker Children's Center and the Harvard Graduate School of Education. Our projects were done under the auspices of a loosely formed collaborative that I call the Group for the Study of Interpersonal Development (GSID). Although the work described here has moved from early studies of children's awareness of interpersonal issues, such as friendship, to studies of their awareness of intergroup and societal issues, such as conflict among factions and ethnic discrimination, nevertheless, much of what is new in this book builds on the GSID's work in an earlier era.

The "Active" Partners

Because our work has been collaborative, I would like to both identify and acknowledge the contributions of several people from the beginning. In the last decade, the major institutional practice partner to our theoretical work has been an organization with the unlikely name Voices of Love and Freedom, Inc. (VLF). Since its inception in 1992, VLF, led by my colleague Patrick Walker, has designed methods to promote social awareness in the heart of the academic curriculum of elementary grade schools. In chapter 5, I introduce Walker, who walked into my office in 1991 with a vision of promoting the ethic of social relationships to prevent violence and drug abuse in troubled communities, and who continues to work at designing a practice to transform that vision into an innovative reality in education.

The research team that has studied the promotion of social awareness in the context of this partnership deserves similar credit. Sarah Shmitt contributed a great deal to the historical and professional analysis of VLF and the observational work on the real lives of teachers in Boston classrooms in chapters 7 and 8. For many years before working with us, Sarah was a social activist working for organizations concerned with the prevention of social injustice and discrimination. Early on in the history of our research-practice partnership, she had been part of the VLF design and implementation team, but she somewhat reluctantly switched to the research side of the partnership when we received a grant from the Carnegie Corporation of New York to study the promotion of social awareness. (It is not always easy to give up the passion of advocacy or the immediacy of practice to take the "neutral" role of an observer.) With her exceptionally good eye for the culture of classrooms and the development of children, Sarah managed our field research in the four Boston public schools and often served as the major communication link between VLF practice and GSID research—not always an easy task.

Cynthia McKeown spent a great deal of time videotaping the classroom of a fifth-grade teacher, Angela Burgos, whom we first meet briefly in chapter 7, and whom we will get to know at greater length in parts IV and V. Cindy is a professional videographer and documentary filmmaker with a strong interest in educational reform and innovation. Cindy also has a long history of activism and advocacy for the disadvantaged; before going to film school, she was a community organizer in Boston. Blessed, like Sarah, with a commitment to social justice, her values resonated with those of VLF. Cindy's documentation of Angela Burgos's teaching provided us with the data we analyze in part IV. Of course, Angela costars in those chapters along with the students in her bilingual education class—especially four of those students, whom we call Marisol, Rosario, Luis, and Felipe.

Lynn Hickey Schultz is a developmental psychologist with whom I have worked for almost twenty years. In fact, Lynn was a major contributor to our conceptual analyses of social interactions among children during the 1980s. She and I wrote a book on that phase of the GSID's research, *Making a Friend in Youth* (1990). Chapter 3 is my attempt to provide a summary of that work that is necessarily brief, in order to move on to the next phase of our theory and practice building. I would refer the reader to that volume, however, since the brief summary here cannot give that work its due.

Our research team usually held research staff meetings on Wednesday afternoons, alternating each week between focusing on student data (chapters 11 through 15) or on teachers' reflections (chapters 8 through 10). Sigrun Adalbjarnardottir, a faculty member at the University of Iceland, is the coauthor of the latter three chapters. Sigrun was the primary initiator of this line of theoretical work in her long-distance partnership with our group; long before the rest of us had turned an empirical eye on teachers' professional development, this was one of her primary interests. As we refined our framework for understanding the professional awareness of teachers, she made regular trips between Reykjavík and Boston to provide advice and consultation.

The same year that Kesia Constantine graduated from Swarthmore College and came to the Risk and Prevention Program, Carolina Buitrago, from Colombia, South America, enrolled in the same program, believing that one place to begin the daunting effort to counter the culture of violence that threatens to engulf her homeland is in its elementary schools. She came to us in hopes of learning all she could about the best educational and prevention practices, determining which of these might be transported back home, and being trained in helping teachers there learn to use them.

Carolina accepted an invitation to work with our research group by helping us pursue the line of analysis on teacher professional awareness that we had begun in Iceland and would be continuing in Boston with our two-year VLF research project funded by the Carnegie Corporation. As this effort got under way, Carolina scoured the transcripts of our tape-recorded interviews with teachers in Boston and chose excerpts for us to consider every other Wednesday. More important, she pushed us to sharpen our thinking about the parallels between our framework for analyzing the reflections of teachers and the framework we had constructed for understanding what children's reflections tell us about their social development.

The last member of our team on the theoretical side of the initiative, Amy Dray, is a doctoral student in human development and psychology. She joined our group in 1998 as a Risk and Prevention Program student and subsequently enrolled in the doctoral program. For the last several years Amy and I have worked together to integrate our work on social awareness, empirically, theoretically, and practically, with language development and literacy. Our ongoing work together is described in the two coauthored chapters of part V.

Obviously, the teachers and students whose voices and actions animate many of the chapters of this book are, in their own way, partners as well. They gave us permission to discuss them in this book, but nevertheless, to protect their right to privacy I have provided them with aliases—all except Angela Burgos, who plays a central role in the lessons we learn about the promotion of social awareness.

Three "Not So Silent" Partners

I also want to say a bit more about other long-standing colleagues of the GSID who contributed a great deal to the collaborative effort that led to this book's publication but were not directly involved in the projects described here. Mira Z. Levitt played a significant role in the construction of the theoretical and empirical aspects of the Risk and Relationship Framework that guides our work (see chapter 4). Mira and I did essential work together on conceptualizing the developmental aspects of the construct of "personal meaning awareness." Together we shaped the risk and relationship model as it stands today. I also want to acknowledge the work of Caroline L. Watts. Her conceptual and practical (service delivery) work on the Pyramid of Prevention also described in chapter 4 was invaluable. Caroline is a former student (from the late 1980s and early 1990s) who has become a colleague of mine at Harvard and at the Department of Psychiatry at the Boston Children's Hospital, two of the institutions that have supported our research over the decades. Another important partner in our work on social awareness has been Dennis Barr. Also a former student, Dennis is now on the staff of Facing History and Ourselves, an organization that for more than twenty-five years has engaged teachers and students of diverse backgrounds in an examination of racism, prejudice, and anti-Semitism in order to promote the development of a more humane and informed citizenry. His work on ostracism and exclusion at the middle-school level has influenced the direction we have taken in this book, and we hope to share that work with readers in the near future.

"A Little Help from My Friends": Further Acknowledgments

The William T. Grant Foundation supported our (still ongoing) research on methods to assess children's social competence when we were doing the work reported here. Betty Hamburg was president of the Grant Foundation at the time; she has supported our work for years. Roger Weissberg, William Cross, and Larry Aber have been valued scientific advisers to our initiative, beginning in the early days when the Carnegie Corporation of New York first funded our study.

Catherine Snow, my colleague at the Harvard Graduate School of Education, provided important suggestions for chapters 14 and 15 and generally acted as a guide for Amy Dray and me as we explored the data we had gathered in the land of literacy. William Beardslee, my colleague at the Harvard Medical School, has been a close personal friend as well as a valuable coworker for the past twenty years. As the chief of psychiatry at Boston's Children's Hospital, Bill has acquired vast experience in research and practice that serve to prevent disorder and despair in children and their families, and I have learned an enormous amount from him about prevention and advocacy.

I also want to express my appreciation to the Judge Baker Children's Center (JBCC), a venerable institution affiliated with the Harvard Medical School. Since 1917, the JBCC has brought together scholarship and service and provided both educational and health services to countless children. The Judge Baker also provided VLF with a home during its early years. I also wish to thank Harvard Graduate School of Education deans Patricia Graham and Jerry Murphy for their support and encouragement, not only of my own scholarship but of the Risk and Prevention Program they helped to nurture. Interim deans John Willett and Judith Singer also supported the completion of this work in significant ways.

Financial support for the work has come from a number of sources. The Carnegie Corporation of New York, when David Hamburg was its president and Michael Levine a senior program officer, gave us the primary funds to analyze the work of the last ten years. The William T. Grant Foundation provided funds to me and to Colette Daiute, who teaches at the Graduate Center of the City University of New York, to continue our respective projects, both focused on culture, literacy, and social development. In addition, the Robert Wood Johnson Foundation and the Spencer Foundation provided support for us, and RWJ also provided direct support to VLF, helping the organization carry out its implementation plan from 1994 to 2000. Many local Boston foundations contributed funds as well. In addition, I was fortunate to twice receive Fulbright Fellowships in the past decade to continue collaborative work with Sigrun Adalbjarnardottir in Iceland. The Harvard Children's Initiative, under the direction of Judith Palfrey, provided support for the final preparation of this manuscript.

The Russell Sage Foundation, ably led by its president, Eric Wanner, is an organization sui generis. Located in the heart of Manhattan, it is one of the most intense, fast-paced, and energetic places on earth, but it provides an oasis of serenity and intellectual stimulation for scholars. My year there, beginning in the fall of 1999, gave me the time and space to begin this book. When I returned to Cambridge, Chris Kochansky, a friend and a superb editor, provided strong and supportive editorial assistance for a year as I completed the first draft. The revised and final draft also benefited from the contributions of graduate students in my classes, with whom I shared my evolving thinking about our ten years of work. It also benefited from the wise judgments of Suzanne Nichols, director of publications at Russell Sage Foundation, the great care and clarification of Cindy Buck, my editor, and the superb attention to detail of Emily Chang, Russell Sage production editor. Anne, my wife, is always helping in ways that are hard to put into words but easy to understand.

Chapter 1

Introduction

SOCIAL interactions—from the intimate and personal to the public and political—are central to the experience of being human. Our development as social beings begins within the family, when we are infants, then continues in ever-wider arenas as we grow through childhood and adolescence into adulthood.

Literature and memory testify to the fact that especially during the school-age years from early childhood through adolescence, our hearts and minds are occupied by our first encounters with fundamental questions about our relationships with other people: What is fair? What is not? How are you and I different? How are we the same? What can I expect from my peers, or from those who are less powerful or more powerful than I am? What rules can I count on to govern human interactions? How should I act when they seem to conflict? And what are the consequences when accepted norms of behavior are violated?

Even as children go to school to learn to read and write and to study the basics of mathematics, science, history, and geography, these social issues preoccupy them. Questions of how to manage matters of trust and loyalty, rivalry and conflict, belonging and exclusion, secrets and lies, concern most children deeply during this period of their lives. Whatever is mandated by the official curriculum of a given school or district, these perennial human questions—what we call, in the parlance of our field, "fundamental relationship issues"—cut across all attempts at teaching and learning and affect students of all kinds of backgrounds and academic abilities. This preoccupation with relationships is both normal and inevitable, since these are crucial years for social development. These are the years not only for learning specific social skills and strategies but also for the growth of our capacities for social understanding and empathy.

I belong to a group of practitioners and researchers concerned with the promotion of social competence and the prevention of the problems associated with impaired social development—primarily in children and youth but also in adults. We believe that these objectives are important not only in the lives of individuals but also in our society's ability to provide—or failure to provide—for the good of all its members. In particular, we are interested in research and practice that help build social competence in children and youth who are growing up under difficult life circumstances—that is, those who face psychopathology in their families, poverty in their neighborhoods, or prejudice in the wider culture in which they must make their way.

This book summarizes the results of thirty years of theoretical work on the social development of children in the elementary and middle school years, focusing on what I now call the coordination of social perspectives—how children come to identify their own needs, wants, and feelings, understand those of others, and act to manage differences and conflicts, as well as closeness, within relationships. It is also a detailed case study of a long partnership between academia and the world outside the walls of the university. It is a story of how research and theory in the psychology of social development helped launch a series of practices—methods and programs for working to promote the social competence of children and adolescents—and then how the implementation of those practices provided a real-world "laboratory" for the ongoing evolution of the theory.

A Short Personal History

I began my professional training in the 1960s as a graduate student in the doctoral program in applied psychology at Boston University, which at the time placed a strong emphasis on the education and training of psychologists as professional practitioners and had a predominantly psychoanalytic orientation. The first group of individuals I was assigned to work with through the BU program were very disturbed adult male patients at a Veterans Administration psychiatric hospital in Brockton, Massachusetts. Most of the people I was trying to "listen to" were blatantly psychotic and heavily drenched in Thorazine. They could hardly say anything coherent that could be understood within a psychoanalytic theoretical framework. That was in 1965.

The next year I was sent by my professors to counsel male inmates incarcerated at the state's maximum-security prison in Walpole, Massachusetts, now officially known as MCI (Massachusetts Correctional Institution)–Cedar Junction. These men looked very different from the inpatients I had seen in Brockton. For the most part, they were tough and physically fit, and some seemed smart and perceptive about both the institution they resided in and the society from which they had been locked away. I remember several who read the newspaper editorials daily, and many had interesting things to say about the sociology of their lives in and out of prison, as well as complex theories about the psychology of their fellow inmates.

What most of these individuals seemed unable to perceive, or at least to talk about, was the effect of their own behavior on other people, even those with whom they had close relationships—family members, girlfriends, wives. It was not that they could not understand another person's situation, but rather that they seemed to lack the capacity to take another person's perspective, in particular on themselves, and especially when such a perspective might prevent them from getting what they thought they wanted. Puzzled and troubled, I went to my clinical professors with my observations and concerns about the futility of my efforts at counseling these individuals. I asked them how my clients at MCI–Cedar Junction got to be the way they were. If you want to know how these guys ended up this way, the professors said, why don't you do some clinical work with children who seem to be heading in that direction?

The following year I worked at the Cambridge Child Guidance Center with troubled children, many of whom were poor and lived in public housing in the city of Cambridge, Massachusetts. There I met kids like Ralph O'Malley, a seven-year-old fire-setter living with his overweight and depressed single mother in a public housing project. Ralph liked to torture (I think "torture" would be the right word) bugs and small animals. I started to ask kids like Ralph not only how they themselves were feeling about things, but also how they thought other people in their lives—people they seemed to need or care about—felt about their behavior in relation to a given event or situation. Like the Cedar Junction inmates, these "troubled" children seemed to have difficulty considering the point of view of other people. Did that difficulty stem from a "natural" immaturity in their social understanding at ages six and seven, or was it a sign that something was lacking in their emotional development? How did their social awareness compare with that of other children their age?

In 1968 Lawrence Kohlberg, a developmental psychologist and researcher at the University of Chicago, visited Harvard for a year. Kohlberg's emerging ideas about what he called stages of moral judgment were attracting a lot of attention. My thesis adviser at Boston University, Freda Rebelsky, suggested that I enroll in an interuniversity seminar that Kohlberg was hosting for a small group of professors and graduate students from Tufts, Clark, BU, and Harvard; in monthly meetings we would consider the latest concepts and research in the field.[1] This seminar gave all of us who participated a new model for social relationships and a new framework for understanding social, moral, and ethical issues from a developmental point of view. It gave me the opportunity to have Kohlberg serve as a reader on my dissertation and also to sponsor my application for a postdoctoral research-training fellowship from the National Institute of Mental Health (NIMH) after I received my Ph.D. NIMH approved my application, and thus I began both my formal training as a researcher of developmental psychology and, although I did not know it at the time, my career as a theorist.

Linking Theory and Practice

My colleagues and I have found that the attempt to link theory and research directly involves putting what we have learned about social development into practice, examining the results, refining the theory, then adjusting the practice. It is this circular research-based practice/ practice-based research enterprise that I describe and advocate in the chapters to follow.

The history of our original theoretical framework, and the research undertaken to test it, begins at the end of the 1960s and covers more than three decades. In each decade our basic theory—I call its present incarnation the Risk and Relationship Framework—was transformed by its interaction with the world of practice in various public schools in the greater Boston area and in a school for children with severe social and emotional problems that I directed from 1975 to 1990 at the Judge Baker Children's Center.[2] In recounting this history, I focus especially on the work of the decade of the 1990s, when our practice-based research group returned to the public schools to explore and address new questions that had emerged from the theory-practice partnership. These questions have special relevance for urban education: How do children develop an ethic of social relationship? How do they put into action their evolving awareness of proper, decent, respectful ways to get along with other people? How do they do this when they are growing up amid social and economic adversity, or when they are treated badly, whether directly by parents or peers or indirectly or incidentally by society at large? How can we help?

In this book, I speak of an "ethic of social relationship" as a general term signifying the nature of the issues we are studying. We want to increase our understanding not only of how children develop this ethic but of what an ethic of social relationship really is. This brings us inevitably into the tricky territory of the promotion of "values." Certain terms are often clustered together—values, character, ethical awareness, moral development, social competence, risky behavior—yet their meanings are somewhat different.

It has always been acknowledged that education involves what has long been called, even to this day, the development of character—that is, the instilling of moral and cultural values in an individual. (Some of us are old enough to remember grammar school report cards with "Deportment" as one of the categories for evaluating our performance in school.) In terms of our theory-practice work, the world of school is not only an important place to promote social awareness and social competence but also a convenient place in which to observe children's growing social awareness and its relationship to their actual social actions.

I report here what we have found in our research and offer suggestions about the implications of these findings for how to help children—and by logical extension, all of us—get along with peers and neighbors. Because children and adolescents spend so much time in the environment of school—which may be primarily designed to promote academic success but is saturated with social interactions—our recommendations about methods and programs will come under close scrutiny by parents, educators, and concerned citizens. This is as it should be. I believe our research is sound, and in this book I address questions of values directly and openly—as I believe researchers or designers of social or educational programs should do.

Many social scientists believe that terms like "affective education," "building self-esteem," and similar popular phrases describe aspects of learning that are too fuzzy to measure or evaluate clearly. To a degree I agree. Yet just as there is an art to getting along with others, I believe there is a science to its analysis. Getting along with others involves concrete and measurable social skills and actions; not only can these be measured and taught, but adults with a wide range of philosophical orientations, political dispositions, and cultural backgrounds and experiences can agree on their importance to social relationships. I believe that there can be a developmental science for the assessment as well as the study of the ethics of children's social relationships. This science can thrive and give rise to initiatives that will make a real contribution to our society, especially in institutional settings designed for the education of our children.

My further goal is to document the value and promote the development of partnerships between research and practice organizations. Often practitioner groups—mental health workers, educators, the makers of social policy—look to researchers for help in two areas: on the front end they look to the implications of research findings for the design of their interventions, and on the back end they look to researchers to help them evaluate programs as they are implemented. Researchers themselves are often eager to try out their ideas in practice, but they do not always seek to revise or expand their ideas through careful observation and evaluation of the results. As practice-based researchers, we do.

By practice-based research I mean that we base our investigations into the nature of the development of children's social understanding in practices designed to promote the very social competence we are studying. Specifically, we are interested in how children growing up come to comprehend, manage, and make personal meaning of certain fundamental social issues and problems we all face in life in one form or another: problems with peers and friends as well as problems with those who may not be our friends, sometimes for reasons that have little or nothing to do with us.

The "we" to whom I refer stands for a group of researchers who share a common, although not identical, way of understanding social development. As I mentioned in the preface, we have given ourselves a name, the Group for the Study of Interpersonal Development, and consider ourselves a collaborative. Besides our understanding of children's social development we also share a set of ideas called the Risk and Relationship Framework. Our intellectual aim is to continue to develop and evaluate this framework and to explore its practical applications. We have functioned for almost thirty years through grants to our members and through our affiliation with a major university. When we receive funds, the university administers the projects. Like many such entities that exist in university settings, our group recruits new members from the ranks of graduate students who come to the university.

What I think has been somewhat unique about our collaborative is that over the past three decades we have entered into partnerships with individuals and institutions interested in the design and implementation of innovative practices, not only to promote social development in the world outside academia but to refine our theoretical framework. Especially in our field, the road connecting theory and practice can be full of potholes. In this book, we acknowledge the difficulties that such partnerships encounter, but by sharing the history of one such endeavor in particular we hope to help widen and smooth that road. As practitioners, that is, as applied developmental psychologists, we want to help young people develop their capacity to relate well with others; as researchers, we want to understand the barriers that hinder that development as well as the experiences that promote it.[3]

Perspective Coordination and Social Competence

I realize that across the globe—or within any city or town in the United States for that matter—people hold many different beliefs about what constitutes proper behavior toward others and how to teach it to kids. The rules and regulations of social relationship are enormously complex, varied, and subtle. They vary from family to family, as well as between cultures. Some believe, for instance, that children should be raised from an early age to anticipate the needs of others; others think it vital to encourage kids to express themselves freely at all times and to assert their own point of view openly if not vociferously. These beliefs are not necessarily contradictory in theory, but they often are in practice. And the rules of appropriate social behavior and demeanor can differ within cultures as well as between them, varying along lines of age, gender, and class.

Yet despite all these diverse expectations of what constitutes appropriate or adaptive behavior, there are, I believe, some basic capacities that are central to the social functioning of individuals in any culture. I call these capacities "core social competencies" and see them as so deeply embedded in the structure of each individual's psyche that to some extent they are hidden from view. We have designed our research, and its methods of inquiry and study, to make these core social competencies more visible.

From the beginning, the common thread that has run through the work of the Group for the Study of Interpersonal Development has been the reciprocity between two core competencies that we believe each individual must develop in tandem—and in harmony with his or her culture—if he or she is to maintain healthy relationships with other people. The first is the capacity to be aware of one's own point of view, to know where it comes from, and to be able to express it or keep it private. The second is the capacity to take, and to keep in mind, the point of view of another person, group, or even society as a whole. Developing each of these competencies is easier said than done. Putting them to work together is even more challenging.

These abilities are no more highly developed in us at birth than the ability to walk. Rather, they are intertwined elements of social awareness that develop over time, and that is why a developmental framework is essential for understanding social competence and the conditions and experiences that foster or hinder its growth in children and adolescents.

The Anatomy of This Book

The first part of this book, "How Children Develop Their Awareness of Risks and Social Relationships: Lessons from Theory," reviews the evolution of the theoretical framework we constructed to help us study social perspective coordination and its role in the social development in children. Here I explain that framework and the research methods we used to test and refine it.

The second part, "Connecting Children's Literature and Social Awareness: Lessons from Practice," tells the story of our partnership with Voices of Love and Freedom (VLF), a program designed to help educators integrate the teaching of literacy and values—or, to put it in our terms, to promote a sound ethic of social relationships among children. In these chapters, we go into the classroom to take a close look at how students responded to VLF's innovative practice. I also discuss the key role of competence and commitment on the part of the teachers we observed, and I begin to address the question of the professional development of teachers.

This topic is further explored in the third part of the book, "Promoting and Analyzing Teachers' Understanding of Students' Social Awareness: Lessons from Iceland." My colleague Sigrun Adalbjarnardottir and I share the saga of how she imported our theoretical framework to her native Iceland as part of her design of a social competence program for use in that country's elementary schools. Very much in the tradition of our group, she soon found herself involved in the circular relation of research and practice—in this instance, in the institutionalization of a strong professional training program for elementary grade teachers, and then in research on teachers' reflections on their own pedagogical vision and professional challenges. The professional challenge of which we speak is in fact a shared challenge: How can practice and research work together to integrate social competence into the curriculum, be it through social studies and history, as in Iceland, or through literacy, as in Boston?

This research in turn connects to the case study on which we report in part IV, "Researching the Social and Ethical Awareness of Students: Lessons from a Fifth-Grade Classroom." Here we integrate our research on students and on teachers by focusing on a single teacher and her implementation of VLF in her fifth-grade classroom. Almost five years ago our research team spent much of the first twelve weeks of school in this classroom, observing a teacher we found to be a masterful instructor in the ethics of social relationships. Over a period of six weeks Angela Burgos used the text of an emotionally powerful and well-crafted chapter book for young readers, *Felita* by Nicholasa

Mohr (1979), and the pedagogy of VLF to promote social perspective coordination skills in her students along with their language and literacy skills. We videotaped the lessons, and in these chapters we share what she, and especially her students, have taught us about the development of social competence through both educational practice and developmental theory.

The last part of the book, "Deepening Social Awareness and Literacy Skills: Lessons from the Integration of Developmental Theory, Research, and Classroom Practice," begins with several questions that are new to us. What is the connection between literacy and social development? What do perspective coordination skills have to do with language skills—comprehending what we hear or read and communicating with others through writing or speaking? What are the standards by which we can judge the progress of students in these areas? Not surprisingly, Amy Dray and I argue in this part of the book that any such standards will have greater validity if they rest on an understanding of the interconnection between the academic and social competencies of children.[4] We also argue that the more opportunities students have to develop basic perspective coordination skills, the more likely they will be to enjoy academic as well as social success.

I use the last chapter to sum up some observations on practice, share some reflections about the possible uses of our ongoing theoretical and research work, and pose some possible directions for establishing scientific foundations of assessment of individuals' growth in social awareness and the evaluation of social competence and moral education programs.

Finally, I want to make it clear here, at the outset, that this is not a book that locates this reprise of our work within the full corpus of the scholarly research and theoretical advances in the field of social development that have occurred over the three decades. Nor is it a book that advocates or is designed to market a particular educational method or approach—although we hope that the research we discuss will be helpful to others in designing educational programs that fit the needs of their schools and districts, and the needs of the students and communities they serve. It is primarily a book about how educational practice transforms developmental theory—in this case, a theory of how to listen to and watch children's growing understanding of their social world, or more precisely, to listen to ourselves listening to children. This is a book about what we have found out about the social awareness of children by attempting to promote it, and about how psychological researchers and educational practitioners can form rewarding partnerships for exploring theoretical issues with real-world implications for children's lives.

Part I

How Children Develop Their Awareness of Risks and Social Relationships: Lessons from Theory

Chapter 2

Social Awareness: The Growth of Interpersonal Understanding

Holly, an athletic eight-year-old girl, is climbing a tree near her suburban house with a group of her friends when she falls from a low branch. Although she is not hurt, her father, just returning home from work, sees her fall and asks her to promise not to climb trees anymore, at least not in the foreseeable future.

Holly agrees to abide by her father's wishes. However, not long afterward, as she walks to a friend's house with some other neighborhood kids, she spots a very young and obviously distressed kitten precariously perched high in the branches of another tree. And this particular kitten, Holly knows, belongs to one of her best friends. None of the other kids with her is capable of climbing up into the tree to get the kitten down, and there is no other obvious way to rescue it. What should she do?

In 1971 the Group for the Study of Interpersonal Development invented Holly and her social and moral dilemma to study children's developing capacities to understand and consider others' social perspectives. Situations that force us to make complex decisions about conflicting principles and loyalties occur in all our lives. Should Holly try to save the kitten of one of her best friends? Or should she obey her father's request to refrain from taking the risk of climbing the tree, thereby leaving the kitten in danger and perhaps also risking damage to a friendship that is important to her? In the 1970s we asked many children, both boys and girls across a range of ages, what they thought would be the best or right thing for Holly to do—and just as important, why they thought so.

Holly emerged during a period when many theorists and researchers in the field of developmental psychology—myself included—were not primarily concerned with how being a girl, as compared with being a boy, might influence a child's reasoning about social relationships and risks. Nor were we much concerned that Holly was white rather than black or brown, or middle-class rather than poor or rich. At the time our field focused its scientific investigations on the discovery of the universal aspects of what was then called social cognitive development—the development of a child's understanding of the social world. Recently the focus has shifted to include comparative explorations of the viewpoints of children of particular or diverse backgrounds (Flavell and Miller 1998).

In the years to come, as our research group deepened and broadened its understanding of the social development of children, issues of particularity and diversity would become important areas of inquiry to be integrated into our theoretical framework and psychological practice. In 1971, during the initial forays of the Group for the Study of Interpersonal Development into this type of research, the questions were much simpler: Could we identify levels (or stages) in the development of social awareness in children? How does a child's level of understanding of different perspectives or points of view influence his or her actions in a given situation? To explore these questions, our research team presented Holly's dilemma to sample groups of children between the ages of six and sixteen and recorded their opinions about what Holly should do, as well as the reasoning behind their choices. Then we set about developing a system for sorting and organizing the data we had collected and a theoretical framework for understanding it.

Theoretical Foundations

During the late 1950s and early 1960s, the theories of the Swiss psychologist and philosopher Jean Piaget and his colleagues crossed the Atlantic Ocean to the United States.[1] Piaget was interested in the development of knowledge (epistemology) as much as he was in intelligence, but his formulations about the sequence of cognitive stages through which each individual progresses as he or she grows in knowledge of the world from infancy to adulthood were immediately recognized as relevant to researchers in all branches of psychology.[2] Among them was Lawrence Kohlberg, a developmental psychologist trained at the University of Chicago (Kohlberg 1964, 1968, 1971). For his dissertation, Kohlberg took an early work of Piaget's, the classic 1932 monograph *The Moral Judgment of the Child* (1965 [1932]), and, using evidence from his own research, built upon it to construct a six-stage theory of the developmental sequence of moral reasoning.[3] For the next thirty years Kohlberg worked to expand and refine this theoretical framework until his tragic and untimely death in 1987.

Kohlberg proposed that the six stages of moral development are universal in that individuals progress through each stage in sequence. However, he did not claim that the stages of moral development that he described are universal in terms of the highest level a given individual can attain—or maintain. He also suggested that the rates at which individuals progress through each stage vary from one individual to the next, in large part owing to what he called their role-taking opportunities. Kohlberg's theory was supported by an empirical method based primarily on interviews. The interviews probed for moral reasoning and action, often using hypothetical moral dilemmas to elicit responses from the individuals who participated in his studies.

Over a ten-year period, from the mid-1960s to the mid-1970s, Kohlberg's cognitive-developmental approach to moral development swept over both the indigenous (American) behaviorist and previously imported (from Vienna) psychoanalytic frameworks for understanding the psychology of moral behavior. On the one hand, Kohlberg's approach challenged the conventional wisdom of social learning theorists that moral behavior, like any other learned behavior, is largely contingent on situational conditions and reinforcements; on the other hand, it called into question the psychoanalytic notion that moral character is largely formed by the end of early childhood through the process of internalization that results from oedipal dynamics within the family.

Kohlberg's research demonstrated how moral judgment develops at least through early adulthood. Moral behavior, Kohlberg suggested, should be understood not only in terms of social cognitive development but also in combination with a given individual's capacity for moral reasoning. By the mid-1970s the proponents of Kohlberg's developmental approach had won some hard-fought intellectual battles and were well represented in the community of researchers who were studying child and adolescent development in academic departments of psychology and education throughout the country.[4]

By this time Kohlberg himself had begun to develop a set of guidelines for pedagogical practice. In fact, in 1969 he moved from the University of Chicago, where he had taught since 1961, to Harvard University, partly to test the practical implications of his theory for moral education. A very basic assumption behind this new work was the importance of perspective taking (Kohlberg called it "role taking") as a critical psychological or social-cognitive skill for the growth of moral reasoning. A second key assumption was that positive peer relationships are an essential environmental or social condition for this growth. And third, the shift in Kohlberg's research signaled by his move to Harvard was based on the notion that participation in institutions that may be "structured" at a higher stage than an individual's own stage is a basic determinant of moral development.[5] These three concepts—perspective taking, peer relationships, and the importance of context in the development of social and moral skills—were the threads that my colleagues and I, as graduate students, teachers, and professors, chose to follow from theory to research to practice—and back again—over the next thirty years.

The Evolution of Practice-Based Research

After completing my doctoral studies at Boston University in clinical, counseling, and community psychology in 1969, I began several years of postdoctoral research with Lawrence Kohlberg at the Laboratory of Human Development within the Center for Moral Education, which he had established at Harvard's Graduate School of Education. In 1972, as my postdoctoral training was coming to its end, Kohlberg introduced me to Julius Richmond, then the director of the Judge Baker Guidance Center in Boston.[6]

Richmond hired me as a half-time staff psychologist at the guidance center. My duties were the same as those of most junior staff clinicians—to provide psychological treatment for children, either in the Judge Baker's outpatient department or in the Manville School, its on-site day treatment school for children with social and emotional problems. It was not my earlier training as a clinician that motivated Richmond to hire me, however, but my more recent work with Kohlberg and others in child development research. He felt that the Judge Baker, with its close affiliation with both a prestigious medical school and a "cutting-edge" teaching hospital, ought to be doing more research on the problems of the children it served.[7] I was able to take the theoretical knowledge and research skills I had learned in my postdoctoral research training and put them to use in clinical practice working with troubled children.

The connection between moral development and the children at the Judge Baker might not be particularly obvious. On a theoretical level, consistent with Piagetian theory, Kohlberg, Richmond, and I all believed that children form their ways of thinking through social experiences, and that these experiences influence their thinking about concepts such as morality, justice, and fairness. Morality, in other words, has its roots in everyday social experiences and children's developing capacity to manage them.[8] Through over thirty years of research, I have come to argue that the cognitive capacity that directs this thinking, the roots of both moral and social development, is the coordination of social perspectives. (I outline the development of the theory in more detail in chapter 3; see Selman 1980; Selman and Schultz 1990.)

On a practical level, there is a second important connection to be made between moral (and social) development and my work at the Judge Baker. My mentorships with Lawrence Kohlberg and Julius Richmond launched the thirty-year partnership between academia and practice that is the focus of this book. As research and theory in the psychology of social development developed, my colleagues and I had the ongoing opportunity to promote the social competence of children through practice—including social programs, therapeutic practice, and curriculum development. As we implemented the practice, we also researched it, the results of which in turn refined the theory.

The Curriculum Project

For the next decade the practice-based research I was involved in focused on two kinds of endeavors. One might be described as clinical: an attempt to understand, and thereby perhaps help to modify, the interpersonal behavior of the troubled children we were seeing in individual therapy at venues like the Judge Baker. The other endeavor was educational: the promotion of the growth of children's social and moral reasoning through the use of "Kohlberg-type" social and moral dilemmas in elementary and middle-school classrooms. The opportunity for applied developmental work in clinical settings was obvious. After all, I was working in a child guidance clinic. But how did my colleagues and I find ourselves in public school classrooms? Again, we must step back a bit in time.

Back in 1970 (halfway through my postdoctoral fellowship), an educational publishing company had approached Kohlberg with a business proposition.[9] Guidance Associates' goal was to produce and market high-quality materials that teachers could use to discuss "values" as part of a social studies curriculum for the early elementary grades. The company had heard about Kohlberg's method of using moral dilemmas to study and promote the development of moral reasoning in adolescents and wondered whether we could construct some stories that would be appropriate for younger children. At the time Kohlberg's primary developmental interest was in the shift from middle adolescence to early adulthood, and he was preoccupied with the application of his theories to the raging moral crises of the day, especially the war in Vietnam. It fell to me to organize a team to pick up this job.[10]

In consultation with Kohlberg, we invented protagonists and situations, including Holly and her story. Then, with funding provided by this commercial endeavor and the cooperation of a group of elementary schools in some Boston suburbs, we set about field-testing our dilemmas—presented through audiovisual filmstrips that are now artifacts of antiquity—to see whether they would generate disagreement among children in the elementary grades as to what was the best thing for the protagonist to do. To climb or not to climb? That was one of the questions we asked first- through fifth-graders from a range of social class backgrounds. It was a tough choice for the children in our pilot sample.

Those of us who worked on this curriculum project believed that the more disagreement a story evoked among the students, and the greater the consternation (or "cognitive conflict") within each child, the better it would work as a social-moral dilemma, both for classroom discussion purposes and for our own research on the growth of children's social understanding.[11] But we also wanted the stories to be relatively simple, and the choices few. Therefore it was important that Holly be the best tree climber (even if she was a girl) in a neighborhood that (tall trees not withstanding) was safe for children playing outside.

We also wrote and produced a teacher-training filmstrip and put together a teacher's guide that described the connection between the developmental theory that we had used to generate the dilemmas and the pedagogical practice of running group discussions among peers to promote children's greater social awareness. Guidance Associates marketed its materials directly to schools and teachers for use in the social studies part of their programs. Individual teachers could lobby their principals to purchase these audiovisual materials, then share them with colleagues. We insisted that the teacher-training materials be part of the package. We also insisted that the curriculum be researched (see Selman and Lieberman 1975).

All the members of our team had a common interest in children's developing capacity to coordinate, that is, to consider and balance their own perspectives with those of other people. Now we had access to a prototype method for listening in on the social development of children as they were growing up, using narratives to ask them how they felt about and understood moral and social issues. Although in actual classroom practice children often complained about the fact that the story had no ending, "the Holly Dilemma" (very much in the tradition of Piaget's "methode clinique") usually provoked a lot of thought and discussion and was ideal for use in our research for just that reason.[12]

For our purposes, what the children who participated in our studies thought Holly should do—climb the tree or not—was less important than their reasons for thinking she should make one choice instead of the other. Back then we believed—class, gender, and cultural differences notwithstanding—that either choice was "reasonable" if it was based on what we understood to be "socially advanced reasoning." Even then not everyone agreed with us on this point. Fewer would now. Nevertheless, in our view, socially advanced reasoning meant first and foremost reasoning based on the capacity to identify the perspectives—including the feelings, needs, and rights—of all the parties involved in a given situation.

For example, a participant's response that "Holly knows her father would understand why she needed to break her promise just this once to save a close friend's kitten" suggested to us a higher level of social perspective taking than did a response that Holly should climb the tree "because she likes kittens so much" or "because kittens are so cute." That is, the first response demonstrates most clearly an awareness of more than one point of view.

For the same reason, the opinion that Holly should not climb the tree "because her father would not understand or think it important enough that she was helping her friend" was seen as more advanced developmentally than saying she should not climb the tree "because she promised" or because "she's allergic to kittens" without any further interpersonal or relational justification. Here too the first response demonstrates clearly the activity of considering another person's perspective in relation to one's own.

The field studies that our team did for the curriculum project taught us a great deal about using hypothetical dilemmas and the conversations they provoke to explore how children think about their relationships with other people. They also seemed to confirm the idea that children's capacities to understand the perspectives of others are central to the choices they make in social situations and that these capacities evolve over time.

Constructing a Theoretical Framework

How, then, could we incorporate our opportunity to do fundamental research on children's social development into the responsibilities and opportunities in the guidance clinic? The team's new task was to compare the growth of interpersonal understanding of children who by most standards would be considered well adjusted socially with that of children whom most of us would agree were "troubled" in their relationships with their peers. We drew our sample of "less well adjusted" children from the Manville School, the day treatment school within the Judge Baker. We then matched these children by age, gender, social class, and intellectual abilities with a group of kids from the Boston public schools.[13] In this first round of cross-sectional studies, we told Holly's story (and others like it) to children between the ages of six and sixteen, then asked them what Holly should do and why.[14]

In addition to these narratives, or "practice-based dilemmas," we used one-on-one interviews to assess the interpersonal understanding—especially the skill of social perspective taking—of children of different ages across our two main sample groups. Again, in assessing our data, we matched children for age, gender, social class, and intellectual abilities.

As we worked out a structure for making sense of our data, we focused on not only the choice of one course of action over another but the reasoning behind it. One important finding was that some children possess a capacity to coordinate perspectives that is not clearly expressed in their initial verbal responses to the dilemmas themselves.[15] For example, building on the possibility that if Holly did not climb the tree she might be letting her friend down, we asked: What makes someone a good friend? What things that happen might break up a friendship? What kinds of things are most important to friends? In answer to the first and last questions, some children mentioned "playing together"; others cited "not telling lies" or "keeping [a friend's] secrets"; still others (usually older kids) framed their thoughts about friendship across all three questions in terms of the word "trust." None of these responses seemed incorrect, but some of them seemed more mature or socially advanced than others.

Seldom does a five-year-old, for instance, explicitly and consciously define trust in a friendship based on the norm of reciprocity—that you should not let a good friend down because you would not want the friend to let you down. More typically, trust means simply doing what you promised, or doing what you were told to do, or not lying. However, this concern with reciprocity—keeping each other's secrets—is very often a preoccupation of a typical third-grader (if there is such a thing as a typical third-grader). By fifth grade, "keeping each other's secrets" not only replaces "not telling lies" as the fundamental basis for trust among friends, but it is framed in a mutuality pact that is even more important than the secrets and lies. For example, one can lie to a third party in order to keep a secret for a friend, so absolute honesty is no longer as highly

Table 2.1 Overview of Social Perspective Taking: A Developmental Analysis

Developmental Levels (Approximate Age of Emergence in Reflective Social Thought)	Levels of Social Perspective Taking Used to Analyze the Understanding of Interpersonal Issues
0: Preschool (ages three to five)	To understand my own perspective (first-person [egocentric] and physicalistic level)
1: Early elementary (ages six to seven)	To understand your perspective, distinct from mine (first-person and subjective level)
2: Upper elementary (ages eight to eleven)	To understand your view of my (subjective) perspective (second-person and reciprocal level)
3: Middle school (ages twelve to fourteen)	To understand her or his view of us (our perspective) (third-person and mutual level)
4: High school (ages fifteen to eighteen)	To understand my own perspective in the context of multiple perspectives (third-person and generalized other level)

Source: Author's compilation.

valued. Framed this way, "keeping secrets" rests on a reflective, reciprocal norm that we would contend requires, theoretically speaking, a second-person perspective capacity. Of course, our framework, we always kept in mind, was a lot cleaner and neater than the facts or data it attempted to organize or explain.

Based on what we had learned by comparing the responses to our social-moral dilemmas of kids identified as "troubled" with those of a sample of matched kids from the public schools, we began to construct a framework that depicted several stages or levels in children's social perspective taking. We grounded our description of these levels in the data we had collected using in-depth interviews with children about problems such as the one Holly faced and on the theoretical principles generated by Piaget and by Kohlberg's ongoing research. The resultant chart—table 2.1—looks somewhat skeletal and simplistic, but we labored long and hard to produce a scoring manual of over three hundred pages that included specific examples of the responses that represented each of the levels of perspective-taking ability as they emerged from our analysis of the data on interpersonal understanding. In the end, our framework had five levels, and it felt, taxonomically speaking, very detailed to us at the time.[16]

Let's go back to Holly's dilemma to see how this framework works.

Table 2.2 To Climb or Not to Climb: An Organization of the Reasons for Holly's Choice

(1) Holly should climb the tree because:	(2) Holly should *not* climb the tree because:
She is a good tree climber.	She is not strong enough to reach that high a branch.
She likes kittens.	She does not like kittens that much.
She does not want her friend to be sad.	She does not want her father to be angry with her.
She thinks her father will understand that she took a small risk to her own safety to help a friend and his kitten, which is very important.	She knows her friend will understand she cannot risk breaking a promise she just made to her father without asking him.

Source: Author's compilation.

Table 2.2 reports eight responses that children between the ages of six and twelve gave to the questions "What should Holly do and why?" The four responders in the left column thought Holly should take the risk to climb the tree and get the kitten down; the four on the right thought she should stay on the ground. Each of the eight respondents cited a primary reason for that choice—and it is those reasons that are relevant to our research.

Since the reasons for the choice were the most important part of our analysis, opposite choices could be considered to reflect the same level of perspective coordination. In table 2.2, we have paired opposite choices at the same level of social understanding, using the developmental framework described in table 2.1. For instance, basing the choice solely on whether or not Holly is a good tree climber (row 1) suggests a primarily egocentric level of social awareness, one that connects the reasons for an individual's social actions only to his or her physical competence. In row 2, liking or not liking kittens as a basis for Holly's decision rests on a first-person or subjective perspective: it reflects only the child's own likes or dislikes. Concern for a friend's sadness or a father's anger, as in row 3, requires taking a second-person or reciprocal perspective. Comparing responses across these first three levels of social awareness (vertically) is as illuminating as are comparisons within rows (horizontally). Our "developmental approach" uses the levels briefly described in table 2.1 as a way to interpret the differences in responses located in the various cells of the grid in table 2.2. In other words, we do not see the levels as fixed capacities, or stages that are stuck within a child's mind, but rather as theoretical tools to organize data—in this case, their reflections in response to an interviewer's questions (see Flavell and Miller 1998).[17]

The Challenges to a Developmental Approach

It is interesting to compare the two most sophisticated "competing" responses in table 2.2 with one another—as well as to the others. One response urges Holly to climb the tree because helping her friend (or saving a kitten's life) is a top priority. The competing response holds that a young daughter's respect for the wishes and concerns of her parents ought to be paramount. Comparing these two responses raises issues about differences among individuals in social thought (and action) that could be analyzed from theoretical linkages very distinct and different from the developmental ones we have designed.

For instance, a purely psychological explanation of the variation between the two responses at this level might interpret the differences in choice—to try or not try to save the kitten—as based on differences in the personalities of two interviewees.[18] The column 1 respondent may be a strong-willed individual who knows her own mind, acts promptly, and has reason to expect that others, her father included, will trust her judgment and good intentions. The column 2 respondent may be an obedient, rule-oriented, and perhaps temperamentally shy individual who does not want to risk the disapprobation, let alone the wrath, of a worried and anxious father.

Alternatively, the advent of cultural and feminist psychology, continued concerns about affirmative action and civil rights, and the early signs of a new great wave of immigration—this time from Asia and Latin America—have led scholars to explain variations in the social thought of individuals from the perspective of systematic group differences—that is, the differences between girls and boys as well as between people of different social classes, ethnicities, and other group identities. Viewed through this kind of framework, the column 2 voice in table 2.2 might be that, not of a shy individual, but of a youngster who comes from a culture that highly values strict family roles and rules and in which, for instance, a father's word is law. Our column 1 respondent might come from a culture that grants its youngsters a great deal of latitude in making decisions and negotiating risk, or perhaps this child is from a culture that places a high value on always being ready to help a friend in need.

Each of these frames (and there are others) provides a potentially useful understanding of patterns of reasoning that individuals might express in thinking about real or imagined social dilemmas. Even in the late 1970s we were aware of these complexities, but because we were convinced of the importance of the information that a developmental approach could provide, we put the complexities aside for the time being.[19] But we knew we eventually would have to get a better handle on how this framework could illuminate the origins of and influences on social awareness. We also knew that we had another important theoretical issue that our approach would need to handle more effectively if it was going to be of practical use.

Thought and Action: A Second Theoretical Challenge

Regardless of which of the two (or more) courses of action our young interviewees chose for Holly, we found in our interviews, not surprisingly, that children who expressed forms of interpersonal understanding that we classified as "low-level" or "undeveloped" usually reported having, or were observed to have, difficulties getting along with their peers. On the other hand, children with more "mature" perspective-taking skills, as compared to those of other kids their age, seemed to enjoy healthy peer relationships. (For a recent comprehensive review of research on the extensive influence of peer relationships on children's social development, see Rubin, Bukowski, and Parker 1998.) This was not always the case, however, and the exceptions were intriguing. Mostly, the exceptional cases came from our clinical sample.

As we continued and expanded this line of research over the next several years, we found that it was indeed safe to predict that children whose social relationships with peers were solid (as measured by a range of methods, including observers and peer nominations) invariably had age-appropriate or mature levels of the capacity to understand the perspectives of others, at least by our standards. They were not necessarily social butterflies, or even social leaders, but they had friends and they got along. Furthermore, it was a good bet that children whose levels of social reasoning were seriously low (or "regressed") for their age (according to our framework) were more likely to have difficulty in their relationships with other kids. Once again, neither of these first two findings was surprising, but they did validate our theoretical framework as it then stood.

However, we continued to find that there were some children whose knowledge of the social world seemed to be perfectly normal—that is, on schedule or even advanced for children their age in terms of our developmental scheme—but who were nevertheless socially reclusive, lonely, and isolated. In addition, other children who seemed to possess age-appropriate levels of interpersonal understanding had difficulties in their relationships with their peers because they were seen as bullies or acted impulsively and aggressively. It was not surprising that by and large the social functioning of the "clinic kids" from the Manville School was low-level much if not most of the time—otherwise they would not have been there. However, they did not necessarily seem low-level or immature in their social or interpersonal understanding. In fact, a few of the children who participated in our studies—invariably those in our clinic sample, who had the most difficulty in their social interactions, at least in the judgment of observers—had among the highest levels of social understanding for children their age.

To many researchers and practitioners, this gap between thought and action in social situations—between "talk and walk," as both the social activists and the corporate consultants put it—is commonplace. Some view it as an artifact or weakness of cognitive or cognitive-developmental approaches to social or moral research questions—as definitive evidence, that is, that when it comes to morality there is little connection between what people say or think and what they do. In effect, critics of a cognitive or developmental approach prioritize actual or observed behavior as the essence of what defines "social" behavior. They elevate the study of the "walk" and ignore the study of the "talk." I believe that it is a mistake to prioritize action over thought—or thought over action, for that matter. In fact, it is the connection—or the disconnection—between thought and action that needs to be better understood, both theoretically and practically. A developmental analysis, although not definitive, has much to contribute to the understanding of that connection, and even more to say about the gap.

Chapter 3

Intimacy and Autonomy: Social Strategies and Interpersonal Orientation

Kathy is ten years old and has been friends with Becky for a long, long time. In fact, Kathy considers Becky to be her closest friend, and she's agreed to go over to Becky's house on Saturday for the afternoon. But Jeanette, a new girl in town, has offered Kathy a "once in a blue moon" opportunity to see a show that Kathy has been longing to see—on that very same afternoon.

Kathy knows that Becky, who's a bit shy, is depending on her company. She wanted to go over to Becky's house, and she's afraid she'll hurt her best friend's feelings if she doesn't, but she really wants to see the show, and she's not sure what she should do or how she can explain her decision to either Becky or Jeanette.

—"Risky Incident No. 2" (synopsis)

FOR THE next decade, from roughly the early 1980s to the beginning of the 1990s, the Group for the Study of Interpersonal Development refocused and expanded its developmental research: we shifted from our original emphasis on social reasoning—what goes on inside individual children's heads—to the arena of social interactions and the behavioral choices of children. Although we were still interested in children's fundamental understanding of social relationships, especially friendship, we also wanted to better understand how children develop the repertoire of interpersonal skills they need to manage these relationships. Our earlier research had shown that the connection between social thought and social action is not a simple one. We realized that if we wanted to provide useful information to practitioners about how to facilitate healthy social development in children in either clinical or educational settings, we would have to know more about how interpersonal skills evolve in relation to interpersonal awareness.

In particular, we were interested in describing children's developing strategies for both staying close and negotiating conflict within relationships. "Risky Incident No. 2" is one of the new dilemmas we invented and presented to the kids who participated in the second phase of our research. In this scenario, Kathy faces both immediate action choices and long-term relationship issues, just as Holly did in our previous dilemma. In fact, Kathy's dilemma is more common than Holly's in the lives of children—and most of us of almost any age—and therefore it may seem more mundane. But with Kathy's story we deliberately took our inquiries a step further: not only does Kathy have to decide in her own mind what to do in this instance, but she must also communicate and negotiate with the other people involved. To put it another way, we turned our attention from asking *why* our protagonists should choose to go or not go (or to climb or not climb the tree, as in chapter 2) to asking *how* they resolve moral-social dilemmas in interactions with other people.

For instance, as adults, we know (have the interpersonal capacity to understand) that Jeanette could be an actual or perceived threat to the close, long-standing relationship between Kathy and Becky. As researchers, we asked not only when (at what age) do children begin to glimpse such a possibility, but also how, at different ages, they then propose to deal with it.

As children grow up and gain higher levels of social awareness, we asked, what strategies do they develop to manage problems such as the one facing Kathy and Becky? Once they are capable of understanding not only their own perspective but the perspectives of others, how do they develop the capacity to balance or coordinate them? For example, and to put it a bit more concretely, how does Kathy learn to balance issues of intimacy—caring about her relationship with Becky—with issues of autonomy, that is, caring about her own interests?[1]

From Perspective Taking to Perspective Coordination: A Modest but Meaningful Conceptual Shift

With the focus now on the relationship between Kathy and Becky (and even Jeanette), we could no longer think of Kathy's dilemma as hers alone. The shift between perspective taking and perspective coordination in our scheme is not just movement up a developmental scale. Theoretically speaking, it is a difference that roughly corresponds to a shift from a focus on the cognitive aspects of the social development of individuals (in the Holly era) to a focus on the social interaction processes at work in interpersonal relationships (exemplified by the tension in the friendship of Kathy and Becky). It is a move from how to understand oneself and others to how one actually relates to others.

We wanted to extend our developmental approach to the study of social interaction as well as social cognition, by looking at both perspective taking and the capacity to coordinate different perspectives at work in social relationships. Perspective taking and perspective coordination are not quite the same thing. For example, some individuals develop a high level of skill at taking the perspective of others—that is, they are able to understand how others look at a given social situation—while seldom if ever being able to integrate these perspectives emotionally with their own actions. Although they can use their knowledge of other people's feelings and points of view to pursue what they perceive to be their own self-interest, their manipulations, being ultimately one-sided, do not always pan out as expected. This was often the case with my clients at the Cedar Junction prison. Or they may simply put their own view aside and yield to the will of others, as was sometimes the case with some of the most withdrawn children in the Manville School.

Back in the 1940s the psychoanalyst Harry Stack Sullivan wrote about this phenomenon in developmental terms. Noting that pre- and early adolescence was a critical "watershed" for this crucial transformation in social development, he maintained that an individual of this age who could not (or would not) learn to move from the normal middle childhood orientation of cooperation with others for self-interest to collaboration for mutual interest (gaining an emotional sense of "we-ness") was heading for interpersonal difficulties. For us, perspective coordination constitutes the path—the means—by which an individual develops the capacity to make this transition from cooperation to collaboration, from thinking in terms of "I" to thinking in terms of "we."[2]

We began to study perspective coordination in two ways. On the one hand, we continued interviewing children about these matters; on the other hand, we began to make direct observations of children at play, both in the classroom and after school in small social groups—and especially in the context of a new treatment method we were using at the Manville School.

Pairing Children for Treatment of Social Relationship Problems

A major impetus and source of data for this next phase of our theoretical work came from a very intense practical context: the pair therapy form of treatment that we had developed for students at the Manville School to try to help these students raise their level of social understanding and close the gap between their understanding of social relationships and their ability to act maturely within them.[3]

Pair therapy involves regular meetings between two children, both of whom have a great deal of difficulty getting along with others, especially their peers. They never meet alone, but always with an adult who is trained in practical ways to help them learn how to have fun together and how to resolve conflicts. Usually the adults are also familiar with our theory and research. The two children who will be paired with one another are carefully matched, and activities are chosen that will not only promote cooperation but engender conflicts that need to be resolved. In most cases, the members of the pair must decide on their activities between themselves, thereby sowing the seeds of conflict and its resolution.

We usually match shy and withdrawn children with aggressive and impulsive ones. The purpose of pairing shy children with aggressive ones—who, in terms of our theoretical framework, have different interpersonal orientations—is to help each kind of child move from his or her position at one extreme of the interpersonal continuum toward the center. With the adult counselor's guidance, the children learn to develop and use strategies for negotiating and sharing experiences with their pair-mates—by learning to express themselves more effectively, jointly planning activities, and practicing compromise and give-and-take. In addition, however, the therapy's aim is not just to teach better social behavior but also to increase children's awareness and understanding of the actions and motivations of others as well as themselves—to be able to take another's perspective and coordinate it with their own, thus linking social thought and action.

Pair therapy was originally designed to treat children and adolescents who had already exhibited extreme difficulties in their social relationships with peers and severe impairment in their social skills. It is usually used in psychiatric day treatment and residential programs for youth with diagnosed psychiatric disorders. Often the course of treatment extends over a lengthy period of time—years rather than weeks or months.

Over the past twenty years, since the inception of this initiative by members of the GSID in the late 1970s, we have written extensively about our work to promote children's social development through the pairing process. (See, for example, Selman and Schultz 1990; Selman, Watts, and Schultz 1997; Selman et al. 1992). We believe it has proven to be an effective method of treatment in clinical or prevention practice. It has also given us an opportunity to observe many children in many social interactions over time, and thus a chance to redesign our theoretical framework.

Social Awareness, Intimacy, and Autonomy: The Story of Kathy and Becky

By the mid-1980s we were using videotapes of pair therapy sessions to help us refine our practice and our theory, and we often presented excerpts from these tapes at professional-academic conferences or in graduate-level courses to illustrate children's social strategies and levels of understanding as we saw them. Our focus had been on "troubled" children with social difficulties and helping them learn how to resolve them. But as we shared these tapes and our ideas, observers pointed out to us that there was a lot going on in these pairs besides conflict and its resolution: these sessions included laughter and gaiety, warmth and affection, caring and consideration.

Of course. It had been one of our assumptions in designing pair therapy that it is in the process of relationship building that social understanding is transformed. If we were going to construct a theory about the relation between social thought and action from a developmental point of view—that is, in terms of evolving levels of understanding and behavior—we needed to look at this aspect of relationship in a similar fashion. To do so we used both our pair therapy videotapes and our ongoing observations of children at play in public school after-school programs.

We chose the terms "relatedness" and "intimacy" to represent that aspect of our social experience that embodies our emotional connectedness with other people. This is a difficult subject to discuss scientifically—the continuing effort to do so that has been part of the work of psychologists of all persuasions from Freud's day to our "postmodern" era has given rise to many different vocabularies and conceptualizations. As "developmentalists" interested in the social interactions of children, we focused on observing "relatedness" in action and on its link to perspective coordination as a key element of social understanding.[4]

As a result of our research, we had come to see friendships such as Kathy and Becky's—and the long-term relationships that any of us

Table 3.1 Developmental Levels of Interpersonal Action Based on Social Perspective Coordination

Shared Experience: Relatedness Aspect	Social Perspective Coordination Levels	Interpersonal Negotiation Strategies: Autonomy Aspect
Unreflective imitation or enmeshment; lack of differentiation	Level 0: Undifferentiated, egocentric	Physical force: impulsive fight or flight or freeze
Unreflective sharing of expressive enthusiasm	Level 1: Differentiated, subjective	One-way, unilateral power: orders or obedience
Reflective sharing of similar perceptions and experiences	Level 2: Reciprocal, self-reflective	Cooperative exchange reciprocity: persuasion or deference
Empathic sharing of beliefs and values	Level 3: Mutual, third-person	Mutual compromise
Interdependent sharing of vulnerabilities and self-identities	Level 4: Intimate, in-depth, societal	Collaborative integration of relationship dynamics (commitment)

Source: Author's compilation.

might participate in at any time in our lives—as inevitably involving a balance between two poles or aspects of social interaction: intimacy and autonomy. During this next phase of our work, we labeled the interactions we observed as "shared experiences" if their function seemed to be to move toward intimacy—relatedness or closeness—between and among the children involved; we labeled them "interpersonal negotiations" if the child or children seemed to be moving toward implementing what we called autonomy—independence or self-assertion—within the dyad (the pair or the friendship) or the group.[5]

In keeping with our developmental focus, we constructed methods to code social interactions as either intimacy-oriented or autonomy-oriented, and we set about organizing our understanding of these interactions along the same lines we had followed in the first phase of our research. Table 3.1 shows how we integrated these new data into our framework. It describes the levels of interpersonal interaction that we observed in six- to sixteen-year-old children in everyday interactions or during the process of pair therapy, that we heard expressed in their discussions of their real-life problems, or that we gleaned from their reflections on the hypothetical dilemmas of protagonists like Kathy in their relationships with friends like Becky.[6]

Shared Experience

Our observations suggested that at its simplest level (level 0 in table 3.1), "shared experience" often appears to be transmitted from one actor to another through a process of contagion—that is, one person's impulsive motoric behavior "spreads" to another person in a direct way that involves little or no reflection or intention on the part of either. This kind of interaction-behavior emerges in infancy and persists in many forms throughout our lives. Think of two five-year-olds engaged in a burping contest, or one adult giving another "the giggles" in a situation that should be a serious one. We would understand this kind of interaction to represent the "unreflective" or "enmeshed-undifferentiated" level of relatedness or shared experience. We might say that at this level it is *impulses* that are shared. This level may be central to all our relationships, beginning when a baby smiles back at a smiling parent.[7] But it would be disconcerting if this were the only kind of shared experience we observed in children of Kathy and Becky's age.

The next level of this aspect of social experience, level 1, is also "unreflective" but involves an invitation from one person to another to join in an activity. This invitation may or may not be direct; in fact, it is often communicated through a kind of "expressive enthusiasm" or exuberance—and through the participation of the second person in that activity. Among younger children we often see this form of shared experience in fantasy or play situations. Power within the relationship is often a part of this kind of interaction. Sometimes one partner is always or usually dominant, and sometimes the two take turns at being in control. For example, when two kids play with dolls or action figures, one of them might always take the role of the parent supervising the son or daughter, or the hero directing the other as sidekick, or they might take turns with these roles. Among preteens and teenagers, one of a pair might take the lead in choosing the music they listen to or where they go to hang out, or the two might alternate. The key point is that, whether reflective or not, shared experience at this level is mostly about doing things together—that is, about *actions* as designated or chosen by one of the two members of the party.

Communication about similar feelings and "in-common" experiences marks level 2 social interactions, in which "relatedness" comes into play. However, although both members of the dyad may participate equally, at this level each is primarily concerned with his or her own personal satisfaction and not strongly or clearly invested in the meaning of the sharing by the other party. The parties in this kind of interaction are primarily concerned with expressing their own feelings and gaining the social support (or "consensual validation") that this kind of interaction can provide. An example would be Kathy and Becky talking about how hard it is to get an A in spelling, or adults commiserating about politics around the proverbial office watercooler.

At level 3, a more mutual form of shared experience, each participant regards the other as part of a jointly experienced "we." We have observed kids like Kathy and Becky talking together about their anxiety about going to middle school and their relief that the other will be there as a friend to count on.

At level 4, the "interdependent" and "collaborative" level, shared experience includes both a willingness to reveal one's intimate thoughts and vulnerabilities and a commitment not only to the other person but to the relationship itself.

Across all levels, our observations suggested that children's capacity for intimacy or relatedness is closely linked to their ability to identify *and coordinate* their own perspectives with those of others. This finding strengthened our belief that situations that foster shared experience also promote the growth of social understanding and development.

Interpersonal Negotiation

Our research also demonstrated that each step in the development of children's capacities for social perspective coordination seems to broaden their social understanding as well as their repertoire of strategies for interpersonal negotiation for the resolution of conflicts within relationships (see table 3.1).

Even in theory, this observation does not suggest that a perspective coordination level has to be firmly in place within a given individual before each parallel level of interpersonal understanding or negotiation can emerge. The interactions between the development of the core capacity of perspective coordination and the associated psychosocial competencies are reciprocal, a theoretical point we return to later. Moreover, in real life none of these aspects of experience are as separate from the others as we conceive them to be for the purposes of theoretical analysis and discussion. Still, our framework for understanding social perspective coordination provided us with a "deep structure" for thinking about how children develop social skills and strategies, and for investigating the relationship between social thought and social action.

As with interpersonal understanding, it is important for parents, clinicians, and educators to know what social skills children can reasonably be expected to have mastered at different ages. What kinds of responses will a kindergartner have available if he or she needs the scissors and a classmate is using them? Disturbed to see his buddies picking on a smaller or younger child, what strategies will a sixth-grader use if he makes an objection and they respond by saying that they are "just fooling around"? And what can a fifteen-year-old do when all her friends are trying to convince her to join in the group's experimentation with alcohol and she does not want to?

In our framework, successive levels of interpersonal skills, like those of interpersonal understanding, are characterized by differing capacities for appreciating the relationship between one's own perspective and that of another person. Unlike the knowledge base that underlies social awareness, however, interpersonal skills are competencies to be directly applied to social interactions, that is, to meeting the (sometimes) conflicting needs for intimacy and autonomy in a social context. With respect to interpersonal understanding, once a child discovers the complexities of a higher level of interpersonal awareness, he or she does not lose this awareness very easily. Consider, for example, the fact that past a certain age, not getting an invitation to a classmate's birthday party hurts most children not only because he or she does not get to eat cake (a level 1 first-person awareness) but also—and more saliently—because he or she feels excluded (a level 2 second-person awareness, one more grounded in social relationships).

Working the Theoretical Framework

Let's return to our original hypothetical dilemma and consider the range of interpersonal negotiation strategies that Kathy—and Becky—might use to deal with the situation that has arisen vis-à-vis Jeanette. Kathy wants to go to a show with Jeanette but has already made a date with Becky. What should she do?

Possible actions at the "impulsive" or least developed level of social strategies (level 0) would include Kathy simply accepting Jeanette's invitation without reflection, or Becky, in reaction, immediately and unreflectively breaking off her friendship with Kathy. Actions oriented only toward getting one's own immediately felt needs met can be characterized as similar to the fight-or-flight response (see the top entry in column 3 in table 3.1). The key element here is that in the moment the action is completely impulsive, thoughtless, or unreflective, even if at some other moment either or both of the girls would "know better."

We characterize the next, slightly more mature level of interpersonal negotiation strategy (level 1) as "one-way" or "unilateral." It involves two opposite yet complementary modes of social action: ordering and obeying. If Becky says, "Don't you ever do this to me again, Kathy," in an overpowering and ordering tone, or if Kathy says, with complete deference, "I'll never break a date with you again, Becky," both girls are employing a unilateral-level strategy. Regardless of which role an individual occupies in the negotiation, he or she is acknowledging the existence of the perspective of the other individual when using this type of social strategy but does not have the skills to deal with the other person's point of view in any way except unilaterally. Even though ordering and obeying are polar opposites in a sense, they are "structurally" at the same level because they have the same level of differentiation. Unilateral-level strategies are based on an awareness of differing intentions or needs between parties but do not involve methods or efforts to reconcile them.

Cooperative and persuasive strategies can first be spotted in an orientation toward taking turns ("You first, then me," or, "Me first, then you") or making trades. If Kathy were to say to Becky, "I'll go with Jeanette this Saturday, but next week I'll get my mom to take you and me to the movies," she would be using a cooperative or persuasive level of interpersonal negotiation. Although her suggestion may prove unrealistic, it demonstrates an intention to resolve the conflict without using unilateral strategies. It is inherent in the nature of the problem between Kathy and Becky that it cannot easily be dealt with using the strategies available at this level. In the end, either Kathy will not get to see the show or Becky will be disappointed. Turn taking cannot completely solve their particular problem.

Similarly, compromise strategies, the next level of interpersonal negotiation, will not yield a perfect solution in this case, although they can be of use to repair any damage done to the relationship between the two girls. Kathy and Becky's problem requires them to focus not only on this particular incident but also on how they are going to communicate with each other about conflicts of interest in the future. In fact, Kathy and Becky are at an age when they must begin to face the challenge of dilemmas in which friends must really collaborate—not simply compromising but working together to redefine how they relate to each other. Within the scope of the framework we are building, collaborative strategies represent the most mature level of interpersonal negotiation to which we have directed our attention.[8]

Our analysis of children's use of various interpersonal negotiation strategies—when scaled along the same developmental lines as those we used to evaluate levels of interpersonal understanding, and especially when observed in actual social interactions—reveals that their choice of one strategy over another is fluid and context-sensitive. Children seem, within the constraints of their highest-level capacity to coordinate perspectives, to move up and down the scale of negotiation strategy levels with relative frequency, if not always with ease or "appropriateness."

For example, children who have attained a reciprocal level of social understanding as a foundation for their concepts of friendship, and who are fully capable of reciprocal approaches to resolving conflicts, may nevertheless move to unilateral orders or threats when they think reciprocity has failed or is unnecessary. Kathy may know she should talk to Becky before deciding what to do about her invitation from Jeanette, but she may not do so. She may act unilaterally, either going off with Jeanette or accommodating to Becky. Either action would demonstrate the gap between Kathy's level of social thought (reciprocal) and level of social action (unilateral), and it is this gap—both a theoretical and a real phenomenon—that led our research into a new dimension.

Interpersonal Orientation: Another Meaningful Dimension

We realized that, within the limits and constraints of her competence in coordinating perspectives, the level of negotiation that Kathy might use with Becky also depends on the confluence of several other factors. These might include Becky's response when Kathy tells her about Jeanette's offer, Kathy's own beliefs about how friends should deal with each other, the advice she gets from her parents (if she were to ask for it), and her perception of the power to be distributed in the friendship. As we began to try to account for the variation in the levels of strategies we saw the same children using across different social contexts, incidents, and relationships, we revised some of our theoretical assumptions.

For example, we observed that the social relationships and interactions of the real children and adolescents in our practices and our research studies were interpretable along another important dimension besides the vertical developmental levels described in table 3.1. (See Selman 1984; for a description of early empirical work on the intersection of levels of negotiation and types of interpersonal orientation in the context of pair therapy, see Selman and Demorest 1984.)

We called this dimension the "interpersonal orientation" of an individual. By interpersonal orientation, we mean a person's tendency either to accommodate to another's wishes or to assert his or her own will. For example, across all age ranges, among the children in our interview studies a greater percentage of girls than boys were prone to suggest that Kathy stay with her earlier commitment to her "old friend." Furthermore, the strategies they offered often leaned toward accommodation at one level or another, whether they suggested that Kathy simply ignore her own desire to see the show or that she ask Becky whether it would be okay if she accepted Jeanette's invitation. Not all the girls took this stance, of course, nor did all the boys opt to leave the old friend in the lurch; clearly other factors besides gender were at play. The key point here is that, independent of the level of the strategies they chose, some children tended to give in to others more readily, while some seemed to be more concerned about serving their own interests first.

Looking back at our earlier framework—and in large part as a result of our pair therapy work at the Judge Baker and the Manville School—we found that at each of the vertical levels we used to classify negotiation strategies, we could also classify strategies reliably along a horizontal dimension. This dimension seemed to involve two types of interpersonal orientation: "self-transforming" and "other-transforming." We used the phrase "self-transforming" to imply some form of accommodation on the part of one party to another (of "the self" to "the other") and "other-transforming" to suggest one party's attempt to bend the will or action of the other party to his or her own (to "transform the other to accommodate the self"). For example, strategies at the impulsive level could be oriented toward either one of two poles: unreflective physical flight (or "frozen fright") or physical fight. Unilateral-level strategies could be oriented along a less extreme set of points on the interpersonal orientation dimension, from ordering to obedience. Reciprocal strategies ranged from accommodation, on the one side, to persuasion on the other, and so on.

At the more mature levels of interpersonal negotiation (or perspective coordination), strategies become both well differentiated and integrated.[9] The integration of the self-transforming and the other-transforming orientations is what we mean by collaboration: the individual pulls together the differentiated perceptions of self and other, blending both assertion and accommodation in his or her negotiations. This is why collaboration is so difficult to achieve and cannot truly be achieved alone.

Table 3.2 describes the relationship of interpersonal orientation to each level of interpersonal negotiation (the autonomy function within the social development model depicted in table 3.1). The structure and wording in table 3.2 reflect an intriguing theoretical and practical finding: with movement toward "higher" or more mature levels of

Table 3.2 Orientation of Interpersonal Strategy at Each Level of Social Perspective Coordination

Interpersonal Negotiation Strategies in the Other-Transforming Orientation	Social Perspective Coordination Competence	Interpersonal Negotiation Strategies in the Self-Transforming Orientation
Strategies that use unreflective, impulsive force to get self's goal ("fight")	Level 0: Undifferentiated, egocentric	Strategies that use unreflective, impulsive withdrawal or obedience to protect self ("fright")
Strategies that use willful one-way orders to control other for self's way	Level 1: Differentiated, subjective	Strategies that use "will-less" submission to comply to wishes of other
Strategies that consciously use psychological influence to change other's perspectives	Level 2: Reciprocal, self-reflective	Strategies that consciously use psychological compliance to accommodate self's wishes to other's
Strategies that advocate letting go of initial goals in order to achieve mutually acceptable goals	Level 3: Mutual, third-person	Strategies that agree to let go of initial goals in order to achieve mutually acceptable goals
	Level 4: Intimate, in-depth, societal	
Strategies that use both self and shared reflection to collaboratively transform (co-construct) both self's and other's goals in the creation of new projects with interdependent goals		

Source: Author's compilation.

negotiation, we believe, comes a natural and inevitable movement toward greater integration of self-transforming and other-transforming orientations.

We realize that this analysis looks complicated, and it may feel both abstract and somewhat academic, but in truth it is quite practical and can be very useful when listening to what children say and observing what they do.

Interpersonal orientation offers a good way to integrate our developmental analysis of a child's capacities for social awareness and repertoire of social skills (that is, his or her psychosocial competence) with a consideration of another behavioral dimension often associated with individual personality but at least partly determined, it would seem, by the dynamics of the particular relationship in question. To put it another way, in thinking about an individual's social behavior, interpersonal orientation fits comfortably as part of what we might call a biographical lens, meaning a lens that looks at variations from the perspective of "individual differences" in personality, or as enduring aspects of an individual's character. Some individuals are more prone to one orientation, somewhat independent of their developmental capacities or any cultural factors that might influence their way of relating to others in different roles.[10]

However, as with our developmental frameworks for understanding the growth of children's capacities for coordinating social perspectives and the acquisition of social skills, we are not claiming that individuals are ever fixed at one level or pole in their interpersonal orientation. We are simply trying to construct a way of describing the dynamics of social interaction using the theoretical tools we already have in hand. Levels of social understanding, repertoires of social skills and strategies to manage intimacy and autonomy, and interpersonal orientation do not work with total dependence on one another. But, as table 3.2 suggests, by the time an individual can function at the mutual and collaborative levels, he or she is capable of integrating self- and other-transforming actions into a relationship, especially if the other individual involved is also operating at that level (admittedly a big "if").

We realize that no social interaction (or relationship) can be reduced to two dimensions. Many other aspects of our individual lives—culture, temperament, and class, to name but a few to stand in for many—influence how we interact with one another. Yet we believe that our two theoretical axes can be very helpful in discussions about the social development, competence, and behavior of children for the very reason that they have been based on careful research and observation, and especially on our experiences with pair therapy, a specialized practice wherein social interaction is easily observed and social competence is put to the test.

Chapter 4

Risk, Relationship, and the Importance of Personal Meaning

Our early pedagogical applications of developmental theory in the classroom began in the early 1970s and were mostly implemented through adult-guided peer-group discussions of moral and social dilemmas like Holly's and Kathy's. These discussions and debates among students were thought to promote deeper levels of social and moral awareness than would have resulted from the children's superficial acquisition of facts or the adults' inculcation of specific cultural values and virtues. The hope was that this kind of learning might even serve as a part of a "new developmental social studies moment."[1]

In the 1970s, when the Group for the Study of Interpersonal Development first began writing dilemmas for filmstrips, the aspect of education that we were interested in was driven by middle-class problems and values. Teachers, administrators, and parents worried about issues such as cheating and stealing (more out of greed or impulsivity than deprivation), teenage sexuality, and excessive alcohol and drug use, but the sense was that these were manageable if not unavoidable problems of everyday life. Concern for the severe difficulties faced by poor urban schools and a sense of the obstacles that impeded their ability to do their job well had not yet traveled much beyond their own local districts and communities.

By the start of the 1980s, especially in the inner cities, increasing numbers of children—even very young children—were coming to our public schools so psychologically traumatized by the effects of poverty, divorce, and an epidemic of drugs and violence that they were finding it difficult to live, let alone learn. Meanwhile, as my colleagues and I continued to work within the Boston public schools and with troubled children in the clinical setting of the Judge Baker Guidance Center and the Manville School, our thinking was changing about the uses of our theory and the direction of our research. Previously, we had used the word "risk" in a purely psychological sense to refer to the uncertainty of outcome that children face as they make decisions about how to act within interpersonal relationships. But our experiences with real children led us to a new appreciation of "risk" as a public health and demographic term, as in the "risk factors" that make some populations of individuals prone to taking actions with very serious consequences—"negative life outcomes"—such as increasing incidence of suicide, peer violence on a deadly scale, incarceration, teen pregnancy, and drug habituation.[2] Actually, we began to use the term both ways.

It seemed that these youngsters, at earlier and earlier ages, were being confronted by risks much greater than climbing a tree to save a kitten or hurting an old and close friend's feelings by going off to a show with a new friend. Yet the problems that Holly and Kathy faced were still part of the day-to-day life of all children, rich or poor. Even in a difficult environment—perhaps *especially* in a difficult environment—the quality of our social relationships, in particular with relation to issues of trust, honesty, and loyalty, matters a great deal.

During the late 1980s and early 1990s school administrators and principals in poor, racially and ethnically diverse urban communities were struggling to educate children under very difficult conditions. The first wave of well-meaning psychologically oriented practitioners to offer assistance based their efforts on informational approaches that may work well enough in other settings, where the social fabric is less frayed and torn, but proved to be very weak medicine for the ailments from which many of the inner-city children were suffering. These kids did not need to be told that drugs are dangerous or that violence produces tragic results: they were well aware of these facts already, from their own personal experience or from that of people in their own neighborhoods. Understandably, it proved impossible to deal with the impact of community-level problems on children through a few short doses of "add-on" lessons. Such efforts were especially inadequate when the problems addressed were fighting and drug use and when the targeted children were the "at-risk" kids who manifested the most severe difficulties. (For a review of risk and prevention programs, see Dryfoos 1990.)

The lack of success of these informational approaches—even when spiced with scare tactics—led to a shift in strategies toward more psychologically oriented approaches to prevention. In addition to providing information about the negative effects of drugs or drinking, psychosocially oriented educators and prevention specialists turned to the promotion of social skills and self-esteem through programs such as peer mediation and life-skills training to ward off negative cultural and peer pressures and give children some help in coping with risk and conflict.

Many of these efforts have undoubtedly benefited children, families, and communities—and they continue to do so. In my opinion, these approaches have proven most successful in schools when they focus on training teachers and aides to help their students deal with peer conflicts on the spot in the classroom or on the playground rather than when they set up special classes or modules for teaching skills like conflict resolution or violence prevention. Yet this approach had little impact on a familiar problem faced by all of us who worked with children, especially those from communities where drugs and violence seemed to be "woven into the fabric of the culture": the difficulty of closing the gap between thought and action, between knowledge and behavior.[3]

Personal Meaning: A Bridge Between Thought and Action

Meanwhile, through the 1980s and into the 1990s, the GSID's attempts to understand the theoretical connections between social thought and action from a developmental point of view and our involvement in practical approaches to moral-social education were running on parallel but somewhat disconnected tracks. We also found that approaches designed either to raise children's levels of understanding of the risks inherent in certain behaviors or to close the gap between higher levels of knowledge and actual behavior in risky situations had been only modestly successful, and then mostly with children who did not carry a full bundle of risk factors. These approaches had been largely ineffective in helping children who lived in harsh environments beset by poverty, violence, or social disintegration.[4]

Our own practical experience with pair therapy in a clinical setting gave us access to the process of relationship building as it unfolds—that is, to children's feelings, thoughts, and actions in the moment. (For a review of pair therapy in clinical and educational prevention settings, see Selman, Watts, and Schultz 1997.) But it had been designed as part of a complete program of treatment for children whose psychological and emotional difficulties were already severe. It was obviously too labor-intensive—and therefore too expensive—to serve as a primary prevention strategy for children "at risk" in general. To address the problems teachers were facing in the public schools, we began to think about more effective ways of putting what we had learned about the anatomy of children's social development into practice on a wider scale.

Pair therapy had been used to treat children who were already exhibiting major social and psychological disorders, but we saw the need to intervene at an earlier point—to use pair therapy in prevention efforts rather than only as a treatment or a cure. Therefore, we shifted to counseling in pairs the public school students who showed signs of serious problems in getting along with their peers and were therefore the most "at risk" for the kind of impairment in their social development that might have long-term consequences. These were the students who also seemed most resistant to the knowledge- and skills-based public school approaches that had been in use for over a decade.

After designing pair counseling for children who seemed to be at risk for developing social problems but did not yet show severe diagnostic indicators of psychiatric disorders, we began to deliver it as a school-based service in public schools, usually for elementary and middle school students. The students are identified by teachers, parents, guidance counselors, or other school staff as angry, withdrawn, impulsive, and/or isolated. The course of the intervention is usually short, most often counted in weeks, but it could be extended over a whole school year. As with pair therapy, a third party—a trained counselor—is always present.

In our practice, pair counseling brings together two children who each have a history of social difficulties, but it is not a mediation effort; we do not pair children to resolve disputes between them. A counselor carefully matches two kids who have problems in relating to their peers with an eye toward how a sharing of their different perspectives might help each child expand his or her understanding of relationships. As in pair therapy, the two children negotiate together their own plans for the pair counseling sessions, including activities they will participate in together; the sessions are focused not just on talk but also on what happens within the relationship between the children.

As valuable as pair counseling might have been on a small scale—helping children two at a time—pair counseling alone was not going to solve national problems of drugs and violence. However, it did have a powerful effect on our theoretical formulations by moving our research out of the realm of clinical cases and into the realm of schools and their communities. As we began to use the pairing technique in new institutional and educational contexts, we recognized another element of the whole developmental picture, one that had been hiding in plain sight, in a sense, and seemed to reside in the problematic space between social thought and social behavior. A story of two students vividly illustrates this emerging element.

Callie and Clarisa: The Importance of Personal Meaning to Our Analysis

As part of our school-based practice, a pair of fifth-grade girls attending a Boston public school, Clarisa and Callie, met for eleven pair counseling sessions. During that relatively short period of time both girls described their ongoing experiences in a low-income neighborhood characterized by a significant degree of violence, including frequent physical fights between children.[5]

Clarisa gave us a theory of fighting that we had heard from many of her peers: one must fight to stay safe. We were struck by the fact that this strategy—which appears to be a paradox, or at least a contradiction—is based on a capacity for taking a second-person or reciprocal perspective. Clarisa was not acting impulsively—her actions were based on her understanding of others in her social world. This strategy is similar to the military strategy of deterrence, which assumes that a show of strength offers the best insurance against being attacked.

Despite whatever else she might have known or heard about fighting—that it is not the best way to deal with conflicts, that she might get hurt, that she might get into trouble with authority figures, that she might do harm to others—Clarisa nonetheless continued to behave according to this unilateral deterrence paradigm. She fought often. Indeed, she got outraged and angry and went "out to get" a different girl every week—a terrifying experience for the targets of her anger. In her own mind and in the minds of her peers, Clarisa had established an image of herself as a tough kid who had many tough friends to "back her up."

Callie, Clarisa's pair partner, also talked about her reasons for fighting, using a similarly self-reflective developmental level. However, over the course of their meetings together in pair counseling, Callie began to try to manage conflict differently. Rather than exercising unilateral displays of force, as she had done previously, Callie tried to negotiate reciprocally and cooperatively with Clarisa and other potential adversaries. She used her experience in pair counseling, for example, to deal with a dispute with another student from her class, a girl who wanted to fight her. Refusing to accept fighting as the only way to resolve the conflict, Callie solicited the support of her mother, and together they went to the girl's home to talk to her and her mother. Callie reported on the success of this strategy in her next session with Clarisa, to whom she had become close; she seemed to want Clarisa too to understand that there was an alternative to preemptive fighting. Clarisa listened attentively and even acknowledged that negotiation had worked for Callie, but she could not accept it as a viable option for herself. It was not as personally meaningful for Clarisa to use negotiation to resolve a conflict.

These two girls had a similar level of social understanding about fighting, and at the beginning of pair counseling they had advocated for social strategies at a similar level as well. Why, then, had they chosen to deal with this issue so differently by the end of their time together? For Clarisa, fighting represented standing up for oneself; it meant not allowing oneself to be pushed around or disrespected. She had siblings who belonged to gangs, and she was taught by her mother to "be tough." To be respected as a person by members of her own family and by the peer group she had chosen, she had to be strong, even an aggressor. It was of utmost importance to Clarisa not to be weak; she saw the weak as less likely to survive in her community.

By contrast, Callie's immediate neighborhood was a bit safer than Clarisa's, and her family supported nonviolent means of resolving conflict. Callie had developed the capacity to look beyond her own security, perhaps because in her experience it was safe to do so. In short, the two girls managed fighting differently because it had a different *personal meaning* for each of them.

This simple but powerful idea is a truism enshrined in proverbs from many cultures: "One man's meat is another man's poison." It has obvious relevance to individual psychology. At any given moment in time—or in any given place—the personal meaning that an individual makes of the risks involved in a social interaction, incident, or relationship provides an important key to understanding whether there will be a gap between the individual's level of interpersonal understanding and his or her level of actual social action.

Charting Children's Growing Awareness of Personal Meaning: Evidence Gathered Through Practice

The practice of pair counseling in schools opened new ways of thinking about the work of the Group for the Study of Interpersonal Development. While our connection to clinical work continued we also considered other ways of promoting social competence in children. We extended our work into public schools, and it is this practice, its subsequent research, and its effect on our theoretical framework that form the subject of part II of this book. Here I will share the story of an institutional invention, a master's degree program we designed, that helped us to establish a home base within which to continue this line of work. It is also the story of the experience of one master's degree student who participated in this program.

In the early 1990s, a group of faculty and doctoral students and I founded the Risk and Prevention Program at the Harvard Graduate School of Education, one of several specialized master's degree programs located within the Human Development and Psychology (HDP) area of that graduate school.[6] We designed it as a vehicle for making our theories useful in practice by training practitioners and developing new methods and programs to help protect children from some of the risks they may face growing up in our society. A quick overview of the Risk and Prevention Program will further explain how the relationship between theory and practice worked in our case and serve to introduce the next phase of our efforts.

Risk and Prevention is designed to be a three-way training and service partnership between a major university (academic training of professionals), a social service or mental health agency (supervision of practice), and urban public school districts (point of service).[7] It made sense that this approach would be largely school-based, not only because that was where the kids were but because we wanted to develop approaches that promoted children's academic and social competencies together. Although it borrows heavily from public health models, the location of Risk and Prevention in a graduate school of education also makes sense. Faculty, research-oriented doctoral candidates, and practice-oriented master's degree students would all share a common purpose, helping at-risk kids make it both academically and socially. We also shared a desire to better understand how children growing up under risky social conditions make meaning of the risks they face and how preventive approaches might work to facilitate and deepen their personal awareness of these risks.

Here is the story of a graduate student who came directly from Swarthmore College to Risk and Prevention several years after it was founded, and how she came to understand the meaning that two elementary school boys made of their predilection to get into fights.

Kesia's Story

When Kesia Constantine enrolled in the Risk and Prevention Program, she was offered a range of options for applied work in her

Figure 4.1 The Pyramid of Prevention Service

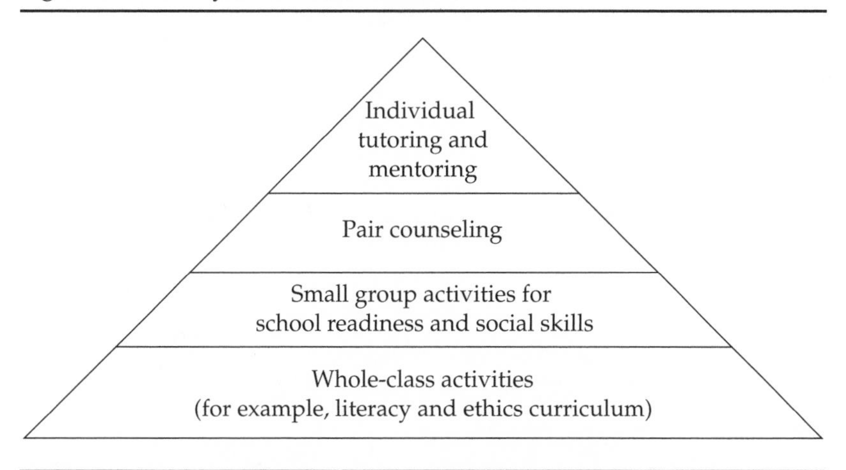

Source: Conceptualized by Caroline Watts and Robert L. Selman.

prevention practitioner training. She chose a service delivery model we called the Pyramid of Prevention Program.[8] Figure 4.1 outlines our approach to providing these services within that model.

Within this service and training practicum, Kesia spent a portion of her practicum time working with children—ethnically diverse, many from immigrant families, mostly urban, and mostly poor—in a public elementary school in the West Roxbury section of Boston, about eight miles from our campus. Her role was to counsel individual students and to provide pair, small-group (secondary prevention), and whole-class (primary prevention) psychosocial services for children across grades one to five. Her "prevention clients," with whom she worked individually or in pairs or small groups, were children whom the school staff, primarily the teachers, believed to be particularly at risk for social difficulties and school failure. As with most schools in the district, this urban elementary school of about six hundred students had little in the way of other social or psychological support services. A site coordinator facilitated Kesia's referral assignments and ran peer supervision meetings attended by Kesia and the three other interns in the Pyramid practicum.[9]

In tandem with this practicum, which ran from early September to late May, Kesia and the other Pyramid interns took a two-semester seminar with me on social development—a research and theory class in which we attempt to connect the Risk and Relationship Framework (described later in the chapter) to their actual practice, focusing on the promotion of children's social competence. The interns entered extensive records of their observations of the children's social actions—and the thoughts the children expressed—in journals. They wrote two summary papers on these social interactions and the social strengths and weaknesses they observed over the course of the year.

Kesia chose to write a case study of two ten-year-old, fourth-grade, public school boys with whom she had worked as a pair counselor. As with Callie and Clarisa, the problematic risky behavior at issue was fighting. Kesia's paper "Mark and Lance: Fighting and the Essence of Being Social," written in February, began by posing some questions:

> My previous [first-semester] paper was guided by my desire to understand the meaning-making process of my fourth-grade boy pair in light of their decisions to engage in the risk-taking behavior of physical fighting. The questions I explored were: Why is it that when conflict arises between them during pair [counseling] they can come up with amicable solutions, but not on the bus, in the cafeteria, the classroom, and, I suspect, in their neighborhoods, with other people? What are the larger implications for pair therapy as an intervention-prevention program? How does this change the way I see my work? Do my work?

Kesia's questions, arising out of her direct experience working with these two boys, are very practical. They are also very challenging theoretically, and to my mind (to turn a famous aphorism often attributed to Kurt Lewin), there is nothing so theoretical as a good practice-based question.[10]

The Personal Meaning of Risk and Relationship: The Importance of Levels of Awareness for Practice and Theory

In Kesia's initial term paper at the end of the first semester, she noted that the excessive fighting of her pair could be classified as "conduct disorder behavior." Kesia described Mark and Lance as "highly regarded fighters among their classmates," who regarded the two "as individuals to be fearful of, to challenge, or to look up to."

> At the Ohrenberger School, at least among the boys, physical fighting is a means by which one gains and loses status. It has been a difficult process to get Mark and Lance to reflect directly on their engagement in physical fights. Through Mark's teacher, for example, I learned Mark feels very unsafe in his neighborhood. To avoid certain people in his neighborhood, Mark would walk several blocks out of his way to avoid

> them, or even stay home. He was quite concerned not to appear to be a "punk" in the eyes of others in his community.[11]

Reviewing the evolution of their counseling sessions, Kesia reported in her February paper that the pair had begun by holding a two-person tournament of sports, alternating between basketball and football. Both boys were talented athletes who prided themselves on their skills. She also noted that both demonstrated a sophisticated understanding of sportsmanship, and that they were able to negotiate to resolve the conflicts that came up during their sports play. Nevertheless, as Kesia reported in her February paper, talking about fighting did not come easily to the boys, owing in part, she suspected, to how other adults had handled their conflicts in the past:

> Mark and Lance . . . were used to the adults in their lives passing judgment and not *really listening* to what they had to say. This is not to say that I didn't make it quite clear to them that I disapproved of their fighting, but I was also able to make the distinction between disapproval of their fighting and my approval of them. When we talked about fighting, it was for us all to gain understanding. I asked questions not only about the facts but also about the emotions. In order to get the boys comfortable with the idea of talking about fighting I made it a ritualized part of all our sessions. Before we played any game, Mark, Lance, and myself would do what we call the "check-in," which consisted of questions about their week, whether they were involved in any fights, if so what happened, and . . . whether they [had] handed in their homework assignments.

It was puzzling to Kesia that, in spite of their work together in pairs, Mark and Lance remained notorious troublemakers and fighters on the school bus. She began a crusade to get the two boys to talk about and reflect on their fights with other kids, hoping to help them make connections between what they accomplished by negotiating when playing sports and what they could get from resolving conflicts they got into elsewhere using similar negotiation skills.

Mark and Lance, however, refused to back down from any challenge, and Kesia was frustrated. It seemed to her that even though Mark, Lance, and the other boys on the bus knew what it takes to stay out of trouble on the bus, they actively went out of their way to find trouble. At this point Kesia learned some interesting information from a teacher who was in charge of the bus arrangements. According to this teacher, Mark was the instigator of many of the fights that he got into, and Mark fought "because he knows that he can win." When Kesia confronted Mark with this information, however, he seemed to see things quite differently. "To hear Mark tell the story, he fights only when he is challenged and he can't back down because he doesn't want to look like a wimp."

The boys' intransigence about fighting led Kesia to an important insight:

> It became apparent to me in our conversations about fighting that the boys get the same rush from fighting that they do from playing sports. For the boys, sports represented the ability to prove that they were better than someone else, "powerful" so to speak, through winning the game; therefore, it was not necessary for them to fight [in this context]. Skill speaks for itself. Over the course of my year with Mark and Lance I have come to realize that fighting shouldn't simply be thought of as the risk-taking behavior that they engage in, but rather it should also be thought of as a skill, something to take pride in.

Practically speaking, Kesia's work offers a striking example of the importance of establishing a nonjudgmental atmosphere that allows children and adolescents to speak openly about their viewpoints and relationships. It also demonstrates the kind of interactions that pushed us to listen for something beyond young people's levels of interpersonal understanding or their repertoires of social skills—and to integrate this new dimension of personal and cultural meaning into our developmental framework.

Theoretically speaking, Kesia's insight enhanced our appreciation of the role that personal meaning plays for children and adolescents in terms of the risks they choose to take and how they act in different social situations. As "data," the material Kesia and her fellow students collected in their day-to-day work helped us to better understand the connections—or seeming disconnection—between levels of social thought and actual behavior. As we began to look more deeply, we saw further evidence from journals such as Kesia's that the seemingly simple concept of personal meaning involves cultural factors as well as familial ones. And it seemed that children's awareness about the personal meanings of their own behaviors—or their ability to think and talk about where their own feelings come from or what an action means to them personally—not only develops over time but also could be organized along an awareness dimension using our developmental framework.[12]

In particular, awareness of personal meaning seems to develop in parallel with the evolution of the core social capacity of perspective coordination. Table 4.1 comes out of our Risk and Relationship research (see next section) about how these levels of awareness of per-

Table 4.1 Awareness of the Personal Meaning of the Risk in Fighting Behavior: Developmental Levels of Interview Responses, by Thematic Orientation

	Orientation to Self (Autonomy)		Orientation to Relationship (Relatedness)	
Level	(Pro) Positive	(Anti) Negative	(Pro) Positive	(Anti) Negative
0: Dismissive	It's fun beating up on people.	Fighting is stupid.	Fighting is cool.	Only jerks fight.
1: Rule-based: impersonal	You have to fight to survive.	Fighting only gets you suspended.	Everyone looks up to those who can fight; they're tough.	Fighting makes you unpopular.
2: Rule-based: personal	I'm a good fighter.	I promised myself never to get into a fight.	Our family is good at fighting; my cousin taught me how.	My girlfriend won't have anything to do with me if I get into fights.
3: Need-based: personal	I fight when I'm tense. Anything will set me off.	I don't fight because I wouldn't respect myself.	If anyone insults my family, I'll fight to defend them.	I worry what others will think of me if I fight.
4: Need-based: integrated	Part of what allows me to keep calm under pressure is the awareness that I will respond if provoked, but sometimes I may have to fight back or may even just lose my temper.	Violence is not a part of me, but I might use it as a last resort, rather than sitting on my hostility and having it expressed elsewhere.	I live in a violent neighborhood, and I have to adapt whether I like it or not, but I don't believe in fighting to solve problems, and it goes against my nature.	I seem to need to keep proving to people that they can't push me around, but I wish there were a better way.
Insightful	I used to tell myself that I needed to fight to survive in this neighborhood, but I took a real good look at myself and realized I needed to look cool to cover up.			

Source: Author's compilation.

sonal meaning find concrete expression in the kinds of comments that children and adolescents make about the particular behavior of fighting. Our overall theoretical model is about to get a bit complicated, but a quick look back at tables 3.1 and 3.2 will provide a rough idea of how levels of awareness of personal meaning correspond to levels of perspective coordination, interpersonal strategies, and interpersonal orientation. We believe this correspondence is not merely theoretical.[13]

In her papers about her pair counseling within the Pyramid of Prevention Program, Kesia's analysis touched upon the cultural meaning of fighting within the social environments—at school and in their neighborhood—in which Mark and Lance operated. Through her intensive work with the two boys, she also gained some access to the personal meaning of fighting for each, and their levels of awareness about that meaning. At midyear, from both a developmental and a cultural perspective, both boys seemed to be in a similar place.

From a cultural perspective, Kesia noted, "fighting seems to provide the opportunity for Mark and Lance to walk down the street with their heads held high . . . and know that now people won't 'mess' with you." From a developmental perspective, she observed that initially both boys seemed to blame the cause of fighting on the behavior of others, or on "the rules of the game" of the street, that is, both seemed to be at what we would call the "rule-based" level (see table 4.1). However, Kesia also reported that by the end of the year she perceived a change in Mark that she did not see in Lance. Unlike Lance, Mark was no longer regularly fighting in the schoolyard, on the bus, or in the neighborhood, for what he told her were "different" reasons than before. "Earlier he [Mark] had been primarily concerned to see that 'no one was messing with me.'" At this later point he told Kesia that he did not engage in physical violence because he did not need to fight to prove he was "cool."

As Kesia understood his statements, making use of a developmental point of view, Mark's understanding of fighting had changed not just conceptually (his theories about why kids fight or not) but in terms of its personal meaning to him (why he himself chose to fight or not). In our theoretical language, (and with reference to table 4.1), Mark's awareness of the personal meaning of fighting for himself had become "need-based." That is, his new awareness was no longer simply rule-based, organized around an inflexible, abstract, and often culture-based rule like "wimps don't fight," but reflected his understanding of his own needs. Unfortunately, Lance did not seem to be able to express a level of awareness we would classify as need-based.

But what do we really mean when we talk about rule-based and need-based levels of awareness of personal meaning? And how does our scheme for understanding personal meaning and its individual and cultural components fit into the larger developmental picture we have been working on all along?

The Risk and Relationship Framework

Generally, we believe that individuals are more likely to take healthy than harmful risks as they grow up if they are able, when considering these risks, to coordinate their own perspective with those of others about whom they care. Further, we believe that this ability develops over time. More specifically, we theorize that an individual's core operational capacity to coordinate points of view toward in-common social experiences develops in reciprocal interaction with each of the three distinct—but closely related—psychosocial competencies we have identified in the brief history of our project given thus far. We now formally introduce them:

1. The *general level of understanding* that individuals have of the facts about the nature of the risk in the context of social relationships
2. The *repertoire of interpersonal strategies* that individuals have available to manage risks
3. The *self-awareness* that individuals have of the *personal meaning* of the risks they take in connection to the quality of the personal relationships they maintain

Examples of these connections between risks and relationships abound. Among pre- and early adolescents, such as Mark and Lance, they include the risk of joining a gang, of repeatedly getting into physical fights, of smoking two packs of cigarettes a day, of trying to do well in school or dropping out, of drinking and getting drunk.

With respect to psychosocial functioning, the mind is never static, never stuck in one level or another; it is always acting within a particular social and cultural context. Although our model is developmental—that is, it represents observed differences in social thought and action in terms of hierarchical levels, each level following and building upon the one that came before—it is understood that few (if any) of us always act in ways that represent the "highest" level of competence we are capable of bringing to bear on a given situation. Nor does the model place greater importance on the level of thought or action expressed (for example, rule-based versus need-based levels of awareness) than on its thematic content (for example, whether one

Figure 4.2 A Developmental View of Risk and Social Relationships: An Analysis of Three Psychosocial Competencies

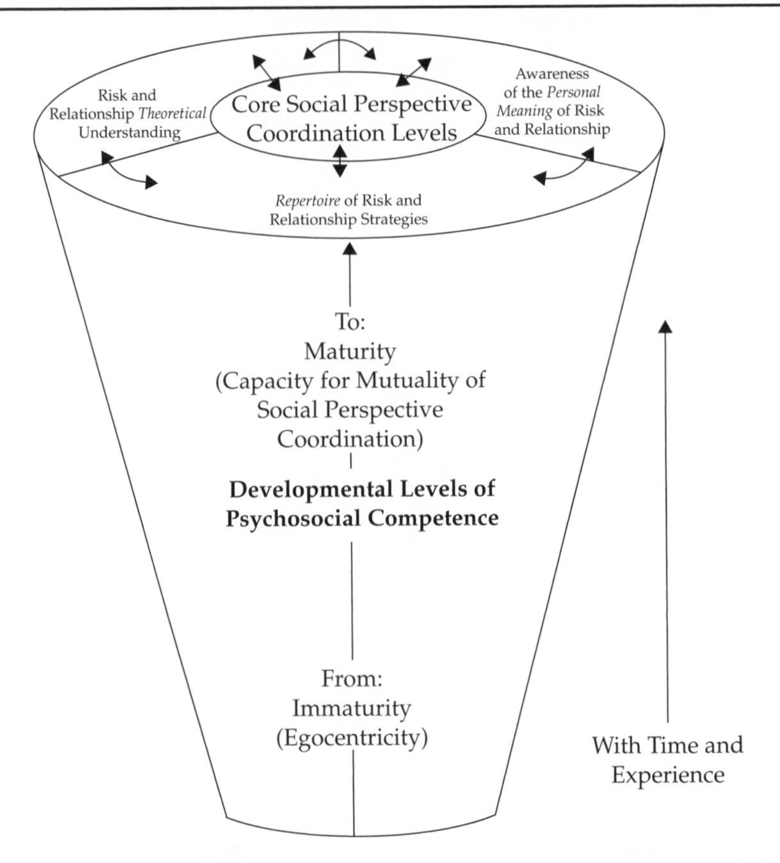

Source: Author's configuration.

has a pro-fighting versus anti-fighting "attitude," as depicted in our picturing of the personal meaning component in table 4.1).

Figure 4.2 represents our attempt to fully depict an anatomy of psychosocial development. Looking down (that is, topographically), the top surface of the figure describes the connections between the core developmental capacity to coordinate social perspectives as it applies to the three psychosocial components of any given risk-relationship. From this bird's-eye view, the reciprocal arrows across areas highlight the relation of the three areas of psychosocial functioning to each other. The arrows to and from the center emphasize the connection of each area of functioning to the core developmental capacity to coordinate social perspectives.

The conical shape of figure 4.2 not only represents the developmental dimension of our conceptual picture but symbolizes the likelihood of increasing differentiation and integration of psychosocial functioning both within and across the three areas with its developmental aspect (the evolution of levels of perspective coordination within the individual). This figure suggests that we can assess independently each of the three psychosocial components along a developmental continuum from immature (undifferentiated and unintegrated) to mature levels (differentiated and hierarchically integrated). By our standards, the potential for growth in an individual's psychosocial functioning is directly related to that individual's capacity to put into perspective the risks he or she must confront and the relationships he or she holds as important.

We realize that for these theoretical terms to be meaningful we must describe in concrete and reliably measurable terms the way in which each level in the coordination of social perspectives manifests itself in each area of psychosocial competence. By knowing in detail the developmental characteristics of each of the three areas of competency, we can analyze how individuals function along each of the three developmental continua, both at any given moment and over time. With these tools, we can chart long-term growth and progress as well as oscillation or regression independently in the understanding, management, and personal meaning of risks to physical and psychological health, and to social relationships. In truth we would need a hologram to do justice to the dynamics of social development as we have come to conceptualize it; for now we will try to sum up the basics of our current Risk and Relationship Framework with the help of one more chart. In table 4.2, we have lined up the corresponding levels of the developmental continuum for each of the aspects of social functioning that we discussed earlier.

Here, to make its relationship to figure 4.2 clear, we have put the "highest" or most developed level at the top, as it is in our cone picture: think of this as the outer skin of the cone, on which these developmental layers have been drawn, unpeeled, and laid flat. This table portrays the specific lineup of levels among the three psychosocial components of the framework. For the theoretically inclined, we point out that levels of interpersonal understanding, once understood, are the most "permanent"; they are not easily lost. Strategies, as discussed previously, can oscillate, once developed. And the awareness of personal meaning is the most elusive aspect of perspective coordination, in part because we can hold multiple personal meanings at the same time but it is challenging to keep all of them in perspective at once.

Table 4.2 Developmental Levels in the Risk and Relationship Framework

				Interpersonal Skills	
Level	Core Levels of Perspective Coordination	Interpersonal Understanding	Personal Meaning	Interpersonal Negotiation Strategies	Shared Experience
0	Egocentric	Momentary playmate	Dismissive	Impulsive	Enmeshed
1	One-way assistance	One-way	Impersonal, rule-based	Unilateral	Unreflective
2	Reciprocal	Fair-weather cooperation	Personal, rule-based	Cooperative	Reflective
3	Mutual	Intimate and mutual sharing	Need-based (personal)	Compromising	Empathic
4	Interdependent	Autonomous interdependence	Need-based (integrated)	Collaborative	Interdependent

Source: Author's compilation.

Putting Theory into Use: Interpreting Lance and Mark Within the Framework

To bring this theoretical discussion down to earth, we return to Kesia's experience with Mark and Lance. First, listening for Lance's and Mark's knowledge, or understanding, of the risks and benefits of fighting, we want to understand the "psychological theories" each held about why people in general (not only their peers and relations) do or do not fight. After listening to the boys (and talking to their teachers), Kesia understood that each of the boys viewed fighting as a means by which one establishes an identity to oneself and others (as a "punk" or a "wimp"), gains and loses status, and defends oneself against both actual danger (unsafe neighborhoods) and one's own fears (that being afraid of certain people marks one as a "wimp"). Developmentally speaking, these boys' view of the risks and benefits of fighting rested upon at least a second-person level of coordination of social perspectives.

With respect to the construct of interpersonal strategies to manage risks, both Mark and Lance were able to go beyond impulsive and unilateral levels in their interactions with peers and engage in cooperation and compromise, but as Kesia pointed out, fighting to the boys was also a skill, a way to negotiate, and "something to take pride in." No wonder that despite the fact that both boys were perfectly capable of cooperation and compromise (key elements of sportsmanship and age-appropriate interpersonal negotiation strategies), when they were playing sports together, they continued to fight with other kids on the bus.

Personal meaning helps explain the gap between social understanding and behavior. Kesia reported that during the year it was difficult for Lance to move beyond a sense that he got into fights because he liked fighting and was good at it, or because to not fight was to be classified automatically as weak (a rule-based response). Mark, on the other hand, seemed to express to Kesia by the end of the year a more differentiated awareness of why and when he fought or not. His awareness included himself in the equation; he did not simply explain his fighting behavior as a function of external forces beyond his own control. Mark's understanding of his behavior changed from fighting so that "no one was messing with me" to not needing to fight to show he was "cool." For us, this is good news not just because we want to discourage physical violence among children, but also because it represents a developmental advance for this particular child.

Mark was demonstrating, at least to us, meaningful differentiations. He could articulate his awareness that fighting with Lance when conflicts arose in pair therapy was a greater risk because it meant losing a friend. On the other hand, not fighting was still the greater risk to him in the neighborhood because by not fighting he would lose power and status in the peer group. Putting it in our theoretical language, we would say that something in his experience allowed Mark to look at the personal meaning that fighting had for him and to take it to a new level of self-awareness, one more in tune with the capacity for social understanding and the social skills he already had at hand.

We realize that Kesia's work with these fourth-graders was only a very small part of their lives. For Mark, however, that work—including what happened between the two boys in a safe setting as they played sports together and talked about fighting—may have been part of the "something" that prompted the change in the personal meaning that fighting had for him, and his awareness of it.

Points of Emphasis and Challenging Questions

As illustrated by the case of Mark and Lance, as well as by the earlier case of Callie and Clarisa, the sources of the way in which an individual makes personal meaning of risks and relationships include his or her history and cultural background as well as his or her level of psychosocial development.

For us, coming upon the concept of personal meaning from a developmental angle completed the theoretical picture we had been trying to draw of the evolution of children's capacities for social relationship—what we had begun to call our Risk and Relationship Framework. First of all, it strengthened two key assumptions regarding both theory and practice: if we want to understand an individual's social actions, we must find out what it means personally to the person who takes it; and the growth of an individual's capacity to understand these complexities at some level is part of being able to take the perspectives of others and coordinate them with the individual's own. Second, this validated our use of the "methode clinique" to investigate not only interpersonal understanding and social behavior but also individuals' level of awareness of the personal meaning of their understanding and action. Third, in terms of both practice and theory, the concept of personal meaning offered a bridge between individual and social experience—and between thought and action.

There are two further points I wish to emphasize. First, whether we consider risks good or bad depends on the personal meaning we make of them. This is especially true of the potentially dangerous but immediately gratifying risky behaviors to which today's children and adolescents are exposed or have easy access at an age that most everyone in society agrees is too early for them to manage. It is the development of these parallel capacities to gain perspective on risks and relationships that we think will serve as a protective factor for those who have achieved it.

In addition—and this is the most critical point of our entire analysis—making the connection between having factual knowledge of social or health risks and taking self-protective action involves two steps. First, factual knowledge becomes deeper developmental understanding when it is "socialized," that is, when it is considered from the perspectives of all those involved, as when Mark realized that fighting was not the only way for someone to gain status in the eyes of others. Second, that deeper social understanding becomes personally meaningful when individuals can see how the risks they take affect not only themselves but also others who care about them. Mark, for example, began to consider how Kesia felt about him. Just as personal meanings are informed by culture and context, they also are informed by the developmental capacities of the individual for self- and social awareness.

My central hunch is that the degree of awareness of personal meaning serves as the linchpin between the individual's understanding of factual knowledge and his or her actual behavior—and between adolescents' perspectives on risk and relationship. Even individuals with sophisticated levels of understanding and a full repertoire of high-level social strategies are vulnerable to the negative outcomes of social risks if they do not have a mature perspective on what those risks mean to them personally. This is why we ground our methodology in directly asking individuals to explain their own social behavior and that of their friends in relation to the risks and relationships involved. The responses we received during our in-depth interviews about risks and relationships—whether through practice or through research—speak to the essential role of maturity of personal meaning in how we manage risk.[14]

As we continue to look for support for our hypothesis that awareness of personal meaning provides a connection between thought and action in the social development of children, our analyses could have important implications for prevention.[15] Telling kids information that does not touch on or reflect what is personally meaningful to them will have little, if any, influence on their actions. In fact, like Mark, they may view prevention initiatives that fail to make the connection between the personal meanings of risk and of critical relationships *to themselves* as boring, or worse, as ultimately irrelevant to their lives.

So how can all children—not just those in specialized programs—

learn to keep perspective and to maintain deeper awareness of the personal meaning of the risks they face and the relationships they hope to maintain, especially in the face of difficult or painful life circumstances?

The Next Step(s)

As the GSID continued to work in schools, our definition of the term "risk" once again expanded, as did our practice. Recall that we chose to construct the Pyramid of Prevention as part of the Risk and Prevention Program because the shape represents, from top to bottom, a range of services that reach larger and larger numbers of children within this practice in the public schools: the top layer stands for working with individual children, the next layer for pair counseling, and the third for similar efforts with small groups of kids (for example, during "lunch groups" focused on discussions about the social life and community atmosphere of the school).

The base of our pyramid, whole-class activities, seems innocuous enough, but it represents an extension of our practical work beyond the prevention of negative outcomes to the positive promotion of social understanding and social skills—especially the core capacity of perspective coordination—among all children.

At the outset we had been content to take Holly's and Kathy's stories and play them out in the relatively narrow confines of the world of basic descriptive research in developmental psychology, simultaneously constructing a theoretical framework we thought would be useful. By the 1990s our efforts to put our theories into practice had taught us a great deal about the social development of children, and our experience with children at risk had expanded our view of the world and the issues that practice might address, specifically in the context of education in the public schools.

At this point in time the use of fictional characters and narratives of their dilemmas emerged as a method for exploring questions about the ethics of social relationships in the classroom, now in new ways designed to promote "resiliency to risk" and to help children cope with their specific real-world concerns, the risky business of social life, and the challenges of a multicultural society. Moreover, the location of one leg of this initiative in a school of education allowed us to take advantage of another valuable resource. We would design this practice so that it moved more to the heart of the elementary grade curriculum; as a way to reach more children, we would integrate it with efforts to promote literacy and with the teaching of reading and writing. This is the story of part II of this book.

Part II

Connecting Children's Literature and Social Awareness: Lessons from Practice

Chapter 5

Voices of Love and Freedom: The Birth and Early Years of a Literature-Based Character Education Program

One day Grace's teacher said they would do the play Peter Pan. *Grace knew who she wanted to be.*

When she raised her hand, Raj said, "You can't be Peter—that's a boy's name."

But Grace kept her hand up.

"You can't be Peter Pan," whispered Natalie. "He isn't black." But Grace kept her hand up.

"All right," said the teacher. "Lots of you want to be Peter Pan, so we'll have auditions next week to choose parts." She gave them words to learn.

—Mary Hoffman, *Amazing Grace*

EDUCATIONAL policies in the United States focus heavily on the promotion of children's literacy—their ability to learn the skills, for example, of reading and writing. To my mind, however, literacy is not merely a matter of being able to master the technical skills of reading and writing. Whether the "literature" in question is a training manual, a newspaper, a voter registration form, or a poem, reading and writing (like speech) are forms of communication and therefore profoundly social. To be truly well educated, children in the United States need to become knowledgeable not only about the rudiments of reading, math, science, and history but also about themselves and the lives of other people. That is, they need to be socially literate.

Historically, successive waves of educational reform in the United States have been marked by a sense of urgency about moral and social education and its place in the public school curriculum. That urgency is fueled by the knowledge that, especially among people who are both young and poor, the rates of interpersonal and intergroup violence, drug and alcohol abuse, and the kinds of sexual behavior that result in unplanned pregnancies and the spread of sexually transmitted diseases (including AIDS) have remained alarmingly high. Moreover, among the children who attend schools like the one in which Kesia worked, we see these risky behaviors occurring at earlier and earlier ages, moving down into the middle and even elementary school grades.[1]

It is not only in the United States that people have found themselves reassessing their assumptions about what it is that their children need to learn about ethics and values. With globalization, value-laden images and sounds from one part of the world now ride on an electronic magic carpet across oceans and over mountains. These images and sounds become part of the vernacular of children who live in vastly different cultures, through the movies they watch, the television shows they devour, the music they listen to, and the print materials they read. And often these free-floating values challenge the basic social and moral beliefs of individual communities and whole societies.

As we confront the challenges of the information age, the debate intensifies about the content of moral and social education. In industrialized countries like our own, this debate includes policy questions about how ethics and values can or should be taught in public schools. Should this aspect of education have its own time and place in the curriculum, or should it infuse the entire atmosphere of the school? Should it be taught at all? If so, should a central administrative body, some ministry or department of education at the national level, select topics and times at which to teach them, as in Japan? Or should the topics be selected locally according to the concerns of each community, as in the United States?[2] These are big questions, and the answers vary widely from nation to nation; in this country they vary from state to state and even from neighborhood to neighborhood and school to school.

Part II tells the story of an approach to school reform in elementary grade classrooms that provided the opportunity for our theory and research to "scale upwards" and move beyond the prevention of "social disorders" to the promotion of social competence more broadly implemented. It tells the story of how our group formed a new partnership in prevention (and ultimately education) that enabled us—urged us—to take our theories a step further, into curriculum design and teacher training. The rest of the book tells the story of how our involvement with this practice pushed our theory and research in new directions.

Toward the Integration of Literacy and Values: A Violence Prevention and Character Education Program

The Voices of Love and Freedom program was conceived in the late winter of 1991 in a living room in Jamaica Plain, Massachusetts. Jamaica Plain is a diverse Boston neighborhood that, at the time, was teetering between gentrification and economic stagnation. Originally called Family, Friends, and Community (FFC), the organization was created in response to local teen violence and drug use as a far-reaching and multifaceted community-based effort that would bring police, school administrators, teachers, parents, and kids together. In the beginning FFC's goal was simply to have these disparate groups talk to each other, in their own voices, about their experiences—to share their perspectives on life in the community and the problems they faced together with those whom they might otherwise consider "the enemy." The FFC's initial focus was on the creation of drug-free schools and neighborhoods through work with families and local community health centers. In 1992 the U.S. Department of Education's "Drug-Free Schools and Communities" initiative provided its initial funding to FFC through the Boston public schools. Since then, the organization, now called Voices of Love and Freedom, has been fundamentally a school reform initiative.

The program's founding director is Patrick Walker, a teacher who was trained as a labor economist and local community activist and had also recently obtained a degree in theology. In 1991 Walker lived in Jamaica Plain next door to a crack house and taught at one of Boston's more embattled high schools, Boston English. The death by shooting of a student at the high school and the experience of watching the goings-on at the crack house next door motivated Walker to approach the zone superintendent in charge of the Jamaica Plain schools with what he called a systems approach to prevention—bring everyone in the neighborhood to the table to address the intertwined issues of drugs and violence.[3]

Discussions held throughout 1991 with educators, students, parents, community activists, and local residents acknowledged that the social problems experienced by this urban community were not unique. But the response would be. Jamaica Plain would take a more radical approach to drug abuse and violence than other zones within the

Boston public school system by training its teachers, especially its elementary school teachers, to teach values through storytelling in the classroom. The values would be pro-social and anti-drugs and -violence. The stories would come from the growing body of contemporary children's literature about young people from a wide range of ethnic, geographic, national, and social-class backgrounds who are confronted with dilemmas and difficulties like the ones that were facing Jamaica Plain's children.

Sometime near the end of 1991 Walker knocked on my door and asked me to help him with his initiative. Today, of course, policymakers across the entire length and breadth of the political spectrum endorse character education (although they often disagree on what its content should be).[4] But in 1991, to propose teaching values in an urban public school as a prophylactic against the alienation and rage caused by social problems in our economically and racially stratified society was a pretty innovative idea.[5] Some elements of Walker's proposal might even have been labeled radical: this program would emphasize the theme of social justice and use contemporary, truly multicultural children's literature rather than resurrected fables from the Western canon to raise these issues in elementary schools. Other elements would seem conservative, especially the inclusion of a developmental approach to multiculturalism that would emphasize a universal social competence—social perspective coordination.

In the fall of 1992, at roughly the same time the Risk and Prevention Program was founded, Voices of Love and Freedom (VLF) was officially baptized with funds from the federal government. For the next four years our research group helped Walker and his colleagues design their first program, which ultimately would be called "Literacy and Values," by using this approach to moral and character education. The program's name reflected Walker's background in theology, but it was also chosen to convey the psychological necessity in all our lives of balancing our need for intimacy with others—or *love*—with the *freedom* to be self-determining, or autonomous. The aim to balance the values of love and freedom fit well with our own theoretical formulation of intimacy and autonomy (see chapter 3), and our developmental framework, especially our focus on the coordination of social perspectives as an educational goal, served as a useful guide as VLF designed its approach.

VLF's initial program had a few basic goals. First, it sought to design a curriculum that would connect moral education to the experience of inner-city children. To make this connection, VLF would use books written about characters with whom these kids could identify to provoke thinking and discussion about issues important in their own lives. Second, VLF would take a developmental approach, focusing on key developmental skills such as the ones described in the first part of this book. And third, VLF would build a bridge between moral education and literacy, a core element of school reform efforts nationwide. As practice-based researchers, we would help with the primary work of selecting the books and writing integrative, theory-driven guides that teachers across several grade levels could use alongside the literature.

An Outline of the Initial VLF Program

The designers of VLF believed that healthy social and moral development centers on the individual's ability to balance the moral values of love and freedom within his or her own cultural identity. Using carefully selected stories about interpersonal and intergroup challenges faced by young people from diverse ethnic and racial backgrounds, its curriculum, which included both written materials and teaching methods, was intended (and still is) to help children discover and develop their own voices and reflect on what is personally meaningful in their lives. Its initial project was to identify books, write in-depth teacher's guides that would link social and ethical awareness to literacy, and design professional development programs to train teachers in using the material effectively. Ultimately VLF would label its curriculum a supplemental literacy program and call it something less evocative than love and freedom: "Literacy and Values." It was considered "supplemental" because it could be used alongside a basal text or other literacy curriculum purchased by the school.

VLF describes the "Literacy and Values" teacher's guides as part of a comprehensive literacy, character education, and prevention program. These teacher's guides put major emphasis on reading-comprehension strategies and literature-based writing while also addressing all the GSID core social competencies. By "prevention" the program's designers mean the promotion in students of the social and intellectual skills that will help them manage their relationships and the psychosocial risks to which they may be exposed. But what do we mean by "literacy," and what do we mean by "values"?

First, the Voices of Love and Freedom program aims to integrate literacy with the promotion of social competence by calling upon children to go beyond remembering and summarizing to reflect on the social and moral questions raised by the stories and books they read in class. Although these questions are basic, they are by no means simple. The process of coming to grips with them—articulating thoughts and feelings and sharing the results with the rest of the class—pushes children to develop their reading, writing, and speaking skills. Ideally a careful choice of materials ensures that what the children read and study engages them personally as well as intellectually.

Second, the VLF program pays attention to both cultural understanding—that is, children's ideas about such culturally variable norms as how they speak in the presence of elders or resolve conflicts with friends—and a developmental understanding of children's capacities to be reflective, to coordinate points of view, to negotiate conflict, and to be aware of the personal meaning of social experiences for themselves and for others.

Third, the program represents a holistic approach to promoting children's communicative and relational competencies. In other words, it aims at helping children learn how to convey to a reader or a listener what they mean in an effective and interpersonally sensitive manner, and in a way that allows them to speak in their own authentic voice. It is a complex and demanding curriculum well suited to use by elementary school teachers, who are usually responsible for educating the "whole child" in all subjects.

To integrate its academic and social goals, VLF relied on a five-step approach that is made explicit in its teacher's guides for the trade books it selects for use in the classroom:[6]

1. "To Connect" emotionally with the moral theme of the story chosen through the sharing of relevant personal experiences by both teachers and students
2. "To Discuss" and reflect on the moral issues raised by the reading selection through open-ended exchanges with the teacher and classmates that build critical thinking skills and through written responses to reading-comprehension questions that promote a deeper understanding of the characters and ethical themes of the story
3. "To Practice" moral reasoning skills and explore attitudes about values in activities with peers, including role-playing, class debates, and art projects
4. "To Express" one's own beliefs through individual writing exercises, dramatic arts, and other forms of creative expression
5. "To Participate" in service-learning activities in school, at home, and through community activism

Certainly none of these practices were new to educators, but the way in which VLF's curriculum integrated social and moral education with the teaching of language arts skills, rather than treating these aspects of learning as "add-ons," was an important difference from other curricula.

Because VLF's program began as a local initiative in a community where well over 60 percent of the children attending public schools were classified as members of minority groups, it takes a multicultural approach. And because one of its main goals is helping those children—and others who live in poor urban neighborhoods—cope with the dangers of drugs and violence, the social aspect of its pedagogy draws heavily on the developmental framework and the Risk and Relationship Framework of our research-practice group.

Connecting Developmental Theory to VLF Practice: Our Initial Influence

The first two pedagogical steps, "To Connect" and "To Discuss," put the critical incidents of a story into context—that is, they call upon students to think about the choices facing the protagonist (and other key characters) in terms of their own *understanding* or *awareness* of relationships and social and personal risks. The third step asks students "To Practice" *interpersonal skills* that include *perspective taking* and *conflict resolution strategies;* they often work in pairs (matched by the teacher along the lines of the pair therapy and counseling model described in chapter 4) to come up with a written or oral presentation to the teacher and the rest of the class. The last two steps, "To Express" and "To Participate," ask students to write a *personally meaningful* story of their own about the issues raised by the book and/or to become involved in other activities in and around the school that speak to these issues, for example, activities that might build a stronger sense of community within the school.

From the beginning VLF chose literature that focuses on themes of family, friendship, and community and whose plots lead up to some sort of moral or social crisis, conflict, or critical incident in order to provide a basis for discussion of the characters' perspectives on the problem. The program's emphasis on helping kids explore the points of view of the various key characters in the stories grew out of GSID research showing that the capacity to coordinate perspectives is necessary, though not sufficient, for building and maintaining healthy interpersonal relationships, without which children are far more likely to succumb to the temptations of drugs and violence (see, for example, Selman et al. 1992; Selman and Adalbjarnardottir 2000).

VLF began to adapt the GSID developmental framework in an attempt to make perspective coordination theory an applied science, something one could learn by doing skills-based exercises. As a result, early versions of the program's teacher's guides suggested role-playing as a way for students to "sample" various viewpoints in the context of the fictional dilemma presented in the narrative. The use of role-playing as a way to learn and practice perspective-taking skills became pretty quickly a standard feature of the program. Students enjoyed having the opportunity to act (out) in class in a sanctioned context. Teachers who had the requisite patience for guiding role-play found that it provided a great vehicle for discussion, and that it allowed some students who were not usually active in class to participate in a meaningful manner.

Well-orchestrated role-playing also succeeded as a way to lead participants away from their own egocentric reactions to a story and toward an increasingly more differentiated view of themselves and others. The process of "getting into character," as actors and drama coaches put it, is an immediate rather than an intellectual experience; the student who is asked to play a particular role must directly engage that character's attitudes, assumptions, and emotions—in other words, move away from his or her own point of view to stand for a while in another person's shoes. The goal is to guide students through and then beyond the perspectives of the story's characters to a "generalized" third-person perspective—their community's view of certain actions or behaviors, for example. Of course, the growth of children's capacities to take a third-person perspective depends on developmental as well as educational factors. Still, one of the basic assumptions of VLF is that having students practice activities that exercise their perspective-taking (-coordinating) skills across all grade levels promotes that growth and enhances their social understanding and competence.

Another Early Influence on VLF: The Developmental Study Center

The idea of infusing literacy with ethics through the study of children's literature in elementary education may have been new to Boston. It may have been new to schools in the heart of distressed communities with high percentages of children of color or from recently immigrated or low-income families. Like many educational innovations and reforms, however, it was not that new in some quarters. In fact, VLF had borrowed the fundamental idea of storytelling and children's literature from an organization that today is a leader in the field of progressive education reform. Here is that story, told in brief, in the spirit of full disclosure, and to give credit where it is due.

It is important to remember that VLF was founded by neither moral educators nor reading and writing specialists. Conceived as the school-based component of a community-oriented approach to the prevention of substance abuse and violence, it was designed by a politically savvy community activist. In hindsight, the community-based component quickly receded in the face of more than ten years of massive national public interest and investment in education. Nevertheless, a strong sense of political activism was reflected in the books VLF selected, as well as in the structure of its teacher's guides.

VLF was also born "poor": it received an initial two-year grant of about $250,000 to the Boston public schools as part of the federal "Drug-Free Schools and Communities" initiative, but it had no fully developed pedagogy of its own. In its early phases the program had to borrow methods and ideas from both the scientific disciplines and the educational professions.

One major contributor to the early development of VLF was an organization now called the Developmental Study Center (DSC). It too had interesting origins, in some ways quite different from VLF's. Its original mission, when founded by Eric Schaps (who is still its president) and his colleagues, was to take the best educational and social science research on pro-social and moral development and use it to design caring elementary schools. Relative to VLF, DSC's first program, called the Child Development Project, was born "middle-class," if not well off. Funded in 1980 by the Hewlitt Foundation for an initial period of seven and a half years, DSC was mandated to evaluate all that it did—and provided with the funds to do so. For more than twenty years the organization has researched how to combine its mission of fostering pro-social development with effective teaching academics. Well funded by comparison with other organizations with similar missions, and with a well-researched program, the DSC now represents the gold standard among innovative organizations in the field of elementary school reform in the tradition of progressive education.[7]

DSC is a nonprofit organization whose mission statement sets forth the goal "to help children develop intellectually, ethically, and socially."[8] In the early days of its own existence VLF looked to DSC's literacy programs for as much help as it could get, especially with the pro-social aspects of its own program. Later on VLF thought it could do it differently—if not better.

In fact, many of the trade books in the "Literacy and Values" program were taken from the long list of books for grades kindergarten through eighth for which DSC provides guides. One such book, *Felita* (Mohr 1979), plays a major part in later chapters of our story. At first glance, and to the untrained eye, the teacher's guides designed by VLF and DSC may appear to be similar. For instance, developmental social psychology provides a foundation for both approaches, stressing, among other things, the importance of fostering perspective taking to resolve social conflicts. But a closer look reveals significant differences that might be explained in part by the origins of each organization and their different theories of individual and organizational development.

It is important to note that from DSC's conception, it has sought to foster social development by creating a school culture in which students experience positive social interactions with peers and adults. It uses its literacy curricula as part of an overall strategy to provide structural scaffolding not only for its pedagogy but also for "whole school renewal" that fosters a sense of community. Schaps writes frequently about the importance to children of feeling close to people at school, being fairly treated by teachers and peers, and contributing to the school culture (see Schaps, Schaeffer, and McDonnell 2001).

VLF would not disagree with those aims, but its pedagogical emphasis has been less on the school environment and increasingly on building the analytical and social skills of the student. Recently it has begun the design of a comprehensive language arts curriculum that includes social skills, but VLF more often focuses on social dilemmas in the context of sociopolitical issues and the direct teaching of social skills than does DSC; it also emphasizes the development of specific conflict resolution skills, often in the context of an awareness of social inequity. DSC relies on the process and pedagogy of its guides to identify and analyze the main theme of a book, but also as structured opportunities for promoting social interaction among students in which the personal meaning of the bonds between students and their peers, teachers, and the school itself is strengthened through the development of the classroom as a caring community. Although each program focuses on social development, VLF guides primarily work on enhancing individuals' literacy and social skills to understand and deal with social context and social change, whereas the aim of CDP guides is to cultivate social relationships within the classroom and the school so as to promote a healthy and cooperative school atmosphere.

Despite these differences, on the full spectrum of approaches to character development these two operations are fairly close together. DSC and VLF have, in a sense, become competitors for a segment of the educational market that may be expanding in absolute terms, as the nation invests in elementary education, but may also be in danger of being marginalized by the push for standardization and high-stakes testing.[9]

Amazing Grace: Putting Theory into Practice and Practice into Theory

As one might imagine, there are many children's books that lend themselves to getting along with others. But few do so while also raising the societal issues that the creators of VLF saw as central to the theme of community, such as discrimination, cultural awareness, and diversity. In 1992 a novel written in 1991 for children of elementary school age struck us as being ideally suited to role-playing and perspective-taking exercises while also providing a platform for an age-appropriate discussion of prejudice—an issue of daily concern to the children whom VLF hoped to reach. That book was *Amazing Grace* (1991), written by Mary Hoffman and illustrated by Caroline Binch.

This novel takes its title—and the name of its protagonist—from the spiritual song "Amazing Grace," written by John Newton, captain of a British ship that plied the slave trade, about a personal awakening that he saw as a manifestation of the mercy or grace of God. But one does not need to be either Christian or religious to grasp the song's message about hope in the face of overwhelming adversity and the possibilities of human understanding and redemption.

The story of third-grader Grace, Hoffman's protagonist, was among the first that our research group and the VLF practice team agreed to work on together in an effort to unify theory and practice in the context of a public school curriculum. The publisher's promotional teaser on the inside flap of the book's dust jacket sets up the narrative this way:

> Grace loves stories, whether they're in books or in movies or the kind her grandmother tells. She acts out the most exciting parts of all sorts of tales . . . sometimes as Hiawatha, or Aladdin, or Joan of Arc. . . . There's nothing that Grace enjoys more.
>
> So when there's the chance to play a part in *Peter Pan,* Grace knows exactly who she wants to be. It's hard when her classmates are doubtful, but Grace has the loving support of her mother and wise grandmother to bolster her own independence. Grace keeps in mind that she can be anything she wants to be—and the results are truly amazing!

The reason that some of Grace's classmates, like Natalie, are "doubtful" is that Grace is black and Peter Pan is white. (Natalie is also white.) The language on the dust jacket is kind, whereas in the book some of Grace's classmates are downright rude. The fact that Grace is also a girl and Peter Pan is a boy also does not sit right with others in her class, like Raj (who may also want the part in the play).

What is "amazing" is not that Grace gets the part—she does—but that she perseveres in the face of these obstacles. It was not the happy ending that appealed to us, however, but the richness of the possibilities that this book offers for both teaching and research on the influence on social and moral development of children's growing awareness of the role that race and gender play in "getting along." For our research group this marked a big leap—from the kind of inclusion issues raised by the dilemmas that Kathy, Becky, and the new girl faced (in chapter 3) to the kind of intergroup inclusion and exclusion faced by individuals from different "factions" within a society.

The first version (circa 1992) of the VLF teacher's guide for *Amazing Grace* (and those for other books like it) focused on the five pedagogical components outlined earlier but said very little about their developmental foundations. Its emphasis was on role-playing in order to enhance and encourage children's self-esteem and creativity—"Be all that you can be" was its main theme. For instance, one three-part exercise designed for children from kindergarten to second grade called on these very young students to tell their parents what they wanted to be when they grew up and to ask the parents to write down how they could help their children realize their dreams; what the parents wrote was then to be read aloud in class.

The second version of the guide (circa 1994) could only be described as heavily focused on the idea of promoting social skills, and it took a very strong and explicit developmental perspective. In fact, *all* teachers in *all* grades, kindergarten through twelfth grade, were expected to teach *Amazing Grace* and use the same set of role-playing exercises, with adjustments according to each teacher's assessment of his or her students' abilities. In part, the decision to teach one book across all grades was driven by political considerations: the administrators of the Boston public school system had just endorsed the idea that character education needed to extend from kindergarten to twelfth grade, and this seemed like a way to make the reach, although not (as it turned out) a very pedagogically sound one.

Despite the challenges presented by the scope of this mandate and the complexities of its stated purpose—"for the student to develop the perspective coordination and conflict resolution skills necessary to overcome the racist and sexist stereotypes which may block her pursuit of her life goals"—the revised VLF guide was only fourteen pages long. (Current "Literacy and Values" guides cover one or two grade levels and average fifty pages.) For early elementary school children the pedagogical theme would remain "Be all you can be"; for older children—say, by fifth or sixth grade—it would be fighting the discrimination that unfairly puts obstacles in the way of some, but not others, who want to be all they can be.

Using a generalized formula and emphasizing role-playing, the "*Amazing Grace* Whole School Guide" instructed teachers to first explore the concept of *point of view* with students. It outlined the five types or levels of POV (perspective-taking skills) but gave teachers little help in choosing which of the activities listed might be appropriate for their particular students. The guide then suggested that students act out their understanding of critical incidents in the book while standing on construction-paper cutouts of different pairs of shoes, representing the various points of view of the characters.

As part of the role-playing exercise, the teacher could act as a reporter and interview the characters about the action; for example, he or she might ask the person playing the character Grace, "Why did you want to be Peter Pan?" To explore "higher-level perspective-taking skills," this guide suggested, teachers should ask the students to "try to get into the heads of those characters and guess how those characters thought about each other." A final assignment was for students to write a story about a time when they were "in Grace's shoes," that is, when they themselves had experienced discrimination or, at least, faced a barrier to achieving their immediate goal.

As with many good books,[10] the central theme of *Amazing Grace* is elusive, or it might be more accurate to say that there are several central themes, depending on one's perspective. One teacher might choose to focus on "Be all that you can be"; another might use this story to discuss issues of fairness or discrimination. From our theoretical perspective, we tend to frame these themes in terms of age-related risks (the risk of going for what one wants, the risk of challenging one's peers) and important relationships (that of Grace to her classmates, or to her grandmother, who encourages her throughout).

Although Grace's situation involves relationships with peers and family, it is much more complex than the problems that GSID invented for Holly and Kathy because it clearly and explicitly involves a cultural dilemma as well as a personal one. We could use *Amazing Grace* as a multicultural text because it featured an Afro-Caribbean heroine with whom American minority students could identify. We could view it as a story about intergroup as well as interpersonal relationships, and it allowed us (as both researchers and practitioners) to bring cultural perspectives into the conversation, even if that conversation was with kids as young as second-graders.

These early teacher's guides, and especially the effort to teach one book at all grade levels, seem crude and clumsy to us now, but our aims were ambitious, and nearly every aspect of the program was experimental. It was particularly important that we find teaching methods that could reach the most marginalized students, the kids who might need this kind of curriculum the most. No one knew what would work and what would not, so everything was fair game. We abandoned some ideas, modified others, and came up with new ones. And we asked ourselves a lot of questions, especially about just what multicultural education should be.

In the classroom, of course, none of our laborious tinkering with these activities was evident to either the teachers or the students. Astute teachers tended to ask about the wording and the emphasis on perspective taking in the guides. Some actually wrote their own worksheets based on those in the guide so that they could assess mechanics like sentence structure or more thoroughly test for reading comprehension.

One of the criticisms of the early versions of the VLF guides was that they did not include specific methods for teaching reading and writing. And in fact, the critics were mostly right: the designers of the guides assumed that the various approaches that teachers were already using for these subjects could easily be married to what was asked for in the VLF program. Furthermore, since the Boston public school system had been without any uniform standards for over a decade, there had been no reasonable way for VLF to negotiate this issue as it sought to expand beyond Jamaica Plain, since the system itself had not shown a preference for any one teaching approach over another.[11]

In the third generation of VLF guides (now officially "Literacy and Values" and published commercially), the overbearing developmental orientation receded into the background. Now each guide—and each book—is designated for a single grade. For example, the guide for *Amazing Grace* (*Literacy and Values Teacher Resource* 1999) targets it for use at the second-grade level. Each guide balances the promotion of social competence and values with a focus on literacy. Each provides exercises to teach reading and reading-comprehension strategies, to develop students' writing skills, and to help students learn to speak clearly and effectively and listen carefully to others. The guides also integrate skills-oriented perspective taking and conflict resolution activities with cultural awareness.[12]

The VLF writing activities that appeared in the teacher's guides emphasized perspective taking and offered a choice of writing genres (autobiography, letter, or essay). The guides explicitly linked each step in the developmental sequence of writing skills to the evolution of social awareness, focusing on what students would most likely be able to achieve at a given grade level. For example, a fourth-grader would be expected to show competence in expressing a second person's viewpoint and its relation to his or her own, and this ability to understand and coordinate perspectives would manifest itself slightly differently in each writing genre. By way of comparison, a kindergartner would only be expected to be able to express his or her first-person viewpoint. To help kids this age master the fundamentals of describing events, people, and settings, the focus would be on speaking (and listening).

This connection between literacy activities and perspective coordination skills was important. However, the fact remained that although this was a literature-based program, VLF's teacher's guides did not completely satisfy the need for an integrated approach that also taught what we might call the nuts and bolts of literacy: phonics, grammar, vocabulary, and the mechanics of spelling and punctuation. And just at this point—in the mid-1990s, as VLF was being offered district-wide to teachers and principals not just in Jamaica Plain but in all the neighborhoods of Boston—the educational tide was turning. In cities and communities nationwide, more and more parents, educators, and politicians were calling for strict, uniform criteria for academic performance in each subject at every grade level and for an increase in standardized testing for both students and teachers. Their focus would be on these "nuts and bolts."

This push toward standards and standardization affected the relationship between the Boston public school system and VLF—and the program itself—in many ways. VLF needed to reassess its teacher training and broaden its language arts component to fulfill the program's promise to be a comprehensive literacy program. Otherwise, VLF might vanish beneath a new wave of the less socially oriented, more standards-based approaches to literacy that were competing for the attention of teachers and the dollars available to schools for curriculum materials and teacher training.

One immediate task for VLF was to reexamine and revise its program guides for teachers. To comply with the new literacy standards that the Boston public school system was still hammering out, the guides had to refer explicitly to character, plot, and setting; they had to list vocabulary words, provide numerous suggestions for journal-writing topics, and offer a "process writing" component and a coherent reading pedagogy. To make matters more complex, the district was also revamping its list of books approved for use in language arts classes—something else that had been neglected for years.

Partly as a result of the negotiations between VLF and the Boston public school system, the new reading list better reflected the diversity of the city's population. It also embraced certain contemporary topics that had previously been avoided by many of the city's teachers, including racism, substance abuse, the Holocaust, and sexism, although some teachers remained uncomfortable addressing these issues in class. Even subjects as seemingly benign as lying and truth-telling took on a controversial veneer during the first months of the debates over book selection and guide content for the VLF program in Boston. For example, some teachers voiced their dismay at the thought that they might have to admit to their students that they had, at some point in their lives, told a lie.[13]

Multicultural Education and a Developmental Approach to the Study of Risk and Relationship

Through all these revisions in the practice, here is how we began to think about these questions from the perspective of a developmental framework. First of all, Grace's story exemplifies a primary dilemma of our time, not only in the United States but everywhere that immigration has played or is playing a defining or redefining role in a national culture. Although the history of civilization is full of the cruelty and tragedy that have resulted from racial, ethnic, and cultural conflict, the United States has ultimately invested in diversity and invited or allowed it into the fabric of society. Today both our national ideals and the reality of who we are demand that we come to terms—over and over again—with the complexity, confusion, and continuing conflict that accompany this invitation. How can we, as educators and researchers, help clarify the developmental and cultural issues involved in a way that allows us to help children make sense of everyday dilemmas such as the one faced by Grace?

In the 1970s our research group asked questions such as, "At what age is it an indication of a serious problem for a child to continue to define a good friend only as someone who does what he or she wants, and at what age is it merely a reflection of a normal phase in the growth of her interpersonal understanding?" In the early 1990s we asked, "At what age is it racism or sexism to believe that to play the part of Peter Pan one must be white or a boy, like the original Peter? Or are such opinions just an outgrowth of the 'normal' literal-mindedness that most children display at early points in life, a developmental stage that most children will outgrow?" How do some children progress beyond such stereotypes, we asked, while others develop prejudiced or racist views?[14]

These are very important research questions, with obvious implications for educational practice if we agree that racism and prejudice are bad for society in that they constitute barriers to the equality of opportunity for individual achievement that we so value as a nation. How can we address these issues appropriately at each grade level? How can we discourage, in its potential perpetrators, what may be incipient discrimination of the kind that faces Grace in her quest to play a role in the school play? And what strategies can we offer to children who are the targets of discrimination to help them cope with it, challenge it, and overcome it?

As part of our developmental research partnership with VLF, we collected data on what children themselves said about Grace's dilemma. We found strongly held differences of opinion on the matter—especially when it came to the concrete actions that Grace could take—even in the elementary grades. For example, two fifth-grade girls from a Boston public elementary school, who came from similar ethnic, neighborhood, and social-class backgrounds and were similar in their capacity for coordinating perspectives, vehemently disagreed with each other about how Grace should deal with her situation. One said, "Just try out and ignore the prejudice." The other took a confrontational, activist position: "Complain to the teacher that Natalie and Raj are wrong that a girl cannot play Peter Pan."

The developmental questions here are: What personal experience leads each of these girls to her point of view and to her choice of interpersonal negotiation strategies—one "other-transforming," the other "self-transforming"—in terms of our developmental framework? To what extent are their choices determined by their individual histories? To what degree is each girl aware of the origins of her own point of view? Or of her peer's point of view?

The use of this kind of material in the classroom provokes other questions as well. We have heard objections from many points on the political spectrum to an educational approach that directly infuses stories like *Amazing Grace* into the public school literacy and language arts curriculum. Some say that by using this story, and by identifying "Be all that you can be" as a central theme, a particular value is promoted, and a certain message is sent: for example, that girls, and particularly girls from poor or ethnic minority backgrounds, should be able to reach their goals, whatever they may be, regardless of the fact that they are female or of a particular ethnic or racial heritage. Some parents may feel that sexism and racism are so pervasive in our culture that their daughters should not take the risk of internalizing false hopes about their futures. On the other hand, others might be disturbed by the use of *Amazing Grace* or other materials like it because their personal beliefs dictate that in matters such as these, girls should not regard themselves as equal to boys.

Cultural values aside (if such a thing is possible), from the developmental perspective that we embrace, the value of a book such as *Amazing Grace* is that it offers different lessons for different developmental phases in children's lives. In the early elementary grades, when children function primarily in a first-person mode of perspective coordination, it seems developmentally appropriate to offer a lesson about hope and perseverance: you can try to be anything; you can achieve a goal that you set your mind to. In the later elementary grades, when most children are moving toward the capacity to take a second-person perspective on relationships, the lesson may be different: it may need to acknowledge the cultural forces that color all our lives and influence the point of view of others, especially points of view toward members of ethnic or cultural groups different from our own.

As they mature, children's perceptions of the culture-based barriers between groups of people within our society become increasingly difficult to put aside. Discrimination in all its many forms is on their minds, especially for minority children growing up in low-income urban environments. In the higher elementary school grades a focus on how to respond to discrimination and disrespect can help students to develop their capacity to take a third-person perspective and to refine their own point of view on matters of fairness between self and others.

Some educational practitioners and theorists, following more directly in Dewey's and Kohlberg's footsteps, would probably claim that to foster social and moral development we must integrate our work into a broader focus on the school as a community rather than simply taking the path that we were choosing by emphasizing curriculum development, teaching practices, and the professional development of individual teachers (see Powers, Higgins, and Kohlberg 1989; Schaps, Solomon, and Watson 1986; Oser, Dick, and Patry 1992). In Kohlberg's framework, this broader focus would be on the school as a "just community." Eric Schaps and his colleagues at the Developmental Studies Center have provided good evidence that intentionally setting schools up as "caring communities" fosters positive academic and social outcomes for students (see, for example, Battistich et al. 1997).

As important as the theories may be, we would respond, we also can use some evidence. A study of these matters as they are raised in classrooms, especially under conditions made possible by a "natural experiment" such as VLF's implementation of its "Literacy and Values" curriculum, is as good a place to start as any.

Chapter 6

Putting "Literacy and Values" into Classroom Practice: Two Teachers and a Lesson Plan

In chapter 5, I described how our theory-research-practice group contributed to the early design and evolution of the "Literacy and Values" program of Voices of Love and Freedom.[1] We had advised VLF on the selection of books and structured its pedagogy around developmental concepts such as perspective coordination levels, conflict resolution strategies, and children's awareness of the personal meaning of risk and relationships. Finally, we hoped, the theory and research developed by the GSID over many years was moving into the public school system.

As Voices of Love and Freedom expanded its reach and the scope of its Literacy and Values curriculum in the mid-1990s, the GSID sought funding to observe the program implementation. Our questions, we thought, were simple: Did the curriculum work? Did teachers like using it? What did perspective-taking exercises look like in action—used by teachers and students in the classroom?

The Carnegie Corporation of New York came through with a research grant that allowed us, over the next several years, to send observers into classrooms in four Boston elementary schools. Our early observations were very much a hands-on effort, and this chapter and the next reflect the collaborative nature of this work as well as the nitty-gritty reality of teachers trying to teach social skills and literacy together in the classroom. In chapter 7, we describe how teachers perceived the practice during a time of massive educational reform, but first, to set the stage, let's take a brief look at the efforts of two teachers to use VLF materials with their students.

The Book They Used: A Brief Description of *A Day's Work*

When we began our observations, each paired book and guide was designed for a single grade. Each guide balanced the promotion of social competence and values with a focus on literacy. The guides provided exercises to teach reading and reading comprehension strategies, to develop students' writing skills, and to help students learn to speak clearly and effectively and listen carefully to others. They also integrated skills-oriented perspective taking and conflict resolution activities with social and cultural awareness.[2]

A Day's Work, by Eve Bunting and illustrated by Ronald Himler (1994), is an example of the pedagogy. Although Bunting's story is only thirty pages in length, half of which are full-page, full-color pictures, it is not a read-aloud book for younger children; its intended audience is children in grades three to five, and it presents a dilemma facing Francisco, a poor young Mexican American boy of about ten or eleven. Here is a synopsis of the story:

> Francisco's grandfather, his Abuelo, has recently come from Mexico to join Francisco and his mother in California. Abuelo is looking for work to help support the family, but he doesn't speak English yet. Francisco, who speaks both English and Spanish, lies to an employer to get himself and Abuelo a gardening job. He works hard beside his grandfather, thinking about how proud his mother will be and about the extra food their earnings will put on the table. But when Ben, the employer, finds all the wrong plants torn out of his garden, he (and Francisco's grandfather) discovers Francisco's lie. Abuelo is a carpenter, not a gardener. "We do not lie for work," Abuelo tells Francisco angrily. Abuelo offers to correct their mistake without pay and teaches Francisco an important lesson about honesty, integrity, and the value of a day's work.

The guide for *A Day's Work* draws on VLF's five-component teaching approach and divides the book into two sections. Reading 1 (pages 1 to 24) takes young readers up to the dramatic climax of the story, when Francisco's lie is discovered. This reading is followed by a "To Practice" activity in which students use role-playing to explore the possible consequences of Francisco's lie, as well as what might have happened if he had told the truth. They then go on to reading 2 (pages 25 to 32), in which the response of Francisco's grandfather—and its results—brings out the central moral theme (as we defined it): that the truth builds trust in social relationships.

"To Discuss" exercises and a second "To Practice" activity (a partner interview) follow in reading 2. The guide concludes with "To Express," which in this case calls on students to write an autobiographical piece.

The GSID and VLF labored over how to put the theory and research of perspective taking into practice in the guides. To show more explicitly how we attempted to integrate perspective-taking, I quote an excerpt from a text, an example of a reading-comprehension question drawn from the guide ("To Discuss") for the story *A Day's Work,* and two students' responses. Together, I hope they show how we used the text to write meaningful comprehension questions that challenged not only the students' literacy skills but also their understanding of social relationships.

After Francisco's lie is discovered, Francisco's grandfather offers to work for free to repair the damage in the garden and the lie. Ben, his employer, responds this way:

> "Look," he said, "if you need money I'll give you half now." He began to pull his wallet from his pocket but Abuelo held up his hand.
>
> (*To Francisco*) "Tell him we take the pay tomorrow when we finish."
>
> Francisco's grandfather and Ben looked at each other and words seemed to pass between them, though there were no words. Ben slid his wallet back into his pocket.
>
> "Tomorrow then. Six A.M.," Ben said. "And tell your grandfather I can always use a good man—for more than just one day's work."
>
> Francisco gave a hop of excitement. More than just a day's work!
>
> Ben was still speaking. "The important things your grandfather knows already. And I can teach him gardening."

A key goal of VLF's reading-comprehension questions was to ask children to talk and write not only about what happened, and what the characters said and did, but more important, about its personal meaning to them. Here is a sample question from the guide accompanying *A Day's Work.*

> At the end of the story, Ben offers Abuelo more than one day of work. He says to Francisco, "The important things your grandfather knows already. And I can teach him gardening" (page 30). What does Ben mean? What important things does Abuelo know?

From our theoretical standpoint, students' answers to these questions may exemplify different levels of understanding of the lesson Francisco has learned and its applicability to their own lives. For instance, here are the responses to this question of two students from a fourth-grade class that we will visit again later in this chapter:

> NORBERTO: Francisco wanted his Abuelo to get a job, and Ben said to take the weeds out but not the flowers. They took the wrong thing out. They took the flowers out. So Ben got mad at Francisco and Abuelo. Ben means that telling a lie is the wrong thing.

> ANGEL: "The important things" means that . . . Francisco shouldn't have lied to his Abuelo because he hurt his Abuelo's feelings. I think Ben learned to trust Abuelo because Abuelo said that he could take care of everything that went wrong. He would put all the good weeds in and out all the bad weeds. Francisco probably lost his grandfather's trust. But Abuelo managed to fix everything that went wrong. I think Abuelo can trust Francisco next time.

Neither Norberto nor Angel is fully correct, nor is either boy totally wrong in his interpretation of Ben's meaning. It is difficult for fourth-graders to express their full understanding of the meaning of concepts like integrity. Most readers, however, would agree that Angel expresses a comprehension of the meaning of Ben's words that, although it may be incomplete, is more sophisticated than Norberto's. But why is Angel's response stronger? From the GSID's standpoint, Norberto's interpretation of the meaning of what Ben said focuses only on the lie as wrong. Angel concentrates on the repair—the truth—as well. Our research group's aim was to develop a rubric or system of classification by which practitioners could articulate the essence of the difference in the social awareness expressed by students like Angel and Norberto. We hoped that the students' responses might capture, or allow us a glimpse of, their own ethics of social relationships. From our point of view, the responses are not simply right or wrong; they are developmentally different. Our subsequent research into students' reading-comprehension and writing exercises is discussed in greater detail in part IV of this book.

As mentioned in chapter 5, students and (most) teachers were unaware at this point in time of our behind-the-scenes work on the guides. And indeed, we had not yet begun to do research in the heart of VLF practice. We simply observed a few classrooms just to see how things were going—as a pilot idea to assist us in our future revisions of the guides. But as will be seen, our observations of the practice not only informed the guides but sent our research in a different direction, one that was not totally unexpected, but not really planned either. To begin to understand how that happened, let's take a look at how two teachers used the VLF materials.

Getting It: Ms. Lewis

Karen Lewis teaches fourth grade at an elementary school in the Dorchester section of Boston. The school, built in the 1920s, is solid and comforting, imparting a sense of safety and coziness. Because of the building's age, the oversized leaded windows actually open, and the wooden floors are pale and smooth from decades of wear. Ms. Lewis's room is sunny, cheerful, and tidy. Though there is little of her students' work on the walls, Ms. Lewis has decorated the bulletin boards with construction-paper flowers, which provide the backdrop for ever-changing book displays. At Thanksgiving all the books are related to Pilgrims, Puritans, Native Americans, or some other aspect of the holiday.

To one side of a chalkboard are lists of vocabulary words for the day: "those, froze, close. . . ." On another is written the date and, behind Ms. Lewis's desk chair, the names of students who have misbehaved during the day. A multiplication table graces a closet door. Two large bookcases contain reference books, word games, and boxes of colored plastic cubes. Desks are arranged in four quads so that students can easily work together in small groups.

To us, Ms. Lewis appeared to be tough and irrepressible. A Boston native, she was welcoming and affectionate but took no lip from her students. Her naturally loud voice came in handy when she needed it, both for disciplining students and for effective teaching and reading aloud. At first glance, Ms. Lewis did not appear to be a particularly progressive teacher. For instance, she seemed to rely on standard teaching methodologies learned fifteen years before in education school and fell back on showing vacuous videos when she could not deal with her students. But her instincts about teaching seemed to surpass those of other veterans, some of whom had been given extensive VLF training. Ms. Lewis just seemed to "get" VLF.

Even if they were enthusiastic about the program, many of the other teachers we observed who were new to VLF struggled to follow the teacher's guides closely and had some trouble making the transition from one section to another. Ms. Lewis demonstrated an uncanny ease with the curriculum, glancing at the guide only rarely, rewording questions to suit her kids' level of understanding, and putting the questions in more natural language, relating students' stories to the book and to her own story, all while remaining faithful to the intent of the guide.

Even though in retrospect Ms. Lewis believed that she spent too much time on the activities, the VLF guide for *A Day's Work* seemed to offer the structure and direction it was intended to provide; the activities, as presented by Ms. Lewis, did not seem hurried. The best way to convey how an effective teacher like Ms. Lewis can use the guides is to excerpt a lesson. Here are our observations from sessions over two days in December.[3]

Session 1: "To Connect"

Ms. Lewis begins by asking her students to get into their partner pairs. Without hesitation or complaint, the students change seats. As they do so, Ms. Lewis writes on the chalkboard: "What happens when we lie?"

When the class has settled in, Ms. Lewis asks the question aloud: "What happens when we lie?" Hands shoot up. She calls on each student in turn.

"You feel guilty."

"You get your mouth washed out with soap."

"You feel bad inside."

"You get a whoopin'."

"You get in trouble."

Ms. Lewis acknowledges each response without being judgmental; she nods her head, says, "Okay, next," or, "What else?" or, "Anyone have another idea?" None of these rejoinders sound dismissive, and it is clear that she is listening carefully to the students' responses. She is meticulous about allowing each student who volunteers to have a turn, even though this takes up a lot of time.

After all willing students have offered their answers, Ms. Lewis asks, "Who here has ever told a lie?" She has her own hand raised, and all the students in the class raise their hands. When our observer, Sarah Shmitt, raises her hand as well, Ms. Lewis chuckles. "See," says Ms. Lewis, "everyone knows what it's like to lie."

Ms. Lewis continues. "What are some examples of a lie?" A tiny black girl named Tamika says in a tiny voice, "Someone asked me if I had a dog, and I said yes." Ms. Lewis asks Tamika for some details. The story is that Tamika told her cousin that her mother had bought her a dog, and the next time the cousin visited she asked Tamika's mother where the dog was. Tamika's lie was discovered. Ms. Lewis repeats what Tamika has said so that everyone can hear. "Why would someone tell a lie like this?" she asks the class.

The replies come:

"So people will like her."

"So no one will tease her."

Turning to Tamika, Ms. Lewis asks her for permission to use her lie as an example in a discussion. Tamika nods. Ms. Lewis, following the suggestions in the guide (though she has not referred to it once in class), writes on the chalkboard: "I HAVE A DOG."

After drawing attention to the fact that she has used quotation marks because she has written something Tamika said, Ms. Lewis asks, "Who was involved in this story?" With a little prompting, the students answer: Tamika, her cousin, and her mom. On the chalkboard below "I HAVE A DOG," Ms. Lewis extends three arrows indicating Tamika, her cousin, and her mom and labels each one appropriately.

"How did your mother feel when your cousin asked her if it was true that you had a dog?" Ms. Lewis asks Tamika. "Shocked," the little girl says. "She was shocked that Tamika had lied," says Ms. Lewis to the class. Ms. Lewis writes "shocked" at the terminus of the mom arrow.

"And how did you feel when your cousin found out you'd told a lie?" Ms. Lewis then addresses this question to the whole class. "How do you think Tamika felt when her cousin found out?"

"Disappointed in herself."

"Angry with herself."

"Scared about being caught."

"Guilty."

Ms. Lewis writes the words "disappointed," "angry," and "guilty" on the chalkboard at the end of the Tamika arrow. "And how do you all think Tamika's cousin felt?"

"Sad."

"Mad."

"Disappointed."

"Let down."

At the end of the cousin arrow, Ms. Lewis writes these responses. "So," Ms. Lewis asks the class, "how did Tamika's mother feel about her lie?" The class offers "disappointed" and "ashamed." Ms. Lewis praises their use of these big vocabulary words and includes them on the mom's chalkboard list.

Turning to the attentive class, Ms. Lewis asks, "Is it wrong to feel ashamed or disappointed?" The meaning of this question is not immediately clear to the class. One boy says, "Yes. She needs to say she's sorry to her cousin."

Rather than dismiss the boy's response because he hasn't answered her question, Ms. Lewis builds on it: "If she says she's sorry, what happens?" she asks.

"She feels encouraged. She feels better."

"Right," says Ms. Lewis, smiling. "When we apologize or say we're sorry for something we feel badly about, we feel better, don't we?" The students nod their heads vigorously. One student rockets her hand up into the air, eager to share a story about a time when she got into trouble for disobeying her mother. Suddenly everyone has a story to tell. Ms. Lewis lets every student who wants to tell a story talk.

Session 1: "To Practice"

Ms. Lewis hands out the first "partner activity" worksheet and asks Tamika to read the instructions aloud, which she does very well. Ms.

Lewis introduces the partner activity by saying, "So talk to your partner in your whisper voices. Where do we look when we talk to our partners?" she asks. The students look blank. "Out the window?" she prompts with evident sarcasm. "At each other!" someone avers. "In the eye!" says another student. Ms. Lewis affirms these responses and repeats the "Look, Listen, Tell" instructions in her own words.

To ease the class into the partner activity, Ms. Lewis shares her own personal story.

> When I was a girl, my family had just moved to Boston and I was eager to make friends, especially with a girl named Kristine. The first time I went to Kristine's house, I wanted desperately to make a good impression, but while we were playing in the living room, I accidentally broke a fancy porcelain figurine. Kristine's mother heard the crash and came to see what had happened. Karen told her that I had broken the figurine. I was sent home immediately, and Kristine was punished.

Ms. Lewis tells the class that she'd felt terrible—she'd been sure Kristine would never be her friend after that.

"What happened?" her students want to know. "Did you apologize?"

Ms. Lewis says she must have apologized, because she and Kristine are friends now. One student says, "She forgave you," and Ms. Lewis writes "FORGIVENESS" on the chalkboard. "Yes," she says. "Kristine forgave me. That's important. Thank you."

Next, Ms. Lewis hands out lined paper so that the students can write a draft of their partner activity answers. "Remember," she says, "that if you get confused about whether or not to say 'mine' or 'his,' what can you do?" Ms. Lewis is addressing an important issue with regard to these partner activities: the confusion about the proper use of pronouns when writing or telling someone else's story. The fact that she brings this up indicates her classroom's familiarity with partnering. Today no one answers. She reframes the question: "What do we do if we don't know which pronoun to use?" After a little prodding, Angel says, "Write the person's name?"

"Right!" Ms. Lewis exclaims. "So you might say, 'Angel lied to his friend,' or, 'Yesenia lied about her homework,' instead of saying, 'She lied,' or, 'He lied.' That way we know who you are talking about."

Ms. Lewis previews the topic and the questions on the partner activity worksheet: "Write about a time when you told a lie to someone you care about, or when someone you care about told a lie. (1) What happened? (2) How did you feel about it? (3) How do you think the people in your story felt? (4) Did lying change any of the characters' feelings toward one another? (5) When you look back on this event from your past, do you think about it differently than you did when it happened? (6) Did you learn anything from it?"

Ms. Lewis uses her own story about Kristine as well as Tamika's story to clarify the questions. The students have trouble with the concepts of questions 4 and 5, but they seem to "get it" once Ms. Lewis has given them an example.

The next twenty-five minutes are happily spent in pairs. Two very sharp students—Angel, whom we met earlier, and Antonio—are paired together, and they choose to work on the reading circle carpet. They get right to work. The other students stay at their desks. Most pairs seem to work fine, but there are two pairs that have difficulty staying on task. Ms. Lewis offers assistance to every pair. She is careful to make sure they understand and respond to the questions. This is very time-consuming (Ms. Lewis glances worriedly at the clock several times) but seems profitable, judging from the students' thoughtful responses.

After she has circulated among all the pairs, Ms. Lewis asks whether anyone would like to share a story with the class. Predictably, no one raises a hand at first, but as soon as Angel volunteers, everyone wants to talk. "Okay," Ms. Lewis says, addressing the whole class, "whose story are you telling? Your own?" The class responds with a collective "No—our partner's!" Ms. Lewis nods at Angel to proceed and asks whether he has Antonio's permission to tell his story. They both nod. Angel stands and confidently reads Antonio's story to the class, beginning with the date: "Twelve, five, ninety-six. Antonio told a lie to his best friend. . . ."

As the students read their partners' stories, Ms. Lewis encourages them to help one another. Some students—particularly, it seems, those for whom English is not their first language—stumble frequently over the pronouns, and Ms. Lewis has to remind them to use their partner's name. Nearly all the students volunteer to tell a story. Some of the stories, like Tamika's story about the dog, are about bragging. Many are about being let down by well-meaning relatives who make promises they cannot keep, like the boy whose uncle promised to take him to a movie and never showed up. Ms. Lewis takes the time to help her class understand that there is a difference between lying and letting someone down, though it is hard to tell whether the class is absorbing this lesson.

One of the students, Marique, has told her partner a story about a time when she told a girl that she liked her when in fact she did not.

Ms. Lewis asks Marique, "Why did you tell her you liked her?" Marique says that she did not want to hurt the girl's feelings. "Well, at least that's a good motivation for telling a lie," Ms. Lewis asserts.

"Okay," Ms. Lewis says after all the students have shared their partner's story, "it's time to read a book." The class hurries excitedly to the back of the classroom where there is a rug and a large easy chair. Ms. Lewis takes a seat in the easy chair, and the students sit in a circle on the rug in front of her. In her lap is a copy of *A Day's Work.* Before she begins reading, she engages the class in a lively and interesting discussion about Mexico, immigration, and Mexican Americans today. Without seeming hurried or concerned that the students will not understand or appreciate the lesson, Ms. Lewis has her class find Mexico on a map; identify the states in the United States into which Mexicans have immigrated; recall the story of the Pilgrims (Thanksgiving having just occurred), who were immigrants from England; and discuss the different kinds of jobs that Mexican Americans do and the concept of day labor. Ms. Lewis spends nearly ten minutes on this introductory material. When she finally begins to read the book, the class is attentive and, for the most part, quiet.

Ms. Lewis reads up to page 24, as instructed in the guide. She stumbles over the pronunciation of the Spanish words in the book, particularly the word "abuelo." Her students, many of whom are bilingual, think her Spanish is hilarious. She laughs at herself and asks the Spanish-speaking students to help her. Every time she reads "abuelo" incorrectly, the students correct her in unison, rolling their eyes and giggling. The class ends with a palpable sense of warmth and mutual respect between Ms. Lewis and her students.

Session 2: "To Discuss"

The next day Ms. Lewis seems a little tired and on edge, though not so much so that her students would necessarily notice. By 10:00 A.M. Ms. Lewis has already been teaching *A Day's Work* for an hour with the help of the resource teacher, Mr. Kaplan. The class has been rewriting their partner activity worksheets based on their drafts from the previous week.

Ms. Lewis reviews with the class what happened at the end of the first reading. "Why does Abuelo say, 'We don't lie for work'?" she asks. Her students hesitate, then respond:

"Lying's breaking the rules."

"Lying is bad."

"He didn't want to hurt Ben's feelings."

Ms. Lewis assembles the class in the reading circle on the carpet and takes her seat in the big chair. She rereads the last few sentences of reading 1 and continues on through the end of the book, meticulously pronouncing "abuelo." ("I practiced," she confides to the class.)

Then Ms. Lewis leads a discussion. "What are some good things Francisco learned?" she asks. "Lying is bad," says one student. "Why?" Ms. Lewis asks. "Why is lying bad?"

"'Cause money can't always get you everything," says one student. "You lose something," says another.

"What do you lose?" Ms. Lewis wants to know.

"Trust."

"And you might regret it [lying] later."

"Why did Ben offer them half their pay? They'd done a really bad job, and still he offers to pay them. Why is he nice?"

"He thought they were so hungry."

"He knew they'd come back and fix it."

"Ben was a compassionate guy."

Ms. Lewis praises these responses, especially the use of the word "compassionate."

"What was the worst thing that happened to Francisco?" (Apparently Ms. Lewis has memorized these questions from the guide, but she asks them without a trace of contrivance.)

"When Abuelo figured out he lied."

"He was sad and disappointed in hisself."

"He almost got fired."

"Abuelo believed in him—to help him get a job."

"How does Abuelo feel?" Ms. Lewis asks.

"Disappointed."

"Francisco was scared he lost his [Abuelo's] job."

"What kind of a person is Ben?"

"A good guy."

"And Abuelo? What kind of a person is he?"

"Generous."

"Thoughtful."

Session 2: "To Express"

Easing into the "To Express" section, Ms. Lewis directs all the students who are wearing black sneakers to tiptoe back to their desks. About half the kids do this, literally tiptoeing to their seats. Next, she says that all the students wearing white or beige jeans should wiggle back to their desks. Again, they do. Finally, she says that everyone else should do the Macarena back to their seats. A line dance begins, with Roberto doing an impressive job leading about five kids in the Macarena. Surprisingly, however, as soon as the students reach their desks, they sit down and turn their attention to Ms. Lewis, who is at the chalkboard now. (In other classrooms the teacher might have had a hard time getting the students' attention after doing the Macarena.)

Ms. Lewis writes the characters' names on the board: Abuelo, Francisco, and Ben. "How do the characters in this story feel?" Ms. Lewis asks. Francisco is "ashamed," the students offer, and Ben is "mad" and "disappointed/shocked" and has "lost trust." Abuelo, they say, is "sad" and "angry."

Responding to the ensuing discussion about Ben's disappointment with Abuelo and Francisco, a boy named James raises his hand and tells a story about a time when his uncle promised him a bike for Christmas but then didn't get it for him. Addressing the class, Ms. Lewis asks, "Why did his uncle do that? Can we know why someone else does something?"

In unison, the class says, "No!"

"Why can't we know?" Ms. Lewis continues.

One student says, "Because we're not them."

"Can we sympathize with others? Can we try to understand why people do what they do?"

Again, in unison: "Yes!"

"Why?" Ms. Lewis prompts.

After a brief silence, Ms. Lewis helps them out. "Because we're all . . ."

"Alike!" the class bellows.

This exchange appears to be one that Ms. Lewis repeats often in class, and she concludes it by summarizing: "That's right, no matter how different we might seem to be, we are really all human beings, right? We are all alike in many ways." The class seems to hear this, though it is impossible to know how they understand it.

Although the students seem to agree that letting somebody down is not the same as lying, they do not fully understand the difference. On the "To Express" worksheets, when asked to write about a time when someone lied to them, most of these students write about being let down by a relative who did not show up as promised, but it is not clear that their aunts or uncles or parents actually intended to deceive them.

At this point Ms. Lewis begins to hand out the "To Express" worksheets and pieces of yellow scrap paper. Again, she takes the time to preview the questions to make sure everyone understands what is being asked of them. The students struggle with the question "Why is this story important?" Ms. Lewis asks them to try to think of another way to say "Why is this story important?" but no one comes up with anything. Ms. Lewis offers her own interpretation: "This question is saying, 'This story is important because of how it made me feel.'"

During the next half-hour Ms. Lewis helps the students with writing—rewording their sentences, organizing their thoughts, clarifying ideas, and correcting their spelling. With some students, she does a lot of the work. Other students have prepared reasonably cogent responses, and Ms. Lewis makes only minor changes. When she senses that the class may have missed an important point, Ms. Lewis uses the "finish the sentence" technique: "Francisco felt . . . what? Sad. Right. And Ben wanted to hire a . . . what? Gardener. Right." (While this technique is useful for jogging kids' memories, it is hard to know how effective it is as a learning tool since the prompting sentences can be worded to make the appropriate answer obvious.)

It is nearly 11:15, and Ms. Lewis wants to bring the unit to an end. As the students put the finishing touches on their writing, Ms. Lewis asks, "So what happens when we know someone lies all the time? Does it help us to know this about a person?"

Angel raises his hand. "Yes," he says. "Because then you can figure out how to deal with the person."

"Right," Ms. Lewis asserts. "It helps us work with that person." Angel asks to share his story with the class. "Of course!" Ms. Lewis says. He stands, and in a loud voice reads:

> "What happened?" My mom lied to me because she did not want to tell me that my father was in jail. "How did the people involved feel about it?" I felt sad because my mom could trust me on anything she tells me. "Why did this person lie?" My mom lied because she didn't want me to be sad. "Why is this story important?" This story is important to me because I love my mother and father.

After Angel reads his story, other students share their writing. Norberto, apparently moved by his classmates' stories, raises his hand and implores, "Why do people lie? People should be nice to each other. It causes so many problems."

While collecting the writing samples from her students, Ms. Lewis opens his question to the class: "What are some reasons people lie?" She reviews all the reasons they have discussed so far—people lie because they want to make friends, because they want to protect others, because they want something, like a puppy, very badly. Sometimes people lie because they are hungry and worried about their family. Although the students did not offer this reason themselves, many of them know exactly what Ms. Lewis means.

Losing It: Ms. Kelly

Cathy Kelly is teaching a fourth-grade class at an elementary school in Roslindale, a neighborhood at the far reaches of Boston that even native Bostonians are hard pressed to locate on a map. Although she is a many-year veteran of the public schools, Ms. Kelly is having a tough first year in her new assignment at this school. There is no direct subway access to Roslindale from where she lives, and Roslindale Center has no thriving businesses, no modern restaurants, and no "services" to lure anyone except locals to its down-at-the-heels main street. Rozzy—as it is affectionately called by those who live there—used to be a white, working-class neighborhood, but in recent years the low cost of housing has attracted soaring numbers of Hispanics, blacks, and gay people. The new demographics disturb many of the old guard residents, who are having trouble adjusting to the changed neighborhood.

Cathy Kelly's attitudes about teaching and about her students seem to reflect something of old Rozzy's parochialism and fear of the future. Though she describes herself as having once been so left of center politically that she was "way over here" (she sweeps her arm to her left, indicating with a flick of her wrist a continuum that extends beyond the room), she says that she has become more conservative as a result of both her experience teaching in the Boston public schools and the effect that some "liberal" social policies, like affirmative action, have had on her family.

Ms. Kelly confided to us, "When I look at my class, I don't see their color—they're all just kids to me." But she talks viciously about the "lefty liberals" who chose to hire a black man for the police force instead of her husband and who, she feels, are threatening the futures of her son and daughter because of "all the minorities they hire."

Right away Ms. Kelly was uncomfortable teaching the first required VLF unit on *A Day's Work* because it provides teachers with a brief and frankly political history of Mexicans in the United States. "My students are too self-centered to understand all this history," she complained. "They won't be interested in this."

Ms. Kelly was willing to talk to us about her refusal to tell her students a personal story, as suggested in the VLF teacher's guide, about a time when she told a lie to someone she cared about. Recalling her strict parochial school upbringing, she insisted, "I never lied, ever. I knew my father would have really punished me if I did, and I was afraid of the nuns at school!" But in subsequent conversations she revealed the subtext to her disquiet: "As a teacher, I'm supposed to hold to a higher standard; I can't be telling my students that I lied. . . . I don't even want them to know that I listen to rock and roll!"

At times our observers felt that Ms. Kelly's room was like a holding cell, a place where everyone was waiting for something to happen. The tense atmosphere was exacerbated by her naturally quiet voice, which, when raised to a volume that could be heard over her students' general clamor, was high-pitched and grating, making her sound perpetually irritated even when she was not. To make matters worse, one student in the class had very serious learning and discipline problems, and he was constantly disrupting class. He was almost never in his seat, and he could not resist the temptation to taunt the other students and to speak loudly and insolently to Ms. Kelly when she tried to control him. By the end of the school year the class was fractured, in large part owing to this one boy's behavior.

"To Connect"

In November, in preparation for the "To Connect" step of VLF, we observe Ms. Kelly lead a discussion about lying. Her students sit at their desks in tidy rows, all facing forward. She opens the discussion by asking who in her class has ever told a lie. Everyone's hand—except hers—goes up. Feigning surprise at the number of raised hands, she asks for volunteers to tell the class a story about a time when they lied.

Though her students are eager to tell their stories, before calling on any of them, Ms. Kelly takes the opportunity presented by the discussion topic to ask, "Who do we know in this classroom who is a liar?" The children look around at one another, somewhat confused. Everyone's hand is up—they are clearly all liars. As hands begin to go down, Ms. Kelly urges, "Don't we know of one boy who lied to the teacher?" The students waver between the urge to please the teacher by naming names and the urge to protect their peers.

Smiling broadly, Ms. Kelly leans over a dark-eyed boy and asks, "Was it you, Donald?" Donald looks away, eyes fixed on a frayed shoelace. To the class Ms. Kelly announces, "Donald told me that his mother hadn't signed his report card because he lost it on the way home from school. But that was a lie! And now it will be hard for me to trust Donald again, won't it?" Several uncertain heads nod. One girl raises her hand. "Marcella?" the teacher prompts. "Donald showed us the report card that same day," Marcella says eagerly. "He never lost it." "See how bad lying is?" Ms. Kelly continues. "None of us can trust Donald now because we all know what a liar he is."[4]

To summarize how the teaching of VLF seemed to be going in this particular classroom, I will be unsparingly forthright: Ms. Kelly was misguided in her beliefs about the population she teaches (that they are all "the same color," for example), had low expectations for their performance, and was unskilled in the basics of classroom management and lesson planning. What she appeared to have going for her was her tenacity and a competitive streak that might ignite the spark that the right teacher trainer could use to once again engage her in her profession. Observing Ms. Kelly was an early warning signal to us that teaching VLF was not going to be so easy for some teachers.

To Understand Rather Than to Evaluate: Implications for Research and Practice

The interpretation of this chapter depends, of course, on one's point of view. Here are the implications I draw from the work described. First, from an educator's point of view, it is clear that pedagogy is not static. Over a period of a decade the structure of the VLF guides was changed several times, owing in part to feedback from classroom observations and in part to policy changes in the larger educational community, especially those focused on raising standards for literacy competence and standardizing the testing of these skills. As we shall see, the VLF curriculum continues to grow and change.

Nevertheless, there are deep philosophical issues and values embedded in the curriculum and instruction. The "central question" of *A Day's Work,* according to the resource guide, is "Why is it important to tell the truth?" According to the guide writers, this question "encourages students to explore how lying affects our relationships with others and our own sense of integrity." Some of the students in this and other classes we visited, especially those who were very poor, thought that lying was okay if they, or their family, were put at risk if they told the truth. How much should the guides or the teachers paint truth and lies in black and white, and how much should they show shades of gray? These are tough issues, and one readily can see why schools and teachers might want to shy away from them.

They also are issues that raise important research questions. Ms. Kelly thought that her students were too "self-centered" to understand issues such as the policies that affect immigration. Is she right? Is this issue too difficult for fourth-graders to understand? What are the developmental and experiential factors that might influence the way elementary school students understand these issues? Ms. Lewis discovered that her students did not clearly differentiate between blatant lies and unfulfilled promises. When do children make these differentiations, and under what conditions? How do Ms. Lewis's and

Ms. Kelly's vastly different readings of the same novel get played out in the classroom?

When Ben, in the story, says, "The important things your grandfather already knows," what are the developmental differences in the meaning that students make of his comment? Besides their teachers' and their own experiences across social class or ethnic differences, what other factors influence how they interpret Ben's comments?

All these questions cry out for systematic study. Sometimes such studies can be done under carefully controlled conditions. However, we also can learn much by doing research of this kind directly in the heart of the practice. We learned a great deal by observing these two teachers in "naturalistic" settings, without controlled conditions, simply watching how they taught and interacted with the curriculum. We planned to do more.

But something unexpected happened when we innocently attempted to observe how the pedagogy worked. We found that we could not ignore the fundamental role that teachers (and schools) play in the developmental process of social awareness in children. What influence were Ms. Kelly and Ms. Lewis having on the social growth of their students? How did their own values, ethics, and opinions about VLF influence how they taught it? In the end, on our way to doing research on children, we found that we needed to focus on the teachers as well. This became both a priority and a challenge. Chapter 7 outlines our plan for research in the heart of the VLF curriculum, and part III of the book details how we attempted to account for variation and development in teachers as well as students.

Chapter 7

The Everyday Lives of Teachers: A New Focus for Practice-Based Research

OUR ORIGINAL research plan was to observe students and teachers during the implementation of VLF over two years in four elementary schools chosen from those that offered teachers the option of using VLF materials. During the first year of the project we worked with teachers in grades two and four; in the second year we observed in third- and fifth-grade classrooms. We selected classrooms for inclusion in this study based on a variety of criteria, including the teacher's willingness to be observed, the dynamics among students, the quality of the relationship between the teacher and his or her students, and, in some cases, the diversity represented by a particular class. The primary assignment of the half-dozen field observers was to record what they saw as they watched teachers using VLF materials with their students as part of their language arts lessons.[1]

For the sake of consistency, we asked that in each grade all the participating teachers use one particular book from the VLF list—and the accompanying teacher's guide—during the fall of the school year, and another in the spring. The fourth-grade teachers, for example, used *A Day's Work* in the fall. In the spring they used *The Hundred Dresses,* a chapter book written in the 1940s about a poor immigrant girl from Poland who is teased by the other girls in an American midwestern town because she always wears the same dress.[2]

At the outset, in September 1996, the participating second- and fourth-grade teachers met with the Carnegie Research Study's project director, Dr. Lynn Schultz, and project manager Sarah Shmitt to discuss the nuts and bolts of the project (how many VLF books to teach, when to administer questionnaires and worksheets, and so on).[3] VLF and research team representatives explained the primary objectives of the project. First, we hoped to gather information on the range of levels of social awareness one might expect to see among second- through fifth-grade students. Second, we wanted to study how literacy and social skills might be related, and whether they could indeed be jointly promoted. Third, we were interested in finding out the measurable effects that VLF—and by extension, other programs like it—might have on students' interpersonal skills and intergroup awareness as well as on their reading and writing abilities.

Observers were encouraged to interview both students and teachers informally to augment their field notes. Field researchers also assisted the research staff in the collection of outcome data. The outcome of primary interest to us at the outset was the growth of students' awareness of the ethics of social relationships. We measured this in several ways. As part of our earlier work with VLF, we had designed student worksheets to provide teachers and program coordinators with information about the social development of the children with whom they were working. These worksheets were integrated into the teacher's guides as reading-comprehension and writing exercises for the students to complete.[4]

The Students and the Teachers

Of the approximately four hundred students in our research sample, well over half were black; of the remaining, most were Hispanic. (Two of our Carnegie research schools were bilingual.) At the third school an April attendance report indicated that only two white students were enrolled; at the bilingual schools a little more than one-quarter of the student body was classified as white. The populations of all four of our research schools were generally poor: at the time of our study roughly 85 percent of their students received reduced-cost or free lunches.

Such statistics tend to imply that the school culture in Boston is monolithic and peopled by despairing children of color. But the picture that the statistics do not and cannot paint is far more varied: Boston's elementary school children, like elementary school children everywhere, are often resilient, poetic, and compassionate. These are the characteristics that good teaching can cultivate.

The principals of four Boston public elementary schools agreed to the participation of their teachers in our research. Most of the teachers who took part in the study were using VLF for the first time while simultaneously struggling to implement several of the many components of the district's ambitious school reform agenda. A lesser number were VLF veterans who had used VLF materials during the early pilot years of the program's development. These teachers relied on the curriculum both as a way of managing discrimination issues among their students and of cultivating careful, critical, and honest forms of expression in their classrooms.

The twenty-one teachers we worked with represented a broad range of teaching experience: one fourth-grade teacher had been teaching in the same school for nearly sixteen years, another had just been certified, and another had been a low-level bureaucrat in the public schools for many years and had decided at the end of her career to try her hand at teaching second-graders. Most of these teachers, not surprisingly, were women; about half were white. There were Spanish-speaking bilingual teachers from Puerto Rico, Ecuador, and Costa Rica, as well as a few Nuyoricans and, for balance, a Boston-Irish lesbian bilingual teacher who was pregnant when we began our study. All of these teachers had attended the mandatory districtwide (pan-Boston) introduction to VLF for elementary school teachers two years earlier.[5]

The Historical Context: Literacy and School Reform in the 1990s

Few teachers object in principle to taking on the responsibility of fostering students' social and ethical development; this is something most teachers feel they have been doing all along, even though most professional training programs do not offer specifics guidelines for teaching interpersonal skills and moral precepts. And though most teachers are enthusiastic supporters of literacy initiatives, almost all have their own, very personal ideas about what ethical development means. Few of the teachers who agreed to take part in our study said that they had thought very much about the ways in which social skills and literacy might be linked in a meaningful, let alone measurable, way. This idea intrigued some of these teachers and seemed to threaten others.

In each of our four research schools, some teachers were drawn to the VLF approach because it seemed to them intuitively right that as children learn to communicate better they also learn to get along better. But others were intimidated by the sheer heft of the newly minted VLF teacher's guides, which seemed to belie the simplicity of the idea that language arts and social skills could be thought of as interdependent. In addition, the long shadows of the words "research" and "observation" fell across the entire project, causing many of the teachers involved, in the beginning at least, to approach the books, pedagogy, and study questionnaires with wariness, or even with resentment.[6]

All of this was occurring against the backdrop of major changes within the Boston public school system, changes that were part of a national push toward educational reform. First of all, as of 1995, the members of the Boston School Committee, who had previously been elected officials, were now mayoral appointees, and the newly constituted school committee had endorsed not only VLF as a systemwide character education program for kindergarten through twelfth grade but other major school reform efforts as well. And after a lengthy, intense, and competitive search the year before, Thomas Payzant, who brought with him a record as a successful reformer in San Diego, had been hired as superintendent to shake up Boston's ever-floundering public school system.

He had immediately set to work: changing the organization of the district; eliminating many middle managers; reviewing the records of all schools and their principals; establishing challenging curriculum standards; and raising money from local private industry for building playgrounds, enhancing libraries, setting up Internet access, restoring dilapidated buildings, and buying books. He chose new standardized tests to assess academic achievement more accurately, switched to a portfolio system of assessment in classrooms, and, in one of his most high-profile initiatives, pushed as many early literacy programs into as many schools as he could, with the goal of bringing the test scores of all third-graders up to grade level in reading and writing as quickly as possible.

The push to raise reading scores in Boston was not an isolated, local phenomenon. Riding the crest of the national wave of educational reform that preceded his tenure, President Clinton had only recently announced his own literacy initiatives, including national (though voluntary) standardized testing, the training of a national corps of literacy volunteers based loosely on Boston's own City Year model, and several new funding sources for literacy-based programs for young children. His high-profile call to action on literacy raised the stakes for nationwide reform in this fundamental educational arena and set into motion a storm of competition for newly available federal funds.

Needless to say, over time all of these trends influenced the shift in VLF's definition of itself as a literature-based multicultural character education program to a program designed to promote literacy skills within a multicultural character education context. Why this shift? Primarily because it made good sense both politically and professionally. A primary mission of teaching, particularly these days and particularly in the elementary grades, is to promote literacy, and educators need to find innovative approaches that are helpful in achieving this essential goal.

It was clear that a notable effect of the local and national focus on literacy was a sudden and immense pressure on teachers and principals to improve students' scores on standardized reading achievement tests such as the Stanford 9 (published by the educational measurement division of Harcourt Brace). Many educators also felt new pressure to deliver high-quality "products," that is, students' stories, essays, art, book reports, and so on, to illustrate the dramatic progress being made in their school or district in the teaching of reading-comprehension and writing skills. Many a superintendent's reputation, it had become clear, would stand or fall on the strength of his or her fourth-graders' levels of achievement as measured in these ways.

In the meantime, all of Boston's elementary school teachers had been asked to adapt to a completely new set of English language arts standards, grapple with the new portfolio assessment system and with the concerns of their principals, and evaluate and choose between half a dozen literacy initiatives suitable for their particular school populations. And they were expected to drive this trainload of required products and processes skillfully and without complaint in the name of school reform.

It was in this climate that the principals of our four Carnegie research schools asked their teachers to participate in a study using a little-understood, often time-consuming, and sometimes emotionally demanding new developmental and cultural approach to improving literacy, social skills, and relationship competencies. And despite what must surely have appeared to them to be improbable expectations, infinite requirements, and unreasonable demands, all of the teachers in our study made the extra effort to help us to better understand the complexities of implementing VLF—or any other new educational approach. A visit with some of these teachers helps to explain what we were beginning to learn.

Sarah Shmitt's Reports from the Schools: The Downside

Across the two-year period of our Carnegie Research Study, Sarah Shmitt was responsible for the collection of our "data," mostly reading comprehension and social awareness worksheets, as described in the last chapter, and writing samples, which we discuss in later chapters. She was also responsible for the team of observers who went to the schools and sat in the classrooms of the teachers who generously agreed to "teach the guides." The rest of this chapter brings into the book some of Sarah's own observations, which give us an idea of how VLF fit into the larger context of the world of elementary grade teachers.

Ms. McDougan

As I approach the door of Darcy McDougan's classroom on this Monday morning just before lunch, I see that her students are all engrossed in a math worksheet. I rap lightly on the door, and a student gestures, signaling me to come in. Ms. McDougan is correcting the worksheets of the few students who have already completed their work. When she sees me, she flashes her signature smile and waves me toward her desk. We speak in whispers as we wait for the remaining five minutes of class time to pass so she can dismiss her students for lunch.

I ask if she has begun *The Hundred Dresses* yet. She rolls her eyes and says, "You know, honey, I would love to get started on that book, but look what we have to have done, and it's already April!" She opens her arms, palms up, indicating the mass of papers and books on her desk. She takes up the basal reader she uses and waves it in front of me. "I have to get through every page of this reader, and, don't get me wrong, I love this reader, it's a really good book, but you know we've got those Stanford 9 tests to get through, and my kids have never taken a test like that, so we have to do practice tests so they know what to expect, and [the principal] wants us to have students write their travel brochures by the end of next week, and I can barely get these kids to find Canada on a map. And we've got all this math to get through, and there's a science fair coming up. And we have this recorder performance that the kids are all excited about, but it takes up time!"

She takes the reader and hides her face from the class as she says to me, "I tell you, I am so stressed out. These kids barely have the basic skills, reading and writing, to get up to fifth grade. Some of them I want to keep back, but I don't think their parents will permit it. I don't know what's going on in the second and third grades, but the kids I'm seeing these past few years can't do the work and should not have been promoted into the fourth grade." I try to reassure her that she still has plenty of time left in which to teach *The Hundred Dresses*. She puts the basal down on her desk, looks up at the clock, and sighs a deep sigh. "I just don't know if I want to teach anymore," she says in a tired voice. "They just expect us to work miracles—they want us to teach all of this stuff with hardly any resources, and they want the students to move on to middle school, and they want them to have stellar personalities. And they have these new standards—and I believe in high standards, I really do—but these kids can't even read and write. How can I get them to meet these new standards?"

The bell rings for lunch.

Under different circumstances, Ms. McDougan might have been a convert to VLF: she was energetic, committed, thorough, warm, creative, and curious. A self-described "lifelong learner," she often asked about the theory behind the program, and she attended at least one of the off-site workshops because she wanted to better understand the VLF pedagogy. Yet she sometimes hinted to the researcher in her class that she was unsupported at her school. She felt the principal played favorites and did not have a very sophisticated leadership style, the result of which was infighting and low morale. At the end of the school year, after more than ten years at the Matthews School, Ms. McDougan left teaching to pursue a career in business.

Ms. Gibbs

If Ms. McDougan is an opportunity lost in a harsh environment, then Eleanor Gibbs might be considered a lost cause, someone for whom VLF was simply not going to work. Sarah's observations suggest some reasons why.

> It is a bone-chilling day, and the sky over Dorchester is a leaden gray, threatening snow. Ms. Gibbs, with a few minutes to spare before her second-grade class returns from lunch, rushes breathlessly around her classroom looking in every cabinet, in every child's desk, in each one of her books and folders, trying to find the stack of "To Express" writing worksheets I've come to collect that her second-grade class completed the previous week. She chatters constantly about her students—about how poorly behaved they are, about their lack of motivation, about their disrespect. She is so disorganized and distracted that I know, as I watch helplessly, she will never find what she is looking for, because she has no idea what the worksheets in question look like. I've noticed that Ms. Gibbs doesn't really pay attention to what she's been teaching, though she believes herself to be an expert of sorts on urban education issues in general, so much so that she has suggested to me several times with a conspiratorial air that we should write a book together on what public schools are really like and get on the *Oprah* show.
>
> When the class returns from lunch, Ms. Gibbs continues her hopeless search, despite my protestations. She tells her class to work on their math homework, which many of them have already completed. They become restless and bored. They ask to go to the bathroom. They begin to speak in loud voices. A student leaves the room without permission. Another deliberately tips over his chair. During all of this, Ms. Gibbs speaks sub voce to me (though loudly enough so that her students can hear) about specific students and their particular troubles—their drug-addicted parents, their poor health, their filthy mouths. She indicates with a raised eyebrow or a tilt of her head the student to whom she is

referring. The students know what she is saying; most look hurt, embarrassed. It is very awkward to be in this position, to be the unwitting confidante of a teacher who is betraying her students as they watch, humiliated.

Gradually, the class's patience for staying seated dissipates. As the forty-five-minute period draws to a close, a class period during which the teacher gave her students no direction and no instruction, the class is completely out of control. Ms. Gibbs is shrieking at her students to behave. One student, who is said to have ADD [attention deficit disorder], has threatened Ms. Gibbs, kicked her, and been sent to the principal's office, where he will simply sit unattended for yet another class period. As I leave, without the worksheets for which I'd originally come, Ms. Gibbs turns the lights out in her room and demands that all of the students put their heads on their desks until they can learn to behave. Another wasted hour is ahead of them.

Ms. Gibbs blamed her problems in the classroom on two external forces. First, she somehow believed, based on her own experience growing up in a mixed neighborhood south of Boston, that her classroom was not "diverse" and that diversity automatically improves student behavior. In fact, her classroom was approximately 75 percent black, and among those children some were Haitian, some Dominican, and some African American; the remaining 25 percent of her students were Hispanic and also represented many countries of origin. Second, she believed that her colleagues and principal were conspiring against her, that she had somehow unwittingly alienated them. Frustrated and demoralized, Ms. Gibbs applied for, and got, a transfer out of the Matthews School to a "more diverse" school in Brighton.

Even with her competence as a teacher bolstered by the best possible skills training to support her use of VLF as part of the curriculum, Ms. Gibbs would still not be likely to be able to make VLF work in her classroom. This is because it is not teaching competence alone that dictates how engaged students will be with the VLF books and activities. It is something that we call teacher engagement.

As our study proceeded, further questions arose. How could we have "hooked" Ms. McDougan on VLF so that it would become the process she used for all of her teaching rather than having it be one more demand she needed to worry about fulfilling? Might there have been a way to engage Ms. Gibbs so that she could have used VLF to improve both her own teaching skills and her students' learning? Why are certain practices or subjects or teaching styles personally meaningful to some teachers and not to others?

The Other Side of the Coin: VLF as Benefit Rather Than Burden

Soraya Loreno and Amy Arbeit are fourth-grade teachers at the Russell School in Allston-Brighton, a neighborhood in the old Boston sense of the word. Its main intersection is dominated by locally owned businesses with Irish names like Rourke's, a pharmacy that still houses a thriving soda fountain augmented to cater to the espresso-and-*New-York-Times* generation. The school's architecture mirrors that of the village square: turn-of-the-century red brick, honey-colored wooden floors, and oversized windows that seal in the warm, mitten-steamy air in winter and open to let in sea breezes to relieve the sudden and stultifying heat of a Boston summer.

Ms. Loreno and Ms. Arbeit

Ms. Loreno has taught at the Russell School for nearly twenty years, and Ms. Arbeit has been there for sixteen. (She has a total of thirty-five years' worth of experience in the classroom.) These teachers have seen this school's population change dramatically as Southeast Asian, Haitian, Dominican, and other immigrant populations have moved into the neighborhood, overwhelming its once-dominant white Irish core. These changes have put unprecedented demands on educators and on the administrators of the schools that serve this community. Ms. Loreno, for example, who speaks both English and Spanish, must do her best to bring all of her students up to grade level in reading in English even though she may have children from six or eight different countries in her classroom at any given time. Some have arrived in the last few months speaking virtually no English. Not too long ago, Ms. Loreno's class would have been far more homogeneous, representing far fewer cultures and languages than it does today.

In the first meeting between the Carnegie research and evaluation team and the Russell faculty, held in the Russell's cramped cafeteria, Ms. Arbeit had no qualms about expressing her opinion about the unilateral, top-down way in which the decision to participate in the VLF study was made. "You realize we were strong-armed into this," she said. We had thought teachers had been asked to be a part of the research and so assumed that teachers would, for the most part, be willing participants. In most cases, however, it seemed that they simply had been told by their principals that their schools would be participating. She did not personalize her comments or malign the program in any direct way, but it was clear that she would be an uncooperative and recalcitrant partner (though one with a sense of humor, as it turned out).

Ms. Arbeit informed us of her long tenure in the Boston public schools and said that she felt she was doing a fine job teaching her students both social and literacy skills, and that she did not need VLF to do it for her. She had her own definition of "critical thinking," which seemed to be synonymous with the more negative meaning of the word "critical." Her students spent a lot of time talking about what they did not like about every book they read and why. (They were disappointed with *A Day's Work* because they felt there was not enough character development of the mother; they had flatly refused to read *Sarah, Plain and Tall.*)

In the end, Ms. Arbeit cooperated fully, turning in copious data, though she made a great show of her disapproval of the activities in the guides. But her initial complaints about the way in which the original decision to participate had been made brought up an implementation variable we had not counted on studying. What had motivated teachers to participate in the Carnegie study in the first place—or, in our GSID developmental model's terms, what was personally meaningful about the research project that led to their participation? For Ms. Arbeit, who had been "strong-armed" into it, the motivation was clear: she felt she had to toe the line or else be punished in some unnamed way by her principal.

Ms. Loreno gave the impression of being someone who had seen, and possibly rejected, just about every trend in teaching to pass through the Russell. She appeared cynical and uncooperative, and in contrast to Ms. Arbeit, rather humorless. Indeed, a researcher in her classroom was more than once greeted icily or ignored entirely, and during the fall data collection period researchers worried that Ms. Loreno might refuse to participate in spite of the principal's directive that she do so. The principal himself, a strong supporter of VLF, warned us that Ms. Loreno might prove to be a tough sell. Her brusque and confident manner could seem authoritarian to one unaccustomed to the cultural norm in a Spanish bilingual class; similarly, her teaching methods could seem didactic and prosaic.

For example, one day as she was speaking with Sarah about her class's experience with one of the VLF books, a student approached her with a writing exercise, apparently with the hope that Ms. Loreno would correct it for her. With a hard stare and a stiff wave of her arm, Ms. Loreno dispatched the girl; her response seemed at first to be one of harsh indifference. But as she walked away, the girl was smiling a guilty smile, aware that she had broken a rule of the roost—do not interrupt—and so deserved to be turned away. As soon as Ms. Loreno and the researcher had finished their discussion, Ms. Loreno immediately called the girl over to her desk and corrected her paper, offering much praise where deserved, and much criticism where she knew this student could have done better. It was clear from this and other interactions that Ms. Loreno demanded of her students the respect and consideration that she, in turn, gave to them, regardless of their life situation or level of academic achievement.

Ms. Loreno's Surprise Endorsement

> It's January, and I approach this school with just a little dread. Ms. Loreno, the fourth-grade bilingual teacher, is never very friendly, and the last time we encountered one another she berated me for failing to give her a copy of the new teacher's guide. . . . When I entered the lunchroom [on a previous occasion, to deliver Spanish-language worksheets], she barely spoke to me. She practically sneered when I gave her the translated worksheets. For these reasons I do not look forward to our meetings.
>
> I find Ms. Loreno in the lunchroom once again. I approach her with caution and, begging her forgiveness for interrupting her lunch, ask how the VLF unit is going. Much to my surprise, she suddenly becomes more animated and engaged than I have ever seen her. "It's going really, really well!" she exclaims enthusiastically. She goes on to tell me how much her students are enjoying the *Day's Work* unit despite how long it is taking to get through it. She requests, for the spring research title, that we supply her class with multiple copies of whatever book we choose, because in a bilingual classroom it makes a huge difference if there are extra copies . . . so that small groups of students can read aloud together or work with an aide on their English reading skills.
>
> When I visit her class again in March, Ms. Loreno wants to show off the work her students have done on their last VLF. Inside a manila folder are the "To Express" activities, letters in which the students wrote to someone about times they felt picked upon. Some of the letters are to friends, others to teachers, some to people outside the school, a few to Ms. Loreno—all of which she has answered, her responses stapled to the students' letters. The level of writing, that is, the sophistication of ideas, the organization, and the execution (mechanics), were all very impressive. We express our delight at the work her students have done; she beams at us, nodding her agreement. "I demand a lot from my students, and they do it. You must set your expectations high, or they won't respond. These kids can do hard work, but no one asks them to!"

Ms. Loreno was the last person that we expected to embrace VLF—she seemed to be among the least motivated to teach the VLF curriculum. And yet by April she was cornering observers to show off the writing her students had done on their VLF units, writing that went far beyond what was suggested in the guides. And most surprising of all, at the end of the school year she chased down the project manager to make sure she could attend—voluntarily—VLF's upcoming two-day summer institute.

Hunches, Obvious and Not So Obvious

As the relationship between the research staff and Ms. Loreno improved over time, we became more aware of the elements of her teaching that seemed to have a positive influence on her students' behavior and motivation to learn, all of which, we also began to realize, were being employed daily by every good teacher we observed:

- *Clarity of instruction:* Making sure students know what is expected of them
- *Follow-through:* Doing what you have said you will do
- *Creative alternatives:* Giving students choices; allowing them to help decide how to achieve agreed-upon goals
- *Smooth transitions:* Taking care not to rush the class from one activity to the next; allowing time for students to make connections and think about the meaning of what they are doing
- *High expectations:* Setting high standards for both academic work and the quality of the social environment in the classroom
- *Respect:* Being respectful of students, their viewpoints, and their ideas

Though there are certainly other practices that define teaching competence, these stood out as we began to analyze teachers' interactions with their students and colleagues and the quality of their students' written work and social skills. This is all well and good, but it is also a bit disconcerting. After all, this list does not seem different from any other list of observations of good teaching, whether teaching of math or geography. The teachers who embraced the VLF approach in a way that seemed to have an effect on their class had something about them that we could not quite put our finger on; there was something about their educational philosophy that was difficult to either quantify or capture.

We also began to draw some conclusions about the other side of the equation. It seemed to us, based on our observations in the classroom, that an unskilled or ineffective teacher is not simply one who has not yet learned these fundamental "tricks of the trade." It goes much deeper than that. The teachers whom we found to be least effective in implementing VLF, or in helping their students to learn and to grow intellectually and emotionally in general, tended to place inordinate emphasis on rules and observable "positive" behaviors like sitting still and talking only when they were called on. These teachers often ignored or even discouraged creative responses or independent thinking on the part of their students. On the whole, they were uncomfortable with children who asked hard questions or showed signs of individuality, as if they believed that a good student is one who does as he or she is told and serves as a passive receptacle for knowledge dispensed from above.

As our study proceeded, it became clear to us that teacher competence needed to be married to the powerful motivation to teach ways of relating to others to initiate the active ingredients in the formula. Together, they drew students most effectively into a classroom where an ethic of social relationships was paramount. But once again, how do teachers become so motivated? Why are certain practices or subjects or teaching styles personally meaningful to some teachers and not to others? The basic concerns embodied in this question—competence, creativity, commitment, and an understanding of child development—lie at the heart of all teacher-training efforts. But by what and whose standards should these abstract concepts be concretely judged or measured?

It began to dawn on us that it was important to understand how teachers become aware of why it is personally meaningful to them to teach students seriously and systematically about dealing with the kinds of issues faced by Grace and Francisco. It became so important that we divided our study, and our resources, into two paths, with the expectation that they eventually would join together. One path was to continue our interest in the social and ethical awareness of children. The other path led to a deeper understanding of teachers' professional development. Not entirely coincidentally, we already were involved in an ongoing practice-based research project two thousand miles north of Boston that focused on the professional awareness of teachers who feel committed to teaching their children how to get along. We describe that research—and how we imported its lessons to Boston—next in part III of this book.

Part III

Promoting and Analyzing Teachers' Understanding of Students' Social Awareness: Lessons from Iceland

Chapter 8

Supporting Teachers' Professional Development

Thorvald rode home from the wedding with his bride [Hallgerd] and Thjostolf [her foster-father]. Thjostolf rode close to Hallgerd, and they talked together all the way [to the place where Thorvald's family lived].

Osvif [Thorvald's father] turned to his son and said, "Are you pleased with the marriage? How did you get on together in conversation?"

"Very well," replied Thorvald. "She was extremely affectionate toward me. You can see that yourself from the way she laughs at every word."

"I do not find her laughter as reassuring as you do," said Osvif. "But time will tell."

—*Njal's Saga,* author unknown

EACH SEPTEMBER, for more than a decade, a group of between fifteen and twenty elementary school teachers in Reykjavík, Iceland, assembled to take part in a yearlong professional development program titled "Fostering Students' Interpersonal Competence and Skills."[1] The aim of this teacher professional development program was to help the participants promote their students' social competencies in conjunction with their academic achievement. These teachers met twenty times or more at regular intervals across the nine months of the public school year and took turns hosting the group at their school. Each year the general aim of these evening "reflective gatherings" was to provide the participating teachers with a supportive venue for sharing professional concerns, discussing their experiences in the classroom, and working together to find ways to improve their understanding of child development and their classroom skills for promoting students' social growth. One important purpose of these meetings was to consider how developmental theory, especially ideas about the growth of interpersonal awareness among children, relates to educational practice. In general, teachers receive little support in considering the relevance of children's levels of social development to their own students, or to the subject matter they teach, or to the part they as teachers might play in helping their students deal with social relationships. A second focus for discussion was on less theoretical matters that all teachers face daily and for which they can always use additional support: school morale; relationships with parents, administrators, and colleagues; and the promotion of specific teaching strategies and management skills pertaining to students' interactions in the classroom.

The program included three parts: teacher training; curriculum development centered on friendship, the school community, and the family; and research to study whether teachers who work constructively on interpersonal issues in the classroom are more capable of improving their students' interpersonal growth than teachers with no such special training. (For more detailed descriptions of this work, see Adalbjarnardottir 1992, 1993, 1994.)

Personal Meaning and Professional Development

When participating Icelandic teachers were interviewed individually at the beginning of the year, they were asked to discuss the interpersonal issues that should be raised in the classroom, and why, and how these issues could be addressed appropriately at each grade level. Should social awareness, moral values, or character education be included in the curriculum for the elementary grades in a formal or explicit way? If so, how? If not, why not? Teachers were also asked how they dealt with interpersonal issues, such as the teasing, tattling, and bullying that inevitably arise during the school year—sometimes brought into the classroom from home, from the neighborhood, or from gym or recess periods. In addition, they were asked about whether any of their students had experienced rejection, exclusion, or discrimination at the hands of their peers because they appeared to others, or perceived themselves to be, "different" in some way. If so, how did the teachers deal with such situations?

When the teachers were interviewed individually again later in the year, the focus was on determining how useful the suggestions offered by the program leader and other participants had been to the teachers in promoting students' social awareness and managing social behavior in the classroom and in the school. Had these suggestions helped teachers resolve conflicts between students? Had teachers seen growth in the social awareness and behavior of their students? Finally, in interviews at the end of the year, in addition to the questions addressed throughout the school year, the teachers were asked whether they felt that their participation in the program had influ-

Table 8.1 Teacher Interview and Report Questions, by Issue and Time

Issue	Primary Time	Key Interview Questions
Motivation (participation, aims)	Beginning of the program	Why do you participate in the intervention program? What expectations do you have toward the program? Why is that important to you?
Classroom management abilities	During the program	Do you feel you are changing in the ways you deal with interpersonal issues in the classroom during the school year? What has changed? How has it changed? Why do you think it has changed?
Pedagogical vision	At the end of the program	Has your attitude toward this kind of work changed during this school year? (If so) How has it changed? Why has it changed? Have you experienced any changes in the students' social interactions as a function of their participation in the program? (If so) How? Why?

Source: Reprinted from Adalbjarnardottir and Selman (1997), with permission from Elsevier Science.

enced their approach to teaching, their pedagogical vision, or their own lives—and if so, how. Table 8.1 provides some examples of the structure of some of the questions in this interview.

Teachers' answers to the questions posed at the beginning of the year—about why they had chosen to participate in the program and what they expected to gain from it "going in"—were always telling, and often prognostic. Here is a representative sample:

> I'm here because the principal said everybody teaching in this grade level in the school should participate.
>
> I felt this program would be fun for me. I need a change in my teaching.
>
> I hope to learn some new methods to improve the social behavior of the boys in my class.

> Teachers spend a lot of energy trying to improve students' social interactions. I want to learn better ways to handle social management problems in my classroom, which I find overwhelming.

> It's important to improve the social atmosphere in the classroom and to improve the social interactions among the students, as well as between teachers and students. . . . The better the social relationships we create, the better the schoolwork will be, and the more pleasant for both students and teachers.

> Students' social interactions are always burning issues, and it's essential to be capable of dealing with them. I really feel I haven't received any instruction or help in this regard. Often I find it hard to know what to do. I hope that participating in the program will help me to improve the social interactions of the students, and that they will be able to transfer that experience to other situations outside school. . . . I hope this will help them later in life with their family [and] friends, at work and in society.

As researchers, we ask first of all how we can interpret such utterances and expressions in a way that sheds light on the question of differences among teachers in their attitudes toward working on interpersonal issues in the classroom—a major concern that had also arisen in our work with Voices of Love and Freedom in the United States. How, for example, do these responses reflect the classroom management skills of the teachers who express them? Or their levels of understanding and commitment regarding the social development of their students? Or their relationship to their students, the school, and the larger society? Or why the professional development program they had signed up for was important to them, either pedagogically or personally?

As theorists interested in social and moral development, we began to ask questions about the professional development of teachers that paralleled those we ask about children's social and ethical growth and maturity. What frameworks can we construct for understanding differences in teachers' expressed pedagogical ideas about and awareness of social and ethical issues, especially with regard to how they address these concerns in their work with students? How can we trace patterns in the development of the professional awareness of teachers before, during, and after their participation in programs designed to help them promote ethical wisdom as well as academic accomplishment among their students? How does what teachers say about these matters correspond to what they do in classrooms?

Very important to our definition of the terms "professional awareness" and "professional development" with regard to this aspect of teaching is the personal meaning that elementary school teachers make of their own experience and its effect on their professional lives in the classroom. To what extent do teachers in these grade levels reflect on how they deal with others in their own social relationships? How do they get along with their own peers under circumstances that are in many ways similar to those faced by their students, that is, in situations that involve sharing, resolving conflicts, or taking the perspective of another person?

This focus on personal meaning is critical to our research on the professional development of teachers because practical approaches such as ours, which emphasize the promotion of children's social and societal understanding, depend on a certain level of awareness among teachers about their own psychological needs, their own cultural biases, and their own social relationships.

The Social Context of the Icelandic Project

Although the social ecology of Reykjavík, the capital of Iceland—a country with a population of 285,000 that is roughly the size of Wyoming and lies two hundred kilometers south of the Arctic Circle—is very different from that of a large ethnically, economically, and racially diverse American city like Boston, the teacher-training and research effort we describe here played a critical part in how we studied the ways in which Boston teachers embraced and implemented VLF. Compared to the United States, and indeed to most places on earth, Iceland is remarkably homogeneous, with regard not only to race and ethnicity but to social class and the distribution of income among its citizens. Few Icelanders possess enormous wealth, but few live in poverty or experience racial or ethnic discrimination. For now, Iceland is a country that enjoys relative serenity, prosperity, and cohesiveness. So is this a place from which we can draw lessons about the promotion of interpersonal and intergroup relations in childhood?

One could argue that the experiences of children in Iceland are not relevant to the kinds of issues faced by students in large urban American cities, some of which have more public school students than Iceland has people. And yet many Icelandic educators are as concerned about social change and the socialization of their students as urban American teachers who work in what we might consider a more difficult social environment. Nevertheless, what we have learned in Iceland—and shared with others in the field—about the professional development of teachers is directly relevant to the lives of educators and students everywhere. The questions of teachers' competence, motivation, and understanding of child development are central to the crucial role they play in the socialization of children in every society.

The Icelandic Project's research and practice had many valuable lessons for our evolving work, not only for our study of the VLF practice but also for our evolving developmental theory. To tell this part of the story we begin by sharing the lessons of the Icelandic Sagas (see Magnusson and Palsson 1960).

The Role of the Sagas in Icelandic Social Studies Reform

In the ninth century a great migration of Vikings invaded and traveled throughout Europe, and even to North Africa (and later to North America). Some of these emigrants settled in Iceland. But, politically, Iceland was not founded as a Viking nation. At the time *Njal's Saga* was written, the country had a population of more than sixty thousand and a unique parliamentary commonwealth first established in the year 930. For several centuries this form of government had worked well. In the thirteenth century, however, years of increasing violence, murder, and strife caused this magnificent initial governance structure to break down and led, in 1262, to the loss of Iceland's independence. It would not be regained until 1918.[2]

As late as the 1970s, Iceland's history curriculum focused on rote memorization of Icelandic lore and historical facts. Children were required, for example, to study parts of the famous Icelandic Sagas, like the excerpt from *Njal's Saga* at the beginning of this chapter, with an emphasis on their chronology, plot lines, and the names of major characters. Less often were they asked to think about the political or social realities behind these texts, or the moral and social dilemmas they reflected. Consider what happens to Hallgerd and Thorvald in a later passage from *Njal's Saga:*

> Hallgerd turned out to be demanding and prodigal. She claimed everything for her own, whether it belonged to her or not, and wasted it all extravagantly. By spring, the household provisions were running out, and there was a shortage of flour and dried fish. Hallgerd went to Thorvald and said, "You won't get anything done by sitting about; we need more flour and dried fish for the larder."
>
> "I laid in no less food this year than usual," replied Thorvald, "and it has always lasted well into the summer."
>
> "I don't care in the least if you and your father starved yourselves for money," said Hallgerd.

At this point in the story, Thorvald angrily slaps Hallgerd in the face and rows out to Bjarn Isles to fetch the dried fish and flour. Hallgerd complains to her foster-father, Thjostolf, who follows Thorvald to the island and kills him. Hearing this, Osvif [Thorvald's father] searches for Thjostolf, who has fled, and not finding him, seeks out his kin and demands compensation. After some debate, Thjostolf's kin pay him two hundred ounces of silver, and, the saga reports, "Osvif thanked him for the gift, and went home well pleased with the outcome. . . . Osvif is now out of this saga."

Throughout *Njal's Saga* the forces of good and evil are in bitter conflict, and physical violence is the most manifest and frequent outcome of this battle. Although Osvif seems content in this chapter of the saga with the compensation he receives for the loss of his son, greed for money and for power generate terrible problems throughout the story.[3] In other words, life is all about human conflict and competing systems of values.

Although Icelandic schoolchildren were asked to learn the names, places, and dates of major events in the saga, they were seldom asked to consider the issues behind these events, or to think about the evolution of their culture by comparing the moral values of the past to those of modern times. How common is it today for a slap to be repaid by a killing? What does it say about the relativity of human values—across time and culture—when the father of a son murdered because he was physically abusive just one time to a verbally abusive wife is satisfied with compensation of two hundred ounces of silver?

Starting in the 1970s, a group of elementary and secondary school teachers participated in a social studies reform project within the Ministry of Education that proposed to move the curriculum in a "developmental direction." Wolfgang Edelstein—then codirector of the Max Planck Institute for Human Development and Education in West Berlin—played an important role in the initiation of the "New Icelandic" social studies curriculum reform. Edelstein had spent the latter part of his childhood and his adolescence in Iceland after arriving in Reykjavík in the late 1930s with his German-Jewish family to escape persecution in Nazi Germany. Like us, he was both a practitioner and a researcher and very much taken with the ideas of Kohlberg and Piaget on cognitive and moral development. Through his strong connections to the educational community in Iceland, Edelstein became involved in educational policymaking and reform, including the effort to transform the traditional curriculum of history and geography into an integrated social studies curriculum. One focus was on the moral values and methods of conflict resolution during the time of the Sagas as compared with the present. The range of topics in this curriculum included comparative discussions about the rights and duties of family and kinship. Edelstein brought to this effort a developmental perspective similar to the one we were working on at roughly the same time. He also played an important role in making a connection between researchers and practitioners in Iceland and those in our group.[4]

By the early 1980s, however, the political climate in Iceland had changed. The new government in power had little sympathy for "left-wing" ideas about educational reform. Conservative forces had attacked this developmental brand of social studies as "value-free" and unpatriotic. This approach, they claimed, emphasized abstract reasoning over concrete and particular Icelandic values and virtues. Conservatives were especially upset that Icelandic students were not required to memorize the names, places, and historical events in the Sagas in chronological order. The shifting tide of politics stopped the further development of the social studies reform program. It was as if conservatives wanted to sweep the reform movement out of the Icelandic elementary schools and into the sea (see Edelstein 1983). Could there be some rapprochement between these two polar forces?

Top-Down Versus Bottom-Up Reform: The Approach of the Icelandic Project

Seeking such rapprochement is one aim of the Icelandic Teacher Professional Development Project.[5] As the project evolved over a decade, each year a new group of Icelandic teachers studied developmental theory and practiced teaching methods that have been demonstrated to be effective in promoting children's social development. (We describe some of these methods in more detail in chapters 11 through 15.) As with VLF (which was just getting under way in Boston in the early 1990s), role-playing, writing, drawing, painting, and storytelling were used to help students explore feelings and ideas about personal relationships and moral questions. The "Icelandic approach" used a set of curriculum materials it constructed around three primary but universal social studies themes for the elementary grades: friendship, the family, and the school as a community (see Adalbjarnardottir and Eliasdottir 1992a–f). These themes may sound familiar; in fact they are identical to the original themes of the Voices of Love and Freedom program. But unlike the designers of VLF, the Icelandic team and the teachers they worked with were not under political pressure to prove a connection between social and intellectual competence by raising student scores on standardized tests of academic performance. Nor were they under pressure to represent different ethnic and racial groups. Iceland was still homogeneous in this regard by Boston standards.

The differences in scale and orientation between these two efforts were also significant. The small size of the Icelandic training program allowed for discussion between researchers and practitioners about developmental ideas (particularly our evolving Risk and Relationship Framework) and about day-to-day events in the classroom. By design the evening "reflective gatherings" were really seminars for a conversation about the ongoing evolution of both theory and practice. In addition, the Icelandic teachers were participating voluntarily and were free to use the curriculum materials offered as they saw fit, whereas by the time of the GSID's Carnegie Research Study (1996 to 1998) the VLF program had been endorsed by the Boston public school system, its far more structured curriculum was required for some teachers in some schools, and the opportunities for personalized training in its use were limited.

In other words, in looking at these two programs from the point of view of what they can tell us about the professional development of teachers, it is important to note that the teachers in Reykjavík experienced the effort to integrate developmental theory and classroom practice as a "bottom-up" process, whereas for most of the teachers in Boston, initially at least, VLF came to them from the top down.

Fundamentally, however, the researchers studying VLF and the Icelandic Project team had a great deal in common—a framework for understanding social and ethical development, a commitment to bringing this understanding into the public schools, and an interest in the professional lives of teachers. The two groups were in constant communication regarding methodology and findings, and we all used some of the same materials and approaches.

In particular, the Icelandic Project was concerned with determining how crucial it is or is not that teachers have a deep understanding of the developmental theory behind a particular method, curriculum, or practice. For example, consider Adalbjarnardottir's report of how one year's cohort of first- through seventh-grade teachers explored the topic of friendship:

> *Meeting Three:* Before introducing to the teachers psychological theories about how children and adolescents develop their ideas about friendship, I asked them, What is a good friend? First they worked individually for a few minutes, wrote down their thoughts, and then shared their ideas in pairs for a few more minutes. Afterward I gathered their ideas together and introduced theories on children's friendship development to the teachers. They took these theoretical frameworks with them to their own classrooms and explored their students' replies to the same question about friendship that they had worked on in their own meeting.
>
> At the next meeting the teachers shared their work from their class-

> rooms with each other. Building on their experiences, we discussed what to expect with regard to how students' comprehension may affect their daily life in interacting with peers, and how their friendship competence and skills could gradually be promoted. In this way, I provided the teachers with a dialogue and context [in which] they could construct and reconstruct their new experiences and professional meaning by going back and forth, integrating their knowledge, understanding, and teaching practice through work with their own students on interpersonal issues.
>
> Then teachers studied how children at different ages resolve . . . conflicts [within a] friendship. Once again, the process began with reflections on their own experience. For example, the group was asked if they had ever been in the same kind of situation that was faced by our hypothetical friendship dilemma of Disa and Anna. . . . The problem there was that Inga, a new girl in town . . . asks Disa to go to a special event at the same time as she and Anna are planning to get together and play. Disa's dilemma [is] not only what to do but also how to deal with Anna if she decide[s] to go off with Inga.

Disa, Anna, and Inga are, of course, the Icelandic equivalents of Kathy, Becky, and Jeanette, whom we met in chapter 3. It bears repeating here that what makes Kathy's (Disa's) dilemma as thought-provoking for teachers as it is for children is its universality: people of all ages and nationalities face this kind of social situation from time to time throughout their lives. Analyzing the comments of children at various grade levels about what Kathy (Disa) should do—and why—had helped us build our developmental framework in the first place. Now the goal of the Icelandic Project was to use the same dilemma to help teachers think about the different social strategies that Disa (Kathy), their students, and they themselves might use in such a situation.

From Theory to Practice and Practice to Theory

An important facet of the developmental research the GSID had done in the 1980s was relating strategies of interpersonal negotiation and levels of social awareness to a five-step method for helping children learn how to resolve social problems and conflicts, designed along the lines of an approach first suggested by John Dewey in the early 1930s.[6] In the course of this earlier research we interviewed children at different ages and asked them questions about each of the steps in their thinking about dilemmas such as the one that had arisen between Kathy and Becky.[7] What is the problem here? How does each girl see it? What can each do about the problem? What do you think is the best solution? How would Kathy or Becky know if their solution worked out well?[8]

In the research-oriented world of the 1980s, Dewey's functional philosophy and pedagogy were translated into a functional psychology, built now upon the newer metaphor of "information processing" in cognitive psychology (see Flavell and Miller 1998). Our research goal was to integrate these two competing approaches with the study of the development of social cognition. One was our own structural approach. (See tables 3.1 and 3.2 for an overview of these aspects of the GSID framework.) The other was a "social information processing" approach that conceptualized the link between social thought and action as a sequence of information-processing steps, from defining the social problem to evaluating the outcome. (For a relatively comprehensive overview of this model at the time, see Dodge et al. 1986.)

In the practice-oriented Icelandic Project, teachers studied the use of specific "open questions" to lead class discussions about social conflicts through a five-step sequence: defining the problem; considering the feelings of each of the participants; generating alternative ways of solving the dilemma; choosing a course of action; and evaluating the probable outcome. Two points were made about this method by the practice-based researchers during the evening teacher-training sessions. The first was that this five-step pedagogy could be used, with appropriate modifications, as a standard or systematic way of thinking about social problem solving across all grade levels. The second was that teachers could learn much from listening with a "developmental ear" to their students' reasoning throughout the process, not just at the "strategy selection" step. The responses of the children in each classroom would differ; the responses of younger children would differ from those of older ones in terms of how they defined the problem, generated solutions, and thought about outcomes; and these responses would vary along a developmental dimension.[9]

In keeping with the program's "bottom-up" orientation, the Reykjavík teachers were asked to begin with their own experience—that is, to apply their own understanding of interpersonal issues, such as friendship, directly in the practical context of group discussions with their students—and to bring their observations from the classroom back into the evening groups to be framed and discussed in theoretical terms derived from our developmental framework. There the cycle of reflection and practice was repeated in a process that mirrored the approach the teachers were taking in the classroom with their students: discussing problems and alternative solutions, making choices about how problems might be solved, and evaluating the outcomes of the actions taken.

From Theory to Practice and Practice to Research: Teachers' Reflections

Researchers of educational change and teacher development have argued that it is essential that teachers reflect on their own theory about teaching, which relates to their values, knowledge, competence, and behavior. Their professional development is also affected by their life environment, gender, personality, age, family situation, working environment, and the policy and aims of government. Moreover, differences among teachers and their different professional competences depend on the ideologies they hold—for instance, whether they adhere to a transmission view of learning in their teaching or to a social constructivist view (see Fullan and Hargraves 1992; Good and Brophy 1997; Hoyle and John 1995; Zeichner and Liston 1996). In this light, over the past twenty years a major shift has occurred in research on teaching. Instead of focusing on teachers' behavior, increasingly interpretive methods are used to understand teachers' reflections on their teaching, that is, the meaning they derive from their work. In this spirit, reflective teaching is becoming a form of inquiry in in-service approaches to teacher development (see Bartlett 1990; Brookfield 1995; Calderhead and Gates 1993; Freire 1998; Korthagen 1993; Louden 1991; Richardson 1994; Russell and Munby 1992; Schön 1987; Shulman 1987; Zeichner 1994).

In the Icelandic Project the major focus of the teacher training was on encouraging the teachers to reflect on their pedagogical ideas, aims, and teaching practices as they related to promoting interpersonal competence and skills in their students. In any profession it may at first seem risky, or at best difficult and discouraging, to reflect on and reevaluate one's approaches and methods, and by and large the Icelandic teachers who participated in the research and training program had already invested many years in developing their classroom skills. A basic goal, therefore, was to create an atmosphere of trust and mutual support in the regular discussion sessions at the evening "reflective gatherings."

Thus, the individual and group consultations, between teachers and the project staff, were an important component of the practice side of the program. It was in these meetings that teachers often seemed most relaxed and willing to reflect openly on their day-to-day experiences, including their attempts to apply the theoretical concepts they were learning to their students' interpersonal orientations or styles (for example, submissive versus assertive, withdrawn versus aggressive) and strategies of interpersonal negotiation (impulsive, unilateral, reciprocal, compromise, collaborative). These consultations also gave teachers the opportunity to talk about any changes they perceived in their students with regard to levels of interpersonal understanding and social competence, participation in class discussions, popularity, self-confidence, and day-to-day changes in mood and outlook. As collaborators in the process of bringing together practice and research and reflecting on the relation between them, the teachers were also asked to complete reports after they tried several specific lesson plans, commenting on how the lesson went step by step, what worked and what did not, and how the plans could be improved. In the interviews the teachers were also given the chance to reflect on their ideas, aims, and practice during the program.[10]

Toward a Developmental Analysis of Teachers' Professional Awareness

In the early years of the Icelandic Project, the emphasis was on encouraging teachers to discuss ideas and reflections about the growth of children's social understanding and interpersonal skills and how these might translate into practice. Gradually, however, the project took on a more specific research focus: the development of conceptual and methodological tools to analyze the pedagogical ideals, aims, and practices that the participants expressed in group discussions in the evenings and individually in their conversations with the research team. In other words, this practical effort to promote reflection among teachers about the social dimension of their work with children led to formal research on teachers' professional awareness in its own right.

There was a reason for this shift in focus. Not surprisingly, but importantly, during their initial research, the Icelandic Project staff found anecdotal evidence that teachers who worked constructively on interpersonal issues during the yearlong professional development program were often more capable when it came to improving their students' level of interpersonal awareness than were teachers with no such special training. Also, in the earlier phases of the research they had documented the teachers' initial reflections, changes in their understanding of students' interpersonal growth over the year, and how the latter affected their teaching skills and attitudes toward working on interpersonal awareness and social skills in the classroom. The six excerpts from teachers' interviews that we presented earlier in this chapter come from these studies (Adalbjarnardottir 1993, 1994).

These early practice-based studies did not, however, use a developmental lens to analyze the pedagogical ideals, aims, or classroom management skills of the teachers who participated in the training program. In fact, there was some reluctance, if not actual resistance, to doing so out of a desire to be respectful of the teachers' daily work and to not judge them by identifying some as possessing a capacity for professional reflection that was more adequate or more sophisticated than that of others without understanding the connections between their reflections and their practice. In a small and close-knit community such as the public school system of Reykjavík, many of the teachers would know who had said what, even if their statements were reported anonymously. It seemed more circumspect for the time being simply to document the range of opinions expressed without putting them in some order or hierarchy that might be construed as valuing some above others.

But this cautious approach would not get us very far in our understanding of the professional development of teachers or of the importance of their levels of social understanding to their ability to foster social development in the classroom. As advocates of social and moral education, we believe that teachers' ability to integrate theoretical and practical knowledge is central to their effectiveness in promoting interpersonal competence and social skills among their students. We needed a way to analyze teachers' reflections on these matters, a theoretical framework that would respect differences in teachers' views about their role as agents of socialization and yet help us to study these differences.

Since one major goal of the Icelandic Project was to enhance each participant's professional development as a teacher, the project leader had developed a sequence of interview and report-form questions that asked teachers at several times during the year to reflect on any changes in their work with their students. These questions, outlined in the next chapter in table 9.1, focus on the three pedagogical issues we mentioned earlier: teachers' initial motivation to participate in the program, any changes they noticed in their aims and classroom management abilities, and any changes they observed in student social interactions.

By 1995 this project had been using questions like these for almost seven years, and the responses had been helpful in providing the research-practice team with the kind of feedback that is very useful for shaping and fine-tuning a professional development program. It was time to do something more with this information. At this point the two of us felt ready to try to devise a theoretical framework for analyzing the reflections the Icelandic teachers had shared with us (Adalbjarnardottir and Selman 1997). In the next chapter, we describe our first attempt to do so.

This chapter was coauthored by Robert Selman and Sigrun Adalbjarnardottir.

Chapter 9

Teachers' Reflections on Promoting Social Competence: Moving Back to Boston

HERE IS what a fifth-grade teacher, Birna, reported about how her participation in the Icelandic Project changed her practice in the classroom:[1]

> I feel that knowledge and understanding of children's social developmental processes has given me new insight into the children's worlds of thought, which will make me a fairer and, I hope, a better educator. Gradually, I have started to make different demands of the students, ones that are better suited to their abilities.

Halla, a fourth-grade teacher wrote:

> I now feel professionally stronger when I deal with social problems because I know more about what is going on, while before I was really groping. I am more aware of how to react to problems that arise. Before I magnified the difficulty of dealing with such issues. I feel I listen more carefully to the children's voices and am more tolerant.

Anna, a third-grade teacher, explained:

> I really think we have to work on interpersonal issues [at school]. It is of vital importance for the classroom work and the school community. The way children manage in the group can affect them the rest of their life; for example, if they feel they are never listened to and are always put down. . . .
>
> In a democratic society like ours we take it for granted that everyone gets the opportunity to participate. But our society is controlled too much by a few people, as in general people don't express themselves on the various issues. Thus, it is important that the children get the

> opportunity to build up self-confidence by expressing themselves about their concerns and by experiencing the feeling that their idea is adopted or that they have to accept the fact that it hasn't been agreed to this time. When I was in elementary school we were not allowed to decide anything by ourselves. That may be part of why our society isn't a very open one. . . . It's important that [children] can stand up for themselves, dare to say no, and not rely on the opinions of others. Dependence can lead to problems like drug abuse. I also think that as a person you must feel better about yourself if you stand by your decision and pursue what you want. . . . You can be independent without putting other people down.

One day during her participation in the program, some of Anna's students learned that three of the girls in their class were suspected of having taken some candy from a store. They felt this had to be discussed in class; in fact, several children called Anna at night to tell her about it and ask her to take up the issue the next day. Anna interpreted this as a reflection of their emerging awareness of their responsibility as members of the group to keep a strong, trusting relationship alive in the classroom and, as she put it, to follow "moral rules." She met with the three girls in question before class, told them what the other students had said, and asked them to discuss among themselves and come to an agreement about how to solve this problem with regard to their classmates.

> They were very [honest] about what they had done. They expressed their own feelings, as well as how they thought their classmates felt about the matter.
>
> When they had come up with a solution, they presented it to their classmates for discussion. They told their classmates that they regretted having taken the candy and that all three of them were equally guilty. They said they felt very sorry about this and that they would never do such a thing again. They also suggested that the problem would not be discussed any further in class. After some consideration and discussion the class agreed to this.
>
> I could feel the relief among all the children that the issue had been dealt with. For example, afterwards two of the boys came to me and expressed how pleased they were.

Anna reported that she felt convinced that the children would not have demonstrated such care and concern as a group, and such competence in solving the problem, had they not taken part in the "program on socio-moral issues."

> The children had become such friends, they felt so secure and were so ready to listen. The boys who told me this weren't tattling; instead they were entrusting me with the problem and asking me to work with them. I am sure if they hadn't been in this program, this situation would have become very difficult. They would have insulted and teased the girls.

Anna was proud of her students. She also mentioned that she herself might not have dealt with the problem so directly at an earlier point in her career. (For one thing, the parents of the three girls were already involved, and some of them felt that the incident wasn't any of the school's business.) As a teacher, Anna reported, she now felt more comfortable about using "real-life" events to promote the children's understanding of moral values and help them think and communicate more effectively about difficult matters. She also spoke about increasing her students' awareness of different points of view and about helping them to coordinate multiple perspectives, comments that showed how receptive she was to the developmental ideas that the training and research team presented for discussion each year.

Perspective Coordination, Conflict Resolution, and Social Awareness

Nearly all of the teachers who participated in the Icelandic Project commented that the "questioning strategy"—the five steps for structuring classroom discussion that they had learned during the evening meetings—had become an indispensable tool for dealing with interpersonal conflicts and for talking about social issues with their students. Here is a report from Elsa, a fourth-grade teacher, about how she addressed a conflict among her students in a systematic way by using the five-step process.

> At the beginning of the school day the students were clearly greatly upset. One of the students, Ragnar, had not shown up and I found out that he had been attacked by most of his classmates and was too scared to come to class. As the students were very upset, I began by asking them to explain their point of view. (What happened? Why did this happen?) Soon after I asked one of the three students who seemed to be on Ragnar's side to see whether he could find him. He came back with Ragnar, and we [all] sat down in our discussion corner. Now Ragnar explained his point of view. The facts of the situation seemed clear. The students had been going to a gym lesson. Since their lesson had not

started, most of the class had climbed up into the spectator area to watch another class in gymnastics. Ragnar thought that this was not permitted and said to his classmates that the teacher had forbidden this. They didn't listen to him. He then went to the gym teacher and told on his classmates. The teacher made no comments about the matter with the class, since the students [had come] down from the spectator seats again before the lesson started. But after the gym lesson Ragnar was attacked—hit, spanked, kicked, and verbally abused. His classmates said he was always a tattletale. Only three of the kids were on Ragnar's side and said he had just been trying to persuade the kids not to do things that were forbidden.

I worked through the steps, having [the students define] the problem and think about the feelings of those involved. Then I asked them to come up with alternative ways to solve the problem and to find the best way to solve the problem. The solution they suggested was that the class agreed to stop teasing Ragnar if he did less tattling. Ragnar agreed to be less meddlesome but thought he should tell someone if it was obvious that his classmates were violating rules. The class agreed to that.

The teacher reported that the effectiveness of this discussion had been obvious: for several months afterward all the parties stuck to their agreement. In addition, the discussion itself had been lively; the students were concerned and eager to find a way to solve the problem. She emphasized how helpful the standard questions of the five-step approach had been for working with her students on a complicated social problem in an organized and constructive way.

It seems clear that this teacher provided her students with an open and comfortable classroom atmosphere, one in which they felt both competent and responsible about coming up with solutions to interpersonal conflict that everyone could agree upon. She also judged correctly that Ragnar could be put in the spotlight and face the pressure of his peers with her support and that of several of his classmates. However, one could reasonably ask what else she did to deal with the children who had assaulted him verbally and physically. No matter that he had broken the unspoken rules of the fourth-grade culture of silence. Should there not have been consequences for his assailants? This part of the story was missing from the teacher's account, but it cannot be missing from our analysis to come.

"My participation in this project has caused many changes in my work," Maria, a seventh-grade teacher, said, and went on to tell the following story about her experience with "the new questioning method."

> Occasionally, one of my students had been bullying younger kids on their way to and from school and on the school playground. Parents had called both me and the principal and had complained about the boy's behavior. The boy's mother had also been contacted. I had already talked with the boy privately, but he kept putting the blame on the other kids. When I realized that his behavior was continuing and also that he had started to bully a visually handicapped child, I changed my approach. I decided to use my new questioning method to run a discussion about the problem in the classroom.
>
> At the beginning of the session I described the situation to the children. I told them that I would not tell them who the bully was, nor which class he attended, but I wanted them to discuss the matter and think about ways to solve the problem. First I asked them to define the problem: What is the problem here? Why is it a problem? Then I asked them to express how they thought the kids who were being bullied felt and why, and how the bully felt and why.
>
> The boy in question took an active and sincere part in the discussion. I noticed that he suggested that the bully might not feel well at home. (In fact there was a lot of tension in the boy's family.) The next step was to find good ways to solve the problem and the best solution. The children suggested that the problem should be discussed with the boy so that he would understand what he was doing. Later that day I talked with the boy and soon found out that he had not realized that the discussion concerned his own behavior. This time we talked about the problem with more understanding of how seriously he took the case.
>
> The next morning his mother called and asked what happened; her son did not want to go to school, and he had complained of a bad stomachache since the day before. I explained the matter to the mother, who already knew that he had been bullying other kids. Then I talked with the boy, repeating that he could trust me not to tell on him in class. He came the next morning and seemed well.

Months later this teacher reported that the boy in question had completely stopped bullying other children. Using the discussion method, she thought, had helped to open his eyes to the feelings of others and enabled him to reflect on both the origins and the consequences of his own behavior. In addition, she commented, it had provided all the children in her class with an opportunity to work constructively together on an interpersonal problem.

Many participants reported that they felt both they and their students had become better listeners and more tolerant of their own limitations and those of others. "I think I listen more carefully to children's opinions and explanations than I did before, and I more often try to get them to think themselves," one said, adding with refreshing honesty, "I guess I only occasionally succeed."

And finally, many of the Reykjavík teachers felt that the time they had devoted to addressing social issues in the classroom was well spent. This particularly enthusiastic account from Disa, a sixth-grade teacher, connects directly to our belief in the importance of bringing basic concepts about social and moral development into public education:

> I feel I am more ready to take time for these issues than I used to be. It is important not to feel that one is taking time from something else. This curriculum is just as important as various other subjects we are working with, and it must be regarded as a valid part. I have been asked what parts of the curriculum I have sacrificed to provide the time needed to deal with socio-moral topics in the classroom. My response is that classroom teachers organize their daily schedule to meet the needs of the students. If we want to classify this curriculum, it can be placed under language, social studies, or ethics.

The Analysis of Teachers' Reflections, Phase 1

All of these excerpts read like testimonials to the effectiveness of the project as a teacher-training program—and since we are not neutral about our ultimate mission we find that gratifying—but it is not our purpose here to prove that the Reykjavík effort produced good results. As researchers, we have another goal in mind. We present these reports from Icelandic classrooms because they tell us something about the professional development of teachers and serve as an introduction to the initially somewhat controversial enterprise we mentioned in chapter 8: classifying, quantifying, and ultimately evaluating (or at least judging) teachers' reflections on why it is important to promote social competence in the classroom.

By 1994 the Icelandic Project had been documenting teachers' reflections on social development in the classroom for six years. It was clear that many of the teachers who had chosen to participate engaged with the project in a deep and powerful way. Yet some seemed less involved, interested only in what the researchers called "teaching tips." We wondered why.

And as many social science researchers have done, we wondered how close a connection there was between what people said about their lives and how they actually behaved—in this case, between teachers' expressed "reflections" and their practices in the classroom. Before we could begin to address this question, however, we needed a framework for thinking about the various dimensions of understanding and experience embodied in the teachers' verbal and written comments. We turned to the approach with which we were most familiar.

Could we now use our "developmental lens" to examine a new kind of landscape? When we studied children growing up, the age differences between them made it relatively easy to see and to conceptualize significant developmental differences. In studying the professional lives of adults, the question of what we meant by "development" would be much more complicated. To be sure, teachers differ in terms of the number of years they have spent in the classroom, but based on our experience, "age" in this sense might have very little to do with an individual's effectiveness as a teacher, no matter how we might define the latter. Still, we believed that our analytical tools would prove useful in the land of adult professional development.

In 1995 we began a collaborative effort to analyze the comments and reports of the teachers who had taken part in the Reykjavík project. The first step was to translate the transcripts of interviews and the written reports by teachers into English so that both of us could read them. Then we began the initial phase of a systematic developmental analysis of the teachers' interviews.

After reading all the materials collected over the previous seven years, we began by identifying what we felt were the primary issues or themes on which teachers had reflected. Not surprisingly, given our theoretical tendencies, three issues emerged. The first we called *motivation,* by which we meant the teacher's motivation to participate in this particular training program, as well as his or her specific aims in working with students on interpersonal issues. The second issue was *classroom management.* In considering the third issue, which we called *pedagogical vision,* we focused on what teachers said about their awareness of a connection between broader understanding of their own pedagogical aims and practices and their work on promoting their students' interpersonal skills—for example, how a teacher used her new knowledge and understanding of students' interpersonal growth to improve her own classroom management skills. In other words, the third issue represented the integration of the other two.

Our goal was to map out differences among the Reykjavík teachers with regard to their views on these issues and to assess the influence of their participation in the program on their professional development. To do so, we built on and adapted our own evolving theoretical framework for the analysis of individual psychosocial development—based primarily on our work with children—and tried to adapt it to adult professional development. Central to this approach was our fundamental assumption that psychosocial maturity—whether among children or adults—is based on an individual's capacity to understand the perspectives of others and to coordinate multiple perspectives.

Table 8.1 in the preceding chapter lists the interview and report-form questions used by the Icelandic training team to elicit teachers' comments at the beginning, middle, and end of their participation in the program each year. In this new phase on the research side of the effort, we sought to analyze those comments with regard to each of our three thematic issues—motivation and aims, management, and pedagogical vision—from a developmental orientation. As we read through the interviews, we identified four perspectives or orientations, which we arranged along what we called an "awareness dimension" because they seemed in some way related to social awareness as we had conceptualized it in our developmental framework. We labeled them as follows:

A. *Student outcome orientation:* Externally based reflection

B. *Teacher outcome orientation:* Personally or internally based reflection

C. *Student-teacher relationship orientation:* Need-based integrative reflection

D. *Orientation toward pedagogical contextualization*

What do these labels imply? In fact, we see the relationship between these different perspectives as being in some sense hierarchical, if not actually developmental. By this we mean that the "higher" or more complex levels build on the "lower" or more concrete and immediate levels, although they do not necessarily replace them. It is important to note that whereas the three content issues—aims, management, and vision—emerged primarily from the teachers' comments in interviews and reports, this hierarchical framework was derived from our developmental approach, and in particular from our focus on perspective coordination as a key element in social interactions. This analysis asks where a teacher's responses about a given issue fall along a developmental continuum with regard to that teacher's capacity to identify and balance, or coordinate, social perspectives (in this case, the teacher's and the students').

For example, consider the question of teachers' professional aims. In responding to questions about this issue, some teachers seemed to focus mostly on overt classroom behavior, others expressed concern about the quality of children's social interactions, and some seemed to look beyond the classroom to consider the role they might play in helping students deal with relationships at home or in the community. Similarly, some teachers seemed concerned only about the immediate situation from day to day, while others spoke and wrote about the effects of their work on their students' social development and future as citizens within the larger society. These were the kinds of differences that shaped our conceptualization of teachers' orientations or levels along the awareness dimension. They also led us to consider whether a given response was outcome-oriented (for example, focused on classroom behavior) or process-oriented (for example, focused on skills to enable children to "get along" in society) or both, as well as to what degree teachers differentiated between their own and their students' perspectives and integrated their own desire to grow as a professional with the idea of promoting social competence among the children in their classroom.

Why do we think the data from the Reykjavík teachers reflect developmental differences in teachers' professional perspectives rather than some other kind of difference, such as individual or cultural differences? This is a crucial question that we revisit and answer differently in the next chapter. For now, we begin by describing in slightly more detail what our "awareness dimension" labels meant to us in the early winter of 1996 as we began the final draft of our first published paper about this phase of our research.

"Awareness Dimension" Labels

The phrase "student outcome orientation (externally based reflection)" refers to a teacher's perspective that focuses only on students' observable behavior in the classroom as a criterion for assessing his or her success as a teacher, and to comments that do not seem to include an expression of the teacher's own point of view or opinion about participating in the training program (comments were couched in terms of "the principal said . . ." rather than "I think . . . .").[2] From a developmental point of view, this narrowness of outlook seems unfortunate. Moreover, at this level of professional awareness, pedagogical ideas and the aims of interpersonal work are not well integrated with overall teaching practices.

The category "teacher outcome orientation (personally based reflection)" represents comments that reflect a teacher's interest in the training program in terms of its professional usefulness (for example, improvements in his or her own teaching skills, more poise, better control of the class). But in this awareness orientation, pedagogical ideas, aims, and practice still focus almost exclusively on students' behavior; they are not integrated with an awareness of the developmental needs of children or their lives beyond the classroom.

"Student-teacher relationship orientation (need-based integrative reflection)" denotes a teacher's capacity to reflect on students' developing social needs as the basis for work on interpersonal issues in the classroom, and on his or her own development as a teacher, including personal strengths and weaknesses. At this level of awareness, teachers are able to consider how to integrate the needs of their students with their own personal and professional needs for understanding, encouragement, and institutional support.

"Orientation to pedagogical contextualization (integrated and context-based reflection)" is the phrase we chose to try to capture the most complex of the perspectives we observed among the Reykjavík teachers. It refers to the expressed understanding that a teacher's role includes the integration of his or her own professional interests with both short-term classroom goals and the long-term educational aim of promoting students' active and effective participation in a democratic society. Included in this form of awareness is an appreciation of the interplay between classroom practice and the development of students' social competence and skills.

How does this developmental framework look in practice? Let's consider the issue of motivation as an example. In our initial analysis, we considered the teachers' comments about their motivation from two angles: their stated reasons for participation in the training (as exemplified by the brief excerpts at the beginning of this chapter) and their general aims regarding the social development of their students. Turning back to chapter 8, where we quoted the remarks of several teachers on why they had joined the evening program, we would classify the responses "I hope to learn some new methods to improve the social behavior of the boys in my class" and "I'm here because the principal said everybody teaching in this grade level . . . should participate" as "student outcome–oriented" or "externally based." With regard to aims, another teacher said, "I find it important that the students are capable of taking the perspectives of other persons. It widens their life experiences, and then this ability may become a part of their nature later in life, to think, How would I feel if I was in her or his shoes?" It should not come as any surprise that we see this statement as characteristic of a higher level of awareness—at least at the level we call a "student-teacher relationship orientation."

Now let us look briefly at the application of our awareness framework to the issue of classroom management. Asked about changes in her own teaching as a result of her participation in the training, one

Table 9.1 An Analysis of Teachers' Levels of Professional Awareness: Themes of "Social Education"

	Thematic Issues			
	Motivation			
Awareness Dimension	Reasons for Participation	Professional Aims	Classroom Management	Pedagogical Vision
Student outcome orientation (externally based reflection)	External, often with a reference to authority	Awareness of improvement in teaching skills as noted by others	Focuses on improving students' classroom behavior, short-term aims, unilateral strategies	Pedagogical ideas, aims, and practices are not differentiated
Teacher outcome orientation (internally based reflection)	Internal, based on wishes and needs of self as teacher	Awareness of improved skills noted by self as teacher	Focuses on improving classroom atmosphere, short-term aims, reciprocal strategies	Pedagogical ideas, aims and practices are differentiated, but not fully integrated
Student-teacher relationship orientation (need-based integrative reflection)	Psychosocial, based on needs of both students and self as teacher	Recognition of interplay between own skills and students' progress, and of own strengths and weaknesses as teacher	Considers students' perspectives, short- and long-term goals; strategies include compromise	Pedagogical ideas and practices are integrated with aims
Orientation to pedagogical contextualization (integrated and context-based reflection)	Pedagogical, with broad perspective on society and the educational system	Focus on own role as teacher with emphasis on effective and responsible teaching in social context	Values students' perspectives and focuses on developing their competence in autonomous thinking and problem solving; uses collaborative strategies	Pedagogical ideas, aims, and practices are both integrated and seen in larger context of society

Source: Reprinted from Adalbjarnardottir and Selman (1997), with permission from Elsevier Science.

teacher said, "The principal feels that I manage the class in a better way." Another said, "I am better at running class discussions." While both these teachers' comments reflect kindly on the program, they do not yield a view into the process by which change occurred for either of them, and we would classify these statements—but not the teachers—as representative of the two less differentiated levels of awareness.

Another teacher who over two years "looped" from first to second grade went on at length to say:

> Before, when problems came up, I was very quick to jump in. Certainly, I asked the kids to express themselves "very briefly" about what happened. But I was quick to judge, to comment, to advise, and to try to reconcile them, for instance, by saying, "Well, now you must be friends." Thus, the students themselves were not active in the problem solution. It was usually I who found the solutions and I who controlled the situation. Now I am not as quick to intervene. I ask the children to stop and think and to express themselves about what has happened, and I listen to them. It is more effective if they themselves face and solve the problems. Then the solution and the whole experience are more likely to stay with them. I feel I have changed a lot in this respect.

For us, these comments reflect a high level of professional awareness with regard to the issue of classroom management. But is it simply the lengthier, more detailed statements that are seen as higher-level in our system, one might ask, or is there something more to this analysis? Table 9.1 frames this analysis by using a matrix similar to those we have used to picture children's social development. However, now the descriptions refer to the reflections of teachers, and they do not have the same developmental characteristics as the figures that attempt to capture growth and development over large periods of time. This does not mean that teachers' reflections cannot deepen, and in that sense develop, over time. In fact, we think they do (or at least they should).

Disa's Pedagogical Vision: The Application of the Framework to the Third Theme

Earlier we excerpted some comments that Disa, a sixth-grade teacher, made at the end of the program for the year. Short excerpts are particularly prone to misunderstanding. Here we present a less abridged version of her reflections on what her experiences working on interpersonal issues in the classroom meant to her personally and professionally:

> By participating in the program, I now realize more clearly the importance of education with regard to emotional and social development than I did before. By seeing how the theories, both of children's social growth and of ways of dealing with interpersonal issues in the classroom, work in practice, I developed a deeper understanding of these theories. I discovered in practice how important it was to get the children to consider different perspectives. I saw how it widened their understanding, and I saw that I had to help them to acquire this understanding by asking them to consider other people's opinions and feelings. It was important for me to experience how much my understanding had improved by seeing things work in practice. As a result I became more secure in dealing with interpersonal issues. I was working within a limited area but hoping that our work would be transferred to other situations in life. [I] see how human beings need much more understanding of each other's point of view. Look at the problems that follow the lack of understanding. See, for example, the low tolerance people in the world have for different religions.
>
> . . . I feel certain that not a minute was wasted in my class when we were dealing with these topics. Positive social interactions among children are the basis for all other work with them. This program provides us with an overview and helps us to work constructively on those serious issues that we constantly have to face at school. I feel I have received a new vision, gathering together various threads and gradually twisting them together into a thick rope, which, I feel when reflecting back, is quite well made!
>
> At home I feel more human also.

Disa's perspective on the importance of work on interpersonal issues in the classroom and how the program helped her in that regard ("I feel I have received a new vision") is, of course, open to interpretation. From our perspective, it led her to develop a deeper integration of the connection between general pedagogical aims ("I now realize more clearly the importance of education with regard to emotional and social development than I did before . . . human beings need much more understanding of each other's point of view") and more specific aims related to classroom practices ("Positive social interactions among children are the basis for all other work with them"). For example, it is interesting to note the changes in Disa's aims. In the beginning, in response to our earlier question about her expectations about her participation in the program, she referred to her relatively undifferentiated aim to "make [her] students good people." In the process of the work she seemed to differentiate and contextualize her aims to a greater extent as these excerpts illustrate, such as: "Look at the problems that follow the lack of understanding. See, for example, the low tolerance people in the world have for different religions."

By the end of the program, Disa claimed that she had deepened her understanding of working on interpersonal issues in the classroom by seeing theories work in practice. Not only did she reflect on the importance of the work for students' interpersonal growth and her role in that respect, but she also realized how essential it was for her to experience directly the relationship between theory and practice as she became more secure in dealing with interpersonal issues ("It was important for me to experience how much my understanding had improved by seeing things work in practice. As a result I became more secure in dealing with interpersonal issues"). In other words, Disa contextualized her pedagogy and experience by connecting improvements in students' interpersonal growth to her own development in understanding its importance, and in her becoming more capable of dealing with interpersonal issues. Furthermore, she saw her self-development transferred to another context ("At home I feel more human also").

In short, as Disa acquired a more profound meaning of the work, she felt that she integrated her pedagogical thoughts and her actions in the classroom. We can argue that her motivation, as reflected in the need she felt to deal with the situation in her classroom and her understanding of its importance, served as a force in finding meaning in the work. To use our theoretical framework, Disa initially experienced a lack of integration between her insightful pedagogical knowledge of what interpersonal education should be about and her own less sophisticated classroom management skills. She found it important to deal with interpersonal situations but felt that the strategies she had been using in the past had not worked well enough. During the intervention program, as she acquired the meaning she derived from her pedagogical ideas, aims, and classroom management skills deepened, the work helped her to bridge the gap between her pedagogical theory and practice.

Hidden Assumptions and the Challenges of a Developmental Approach

With this abridged sketch of how we initially constructed our theoretical framework as background, let's take a look at some of its assumptions, benefits, and limitations.

The first assumption we have already mentioned: that each level of awareness regarding each issue is in some sense built on (reconstructs) the level "below" it. As we have stated, we view differences along the awareness dimension as developmental, but not in the sense that they represent stages; that is, we do not mean to imply that as individuals the teachers in the program tended to operate at the same (or only one) level of awareness across all issues or across all conversations. In fact, it is important to note that with regard to each issue (motivation, classroom management, pedagogical vision), teachers often expressed ideas that ranged across multiple levels of awareness. Sometimes, in interviews, teachers began with simpler comments and then moved on to more deeply reflective responses, and sometimes immediate life experiences seemed to color their views, influencing them to think differently about a given matter than they might have done at another time. Nonetheless, we assumed that some teachers might reach a higher level of awareness about their new professional experience more quickly than others.

In addition, we found the question of how consistently teachers expressed each of the levels of awareness over time and in different situations to be an important one. In particular, there seemed to be a significant difference between teachers whose expressions tended to stay within the lower two levels of professional awareness (A and B) and those whose comments we saw as indicative of one or both of the higher two levels (C and D). For each of the first two levels on our awareness dimension, the primary focus is on observable *outcomes* regarding students' interpersonal competence and skills (for example, classroom behavior); comments at each of the second two levels involve an awareness of developmental *processes,* as they relate to experiences that go beyond the classroom, and of societal needs as well as individual ones. Thus, we might consider responses at levels A and B to be more concrete and those at levels C and D more abstract. We hasten to add that this does not mean that we think abstract is better than concrete: concrete and practical ideas can of course be as useful as theoretical or abstract ones. But we do hypothesize a meaningful difference in terms of professional development between teachers who *only* speak about student or personal outcomes—that is, whose thinking seems always to be concrete—and teachers who also express an interest in such abstract matters as developmental processes, connections between their own interpersonal understanding and that of their students, and larger questions about society and the future of their students.

But we need to take our inquiry a bit further. The more difficult question is whether we can rely on our interpretation of statements like these to be accurate reflections of developmental differences in professional awareness in a way that tells us something about the actual work of teachers on interpersonal issues in real classrooms. The voice of the skeptic, always present in every good researcher, raises two points for starters.

First, we know that *individuals*—teachers included—*do not always say what they mean, or all of what they mean.* For example, remember the initial comment of one teacher, quoted in chapter 8, when asked why she had joined the "reflective gathering": "I'm here because the principal said everybody teaching in this grade level in the school should participate." If it is true that the principal did say that all the teachers needed to participate in the program, we might hear the comments of the first teacher as simply "telling it like it is." Why, one might ask, is that any "lower-level" than what any of the other teachers had to say about their participation? Is she not just being more honest, more straightforward? Or perhaps she is just as aware as some of the other teachers of the potential benefits of the program to herself and her students but is so annoyed at what she perceives as the "top-down" nature of the mandate that she says no more, even though she intends to participate fully.

Obviously, analyzing anyone's reflections out of context and then putting a label on them (either the reflections or the person, but especially the person) is a very risky business. Maybe this teacher feels that she already has the knowledge and skills she needs to deal with social issues in the classroom—and maybe she does. But we doubt it. If that had been the case, we think she would have said so. In the end, even though we are aware that it may not have been complete, we take this response at face value and see it as reflecting a fairly rule-based—that is, *externally based*—orientation toward the issue of motivation.

A second potential problem is that we know that *individuals*—once again, teachers included—*do not always mean* (read "do") *what they say.* For example, one fourth-grade teacher provided a more complex and differentiated response to our question about her motivation for participating in the professional development program: "Teachers spend a lot of energy trying to improve students' social interactions. I want to learn better ways to handle social management problems in my classroom, which I find overwhelming." But is this teacher any less likely to act impulsively or unilaterally with students when under pressure than her colleagues are? Included within her motivation to participate is an orientation toward helping her students develop the skills they apparently lack; she reflects on her desire to improve her own skills as a teacher; and her comments make a connection between the two. These are markers of what we called a *need-based integrative* level of professional awareness. But what kind of teacher is she? What does she really do in the classroom, or in her work with parents and fellow teachers?

Clearly, before we made sweeping pronouncements about the professional competence of teachers we needed to take a second look at our framework and gather more information.[3]

A Critical Look at Our Framework: The Benefits and Risks of a Developmental Analysis

In the meantime, a third concern had arisen—or it might be more accurate to say that it had resurfaced. In our short history of the Reykjavík training and research project in chapter 8, we mentioned that there was "some reluctance, if not actual resistance," to analyzing teachers' aims or skills in a way that, no matter how delicately stated, valued some expressed attitudes, ideas, and approaches over others. Now we needed to revisit this issue.

One limitation of our analysis, we could all agree, was the imposition of a theoretical framework "from the top down" on the statements gathered from teachers in the course of the Icelandic Project—a framework that, regardless of our protestations, still prioritized abstraction over the concrete. By whose standards did we judge these teachers' reflections? Were we really able to "walk in their shoes," or might it be that we were overly partial to those whose statements reflected our own ideology and educational agenda? These were good questions.

We think a developmental analysis—with its various awareness levels building one upon the other—is a useful tool for research on the general topic of teachers' professional lives, one with important implications for practice. For one thing, it forces us to articulate the standards and indices we use for classifying teachers' reflections about their work. For another, it allows us to quantify these in ways that are open to public scrutiny; others can then validate or refute them. And in the long run, we believe, this approach can be useful to practitioners and to designers of programs that support teachers' professional development. (After all, by definition, to develop is to change.) It can guide programs to train teachers in the first place and help them refine and freshen their skills throughout their careers.

However, there are also real risks to this kind of approach. Top-down analyses involve trying to fit data—in our case, evidence from teachers' narratives—into a preconceived framework, but sometimes these data do not fit well into any of the slots available. Sometimes they do not belong in the framework at all.

With regard to the questions of fairness and judgment raised by a hierarchical system of classification, one safeguard is our constant awareness that we are looking at expressions, not people. A second is our awareness that we are doing so, at least so far, in the context of very limited amounts of data—in these cases, only one interview. This qualification—that we are not judging the individual, only listening carefully to the words he or she uses at one point in time—is important, if not entirely satisfactory. Ultimately, however, we are interested in more than the analysis of disembodied responses—we are interested in teaching and in enhancing the professional competence of teachers as individuals.

To this end, we are committed to practicing what we preach by keeping the larger context in mind as we listen to what teachers say. For instance, historical and political circumstances have an influence on individuals' decisions to go into teaching, and these change over time, as do people's personal circumstances and motivations. Some men and women enter—or stay in—the profession, especially in poor communities, in large part because they feel committed to the ideal of social equity; they want to "empower" children who are growing up under conditions of unequal opportunity, to provide them with tools that will help them transcend their disadvantages. Others commit themselves to teaching because they feel a deep and abiding affection for all children. They may not be as politically minded, nor as oriented toward issues of social justice. They may not focus on the broader societal context; we might even say that they are more exclusively child-oriented. But who is to say whether one set of motivations is worthier, let alone "higher-level," than the other? Who is to say which motivation will make for better teaching?

Furthermore, personal, social, and economic factors often had a prominent place in what teachers told us. For example, in our small sample, many of the teachers were women who had begun their careers in the 1960s and 1970s, and they tended to cite reasons for becoming a teacher that were different from those of individuals who had entered the profession in the 1980s and 1990s. Because the comments of the older teachers reflected the fact that there were fewer professional choices for women during the earlier decades, they may sound more passive and externally driven than was really the case.

We also realize that teachers' views about their engagement in the profession may change over time, even fluctuate from day to day: teaching is a demanding job, and some days are better than others. Sometimes teachers' views vary in relation to the number of years of experience they have in the field—or as a function of the grade level they teach. Some years they may have a difficult class, or child, or principal, or colleague, and this experience may shake their sense of commitment. So even if we can construct a valid developmental dimension on which to locate teachers' expressions of engagement with the profession, we must be cautious in interpreting what these words mean.

The settings in which teachers do their work are also reflected in their comments. The challenges described by suburban teachers are real and often grueling, but they are different from the ones that teachers experience in poor urban or rural communities. Social class makes a difference. So too does gender. The overwhelming predominance of women in the teaching profession in the elementary grades powerfully influences the general tenor of the reflections of the teachers we interviewed. Only two Boston public elementary school teachers in our study were men. In the Icelandic study no men at all took part in the training program during the decade in question, although this had not been the case in years past. All these factors need to be considered when we interpret the meaning of the narratives or interview responses.

The Antidote to "Developmental Reductionism"

We think we have found an antidote to the "top-heaviness" of our initial theoretical approach to studying the professional development of teachers, a method that can counter the tendency of any developmental framework to reduce the statements and behavior of individuals to nothing more than points on a hierarchical continuum. We describe this method, which involves working to interpret the reflections of teachers "from the bottom up" as well as from the top down, in the next chapter.

This chapter was coauthored by Robert L. Selman and Sigrun Adalbjarnardottir. Significant portions of this chapter appeared previously in Adalbjarnardottir and Selman (1977).

Chapter 10

Terms of Engagement: Personal Meaning and the Professional Lives of Teachers

I sort of feel like I'm the director of an orchestra and I give the students the instruments, and together we play the symphony and I have them take the risk and support them. I don't think it's an easy thing to do. I think you have to be willing to take a risk and try something new, which I think is not easy.
—Angela Burgos, fifth-grade teacher, Russell Elementary School

To me, reading books like Felita is something that helps me to take the chance to get out everything that I felt inside that was hurting me a lot. It helps me through making new friends and knowing what to do. It gives me messages. Ms. Burgos helps me say what I think Felita should do.
—Juanita, age eleven

ACROSS THE chapters of this book, we have used the term "risk" in several ways. In the name we gave our basic developmental framework in chapter 4, it refers to "the uncertainty of outcome that children face as they make decisions about how to act within interpersonal relationships." When we speak about "risk factors," however, the term has an inherently negative connotation. These factors—poverty, disruption within the family, and racial or ethnic discrimination—when piled on the shoulders of an individual, often lead to poor life outcomes. In this context the phrase "risk-taking behavior" refers to those actions, such as chronic fighting, promiscuous sexual behavior, and addiction to cigarettes, drugs, or alcohol, that most often prove to be dangerous to the individual and to others.

But when Angela Burgos uses the word "risk" in speaking of what she asks her students to do—and what she does herself as a teacher—its connotations are quite different: she is referring to the healthy risks we all must take if we are to grow as individuals and in our relationships with other people. She believes that it is a good thing for her students to stretch their academic abilities and for them—as for all of us—to dare to reveal personal thoughts and feelings. She also knows that her students need her support in taking these risks.

Ms. Burgos knows that she is taking a chance in selecting a book like *Felita* for her class to discuss in depth. Many teachers might think the classroom is not an appropriate place for a fifth-grader to "get out" painful feelings. They might be concerned that children would become embarrassed or be put in a vulnerable position; they also might be worried that they would encounter problems they are not willing or qualified to deal with. And of course, they know that some parents might vigorously object on any number of grounds. On the other hand, selecting text materials for children to read and write about or discuss in class that they find boring and irrelevant is also inherently risky: the students may fall asleep in school and not wake up until it is too late. It should be acknowledged, however, that even when teachers work under the best of conditions—with manageable class sizes and good supports and resources—their professional lives are full of difficult choices and social dilemmas both large and small.

In 1996 we asked a small group of teachers in Boston to take the risk of allowing us to observe in the classroom as they taught VLF, which was new to many of them. We also asked them to share with us their thoughts and feelings about their profession and about the effort to integrate literacy and values, that is, to connect reading and writing with the promotion of social competence and conflict resolution skills. In our conversations with these practitioners, we found that their reflections on why they had gone into teaching, and what kept them committed to it, seemed related in important ways to how willing they were to take on the challenge of an approach such as VLF—and how well they taught this curriculum. But as we entered their classrooms—and their lives—we did not yet have a firm place for any of this in our theoretical model of teachers' professional awareness. Fortunately, we did have our experience with the teachers in Reykjavík to build on.

Revising Our Model, Step 1: From the Top Down—A Developmental Approach

In the fall of 1996, as we began our study of the implementation of the VLF approach, we were well aware that its subject matter was challenging, that some of its methods would be unfamiliar to some teachers at first, and that the commitment of teachers was key to the program's success. As we put in more and more hours observing in classrooms, we realized that our understanding of the program would be incomplete without a deeper understanding of teachers' perspectives on a range of professional issues. But it was not until December 1997, a year and a half after we began our study, that we were able to interview teachers systematically. It had taken our team that long to decide what questions we wanted to ask. How could we modify the interview protocol developed for the Icelandic Project in a way that would fit our new research questions and these new circumstances?

We decided to design a method of analysis that would expand our approach for assessing teachers' views about their participation in *any* school-based practice that integrated the promotion of social competence into the academic curriculum. To help us formulate our research protocol, we turned again to our basic developmental framework. The new "Boston" interview, we decided, would focus on teachers' general reflections on their role in promoting social competence rather than ask about any specific practice or professional development experience.

Broadening our questions allowed us to reconceptualize what we hoped to discover. Teaching is a profoundly social occupation. We wondered whether the three basic psychosocial components of our Risk and Relationship Framework—understanding, strategies, and awareness of the personal meaning of events and interactions—would also apply in the domain of elementary school teaching and teachers' professional awareness. Thinking about the subject from this angle resulted in a seemingly modest but nevertheless quite meaningful conceptual shift in our thinking and a reformulation of our three central "issues."

In this slightly revised scheme, the issue of "aims," as in the Reykjavík study, represents what teachers have to say about the connection between a curriculum they are using (like VLF) and the teaching process, and about their goals for themselves and for their students—that is, their pedagogical *understanding*. The issue or category "teaching *strategies*" encompasses the methods and techniques that teachers use to achieve the pedagogical goals of promoting social awareness and competence, as well as how they deal with difficult issues and social conflict in the classroom. This conceptualization of strategies is also similar to our earlier approach. It is the third issue that marks the most significant revision in our analysis. This issue, "terms of engagement," includes teachers' reflections on their commitment to the profession: Is it a job? A career? A profession? A calling? This issue represents the *personal meaning* that teachers make of their work.[1]

Looking again at our earlier formulation, we felt that "pedagogical vision" now belonged at a different place on our new conceptual map. We saw it as an integrative meta-issue—or to put it another

Figure 10.1 Teachers' Professional Reflection: Levels of Awareness by Professional Issues

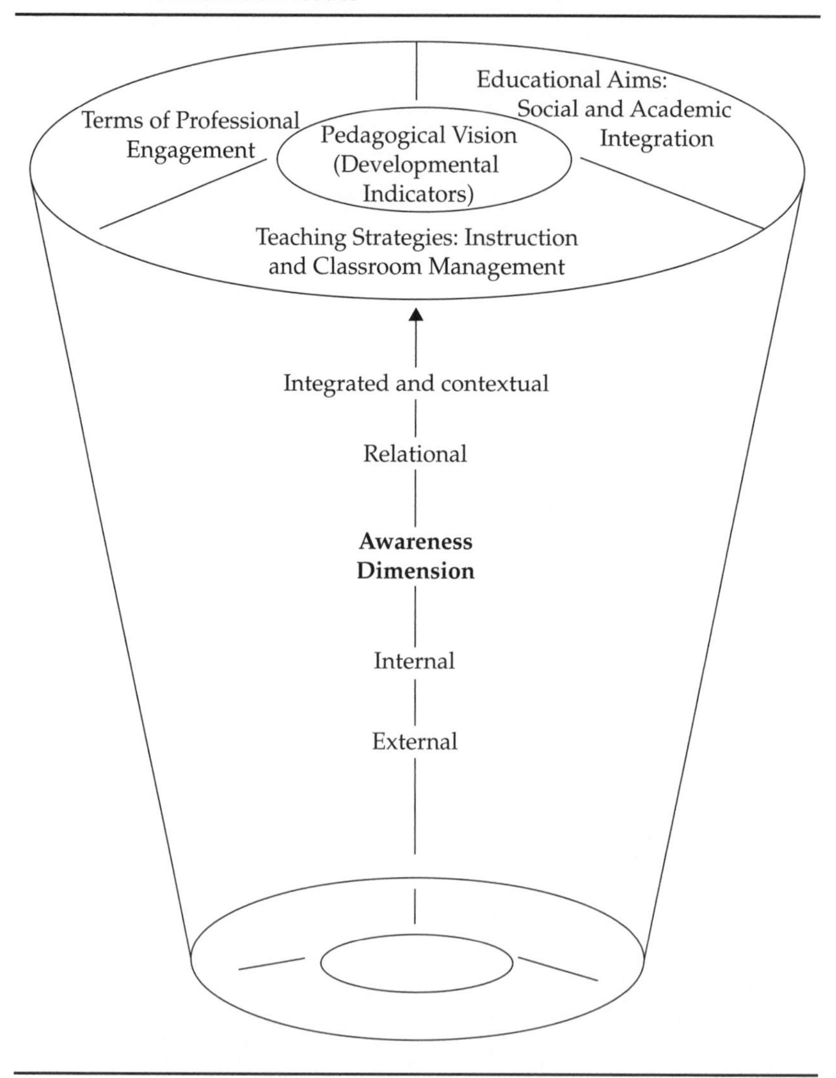

Source: Authors' configuration.

way, a coordinating operation that crosses the three domains of teachers' professional awareness. Figure 10.1 portrays this revised theoretical framework in both developmental and issue-oriented terms. Its resemblance to figure 4.2 is not accidental.

What does it mean to say that pedagogical vision is now the core operational structure of this model, equivalent to social perspective coordination in our psychosocial development framework? How does it underlie professional development along the three component dimensions of teachers' professional awareness—aims, strategies, and engagement?

Recall that within our psychosocial Risk and Relationship Framework (see chapter 4) the core operational function of perspective coordination expresses itself through the various psychosocial components (social understanding, social skills and strategies, and the awareness of personal meaning) that influence or determine how individuals relate to one another. Since we believe that teaching is essentially a relationship-oriented activity, we think it makes sense to extend the parallel here. We define "pedagogical vision" as centering on the teacher's reflective coordination of his or her own perspective on learning processes with the perspectives of his or her students.

In the case of the Icelandic Project or VLF, of course, the learning is as much about the ethic of social relationships as it is about grammar, vocabulary, and spelling. However, whether the specific content being taught is literacy, math, science, or history, good teaching requires a meaningful relationship between those who teach and those who are learning—an engagement of teacher and student alike—that depends on the specific professional competencies we are studying.

Our approach does not ignore the current debate about educational reform and the goal of holding teachers accountable for the performance of their students in terms of reading and writing skills, basic competence in mathematics, and knowledge of history and science. Instead, we explore whether teachers' professional awareness—their understanding and aims with regard to a particular curriculum, the specific practices they use, and the personal meaning that teaching that curriculum has for them—may be fueled by their capacity to integrate their own perspective on learning with that of their students.

To refine this model of teachers' professional awareness, we interviewed the twenty teachers who participated in year 2 of the implementation of the VLF curriculum in 1997 to 1998. We used a redesigned interview that fit our new conceptualization. Table 10.1 shows how the revised questions relate to the evolving model depicted in figure 10.1. (Designing interview questions to elicit comments about the specific issues of teachers' aims, strategies, and professional engagement, and about "pedagogical vision," is part of what we mean when we describe this as a "top-down" approach.)

Table 10.1 Teacher Interview Protocol

1. What made you decide to become a teacher? (E)
2. What keeps you teaching? What makes your job good? What makes it hard? (E)
3. How do *you* define good teaching? What's the most important part of teaching to you? (A)
4. How would you define success for a student in your classroom? (A)
5. Describe the climate of your classroom. How do you think students and teachers should interact? How are decisions made in your classroom? (S)
6. What do *you* do when conflict arises in the classroom? (S)
7. What do you think fosters:

    a. Open classroom discussion of difficult issues?
    b. Respect for others who hold different or opposing views?
    c. Deep engagement and critical thinking? (S)

8. How was this project [the research] introduced to you? How do you feel about that? (E)
9. What do you hope to get out of participating in this research project? (A)
10. What do you think will be:

    a. Compelling aspects of VLF for your students?
    b. Challenging aspects of VLF for your students? (PV)

11. Do you think the classroom is an appropriate place for kids to learn about values? Are you comfortable in the role of teaching a curriculum that explores personal and social values such as discrimination, social conflict, and race? (A)
12. Do you feel that there are connections between children's literacy skills—or their ability to communicate through reading and writing—and their interpersonal skills? Explain. (PV)
13. What do you do to improve your teaching? (S/A)

Source: Authors' compilation (Group for the Study of Interpersonal Development).
Note: The professional issues tapped by each question are abbreviated as follows:

E = Engagement
A = Aims
S = Teaching strategies
PV = Pedagogical vision

Personal Meaning Redefined as "Teachers' Professional Engagement"

Before discussing the role of pedagogical vision in depth, we wish to clarify the introduction of a concept that became integral to the Boston study. Chapter 9 described the application of our developmental analysis to the issues of the Icelandic teachers' aims and motivation and their strategies for promoting children's social competence. There is enough similarity between the new and old conceptualizations of these issues that we need not revisit them here. What is new is a focus on engagement—the *personal meaning* of the work of teaching for each individual. When we began interviewing teachers, their responses to certain questions gave us new insights into their professional lives. We addressed what we had begun to call "terms of engagement" most directly in two questions on the new interview protocol:

- What influenced you to become a teacher?
- What keeps you teaching?

Narratives A, B, and C are brief excerpts from three interviews in which teachers reflect on why they entered the profession and why they remain committed to it. We present them as snapshots of what is in reality a much more complex picture. Even though they are brief and taken out of context, and therefore subject to misinterpretation, we think that comparing the excerpts helps us to make a point about ways to analyze teachers' professional reflections.

> *Narrative A:* Well, originally, ah, I used to . . . when I was younger, I used to always baby-sit—you know, relatives' kids, and things like that—and I used to love doing that, and, um, I wanted to be a pediatrician. And when I got to high school and I started taking chemistry [*laughs*], I said, "Now wait a minute! I don't need to know all this stuff!" . . . And it wasn't until my junior year that one of the professors said, Why [didn't I] just go for the whole certification instead of . . . you know, 'cause I wanted to do social work and work with families and things like that. And I started thinking about it. I guess I was afraid to, you know, the first time, being in the front of the class—all those little eyes on you, everything you say. But once I started, I got into the hang of it. I realized I had the knack of it.

> *Narrative B:* I think when we were sophomores we had to put on this demonstration lesson over [at] the school, because I went to Boston State, which is not there anymore, but anyway, I used to practice with

my brothers and sisters. I used to practice my lessons in front of them, and that was kind of funny, but I think that there's nothing that can really prepare you for being in the classroom. I think that the best experience is being in the classroom—that is where you learn the most. You don't get it from a textbook, and I think it's something that you [just] really feel inside you and that is really what you want to do, because I don't think everybody is cut out to do this, because there is so much work, you take it home with you, you take the kids in your mind home with you, so it's just constant, and it's very emotionally draining, but I think if that is you, you just really want to do it—you want to be the teacher. I think I have always been cut out for teaching. I just love it, I really do.

Narrative C: Thinking back, it was something that was decided within myself as a young child, that—I think I was five years old—I knew. I had a calling. And that was something that I never deviated from. . . . It wasn't for the money. I think it's the gratification you get, the reward you probably don't experience in a regular job setting. To open a child's eyes into learning, and sharing and growing with them as they meet the challenges—I don't know, it's gratifying to me. I don't know if it answers the question. . . . I sort of feel like I'm the director of an orchestra and I give the students the instruments, and together we play the symphony. . . . It's a way to help them use what they learn, to empower them. . . . My family always raised me to respect teachers, and it fit with my own instincts to nurture and support. It's just in me.

Developmental Indicators of Professional Awareness: A Methodological Advance

In chapter 9, we described our attempt to analyze and compare Icelandic teachers' reflections on professional awareness issues along a one-dimensional developmental line, using the coordination of teacher and student perspectives as our fundamental conceptual tool to classify them. With the new material we were gathering in Boston, we began to add breadth to that approach. Reading through the initial round of interviews, we came up with three ways to think about what the teachers were saying that lent themselves to a developmental analysis. Calling these three analyses "developmental indicators," we felt that they enabled us to interpret teachers' reflections from a developmental standpoint whether the topic was aims and motivation, strategies, or terms of engagement.

The first of these we have already pointed out in chapter 9: *the quality of the teacher's perspective on student-teacher relationships.* By this we mean the teacher's (level of) awareness of her own perspective, her students' perspectives, and the extent to which they connect and integrate with one another. In chapter 9, we also described how we classified teachers' reflections as student-oriented when teachers emphasized the children's perspective, as teacher-oriented when teachers emphasized their own point of view, and as student-teacher-oriented when the teachers integrated their perspectives with those of their students and emphasized relationship issues.

A second indicator we call *the quality of a teacher's view of children and their development.* In reading narrative texts like these three excerpts, we identified differences among teachers regarding the level of complexity of their understanding of child development. Some teachers tended to focus their conception of children's development on observable outcomes and the skills they expected their students to have or to acquire through classwork. At more complex levels of understanding, teachers recognized the psychosocial needs of students and how these relate to students' behavior and to their own work with children in the classroom.

The third indicator we called *the teacher's capacity to take a contextual view,* that is, the potential that teachers have for taking into consideration the perspective of the larger society. Teachers with this capacity were aware of the developmental and cultural characteristics of their students, the future role of their students in society, and the historical and political conditions that shape students' lives and learning.

We believe that using these three indicators as we read interviews helped us broaden our developmental analysis of teachers' professional awareness. The three interview excerpts quoted here are far too brief to provide a full picture, but we can use them to demonstrate this revised approach as it might be applied to the analysis of teachers' engagement, the newest of our professional issues.

Narrative C should sound familiar: it includes part of this chapter's epigraph quote from Angela Burgos's interview. Some of Ms. Burgos's additional comments—that she "had a calling," for instance, and found "sharing and growing with [children] as they meet the challenges" personally gratifying—suggest that she is aware of an internal source of commitment, and that she has a refined notion of her students' development in conjunction with her own. Her assertion that teaching is a calling, or "something that was decided within myself as a young child," would not be enough to lead us to classify her comments as reflecting a "high level" of professional awareness with regard to the issue of engagement. We do, however, find such a high level of awareness reflected in Ms. Burgos's differentiation between an intrinsic and an extrinsic source of her commitment to teaching.

We would place narrative B at the middle level along the professional awareness dimension. Comments like, "If that is you, you just really want to do it," and, "I don't think everybody is cut out to do this," suggest to us a dichotomous and concrete conception of an individual's attraction to teaching and ability: either you have it or you don't. This teacher does say, "I just love it, I really do," but her view of the profession and her engagement with it seem fixed and categorical rather than dynamic and evolving.

Finally, a comment like, "The professors said, Why didn't I just go for the whole certification. . . . Once I started, I got into the hang of it," and other such comments from narrative A suggest the experience of having fallen into the job rather than selected it for reasons connected to personal passions or values. In this narrative, external forces seem to prevail over inner direction. We would say that of the three excerpts, narrative A reflects the weakest sense of engagement with the profession, combined with a lower level of professional awareness.

Theoretical Revisions in Developmental Levels: Defining What We Mean by "Pedagogical Vision"

The first two of the theoretical changes we made between Reykjavík and Boston—defining pedagogical vision as operating across the domains of teachers' professional awareness and using the concept of personal meaning to reframe the issue of motivation as "terms of professional engagement"—resulted from our effort to think more three-dimensionally and to align our model of adult professional development with the one we had constructed to help us understand the social development of children. Here "development" is a key word, reflecting our interest in a fourth dimension: how awareness and behavior change over time.

Although these analytic changes and the resulting shifts in methods were useful and meaningful to us as theorists and researchers, it is important to remember that the distinctions and categories we devise are not etched in stone. This becomes even clearer in the second major theoretical "move" we decided to make, one rooted in even more practical considerations.

For example, in Iceland we had begun to find ways to "soften" the hard edges of our "developmentalism" to fit a new set of research aims, working with adult professionals. In the context of the Boston study, we continued to push in this direction. We found less practical utility in trying to squeeze each and every one of our teachers' responses or narratives into one of four supposedly distinct levels that, in appearance at least, might seem iron-clad. Were all of the fine distinctions captured in table 9.1 useful for practitioners or for ourselves? From our earlier experiences with this type of work our answer was, not atypically, "It depends." It depended on what we were trying to understand. If we were primarily trying to do theory, perhaps yes. If we were trying to bridge theory and practice, probably no.

Since ultimately the goal of our research was to study the implementation of a literacy and values curriculum, we decided it was adequate for us to think about teachers' professional awareness as it related to their students' social development in terms of three levels rather than the four depicted in chapter 9. We noticed that the first two orientations along the awareness dimension (see table 9.1) actually describe the same level of awareness with different orientations: student or teacher outcomes. However, whether a teacher focuses only on student outcomes or only on teacher outcomes did not make much difference from a developmental perspective, since both orientations are toward external results only.

Then we looked more carefully at this formulation. It seemed that the distinction we had really been making at those two levels was between focusing on external outcomes alone (at the first level) and focusing on both outcomes and internal processes (at the second). We reworked our descriptions to reflect this shift in the way we made the distinction. We looked at comments indicating a concern for inner experience and acknowledging its growth and connection to overt behavior as a level above comments focused only on external manifestations of behavior.

In addition, we did not think the distinction between a student-teacher relationship orientation and what we had called "pedagogical contextualization" would prove very useful for working with teachers in the everyday world. For one thing, it set up a very elite "highest" level, one that relied to a great extent on verbal gymnastics. For another, few people other than researchers or theoreticians use this degree of abstraction in thinking, let alone talking, about their professional lives. So we chose to blur the distinction and merge these two levels into one.

In the end, we came up with the terms "external," "internal," and "relational" to give these three levels (or stages) of professional awareness labels that better capture our definitions of what they mean. Let's see how our new theoretical framework looked when we got done with all this heavy conceptual lifting. We know that with its particular focus—promoting students' social competence and the connection between this aspect of classroom work and teachers' terms of engagement with their profession—it is not a complete picture of all the facets of elementary school pedagogy. Think of it as an impressionist sketch of how different teachers conceptualize and approach their teaching of social competence.

The External Orientation

An external pedagogical vision of social competence tends to focus on the importance of teaching "good social behavior" so that students are able to learn academic subjects. The teachers' aim is to "control" students' individual behavior (impulses, attention) so that they can learn the academic content.

Management strategies at this level are focused on eliminating negative behavior in a *reactive* way: the teacher reacts to the students' poor behavior. Strategies to improve students' behavior tend to be unilateral (get students to get along, not fight) regardless of the context. Students' social skills are interpreted as additive and individualistic (*more* control, *better* behavior, *less* withdrawn).

As expressed at this level, engagement with teaching is as a job, with fixed parameters largely defined by external forces (for example, the principal's orders, pre-service training requirements), and this job works well when it fits with personal schedules ("home by four") and personal skills ("good with children").

The Internal Orientation

The internal view of academic and social competence is based on an awareness that learning in school must include promoting the understanding of social and societal relationships, which are as important as literacy, math, or science. The aim, as expressed at this level, is to educate students to "get along" with one another and to provide them with life skills and the "inner strength" to manage the societal issues they will face in and outside of school.

Teachers with a classroom management focus work to promote students' social understanding and skills in a *proactive* way. They strive to improve classroom atmosphere by using strategies that improve students' ability to be *interactive:* for example, they train students in the skills needed to recognize interpersonal problems in the class as well as to manage their own behavior with others. Teachers who practice an internal pedagogy emphasize teaching students how to resolve conflicts with peers and authorities.

At this level, engagement with teaching is as a *profession* (long-term career path). These teachers often express their commitment to improving their own teaching skills as a personal and professional commitment to promoting children's development and providing students with the tools to function in society.

The Relational Orientation

The most sophisticated level (at least by our standards) of the revised framework we label "relational." It starts with the awareness that strong academic and social competence is necessary *in the service of* educating students to be able to maintain and improve society. As they gain a broad perspective on the educational and cultural system within which students and teachers operate, teachers at this level of awareness strive to empower students to *participate* actively in society by fostering their capacity for autonomy (freedom) and caring (love).

These teachers focus on fostering relational competencies and skills in a *transactional* way. Their strategies employ their own capacity to listen to students' perspectives on social issues (at any level) as they express their own. They also work to develop students' competence in autonomous self-control and expression of personal concern about social issues. These teachers train students in taking collaborative approaches to debate (where developmentally and contextually appropriate) and foster communicative and relational competencies in students that enable them to develop trusting relationships beyond individual instrumental gains—in both social and societal contexts.

Engagement with teaching is often seen by those who practice a relational pedagogy as a *calling*, or as *service*, that is, as part of a larger vision of the professional development of the self in society. Their awareness of teaching as providing a critical function within society connects with their own ability to develop their personal and professional qualities.

Revising Our Model, Step 2: From the Bottom Up—A Thematic Approach

This analysis is defined by our own standards; perhaps not everyone would agree with it. Even though both the reliability and validity of our developmental analysis can be challenged, we do not think it is a wrong or bad approach. In fact, we think it is very useful. But we need to take care and avoid simply assigning a teacher's comment to a certain level and then leaving it at that.

To protect against this conceptual pitfall—and to broaden our understanding—we decided to look at the teacher interviews in our study from a very different perspective—from what many would call the bottom up. Using a bottom-up approach, we put our theoretical developmental framework aside for a while and read the interviews for common themes without immediately trying to put them into a developmental order or quantitative hierarchy. This effort was a bit of a challenge, but more than worthwhile. To help illustrate why, we present three more brief interview excerpts that touch on the issue of professional engagement. These teachers are responding to the interview questions: What influenced you to become a teacher? What keeps you teaching?

> *Narrative D:* Yeah, . . . there are a lot of things, as I think about it. I really like the fact that teaching is really the synthesis between theory and practice. The one thing that really frustrated me in the university was talking about theory and not being able to [know] how to apply it, and I would get really upset with my professors and write these papers about how useless all these books were . . . because they did not apply to the real world, nobody can use them in their lives. . . . And I really like the fact that teachers can take ideas and turn them into reality. Intellectually it is very challenging, being able to take an abstract idea or a concept and turn [it] into a lesson . . . trying to break it down into its component parts so that an eight-year-old can understand it. . . .
>
> I enjoy the politics a little. Some of the politics I enjoy—the idea that you are involved in something that is making a difference in children's lives and that in a small way there is a personal involvement in changing society is a good thing, and, you know, everything else is just the kids. It is just so fascinating that they can learn something every day.

> *Narrative E:* I came here in 1985 from Panama, and I never thought about being a teacher [*laughs*]. I thought that would be the last thing I would ever do. So when I came here, because I had two children—they were three and almost six years old, and it was time for them to go to school—so I found a job as a paraprofessional in a school [because] it was easy for me to have them in the school while I was working. So when I went to the classroom, I felt so many needs that the children had, so I kept looking and thinking and . . . that was the reason I decided to become a teacher, to help these children. And I always remember, my second year, I was teaching a fifth grade, the teacher [had just reprimanded] the children because they were teasing, and I remember this boy came to me to ask me something, and the teacher said, "Why do you always go to Ms. Fuentes and not to me?" and they said, "Because Ms. Fuentes has children and she knows what is going on in our lives."
>
> So she was surprised, because she doesn't have children, and I started to think that it was better for me to become a teacher to help these children. And sometimes, when you have too many issues in your

classroom, you ask, Why am I a teacher? Why can't I change to another thing? And then I go back and say, Well, maybe I'm the only person who can help them, and if I leave the system, there is another group of children who maybe don't have anyone to help them. I think my background, my interest, and my calm nature combine to make me a good teacher.

So that's my story.

Narrative F: Well, when I started teaching in the early sixties, there wasn't much else that a female could do. You could either become a teacher, a nurse, or a secretary. So I became a teacher. I started teaching in 1961.

What do we find when we look for common or distinct themes in these teachers' responses? To begin with, in the longer interviews we see life stories beginning to emerge; as is often the case, the questions led these three teachers to include anecdotes, turning-point incidents, and references to their families and personal histories.

Sometimes teachers touched on more than one theme to explain their professional choices and actions. Sometimes they seemed to speak to the same theme from different angles. Nevertheless, across the narratives in our sample we were able to identify five distinct and recurring themes. As we shall see, the characterization of the interviews by themes looks quite different from their classification by levels.

The Five Terms of Engagement

The first theme we call a *good fit,* as when teachers commented on the good match between their own inclinations and the primary activities involved in teaching children of elementary school age. A common perception of a good fit was a basic enjoyment of working with children ("I used to love to baby-sit," or, "It seemed natural that I would go into teaching and be around children"). This perception often included a belief that she or he had certain essential attributes—like patience, nurturing, or caring—that define being a good elementary grade teacher. "Good fit" captures the theme of the speaker in narrative A, for whom teaching became an option late in her college years, and who, despite some fears, "got into the hang of it." It also captures some of what is expressed by narrator B, who talks about some people being "cut out" for teaching.

Whenever a teacher spoke about having gone into teaching for practical reasons, such as wanting a schedule that fit in with his or her professional and personal commitments, we heard the second theme: *convenience.* Parts of narrative E reflect this theme ("It was easy for me to have them [her own children] in the school while I was working"), although even this brief excerpt provides evidence that this was not the only reason she went into teaching.

A third theme is *a desire to change society.* Several of the teachers in our small sample told us that going into teaching was an expression of their political commitment to changing things for the better. Some of narrator D's responses reflect this theme: "The idea that you are involved in something that is making a difference in children's lives and that in a small way there is a personal involvement in changing society is a good thing."

A fourth theme we call *default,* represented here by narrator F, a teacher who curtly responded to our questions by saying, "In the early sixties, there wasn't much else that a female could do."

A fifth theme we heard as a *calling.* Some teachers simply—but often emphatically—pointed out that teaching was what they had always wanted to do. Many of these teachers remembered identifying with teachers from very early childhood. This is a prominent theme in narratives B and C. But, one may ask, a calling to what? To transform society through education? To educate poor children? Our thematic analyses rest on our understanding of the personal meaning these teachers derive from teaching. In that sense, personal meaning is the corner where thematic and developmental analyses meet.

In some ways, using this thematic approach is more comfortable than using levels to classify or categorize what teachers had to say in the interviews. It feels legitimate simply to note which theme—or themes—were expressed in each narrative. For example, narrators A and B seemed to stress the good fit theme. Narrator E seemed to be saying that she had become a teacher in part because of its convenience with relation to the rest of her life. Narrator D saw teaching as a way to change society. Narrator F described her entry into the profession as happening pretty much by default. (Even if her response accurately reflects the realities of the times, one wonders about the implications of her dismissive tone.) Two of these teachers suggested that teaching was a calling: narrator B also suggested other reasons for going into the profession, but for narrator C this theme seemed to be a priority.

Coordinating Analyses: Developmental Levels and Qualitative Themes

What, then, are the advantages and disadvantages of these seemingly opposite approaches? When we juxtapose the two ways of looking at our data, the developmental approach seems to risk being too bold, too imposing of its values on the narratives of others. On the other hand, the thematic approach may be too cautious: Does it give enough value to those narratives that demonstrate deeper reflection and greater awareness? Does it acknowledge that some of the teachers' responses are actually quite banal, dismissive, or superficial? And do the five themes really lie flat on the same plane? In truth, don't some themes suggest a deeper sense of engagement and greater professional awareness, if not a greater commitment to teaching, than others? If so, what keeps us from saying so?

Surely a teacher who sees her or his work as a calling is more likely to be truly engaged in the work than the teacher who says he or she entered the profession because it offered a safe job, a decent paycheck, and the long summer vacation. Surely the person who has a sense of vocation and a passion for children's development is more likely to be able to inspire students than the person who seems less interested in them.

Perhaps so, but we can argue that such a comparison is one of extremes. How do we compare themes that are a bit more complicated? What about the teacher who entered the profession because it was a good fit with her affection for children and her perception of her abilities? How does she rank in comparison with the teacher who sees teaching as an ideological (political) as well as a professional endeavor and a chance to change society? Without abandoning our interest in the themes that have emerged from our teacher interviews, we need to tackle these questions by returning to our developmental framework and seeing whether we can integrate the two approaches.

We think that it is a mistake to assume that a teacher who says that her choice of teaching as a profession reflects her desire to change society demonstrates a higher level of engagement than a teacher who recognizes a general love for children as a motivating force in her choice. If each expresses an awareness that their motivation originates in their own personal, professional, and political biographies, our developmental analysis would give them equal credit, since self-awareness (in the context of society) lies at the heart of our developmental framework. (To do this more in-depth analysis we would, of course, need more information than we have provided in the short interview excerpts included in this chapter.)

We have reached the conclusion that each kind of analysis—quantitative as to developmental levels, and qualitative according to thematic categories—is necessary and illuminates the other. We do not believe that thematic and developmental analyses are like oil and water. Not only can they mix, but by combining the two we can achieve an even deeper and more accurate understanding of a teacher's com-

Table 10.2 Teachers' Terms of Engagement with Their Profession: A Joint Analysis by Awareness Levels and by Recurrent Themes

	Recurrent Themes Across Interviews with Elementary Grade Teachers, Grades Two to Five				
Levels of Awareness (As Interpreted Using Our Developmental Indicators)	Good Fit with *My* Abilities	Convenient to *My* Life Circumstance	Vehicle Driven by *My* Inner Desire to Change Society	Default Option Due to *My* Limited Choice of Profession	A Calling: *I* Have Always Wanted to Teach
Low marks on the awareness indicators (external outcome only orientation)				F	
Moderate marks on the awareness indicators (internal process orientation)	A B	E			B
High marks on the awareness indicators (relational-contextual orientation)	E		D		C

Source: Authors' compilation.

Notes: Our stress on the words "my" and "our" in the column heads is intended to make two points. "My" in the theme headings suggests that the domain of personal meaning lies mostly with the narrator. The use of "our" and "as interpreted" under the head "Levels of Awareness" acknowledges that the developmental indicators we use are constructions of the analyzers, as in "our theoretical framework."

The letters within each cell refer to the "narratives of engagement" of each of the six teachers whose narratives we excerpt in chapter 10. Awareness indicators: perspective on student-teacher relationships; view of children and their development; capacity to take a contextual view.

petence and commitment than if we use only one or the other. In other words, we believe that an analysis that integrates the two approaches yields valuable insights about teachers' professional awareness and engagement that are greater than the sum of the two parts.

Table 10.2 suggests how an integration of qualitative themes and quantitative (meaning ordered) levels might look.

To understand this chart requires a word about how it differs from all the other charts and figures in this book, which are attempts to describe differences *within* individuals, that is, developmental pathways and changes or fluctuations within individuals over time or in different situations. Table 10.2 is different because its purpose is to help us use our two types of analysis to compare differences *between* and *among* individuals. We have indicated where we might locate each of the narratives quoted in this chapter at the intersections of the thematic plane with our developmental awareness dimension.

Table 10.2 illustrates two important points about our dual or integrative analysis. First, as we mentioned previously, it is possible for a teacher to express more than one term of engagement with his or her profession—that is, more than one theme or comment on personal meaning—at a time. Each of these themes might be expressed at the same—or at a different—level of awareness. Narratives B and E exemplify this possibility. Narrative B expresses two themes—"good fit" and "calling"—at the same level; in narrative E, two different themes—"good fit" and "convenience"—are expressed at two different levels.

Second, when we compare themes across different narrators, we see that two teachers may focus on the same theme, but with different levels of awareness. Compare narrative B, for example, with narrative C. Both teachers spoke of teaching in a way that reflects the theme we've labeled "calling" (narrator C actually used the term), but did so, in our opinion, with different levels of awareness. Narrator B focused only on her own subjective experience, whereas Narrator C included reflections on her role as a teacher and her relationship with her students.

These comparisons illustrate the risk of doing only one kind of analysis without the other in studying such a complex subject as teachers' professional awareness. There is no getting around it. Developmental analysis classifies narratives in terms of a hierarchy in which one level is *higher or lower* than another: the metaphor is vertical, like a ladder. Thematic analysis allows us to look at the same narrative in terms of *similarities and differences:* the metaphor here is horizontal, a circle of themes, suggesting no automatic hierarchy for ranking them. To make a meaningful contribution to the study of teachers' professional lives, we need both.

As a research tool, the revised framework we have described in this chapter requires extensive engagement on our part and a much more complex analysis than we have done (or reported) to date. But we think our pilot study and the examples we have presented make the following points quite well. Developmental and thematic analyses are not simply two different ways to code the same information (in this case, the interviews with the teachers in our study). They are ways to extract different kinds of information from the same source and to look at the same data from two different angles. When we integrate them, these analyses interact and each illuminates the other. (Think of M. C. Escher's well-known picture in which two hands are drawing each other.) Together they provide us with a way to understand the narratives of each teacher over time, in different contexts, and in comparison to others. And each approach safeguards us against the errors—or weaknesses—to which the other is prone.

Remembering Our Ultimate Purposes

What about educational practice? What will teachers think, reading this long and detailed theoretical analysis of "terms of professional engagement," when we are through refining it? What do we want them to get out of this effort? Frankly, we feel that the developmental aspect of our dual approach tends to overpower the thematic side. Teachers can get preoccupied with asking: What level am I? What level are you? This is not necessarily a terrible state of mind, but it can lead to a feeling that one is stuck in some conceptual elevator trapped at a particular floor.

We feel we have a responsibility to provide teachers with opportunities for professional self-reflection, to do more than bombard them with classifications that can easily be interpreted as judgmental and oversimplified considering the complexity of the profession and the people in it. Therefore, instead of framing the developmental side of the analysis solely, or even primarily, in terms of a language of levels, we can take our effort to integrate the two approaches a step further and begin to speak about *awareness profiles* rather than awareness levels.

A profile is by definition an outline, or a summary of data relevant to a particular person or thing, but the word also means "a short, vivid biographical or character sketch"—something that has a bit more life to it than a developmental chart (as useful as those continue to be to us). Because the word "profile" refers to a view from a single perspective (think of a Renaissance portrait or a nineteenth-century cut-paper silhouette), it implies that there are other perspectives to be explored. Instead of offering an analysis that reduces individual differences among teachers to levels along a single dimension (points on a line), table 10.2 suggests that we can hope to capture at least two dimensions (as a drawing or a painting does) *and* to imply a third—the potential for change over time.

It also downplays the "levels" approach by dropping the attempt to specify mutually exclusive distinctions across levels and to give each a name with the expectation that responses will fit within each named level. In both figure 10.1 and table 10.2, we have become more imprecise on purpose, calling the levels "external," "internal," or "personalized," and "relational" to suggest the path from a focus on outer behavior to inner psychological processes and the connection of the two with development.

Teachers' Reflections and Their Practice: The Next Step

One of our ultimate purposes in looking at teachers' reflections using combined developmental and thematic points of view has been to determine whether there is a connection between professional awareness and what teachers do in the classroom. We are particularly interested in determining their effectiveness in teaching curriculum that focuses on literacy and social competence—the kind of curriculum VLF embodies. The concept of awareness profiles stresses both personal themes and the meaning and origins of these themes for individual teachers in a way that adds texture to and deepens our inquiry.

We know that individuals who say lofty things about teaching and about kids may not follow through in their practice. We also know that teaching occurs in a social and political context, and that there is great pressure to fit the teaching into that context. Viewpoints and perspectives are influenced by historical circumstance. The atmosphere of the Reykjavík schools in the early 1990s, for example, was quite different from the atmosphere in Boston in more recent years. In Reykjavík there was room for the kind of exploration that occurred in the evening training seminars at teachers' schools and for focusing on children's social development in the classroom. In Boston the current push to raise academic standards may be all to the good, but unfortunately it may make for less flexibility to teach in ways that integrate social and academic development than existed in the city ten years ago, when we first helped design the VLF approach.

The concept of awareness profiles allows us, in a more natural way, to integrate a bottom-up with a top-down approach to understanding the professional development of teachers in general, as well as the relationship between literacy and children's social development, all of which we discuss in chapters to come. With an integrative approach, our own standards and values as researchers still inform our analyses, but at the same time the voices of teachers and children come through more clearly.

For example, how can we affirm that in terms of her awareness profile, Ms. Burgos (narrative C) understands her teaching from a perspective that goes beyond the classroom and the school to include the sociohistorical context of her work? At the same time, how can we illustrate how her desire to empower her students shapes her mission as a teacher? Working from the idea of a profile, we can combine interview data with classroom observations to see how these themes influence her teaching style and how consistent that style is. In this way we can begin to sketch in the ever-present leitmotif of thought and action in what this teacher says and does.

Profiles also allow us to integrate information about the various settings in which teachers teach (urban, rural; public, private; rich, poor), their political agendas, their gender, their biographies, and their cultural backgrounds with what they have to say about their lives and work. Profiles may even allow us to develop a better sense of that metaphysical and elusive "meta-issue" we called pedagogical vision.

Finally, a more descriptive and less purely analytical approach to teachers' reflections allows us to reduce the tension between thematic content and the reflective awareness structure of our analysis, on the one hand, and the discomfort that arises from classifying and judging teachers' words and deeds, their reflections, and their practices, on the other. Using this integrative approach, we can still focus on teachers' sense of engagement with their profession, their teaching aims, and their practical skills and teaching styles. And we can use developmental indicators to test our hypothesis that a teacher who is able to think beyond the day-to-day routine of the classroom and consider the broader social context is more likely to be an effective teacher of a curriculum like VLF, in Boston, Iceland, or anywhere else.

Teaching is an uncertain profession in many ways. Sometimes, and for some teachers, it means nothing more—or less—than an honest day's work for a day's pay. It's also a frontline job that is all too often woefully undervalued and poorly supported by a society that gives lip service to its importance. Many teachers work under difficult conditions—without adequate resources, with students who are disadvantaged in one way or another, with classes that are too large, with conflicting demands from parents, administrators, and politicians about what they should be teaching, and under pressure to help their students meet ever-higher standards on high-stakes tests. It is no wonder that burnout is a well-known professional hazard.

Teaching is also a highly sophisticated and complex profession that affects us all profoundly, whether we ourselves are parents or not, because teachers care for our most important resource—the children who represent our collective future. Being a good teacher demands the nerves of a highly skilled surgeon, a knowledge base equivalent to rocket science, and the round-the-clock dedication of an investment banker. From our position, perched in the relatively serene venue of an academic ivory tower, we hope to convince the public to take real steps to encourage teachers to aspire to a highly professional vision of their role, even in the midst of the nitty-gritty realities of their everyday working lives.

In part IV of this book, we use a case study approach to illustrate in some detail what we mean by "highly professional" and "nitty-gritty." We develop the idea of an awareness profile by spending time with Angela Burgos, whose comments about teaching and actions in her classroom fit our idea of a committed and competent teacher.

Carolina Buitrago joins Robert L. Selman and Sigrun Adalbjarnardottir in the authorship of this chapter.

Part IV

Researching the Social and Ethical Awareness of Students: Lessons from a Fifth-Grade Classroom

Chapter 11

To Connect: A Teacher's Pedagogical Vision and Her Empowerment of Students' Points of View

IN THE fall term of 1997, between early November and the beginning of the Christmas holidays in December, our Carnegie Research Study video crew spent many hours in the classroom of the elementary school teacher Angela Burgos at the Russell School in the Allston-Brighton neighborhood of Boston. Our goal for this part of the study was to understand the effectiveness of the kind of approach used by the Voices of Love and Freedom program, to learn more about children's social development, and to increase our understanding of the professional development of teachers.

In chapter 10, we introduced teacher awareness profiles as a way of capturing how teachers' reflections may influence their teaching practice. Now we turn to the classroom to see how our three domains—the teacher's aims, engagement with the profession, and personal meaning associated with the VLF curriculum—plays out in practice. We chose to videotape one teacher, Angela Burgos, and her class for six weeks. Direct observation has been an important part of the work of the Group for the Study of Interpersonal Development—from the early studies upon which we built our basic developmental framework, to the Risk and Prevention Program and our consultation with the developers of VLF. For us the issue of the connection between thought and action is not only a central concern in designing our methodology but also a key research question. While videotaping consumed a significant part of our budget and is not necessarily better than the field notes of a trained observer, it captures the interactions between children and teachers in a special way and for future use: we can look at the tapes more than once, and we can share them with fellow researchers and practitioners, as well as graduate students, who can then contribute their insights to our analysis.[1]

I suggest that you read each of the three chapters of part IV from several perspectives. First, if you are a teacher, you might compare your teaching philosophy and methods with those of Angela Burgos. We do not feature her teaching and class because we think she is a perfect teacher. In fact, some viewers of the video have made strong critiques of her teaching. Nevertheless, one purpose of this chapter is to use her teaching and class as a case study of a teacher who the members of our research team believe implements her pedagogical vision in practice at a high level by the standards we articulated in chapter 10. You may disagree.

Second, see whether you can put yourself in the shoes of a developmental, cultural, or educational psychologist. Reading these chapters as a researcher interested in the growth of children's social competence and awareness, you may be able to view them as a pilot study of one classroom. From this perspective, the aim is to better understand how children understand, negotiate, and become aware of the meaning of social issues in the family (chapter 11), among friends (chapter 12), and in the community (chapter 13). Please be aware that we need to observe and collect data in many more classrooms before we are through.

I hope that you will not read these chapters as infomercials for VLF, for as much as we stand behind most aspects of its design, these chapters are not designed to feature its pedagogy. They are designed to provide a window into teaching and learning—the subject in this case being the ethics of social relationships.

The Teacher: Angela Burgos

In part IV of the book, we are going to spend our time with Ms. Burgos and her students. We will observe several morning meetings in which she covers language arts, reading, writing, spelling, and oral language. We selected Ms. Burgos's class for intensive videotaping for a number of reasons. First, many of her students had experienced the VLF curriculum the previous year, as fourth-graders in Ms. Loreno's classroom at the Russell School. Therefore, the students were already comfortable sharing personal stories, practicing perspective-taking and conflict resolution skills, and working in pairs. In addition, based on our observations from the year before, we thought Ms. Burgos was extremely competent and taught with a method and style well suited to the VLF curriculum, and she seemed sympathetic to its content. Furthermore, we were impressed by the comments she made during our interview with her at the end of the year.

During our interview with Ms. Burgos, when she spoke about her work, she touched on personal, political, and professional issues, and she frequently referred to what she does as *empowering* her students. Asked how she would describe success in the classroom, she replied: "Well, success for me is when I see [an increase in] a student's self-confidence, self-esteem . . . and [see the student] become empowered, [when] he recognizes that no matter what obstacles he may encounter, he will still make a difference, and he will be somebody."[2]

According to the framework outlined in chapter 10, Ms. Burgos demonstrated a strong level of reflection and awareness during her interviews. But how would that awareness play out in practice? We needed to explore whether our hunch—that a high level of teacher awareness leads to better teaching practices—would hold up. What were the specific practices that Ms. Burgos used to connect her pedagogical vision to her teaching, and what was the effect on her students' learning? We decided to focus on her classroom in depth to find out.

Ms. Burgos is a native of New York City whose family came to the mainland from Puerto Rico after the Second World War. As of 1997 she had accumulated nearly twenty years of experience teaching in the Boston public schools. That year the twenty-one students in her fifth-grade class were part of Russell's transitional bilingual program; most were from Puerto Rico or the Dominican Republic (though several had been born in the United States), Spanish was their first language, and some who were recent arrivals from South and Central America had English-language speaking and writing skills that were minimal at best. As you will observe in this chapter and the next, Ms. Burgos is not shy about sharing her own background and experiences with her students. The common experiences they share create a particularly trusting classroom.

The video crew and researchers arrived each chilly New England morning at 8:30 A.M. to videotape the day's lesson. The language arts period lasted anywhere from forty-five minutes to an hour and a half, depending on Ms. Burgos's schedule for the day. The lesson consisted of reading aloud from the book; whole-class discussions that focused on reading comprehension and on the personal meaning to the students of the issues raised by the narrative; individual, pair, and group perspective-taking and conflict resolution activities; and exercises in writing and composition.

We have faith that the "ethnographic material" collected by our video crew provides a useful case study of the implementation of a VLF title in a real classroom by a highly motivated and competent teacher. Seeing the video crew daily over a period of six weeks mitigated any initial self-consciousness on the part of both Ms. Burgos and her students; in fact, by the end of the first week they seemed to be so accustomed to the camera that they often forgot it was there. Toward the end of the six-week period, we interviewed Ms. Burgos again about her teaching philosophy and classroom practice. In this and the chapters to follow, we see that the views she expressed in her two interviews correspond to her actual practice as captured by the video crew—that is, the *awareness profile* we would construct based on her comments was indeed closely related to her performance in the classroom.

Introducing *Felita*

The VLF novel, *Felita* by Nicholasa Mohr (1979), was the focus of the language arts lessons for this particular six weeks.[3] Felita, the novel's narrator, is an eight-year-old Puerto Rican girl growing up in New York City in the 1950s, during the first wave of large-scale Puerto Rican immigration to the United States. Her neighborhood, although poor and dilapidated, is comfortable and familiar. Filled with the sights, sounds, and smells of the island, it is home to Abuelita and Abuelo, her grandmother and grandfather, and her best friend Gigi. It is also a neighborhood of crowded tenements and inadequate schools. In chapter 1 of the novel, Felita's parents, concerned about the limited future that their daughter and her two brothers might face, decide to move the family to a neighborhood where the streets are cleaner, the apartments roomier, and the schools better equipped. The children are very distressed about moving, especially Felita. For her, all the advantages of the new neighborhood cannot make up for the loss of contact with her closest friends.

In keeping with VLF's literacy and values curriculum for the elementary grades, *Felita* begins with the basics of social relationships—family, friends, and neighborhood—but goes on to place its characters in situations that involve intergroup issues of prejudice, discrimination, and cultural identity. The content of the novel lends itself very well to exercises in perspective taking and the development of conflict resolution strategies with regard to both interpersonal and intergroup conflicts, and to writing assignments and classroom discussion focused on these issues.

Day 3 of *Felita:* Leaving the Old Neighborhood

It is the beginning of our six-week videotaped session. So far, the class has read only chapter 1 of *Felita,* which introduces the characters, describes the setting, and sets up the first part of the plot. At the start of this morning's session, Ms. Burgos divides her class into four reading groups of four to six students, one of whom she designates as the group's spokesperson. She has arranged their desks in clusters so that the members of each group face each other. The students' assignment is to share their feelings and exchange opinions within their group about how they think Felita feels about moving away from her neighborhood. They talk together for about fifteen minutes as Ms. Burgos circulates around the room from group to group; she then asks the kids to shift their chairs around so that they all face the front.

After each spokesperson reports to the whole class on the opinions of his or her reading group's members, Ms. Burgos opens the discussion to all. To start, she reflects on a comment made by Rosario, the spokesperson for group 4: "It's very interesting to me that Rosario's group has brought up the subject of the parents not talking to Felita about the move before they were ready to leave the old neighborhood. What do you think of that? Why do you think she is saying that?"

At first, this seems like an unremarkable introduction to a discussion of the character Felita, about whom the class knows very little, having read only the thirteen pages of the novel's first chapter. However, it is significant that Ms. Burgos begins by citing comments from *students* and asking the others what *they* think. It is one example of how Ms. Burgos has integrated her pedagogical vision of student empowerment into her teaching practice. Because she has opened the discussion by making it clear that what they think and feel is important, Ms. Burgos's students feel free to share their own ideas about Felita and her situation.

Luis: I think Felita was a little bit angry at her mom, because she didn't care about the move, but Felita did. She just kept on thinking about packing up things and going to the new neighborhood. That's why they brought it up, because Felita was sort of in a bad mood because she didn't want to move, but her mother didn't care about that.

Ms. Burgos: Okay. [*She points to Juanita, who has raised her hand.*]

Juanita: I think her parents told her on the last day because if they told her more earlier she would have been more upset and done terrible stuff to not move away.

MS. BURGOS: She would have done terrible stuff not to move away—and in that sense, her parents were sort of protecting her from being hurt early and going through the process. Do you think that's fair for her to be—what do you think about her feelings? Being angry at her parents, or her mother? Who has a . . . [*points to Flora*] . . . yes?

FLORA: I think it's not fair because she doesn't know what it feels [like] . . . to Felita. She's just thinking by herself, her mother.

MS. BURGOS: So you don't think that Felita—I want to hear what you're saying—you agree with Felita? Is it okay for Felita to be angry?

FLORA: Yeah, because they didn't say—she doesn't feel what Felita feels about the neighborhood.

MS. BURGOS: Okay, so the parents are not taking Felita's feelings [about] her friends into consideration. Who else has something to say? Does Felita have a right to feel the way she does—anger?

CLASS (*in chorus*): Yes!

MS. BURGOS: Yes? Okay, what are those reasons? . . . Yes?

LUIS: Well, I think Felita should speak up and tell her mom, her parents, about what she feels inside, about the move. And she's not speaking up, so that's why they're not paying attention to her. She has to speak up—that's what I think—and do something about it.

MS. BURGOS: Okay, she's not speaking up. Anyone else have any thoughts about Felita being angry at her parents?

FELIPE: I agree that she's mad, because if my parents didn't tell me I was moving, I'll do the same thing that she's doing.

For the most part this morning, the children are responding from their own "unilateral" perspectives. They see the parents as "unfair." Flora thinks the mother is being selfish, "thinking only of herself." Being able to see only Felita's perspective is developmentally appropriate for fifth-graders, although a few students seem to be able to understand why Felita's parents chose not to tell their children about the move. Had this been a peer conflict, Ms. Burgos's students might not have had nearly as much difficulty taking another, even opposing, point of view. When a conflict involves children and their parents—or others in power or authority—the child's capacity for taking the perspective of the other party is often significantly lower than it would be in the case of a conflict involving other children. It is easier for children to negotiate with, or take the perspective of, a peer than an adult, including parents and teachers.

From VLF's standpoint, this initial exercise has a dual purpose. First, it aims at helping children understand a text in terms of the motivations, intentions, and context of the story's characters, thus deepening the students' comprehension of the story. Second, by asking the students to imagine what it feels like to be Felita, to reflect on how they themselves would feel, or have felt, in a similar situation, it stresses the concept of "point of view" and encourages the students to exercise and expand their capacity for social perspective taking and coordination.

Many teachers understand the literacy value of examining a fictional character's motives and personality by asking students to respond to provocative questions. However, Ms. Burgos has taken the discussion a step further. Listening to the students empathize with Felita, she asks, "Does Felita have a right to feel the way she does?" By asking the question, she has moved the discussion into the domain of the ethics of social relationships, a territory laden with potential cultural and personal land mines. Some teachers may avoid this territory. For instance, in certain cultures that do not expect children to participate in the kind of family decision Felita's parents have made, Ms. Burgos's question—especially her use of the term "have a right"—might seem strange at best; some real-life parents might even dismiss it as a challenge to their authority.

But by explicitly adding moral content to the question of Felita's feelings, by making this discussion more than just a conversation about a fictional character, Ms. Burgos intends to help her students consider the complexity of the situation, and in particular the various perspectives involved. Justification for Felita's right to be angry lies in the students' interpretation of the intentions of her parents. If the parents are simply being cavalier about Felita's emotional pain at having to leave her friends for another neighborhood that they prefer, we would find it easy to grant her the "right" to be angry. However, if her parents are acting out of ultimate concern for their family—as the narrator indirectly states—such a motivation does not necessarily negate Felita's feelings, but it certainly changes the context, and thus the "appropriate" emotional response on the part of the reader. (The term "appropriate" reflects my own cultural bias, but there is no bias in having the students better understand Felita's point of view.)

Ms. Burgos's challenge is to help her students make their own meaning of both Felita's and her parents' points of view so that they will fully comprehend both the narrative and the interpersonal lessons the book holds. In our interview with Ms. Burgos, she explained how this goal fits into her teaching strategy. By not just giving them information but "having them take responsibility and empower[ing] them," letting them know "that they're also going to play a major role during the day," she keeps them "motivated and engaged." Her vision of herself as an orchestra director ("I sort of feel like I'm the director of an orchestra and I give the students the instruments, and together we play the symphony") reflects her desire to lead students to consider their own meaning rather than to spoon-feed it to them.

The students' predictable embrace of a Felita-only perspective at the beginning of the discussion limits their understanding and initial exploration of the conflict between Felita and her parents. A shift occurs in Ms. Burgos's classroom, however, when Felipe demonstrates an ability to stand authentically in Felita's shoes by using an "I" statement: "If *my* parents didn't tell me *I* was moving," he remarks, "*I'll* do the same thing that she's doing" (*emphasis added*). Although students seemed to project their own feelings onto Felita ("Felita was sort of in a bad mood"), Felipe's statement is different developmentally because it changes the meaning of the story. *Felita* becomes not only abstractly meaningful as a good book but also personally meaningful: it is no longer simply a story about a Puerto Rican girl in New York, it is also about Felipe himself, his relationships, and his ability to make his way in the world.

The Power of Personal Meaning

In recognition of the power that the personal meaning of a story has to enhance a child's experience of literature, VLF incorporated this component of our developmental theory into its pedagogical framework in at least two ways. First, using personal meaning as a motivational device, the VLF teacher's guides encourage teachers to tell stories about experiences they themselves have had that in some way elucidate a theme in the book or story their class is studying. Second, as a developmental device, the investigation of personal meaning helps children cultivate their own narrative voices and encourages acts of social perspective coordination. In other words, an awareness of the personal meaning to themselves of the literary materials they are studying helps students learn how to tell or write parallel stories, share these stories with their peers, and understand the stories of others.

Ms. Burgos intuitively already incorporated the investigation of personal meaning into her teaching style and shared stories of her own life with her students long before she had ever heard of VLF: "For me, [this is] empowering. . . . We are role models for them, and for them to see the sharing of my stories, personal experiences with them, brings them that much closer to connecting, to saying, 'You know, when she was our age, she went through something like this.'"

It became clear to us early on that the goal of empowering her students informs every decision that Ms. Burgos makes in the classroom, and that she sees the practice of perspective taking as a means to achieving that goal. In speaking of how she hoped to help her students develop a sense of mastery and competence, she told our interviewer:

> If we look at the initial stages of getting kids to speak on certain issues, they were . . . sort of taking a light approach, and then as we started including those exercises of perspective taking and allowing them to share with each other their points of view within a group setting, responding and getting support, then they were able to focus and take charge and become involved, put themselves into the real context of their world and say, "What are the issues affecting us and what could we do to make it better?"

Day 3 of *Felita:* The Conversation Continues

Consistent with her philosophy of teaching—her pedagogical vision of connecting real life to literature, as she expressed it in interviews—Ms. Burgos reinforces Felipe's personalized response about being angry. "I'm glad you brought that up, Felipe," she says, then turns to the class: "How many of you have ever been angry at your parents for a certain decision that is made that is beyond your control?"

This is not the kind of question that teachers ordinarily asked elementary school children in previous generations, and certainly there is a risk in posing it to a roomful of children who represent the cultures of nearly a dozen nations. Can a teacher be sure that no child is going to feel that speaking of their anger at their parents would be a betrayal of something very deep and private? How might a Southeast Asian child in an even more diverse class respond as compared with a Dominican or Puerto Rican or Boston Irish child? Some parents might be uncomfortable with the idea of engaging a group of public school children in a discussion of difficult personal, cultural, and political issues. Some teachers may feel that it is not their job to bring cultural and personal issues into the academic classroom.

What keeps such questions from being too risky for most of us is that they are asked in the context of a discussion that is literature-based and develops from *Felita.* The tension between youth and the previous generation exists in all cultures, even the most stable and traditional, and this theme has found expression in myths and folktales from around the world precisely because using stories is a good way to talk about this tension, to understand it, and to defuse it. Ms. Burgos recognizes that the exploration of the personal meaning of a story to her students is a risk worth taking to help prepare her students for life in a rapidly changing multicultural society. For instance, during an interview, she says:

> Within the classroom setting, my experience has been [that] here it's a family, it's a community setting where we work together, and so there are certain issues that affect them in the real world. If we wanted to

> think back ten, twenty years ago, it would be a different story. But now . . . kids walk in with extra baggage that maybe they have never had anyone to really talk to and open up to [about]. . . . To provide these students with a platform to explore and share ideas . . . gives them confidence to express an opinion that maybe in the past was never asked.

As the class discussion continues, quite a few students raise their hands after Ms. Burgos asks whether any of them have ever been angry with their parents about parental decisions.

> Ms. Burgos: How many of you would like to share? [*Most students put their hands down.*] How many of you told your parents that you were angry? [*Several students raise their hands.*] . . . Rosario?
>
> Rosario: I told my parents I was angry at them because they never talk to me, they only just do it like that.
>
> Ms. Burgos: So they don't take your feelings into consideration when making a decision? [*Rosario nods.*] And how do they react when you tell that to them?
>
> Rosario: My mother said, "Well, I don't know. I just did it."
>
> Ms. Burgos: Okay. Anybody in group 3? Any time you want to share when you were angry? At your parents or [another] adult?
>
> Pedro: I was angry when I was moving to Mission Park because I didn't want to leave my neighborhood and I liked playing with my friends and there was a lot of kids there that would play. And then when I move over there, I got more friends from over there, and then I was enjoying it, and then I got happy.

The relevance of the issue at hand is clear. Although only Rosario and Pedro are willing to share the details of their experience, nearly all of the students have raised their hands to indicate that at some point they have been angry at their parents. Now Ms. Burgos moves the discussion even more directly toward considering the parents' perspective. To help make this leap—and because this is a language arts lesson—she brings the class back to the text. "Let's take the parents' point of view. . . . The parents are moving. Did they just decide one day, 'Oh, it's time for us to move'? According to chapter 1, what did we find out?"

Again, on the surface this may seem like a simple question, but as is evidenced by the students' difficulty in articulating the parents' perspective, this exercise is far more complex and demanding than it appears. At first, the class as a whole resists moving away from its initial unilateral bias, but Ms. Burgos keeps the discussion focused on the parents' point of view, and she returns the students to the text to find their answer.

FILOMENA: [We found out] that the parents should tell Felita in more time instead of one day when they gonna move, and she don't have time to say good-bye to her friends.

MS. BURGOS: Okay, that's going back to—the parents should have taken more consideration, they should have. But what now I'd like to know—we looked through the eyes of Felita, her feelings. Now what we're going to do is take the parents. Let's look at the parents' side. Let's do a balancing act. Remember the balance that we used with *The King's Equal*?[4]

CLASS: Yes.

MS. BURGOS: Remember how we took Felita's position? Now let's look at the parents. What are the reasons for the parents making this move? Marisol?

MARISOL: Sometimes they need to move because they need bigger space so that they can have more space for their kids, and [when] the kids they are bigger, they can have their own room so that they won't have to share their room with small kids.

Ms. Burgos writes Marisol's response on the board as "Bigger Apartment" and again steers the discussion back to the words on the page. Picking up on a student's earlier mention of Dona Josefina, a character introduced in chapter 1 who expresses support for Felita's parents' decision, Ms. Burgos suggests, "Let's bring Dona Josefina to life by having someone read that dialogue for me."

Ms. Burgos recognizes that verbalization of an idea increases both comprehension and recall. Having students read aloud has always been a key component in the teaching of literacy, and speaking a character's words is a form of role-playing, a valuable technique for exploring different points of view. Ms. Burgos appreciates the role-playing opportunities in the VLF curriculum: "Kids enjoy role-playing because . . . it opens discussion and opportunities for kids to exchange views. They may not agree, but they come to a consensus or understanding of that other person's experiences. . . . This will remain with them."

As Ms. Burgos realizes, social awareness does not develop in a vacuum. At the same time that awareness guides action, action can open up new ways of understanding social relationships. Role-playing is one safe way in which children can act out different positions on important social topics. Ms. Burgos has her sights firmly focused on the future ("this will remain with them"). She clearly has a vision of education, and the VLF curriculum, as extending, like her notion of empowerment, beyond the immediate world of the classroom.

Back in the classroom, Ms. Burgos picks two students to take the two roles in this brief dialogue scene from the book. Rosario reads Dona Josefina's opening remark, "I heard you going to live in a better neighborhood." When the students have finished reading the excerpt out loud, Ms. Burgos repeats that remark and restarts the discussion.

MS. BURGOS: What's wrong with her [Felita's] neighborhood? What else do we find out that the parents reveal, that we didn't actually know at the beginning? . . . Luis?

LUIS: Her parents want to move to another neighborhood so they can give a better future to their children because they want a better life for them, because maybe in the neighborhood where they are it isn't good, so they want—her father wants Felita and her brothers to grow up to a better future—a better neighborhood.

Ms. Burgos writes a two-word summary of Luis's observations on the board—"Better Neighborhood"—and again addresses her next questions to the whole class.

MS. BURGOS: So, the parents are looking out for whose best interests? Have they not taken the children into consideration?

FELIPE: They did the decision by themselves.

MS. BURGOS: Well, think about [*points to the list on the board*] bigger apartment, better neighborhood. We don't know what dangers are within their old neighborhood. A better future. Think about [that] as parents. Pretend you *are* parents. Does that mean that you're ignoring your children's feelings?

CLASS: No!

MS. BURGOS: You're taking them into consideration. Think about your parents. What does that tell us here?

LUIS: They want the best for their children.

MS. BURGOS: That's right, and sometimes . . .

LUIS: Sometimes their parents, like they want to—sometimes parents give you something that you don't want but they do it because they love you. That's to help you.

MS. BURGOS: Okay, they know you and they love you. What other reasons?

ROSARIO: Sometimes parents do mistakes, but they always want to get you with good stuff.

MS. BURGOS: You might not understand it at the time, you might be angry, but then later on, it seems you're able to understand that mistake because you're looking at it from [another] point? . . . Right?

Text, Context, and Point of View

In part, Ms. Burgos asks her initial question—"What's wrong with [Felita's] neighborhood?"—to get the kids to refer back to their books, to find places in the text in which the parents' point of view is expressed or substantiated. But in asking this question she also deliberately hints at larger societal issues. By the time they're in fifth grade, children know that certain neighborhoods are safer, cleaner, and more attractive than others. But why do certain ethnic or racial groups seem to inhabit the better or worse neighborhoods? And what do we value more, prosperity or a sense of community?

These are questions to be addressed later, as the class reads about Felita's move to a part of the city where hers is the only Spanish-speaking family, and about the discrimination that finally compels them to move back to their old neighborhood. Then Ms. Burgos will ask her students more difficult questions. She will move toward the heavy lifting of interpersonal development in time with the novel. Right now, however, she is scaffolding their understanding of the basic familial relationships in the novel. It is important not to overlook the strategies she is using here, because they will return later. Role-playing, asking tough questions, encouraging the children to take others' points of view—Ms. Burgos will rely on these teaching strategies over and over again, regardless of how difficult the topic at hand. And she will do so with an endpoint firmly in mind—to empower the students to develop skills that will last them throughout their lives. Here is strong evidence that her awareness—in fact, her pedagogical vision—is directing her day-to-day teaching practice, whether she is conscious of it or not.

For Ms. Burgos, the meaning of what it is to be literate extends beyond narrative and into the real world. The novel *Felita* offers opportunities to raise students' awareness of their own and others' political and social histories—to give them a glimpse of the larger social context that frames the circumstances in which they live. For now, however, Ms. Burgos has followed her students' lead and kept the focus on the coordination of points of view.

To summarize, Marisol's response, which acknowledges a concrete reason to move ("bigger space"), signals the beginnings of an understanding of Felita's parents' perspective. Felipe seems to see the problem as the parents' unilateral approach ("They did the decision by themselves") rather than the move itself, but his response does suggest that he too can now consider the parents' motives (their aims) even if he disagrees with their methods (their strategies). Rosario, while steadfastly maintaining her own understanding of the situation—it was a "mistake" for the parents not to include Felita in the discussion about moving—acknowledges the parents' good intentions: "Sometimes parents do mistakes, but they always want to get you with good stuff." Luis, one of the more articulate students in the class, has managed the most abstract response: "They want what's best for their children." (However, we must remember that the capacity to think abstractly does not always mean a greater capacity for emotional understanding or the capacity to relate well to others under difficult conditions; see Selman and Schultz 1990; Selman, Watts, and Schultz 1997).

Whereas another teacher might stop here, figuring the students have gone as far as possible in their understanding of the chapter and the parents' perspective, Ms. Burgos does not settle for these answers. She returns to another teaching strategy in her tool kit: personal meaning. "How many of you were born here?" she asks the students. Several kids raise their hand. "How many of you were not?" Others raise a hand. "Okay, do you remember when you came to this country?"

Under Ms. Burgos's gentle prompting, several students admit to having been afraid about moving to a new, foreign environment, and she connects their responses to the novel: "So you yourselves have been in sort of Felita's shoes, have gone through that experience?" The students seem reluctant to share further, so she makes the choice to offer a personal story from her own life. By using this strategy, Ms. Burgos deepens the trust between her students and herself: she does not expect them to always share difficult personal stories; she will do it too.

This time it is a story about being afraid about moving—first when she was seven years old, moving from New York, where she was born, to Puerto Rico, and then later, when she was ten, moving back to New York.

> I remember when I was seven years old and my parents—we lived in New York—and my mother said, "We're moving to Puerto Rico." I was born in New York. I was excited because of the warm weather, but I was leaving my friends. And I would live there for two years. I adjusted—and after living there and adjusting for two years, I was told, "We're moving back to New York." No one consulted me. I was about nine or ten, just like Felita. But sometimes you have to—there are some decisions that as children we cannot make. But we can understand that anger [that children feel when they are not included in decisions]. And do you think the parents are not aware of what the kids are giving up? What do you think?

Ms. Burgos has helped her students place themselves in Felita's shoes; now, by giving them an example from her own experience, she invites them to take the next step *with* her. Even as she validates her students' experiences of fear and anger by sharing her own, she introduces the idea that though their feelings and hers and Felita's are real and understandable, Felita's parents may have been right in making such an important decision as moving to a new neighborhood without consulting their children.

The fact that this conclusion is "context-dependent"—that is, that one must consider the context of other people's behavior in addition to its effects on oneself—is important. In the realm of relationships with others, children cannot learn to think critically unless they are capable of discernment and discretion; they must be able to take the time to read a situation carefully before determining the proper response. In other words, there are no moral absolutes in this classroom, but there are clear moral guidelines and a challenge to understand social situations as fully as possible.

The discussion continues:

MS. BURGOS: Do you think the mother is totally ignoring Felita's feelings?

CLASS: No!! Yes!! [*The response is mixed.*]

JUANITA: She won't tell her—like, they're about to move, [but] she don't tell her, "Oh, I know you're going to miss your friends." She don't talk to her about it.

MS. BURGOS: Okay, that's right. And those of you who say no . . . who says no, that the parents really—it's not that. What is it? Marisol?

MARISOL: They just want the best for their childrens, and that's why they do it. Sometimes they don't consult with us so that it could be a surprise for us, and then when we get to the point where they want the best for us, that's when we understand.

This last comment suggests to us that Marisol, for whom reading and speaking in English still presents a significant challenge, has a more complex and sophisticated developmental understanding of the parents' perspective in *Felita* than was indicated by her previous, "more concrete" observation that the parents wanted a "bigger space." Ms. Burgos's teaching practice—the many and varied questions she asks—and the respect and attention she gives her students' answers push them toward learning to express ever more complex thoughts as they increase both their conceptual understanding of the text and their vocabularies.

As she ends the discussion for the day, Ms. Burgos makes one last point about Felita's mother's apparent lack of attention to her daughter: "You have moved—remember what it's like? . . . Does the mother have time to stop and say, 'Felita, what's wrong?'"

Once again she personalizes the story, making a comparison between all the work Felita's mother has to do to get her family organized and packed and her own busyness when teaching: "Sometimes Ms. Burgos is busy running around from each desk and maybe sometimes you may think that I'm overlooking you." But in the end, she says, she never forgets any of her students.

Connecting Vision and Practice

It is our assumption that helping students practice perspective coordination in the context of literary materials to which they can personally relate promotes the improvement and transference of this skill to real-life situations. In terms of our analysis of VLF's approach and the usefulness of the novel *Felita* in its curriculum, it certainly seems that this book engages students on a personal as well as an intellectual level. Furthermore, we believe that this classroom session demonstrates how a skilled teacher's guidance can foster the growth of social awareness and help students progress from an exclusive focus on their own point of view—by proxy, Felita's—to a consideration and understanding of the perspectives of others.

We also feel that this videotaped class meeting illustrates Ms. Burgos's ability to connect her pedagogical vision to her classroom practice consistently and effectively. We do not yet know what happens when her students are not as responsive to her teaching as they have been on this morning, and surely she must have days when she herself is less engaged and not as focused. But in terms of our ongoing research on teachers' professional awareness and development, her teaching style and strategies—asking questions, respecting and affirming different points of view, continually reminding her class of the larger context—are consonant with her goal of empowering her students.

Of course, the transcript from this classroom discussion reveals certain risks as well as benefits to these strategies. Marisol seems to demonstrate development before our eyes as she moves from interpreting Felita's parents' motivation in terms of physical space to seeing it in terms of psychological caring. But what about the student whose experience of her parents is that they do not really "want the best for us"? That student would join the conversation from an uncomfortable position, and it takes a skilled teacher to help her feel safe and secure. What if Ms. Burgos does not listen carefully to what the students are saying or misunderstands their comments?

However, it seems to me that when teachers listen carefully and can understand both the developmental limitations and developmental strengths in their students' comments, there is much to be gained. The kinds of issues this class is discussing, because they are so personally meaningful, invariably lend themselves to misunderstanding, miscommunication, and misinterpretation. But the class can serve as a laboratory for children to practice expressing themselves in this kind of experience, which inevitably will be part of their lives.

Additionally, the videotaped class demonstrates the power of relationship—in this case not so much between Felita and her parents, the students and their own parents, or even between the students themselves (as discussed in chapter 12). Instead, what has been revealed is the power of a connection between a teacher and a class.

Often teaching has been conceptualized as moving in one direction—from teacher to student. Teachers, as we have discussed, may be afraid of losing their authority, or bringing too much of themselves as individuals into the classroom, if they discuss social issues or their own lives. Here we see how Ms. Burgos has created a two-way connection from her students to herself. In chapter 10, my colleagues and I hypothesized about the importance of a pedagogical vision: the reflective coordination of a teacher's perspective on learning with that of his or her students. We have seen it in practice in this chapter. And it is not an abstract, cold, theoretical process. Instead, a pedagogical vision put into practice is strong, occasionally directive, and often challenging for student and teacher alike. But it is real. It is a relationship that is energizing and transformative for both teacher and student. I believe it is the presence of this relationship that allows the students to grow, change, and develop in their learning of both the academic and social skills they will need throughout their lives.

Chapter 12

The Power of Peers: Communication, Engagement, and Commitment

IT'S THE beginning of another school day at Russell Elementary. Even the most casual observer can note the differences among the students as they come down the block or pile off the bus. Two smiling girls skip hand in hand; a young boy charges toward the school, pushing past the girls and through the knot of kids at the front door; other children walk solemnly to the building alone, looking as though they were approaching their doom. As I discussed in part I of this book, for all of these children social experiences with peers—including their interactions in the classroom and on the playground—play a pivotal role in their education and development during these critical years.

As Ms. Burgos knows, the fifth-graders in her class focus much of their energy and attention on their friendships and other relationships with peers. As with preteens everywhere, sometimes it seems as if their preoccupation with "fitting in" distracts them from their academic studies. I believe, however, that intense peer focus at this age not only is a natural part of psychosocial development but can be used to promote both academic and social learning.

We often hear about (and most of us can remember from our own early lives) the less than happy experiences of children at the hands of others who bully, harass, or intimidate them (see Olweus 1993; Wolke and Stanford 1999). And the detrimental effects of peer pressure—to participate in such behavior, or, in adolescence, to join gangs, experiment with drugs, or become sexually promiscuous—have been well chronicled. (For more information on risk-taking behavior in preadolescence, see Jessor and Jessor 1977; Kandel et al. 1997.) But in observing Ms. Burgos teach from the VLF title *Felita,* we have the opportunity to study the positive influence that peer relationships can have on children's lives.

When the ten-year-olds in Ms. Burgos's class were a bit younger, they were content to define a good friend as someone who played nicely and shared their toys. Now, as these students fast approach adolescence, friendship has assumed a deeper meaning for most of them: a good friend is someone to confide in, someone who will keep your secrets, someone you can trust. And as their desire to be included in a peer group—and their fear of being excluded—intensifies with the growing complexity of the social scene, a good friend is an ally and a comforter, a bulwark of stability (see Selman, Watts, and Schultz 1997). But what about the painful experiences that can intrude on friendship, stemming from competition or jealousy? And what happens when good friends find themselves in conflict for one reason or another?

How, then, is friendship understood by preteens? The goal of this chapter is to demonstrate how teachers can harness children's natural focus on peer relationships—and their concerns about being part of the group—to promote academic and social learning in the classroom.

Listening to a Partner's Perspective

Throughout the VLF language arts unit, Ms. Burgos's students have been asked to record their thoughts and feelings about Felita's story in homework journals. Journaling helps them work on reading and writing skills and teaches them to articulate and express points of view—their own and those of the fictional characters. In addition, Ms. Burgos has paired each of her students with a classroom partner, carefully taking into account their interests, their abilities, and their personalities. She knows that a good pair match can foster her students' social growth—especially with regard to active and responsive listening—as well as their academic skills.

The classroom partnerships usually last from the beginning to the end of the school year. On most days Ms. Burgos's students share their at-home assignments with their assigned partners. This gives the students an added incentive to do their homework seriously and bring it into class. Not only do they know that their teacher will examine it for spelling, punctuation, and grammar, but they also know that their partner depends on them to be prepared. This partner-learning technique is widely used in all sorts of educational settings, but it is particularly well suited for promoting social skills, one of the basic goals of the VLF curriculum.[1] Ms. Burgos explains her understanding of the partner-learning process this way:

> As we look at the standard tests given to evaluate all children across the state and at how students have to demonstrate their learning, what better way to have them work than in partners and share information—my point of view, your point of view—and then take it a little step further and work in a group, have each one express, collect and summarize, present. . . . [This] provides students with the opportunity to learn again, from each other, and also support each other in the process, which sometimes gets overlooked. It's fair ground for each of them to shine and be supported, and I think that's very important.

In the course of our research, we asked the students in Ms. Burgos's class about the benefits and disadvantages of working in pairs with one partner. Juanita affirms that she acquires solace from her peer partnership in class: "I didn't know Alegria that much, and now that I know her a lot she's like a good friend, and she has been going through many things just like me. And I learned that you don't be afraid to tell anybody [about these things], 'cause they're not going to make fun of you." Creating an environment where children can trust one another encourages academic achievement as well as the respectful exchange of opinions. And linking partner sharing to whole-class discussions—the next step in the VLF process—gives students the opportunity to hear many different perspectives and to learn from each other.

Felita and the Question of Friendship

It has been four weeks since Ms. Burgos's students began their study of the novel *Felita*. They have read about the problems that Felita and her family faced in their new neighborhood, where they were the only Spanish-speaking residents, and about the family's decision to move back to the old neighborhood. The experience of being discriminated against is one that the children in Ms. Burgos's class can relate to on a personal level, and by drawing on her own life history and the resources of the VLF teacher's guide, Ms. Burgos has helped them to discuss racial and ethnic prejudice (including prejudices they themselves may hold) and to think carefully about the best courses of action when they encounter similar situations in real life. (We take a close look at the unfolding of this classroom discussion in chapter 13.)

Now the students in Ms. Burgos's class are reading about a serious threat to the friendship between Felita and her best friend Gigi. Each girl has decided to audition for the lead role of Priscilla Mullin in the school's drama production of the Thanksgiving story "The Courtship of Miles Standish." But whereas Felita told Gigi about her plans to audition, Gigi did not similarly confide in Felita. This adds to the tension between them when Gigi ends up getting the starring role of Priscilla and Felita is left with the job of designing the costumes and the set.

In one way or another, most of Ms. Burgos's students have faced friendship problems similar to this one, and it is not surprising that this situation evokes strong reactions from many of them. Their enthusiasm for the discussion was captured by our video crew.[2]

Exploring the Problem: What Is a Friend?

Ms. Burgos begins this day's class discussion by asking her students what it means to be a good friend. She writes "Best Friends" in the center of the blackboard at the front of the room and circles the words. Then she turns to face the class: "When you are best friends, what do you expect from each other?"

As the students volunteer their ideas, she picks up key words, and soon the central phrase on the blackboard looks like a pinwheel, surrounded by the words "equal," "share thoughts," "trust," "love," "keep secrets," "help," and "play."

Ms. Burgos encourages the class to reflect on the conflict between the two friends Felita and Gigi. What are these fictional characters arguing about? She coaxes her students with questions.

"I want to hear your reactions. What happens to Felita in this chapter,[3] and what was your reaction—because—what does Gigi do that surprises Felita?"

"She gets into the play," Juanita volunteers.

"She gets, like, the better part," Luis adds.

Ms. Burgos challenges her students to expand on these statements: "What do you mean by a 'better part'?"

There is some confusion, apparently, about exactly what she is asking. (In the novel Gigi learns the play's lines more quickly, and this may be why she wins the starring role; at least, that is what Felita thinks.) "She knows her part," one student suggests again. Ms. Burgos brings the focus back to what has happened between the two girls; for her, this is the crux of the chapter, and she wants to focus the discussion on it. "Did Felita know that Gigi was going out for the same part?" Ms. Burgos asks. The class responds, "No," in chorus.

Ms. Burgos tries another approach to zero in on the key issues. She connects the story to their own personal lives. Jorge and Jose are close friends in and outside the class. Ms. Burgos directs her next question to them. "If you were in her shoes and let's say . . . Jorge and Jose, you've been working as partners in different activities we do in class—and let's say . . . you share everything. All of a sudden, there's an activity that you—oh, you want to do this! And he wants to do the same, but he doesn't tell you."

She recasts the dilemma to make it even more relevant: "It's like in sports. You want to try out for being the pitcher. He does too. He doesn't tell you. And the coach says, 'Okay, Jose, you are the pitcher.' Meanwhile, he hasn't told you that he's interested in that; he's kept it to himself. Next thing you know, the tryouts come out and Jose is selected the pitcher. How do you feel?"

Jorge reflects for a moment. "Angry?"

"Aha." Ms. Burgos nods. "Would you still talk to him? Would you ask him why?"

"I would ask him why did he did that," Jorge affirms.

Ms. Burgos follows up: "You would ask him why—why he didn't tell you earlier?" Jose nods. "Okay."

The students' homework assignment due this day was reading the chapter and writing down their thoughts about what has happened between Felita and Gigi so far. After a few more minutes of discussion, Ms. Burgos asks them to share those thoughts with the class: "How did Felita feel at the end of the chapter? Were they friends—did they make up in chapter 5?"

Marisol reads from her homework journal and quotes from the novel itself:

> They don't make up because still Felita is mad with Gigi because she said [*Marisol reads from the place she has marked in the book*], "'Felita, are you mad at me?' 'Why should I be mad at you?' 'Well, I did get the leading part, but . . .' 'Big deal,' I said. 'I don't really care.' 'You don't? But . . . I . . .'"
>
> [*Marisol stops reading from the book.*] And she doesn't says nothing. And she wanna say, "I *do* care because I wanted to do the part," but Gigi doesn't know Felita is mad at her because Felita tries to hide it away from her.

Marisol's English may not yet be fully grammatical, but she has obviously read the text very carefully and uses it to support her point. Marisol's ability to empathize with both Felita and Gigi (and not take sides) is powerful and demonstrates the maturity of her understanding of the friendship depicted in the novel.

Not all of the students are on the same page with Marisol. Ms. Burgos, clearly pleased with Marisol's answer, attempts to pull in students who are more reluctant to speak up in the classroom. She calls on Manuel, who seems a bit shy but is ready with his answer: "Felita is mad at Gigi because Gigi took her, her . . . [*Manuel searches for the word and finds it*] place, and Felita couldn't be Priscilla because she . . . [*another pause*] she couldn't learn the lines." Felipe, Manuel's peer partner, displays more confidence as he carefully reads what he has written in his homework journal: "In chapter 5, Felita and her friends are in the same class. They make [tryouts] for the Thanksgiving play. Felita breaks up with Gigi because of the play of Thanksgiving. Gigi couldn't tell her that she wanted to be Priscilla because she thought telling her will break Felita's heart. But it didn't. What broke her heart was Gigi not telling her that she wanted to be Priscilla."

Felipe's response reflects a high level of perspective taking in addition to impressive English-language skills. Like Marisol, he goes beyond identifying the problem to consider the interplay between each girl's thoughts and feelings.

It's significant, however, that Ms. Burgos seeks contributions from *all* of her students, not just those whom she knows from experience are likely to be the most articulate or to offer the most "mature" responses. Engaging each child and getting each to participate is part of what she means when she talks about empowerment to our research team:

> It's a process that starts from day one, where you build that community of learners, and within that community . . . you provide them with the tools and the encouragement that *they* have a voice, that they are part of this classroom. They have a responsibility not only to their work but to contributing to the learning process and not just relying on my providing them with information.

Looking for Solutions

Once the class has identified the problem between Felita and Gigi and begun to discuss each girl's point of view, Ms. Burgos turns to the question of what a solution might be—how the two fictional characters might have prevented damage to their friendship in the first place and how they might repair it now.

An activity called the "conflict escalator" is used in many programs designed to teach conflict resolution skills, including VLF. The conflict escalator is a way of looking at the incidents in a story (or a real-life event) step by step in order to determine what might have been done at each point (or what could be done in a similar situation in the future) to change the outcome. Like Juanita, whose worksheet (figure 12.1) describes her sense of how the escalation might occur,

Figure 12.1 The Conflict Escalator

READING 5, WORKSHEET 1

Story-Mapping Activity:
The Conflict Escalator: Going Up!

Name Juanita Date 12/5/97

Map the conflict between Felita and Gigi on the conflict escalator. On each step, mark what each character said or did to make the conflict worse (or better). If you like, use dialogue from the book and note the page numbers. Below each step, note how each character might have been feeling. Feel free to add additional steps.

Well good!!

After all I am Pricella!!

Now if you may I have to go

Sorry!! I just wanted you to be happy.

Go and be Pricella see if I care!!

I think you should be a pilgrim

Well I'm not!!

We all didn't think you're good for the part-Felita

I don't want to be a pilgrim!!

Why, not? Gigi.

Source: Author's data set, adopted from "Literacy and Values," Teacher's Resource: *Felita*. © 1999 Voices of Love and Freedom, Inc.

most of Ms. Burgos's students are familiar with this teaching-learning device, but she reviews the process again before passing out worksheets for them to take home and use to prepare for the next day's discussion. (For reviews of research and practice on cooperative learning in the classroom, see Kohn 1992, 1998a; Kreidler 1994; Kreidler and Educators for Social Responsibility 1991.)

The next morning's session begins with partner sharing. "Take out that sheet," Ms. Burgos instructs her students, "and share with your partner which step you would have changed—maybe with [what] the character Felita, or Gigi, would have said—and then you'll share with the class. Okay?" Some of the pairs that have been working together this year are Juanita and Alegria, Luis and Antonio, Jorge and Jose, Felipe and Manuel, and Marisol and Rosario.

Our video crew eavesdrops on several of the pairs as they read their brief statements to each other about what Felita or Gigi could have done differently. The crew comes in close; the kids, aware of being filmed, are undoubtedly more self-conscious than they would otherwise be, but they seem proud rather than reluctant to present their work in the presence of the camera.

The students' thinking is right where we would expect it to be developmentally: some of their comments on the personal meaning of the incident to Felita and to Gigi reflect a rule-based orientation ("Felita shouldn't be jealous," Gigi "shouldn't lie" [to Felita] "just because of a play"); others involve more skill at perspective taking ("[Gigi] didn't know the Priscilla part was a big deal for Felita"), or an even more sophisticated focus on the relationship itself ("It hurt Felita's feelings that Gigi had lied to her").

Here it is important to note that in terms of our framework for understanding the growth of social awareness, a child's statement at a given time often represents more than one level of awareness. For instance, why does it hurt Felita's feelings, and did Gigi really lie? Some students may be aware that Felita feels hurt because Gigi kept her desire for the part a secret from her best friend. But how many fifth-graders are aware that Felita might also be hurt because Gigi feels she is too domineering? (Felita herself does not seem to be aware of this possibility, or at least she does not mention it.)

As Ms. Burgos brings the whole class together for a general discussion, she calls for volunteers to identify a turning point in the chapter and to say what they think might have happened differently to prevent the estrangement between the two friends. "Who wants to share?" she asks. (This is a question we hear her ask many times during our six weeks of observation in her classroom.)

As a starting point on her escalator, Flora picks Felita's remark about Gigi, "She's getting on my nerves."

"Everyone remember that?" Ms. Burgos asks the class. Murmurs and nods of assent. Flora continues:

> Felita might talk to her why she's angry with her, and then Gigi talk. Gigi could tell her she didn't mean she only wants to take the part. But she didn't [know] the Priscilla part was a big deal for Felita, although it *was* a big deal for Felita.

Ms. Burgos writes quickly on the blackboard in big letters, then turns back to the class. "I put the word up 'Communication.'" She gestures toward the board. "And that's exactly what Flora is emphasizing between Felita and Gigi."

As the discussion continues, Ms. Burgos calls on Marisol, who has selected Felita's earlier comment, "Gigi, are you going out for the play?" Marisol has rewritten the novel's dialogue from that scene and reads it to the class from her worksheet:

> "I don't know. Are you, Felita?"
>
> "Yes, I want to be Priscilla. Gigi, you know you would be good for Priscilla."
>
> "You too, Felita. You know, Felita, maybe I will try out for that part. Felita, will you get mad at me if they choose me to be Priscilla?"
>
> "Of course I will be sad but not mad."
>
> "I will thank the Lord for giving me a friend like you, Felita."
>
> "Me too, Gigi."

Marisol is working hard at coordinating the different points of view of the two characters, and her effort implicitly includes what we would call the next level of perspective coordination—an awareness of the importance to each party of preserving a positive relationship between them.

Ms. Burgos picks up on a key point: "[What] Marisol is demonstrating here is someone who is forthcoming. We're talking about telling the truth, but in this instance it wasn't that [Gigi] is lying, or anything. It was just keeping a secret." Ms. Burgos then asks, "Why would Gigi do this?" The ensuing discussion brings up the question of the difference between a person's intentions and the consequences of his or her actions.

The next morning Ms. Burgos seizes another opportunity to make a connection between the fictional narrative and the real lives of her students. "Yesterday I was trying to make you understand that when we have problems we have to find ways of resolving them," she says. "And sometimes we do the first thing that comes to our mind. When you have a problem with someone, what's the first thing you do?"

From the flurry of tentative responses from the class, Ms. Burgos picks one to repeat. "React. But do you think out your reaction?" A chorus of "No." "That's right," she continues. "And I used Filomena and Jose as an example. Will you allow me to tell the story again?" The two students nod. They seem perfectly comfortable about having the incident between them discussed in class.

"Last week they were at physical education, right? And for some reason, there was a little misunderstanding. Well, it ended up that it was sort of like . . . a little fight. They were playing on the monkey bars, and Filomena fell. And her reaction was—when she looked and saw Jose, she thought, 'He pushed me.' But unbeknownst to Filomena, he didn't realize that he accidentally hit her, or pushed her, and caused her to fall . . . because he kept on playing with his friend Jorge. And next thing you know—Filomena, what did you do? Do you remember?"

"I hit him," says Filomena.

"Yeah, she ran to him and was shaking him, and he was like, 'Hey!'—this is the way he told me the story—'I didn't know. . . .' And then I called Filomena, and we told the story, we went through explaining Jose's point of view. And then we listened to Filomena, and we said, 'You know, let's pretend that you are Jose, and you're the one behind. And Jose's here and you accidentally did that to him.' So [*turning to Filomena*], what ended up happening after you put yourself in Jose's shoes? That you . . ." Ms. Burgos pauses.

"That I noticed that he probably pushed me by mistake."

Ms. Burgos underscores Filomena's realization by repeating it to the class. Then she turns to Jose and asks him to tell what happened next, how the problem was resolved. "We talked," he says, "and we shake hands and we say, 'Sorry.'" Ms. Burgos points out to the class that once they understood each other's perspective, Filomena and Jose both apologized, she for overreacting and he for causing her to fall.

The ABC Approach: Relationship Repair

Another common teaching device recommended in VLF's curriculum guides and used by Ms. Burgos to help students develop strategies for dealing with difficulties in peer relationships is the ABC approach. While the conflict escalator concentrates on the prevention of problems and disputes, the ABC approach focuses on the repair of relationships. The first step in this activity is to *ask* what the problem is; the second step is to *brainstorm* solutions to the problem; the third step is to *choose* the best solution.[4]

Ms. Burgos combines the ABC approach with partner learning and role-playing as a way for students to practice their conflict resolution skills. Now, as part of Ms. Burgos's activities for this chapter of the novel, one student in each pair takes on the role of Felita while the other plays Gigi. First, speaking from each character's point of view, the partners tell each other what they think the problem is. Second, they discuss different ways to solve it. Finally, the partners choose what they think is the best way to resolve the conflict and act it out.

"If you look up here," Ms. Burgos points to a large sheet of paper on which the steps in the process are written, "we have a problem-solving chart called ABC. And this is what we're gonna do today. We've been talking—for the last week—talking about perspective taking. Who remembers perspective, when you take a character's perspective? Does anyone remember? Luis?"

"When you take the character's point of view."

"You put yourself . . ."

Luis completes the sentence: ". . . in their shoes—like feel what they felt, to become them, to become part of them."

The designers of the VLF curriculum emphasize role-playing as a way to help students go beyond talking about how a conflict might be resolved and give them a chance to practice the skills that are necessary to make that happen. It is not easy. As Ms. Burgos tells our interviewer, "[This activity] is a challenge . . . but it helps solidify the experience of perspective taking and critical thinking."

Holding up a copy of the ABC worksheet she has passed out as a guide for this role-playing activity, Ms. Burgos explains that the goal is to figure out how the two fictional characters might become friends again, and that each set of partners will decide together who will take the part of Gigi and who will be Felita. Some of the boys start to giggle.

"The boys are giggling and laughing," she says. "Just can't imagine themselves taking the role of a female, but I'll tell you one thing. . . . In the olden days when they used to do plays, especially, you know, like Shakespeare [*there are murmurs of recognition*], like *Hamlet* and *Romeo and Juliet,* the roles of females were played by men." More giggles. "*Yes.* So this is not any different. . . . It's only an exercise in perspective—ways of thinking." This seems to defuse the issue, and the students get to work with their partners. For the rest of the morning's session Ms. Burgos circulates around the room, listening in on the pairs, sometimes lingering to help them with this assignment.

The Teacher's Role

It should come as no surprise that based on our Carnegie study of the implementation of VLF, including the Russell School videotapes, we would say that although exercises like the conflict escalator and the ABC approach are indeed valuable, children need help in learning how to use them in a way that will carry over to real-life situations outside the classroom. Well-trained and committed teachers are a key component of the success of any program that addresses such complex issues as social development and conflict resolution. We offer the following scenes from Ms. Burgos's classroom as evidence to support that conclusion.

Following the instructions on her worksheet, Alegria, as Felita, asks her partner to list the ways in which the two fictional friends might heal the breach between them. As Gigi, Juanita responds: "I think the different ways to solve the problem is that—I give the role to someone else and we can both do drawings and backgrounds, and we can make up for everything before. We can think more of each other than ourselves." She consults the worksheet. "What do you think is the best solution? Why?"

Alegria (Felita) seems a little anxious as she responds. "I think the best solution is that maybe I should wait for another play and maybe I could be the star, 'cause in this play you're Miss Priscilla, and maybe we don't have to be fighting because you want to be in this one and I want to be in the other one."

In their role-play, both girls are eager to please the other. As Juanita says, "We can think more of each other than ourselves." On the surface, this answer sounds cooperative or even altruistic. Giving up the part, or taking turns, may sound like a good compromise. But does the strategy of avoiding conflict at any cost really represent either cooperation or a compromise? Our video crew captured this interchange while Ms. Burgos was elsewhere in the classroom. We doubt whether these answers—especially Alegria's—would satisfy either Ms. Burgos's desire to empower her students or VLF's aims. It seems to us that instead of grappling with the problem of how to resolve conflict, Juanita and Alegria have simply avoided the exercise. Determining why they chose this strategy is complex. The problem may not be very meaningful to either of them, or perhaps it's a matter of individual interpersonal style (which we might relate to). Avoiding conflict could also be the way these girls have been socialized to deal with complicated interpersonal dilemmas.

It is not only the more accommodating students who could benefit from help as they try to address the Felita-Gigi impasse. For example, Rosario and Marisol, two confident and opinionated girls who show little fear of conflict, get stuck on the very first step of the ABC approach.

When Marisol, playing Gigi, begins by asking her partner what she thinks the problem is, Rosario, as Felita, responds, "I think the problem is that you didn't tell me that you wanted to be Priscilla and you caused all this problem. Gigi, what do you think the problem is?"

Marisol responds that she thinks Felita is simply jealous that she won the role of Priscilla. Rosario retorts, "That's not true!" Then she turns back to the worksheet. "Can we both agree on what the problem is?"

Marisol states, rather forcefully, "No, we cannot agree on what the problem is." The girls immediately move to step B: brainstorming.

Rosario reads from the worksheet: "What are the different ways to solve the problem? List what the different ways to solve the problem are." Marisol speaks first: "Okay, by calming down and talking it over we could—"

"Okay," Rosario interjects. "What do we think is the best solution?"

"Talking it over," Marisol responds.

Rosario nods and they're done.

Meanwhile, Ms. Burgos has been working with Antonio and Luis. Antonio looks down at his worksheet and, as Gigi, takes the first step. "Felita," he says a little self-consciously, "what do you think the problem is?"

"I think the problem is that Gigi isn't being fair by not telling me her secrets," says Luis, as Felita, "and just, like, being in the play without telling me." Then he asks in turn, "Gigi, what do you think the problem is?"

"I think the problem is that Felita and me are having problems." Antonio pauses. "There's been too many lies."

Ms. Burgos interrupts. "Felita is telling you lies?"

Antonio, in the role of Gigi, says, "I'm telling *her* lies."

Ms. Burgos pushes him to reconsider his answer. "You're telling her lies? What lie did you tell?"

Antonio responds, "That I'm not going to be in the play—that I wasn't."

"Was that really what Gigi said?" asks Ms. Burgos, breaking out of the role-play assumption for the moment. "Can you find it in the book where she said that—or was it something else?" She turns to Luis. "Felita, do you want to help her out? I think Gigi needs a little help. Did Gigi ever tell you [that]?"

Luis answers, "No, she's keeping a secret. She's not really lying—but she's just keeping a secret."

Ms. Burgos encourages Antonio to consider the distinction Luis has made. "Did you listen to what the problem, from Felita's point of view, is?"

Antonio confirms, "I see that I'm keeping too many secrets from Felita . . . I'm not really telling her everything I know."

"And? And what has happened as a result?"

Antonio answers, "Felita and I have been friends for almost forever, so I shouldn't be keeping secrets from her—I should tell her."

Ms. Burgos keeps the focus on simply defining the problem for the time being. "Don't tell me your solution yet, just tell me, because of keeping these secrets, what has it caused between the two of you?"

"We're not being friends anymore."

We can see how Ms. Burgos has held the ladder of social awareness for Antonio to climb. She encourages him, with a little help from his friend Luis, to deepen both his understanding of the problem and his vocabulary: when Gigi does not tell Felita she is going out for the part, this omission is not exactly a lie, as Antonio first frames it, but it is a deception that drives a wedge between them. By going carefully, step by step, and emphasizing that each person needs to listen to the perspective of the other, she has helped them with the first part of the ABC approach, which is confronting and coming to an agreement about the critical issue at hand: a friendship in jeopardy.

Beyond the Worksheet

These three scenes point to the importance of the teacher's role as a guide for students working with a curriculum like VLF. Simple solutions are not adequate to deal with complex social problems. For example, "talking it over" may sound good in hypothetical discussions, but what does "talk it over" really mean? Ms. Burgos cannot be everywhere at once; she cannot coach each pair through this process from beginning to end. But by addressing a key question with the whole class, she can help them bridge the gap between social thought and social action.

Ms. Burgos calls the class to order. She then asks Marisol and Rosario to stand up in front of the class and share their discussion.

As we have seen, Rosario and Marisol are strong-willed girls who hold different explanations of the problem between Felita and Gigi, and each seems entrenched in her own position. By choosing this partner pair to work with in front of the whole class, Ms. Burgos is taking a risk. But if she can get these two to reexamine their points of view and really listen to each other, it will be a meaningful experience not only for them but for the rest of the class as well. Rosario and Marisol stand side by side in front of the class and our video crew.

> Ms. Burgos: So. What do you think the problem is, Felita?
>
> Rosario: I think the problem is that Gigi did not tell me that she wanted to be Priscilla and she caused this problem.
>
> Ms. Burgos: Oh. Okay. And Gigi, what do *you* think the problem is?
>
> Marisol: I think the problem is that Felita is jealous because she couldn't get the part that she wanted to get.

Ms. Burgos: And so can you both agree on what the problem is?
Marisol and Rosario (*together*): No.
Rosario: We cannot agree on what the problem is.
Ms. Burgos: You can*not* agree? Why not? That's interesting. Why can't you agree?

Up to this point, the girls have been consulting their worksheets and essentially reading their answers. But Mrs. Burgos has asked a question they have not considered. Now Marisol and Rosario are forced to abandon the script, and there is a subtle change in the tone of their voices. It is almost as if they themselves are having the disagreement.

Rosario: We cannot agree why because she's saying that I'm jealous and I'm not jealous.
Ms. Burgos: Okay. [*She nods at Rosario.*] So you say you're not jealous, and [*to Marisol*] you say she is?
Marisol: Yeah, she's jealous.
Ms. Burgos: Why do you say she's jealous?
Marisol: Because when I told her that I wasn't going to get the part, she was happy, and when I told her that, yes, I was going to get the part, she got mad at me and didn't want to talk to me.
Ms. Burgos: So you think she's jealous because you got the part?
Marisol: Yes.
Ms. Burgos (*turning to Rosario*): And you're saying, no, it's not. Why is it not?
Rosario: It's not, because I could have had another opportunity on another play. . . .
Ms. Burgos: Yeah, but what *really* bothered you? What was the problem that you felt? Was it that she got the part in the play or that she didn't tell you?
Rosario: That she didn't tell me.
Ms. Burgos: So can you both agree on what the problem really is?
Rosario and Marisol (*together*): No.
Ms. Burgos: You can't still? Okay, we need to work on that. It would be interesting to see—since you can't really define what the problem is—what you've brainstormed for ways of solving it. What did you come up with?
Rosario (*reading again from her worksheet*): We could solve this problem by talking it over.

Some teachers might be satisfied with getting their students to articulate this message—don't fight, just talk it over. Ms. Burgos is not. She knows that communication sometimes involves the hard work of listening to others as well as expressing oneself, of being open to changing one's position. She also knows that as a teacher she may need to push her students to go to a place that may not feel comfortable to them. Conflict situations evoke strong feelings, but she can support her students by providing them with a safe environment for exploring those feelings.

Ms. Burgos: Okay, and in talking it over, what would you accomplish? What would you get out of it? By doing that, what would happen?
Marisol: We could just calm down and talk it over and see—
Ms. Burgos: Okay, pretend you have that opportunity to do it right now, without a script. You haven't written it down, use what you know of the information. I know I'm putting you on the spot right now, but this is an opportunity to do improvisation. Improvisation is, given information you already know from the book, you pretend that you are talking it over—without a script. What would you say, Gigi, to her?

For the first time the girls turn to face each other. The papers in their hands are forgotten for the moment.

Marisol: I think that you're just jealous because I got the best part and you couldn't get the part that you wanted to get.
Rosario: That's not true, I'm not jealous. I'm just mad at you because you didn't tell me.
Marisol: I just changed my mind when I went home and thought about it all over.
Rosario: Yeah, but best friends is for to share and tell secrets.
Marisol: When I went to look for you, you didn't want to talk to me or nothing.
Rosario: Because I was mad at you.

By now the girls are smiling, and their teacher commends them on their impromptu performance.

Ms. Burgos: Ahh. [*She pauses for a moment.*] Let's give them a hand because that was hard to do, but they did it. Now don't go anywhere. Very good! Now—let's go back . . . because I think that now that you talked it over, can you agree on what the problem really was between you?
Marisol: We was both mad, and we didn't want to know what the problem was because we didn't want to talk it over.

Through reflection on their role-play, Ms. Burgos invites Rosario and Marisol to analyze their work and pushes them to find the language for what the conflict was really about. It becomes personally meaningful. This helps the girls to internalize the lessons of the conflict and to respond to the situation in the book as they would respond to a similar situation in their own lives. When Marisol further explains, "We were just mad, and we didn't want to know the truth of who started it first," she acknowledges mutual responsibility for a conflict in which neither person wanted to give up her position or change her point of view. This statement also suggests the movement from a unilateral to a reciprocal level of perspective coordination. It even may have tinges of mutuality in the structure of its awareness.[5]

Rosario and Marisol—and, we hope, their fellow students—have come to a new level of understanding about what "talking it over" means: honestly articulating one's own thoughts and feelings and being able to listen to and consider the perspective of the other person. Their engagement with the emotional world of the fictional characters so skillfully drawn in the novel *Felita*—and their teacher's patience and persistence—have pushed them beyond satisfying the superficial requirements of this classroom assignment, toward growth and change that may well carry over into their own social relationships.

The "Physiology" and the "Chemistry" of Social Relationships

I have attempted to show in this chapter that, because it involves conversation and collaboration, partner learning gives children the opportunity to practice the social skills they need for interpersonal and intergroup negotiation. Learning by doing—dealing with issues and themes directly with peers—increases the likelihood that these skills will become part of a child's behavioral repertoire and be put to use in their lives beyond school. In fact, regardless of the content of the material being studied, pairing students to work together (presuming the pairs are chosen with reasonable care) helps them learn *how* to work together.

This all makes sense intuitively, but as we continued our observations in various classrooms as part of our study of VLF, we became increasingly interested in taking a closer look at how these interactions work. How do they fit in with our developmental models?

As an example, Marisol and Rosario's successful role-play about the conflict between Felita and Gigi invites us to think hard (that is, theoretically) about the connection between social thought and action from a different angle. It pushes us to go beyond our previous, limited focus on the social awareness and skills of single individuals. How can we expand our set of interrelated theoretical frameworks to capture the essentially dyadic nature of the kinds of social interactions that seem to lead to a positive outcome and gains in awareness or understanding for each party?

To keep to our example, we hope that Marisol and Rosario will "internalize" what we saw as the new, more mutual level of social awareness they achieved—that this new awareness will become part of how each girl approaches difficulties in relationships in her own life in the future. But how did this awareness arise, and where is "the future" located in our Risk and Relationship Framework?

The figures and tables back in chapter 4 represented our view of the anatomy of social development. Figure 12.2 represents an initial attempt to encompass the "basics" of our Risk and Relationship Framework for understanding the "physiology" of individual psychosocial development as it has evolved over the years to include such influences as temperament, personal history, and family and peer culture.

This is a complicated figure not only because it includes so many elements—nature, nurture, psychosocial development, and "social performance"—but also because we have tried to depict the interactions between these elements in terms of a time perspective, both the influence of the past on the present and the influence that present interactions have on understanding and awareness, and therefore on future thought and action.

Most of the time, as psychologists, we tend to think about how past experience and genetic determinants affect the current psychosocial status of individuals: How did Rosario and Marisol get to be the way they are? In this mode of thought, time goes from left to right in our figure. However, if our conception of time starts with the observation of events or social interactions that occur in the present (here depicted on the right), we must reverse the arrows to indicate that these—more specifically, experiences and relationships that carry new meaning—influence the developing psyche, future behavior, and even our conception of the past.

Figure 12.3 describes a next step in our exploration and mapping of the chemistry of a relationship or an interaction rather than an individual as the object of study. Thinking theoretically in terms of analysis, intervention, or prevention, the chemistry of the pair—the partnership—is our client-focus. What initially was the transformation of theory through the practice of psychological treatment (pair therapy in chapter 3) and then psychological prevention practice (pair counseling in chapter 4) is now, through the catalyst of programs such as VLF, applicable to social development—generally speaking, through education.

For example, we watched Marisol and Rosario as they engaged

Figure 12.2 The Risk and Relationship Framework: A Model of the Relations Among Spheres of Influence

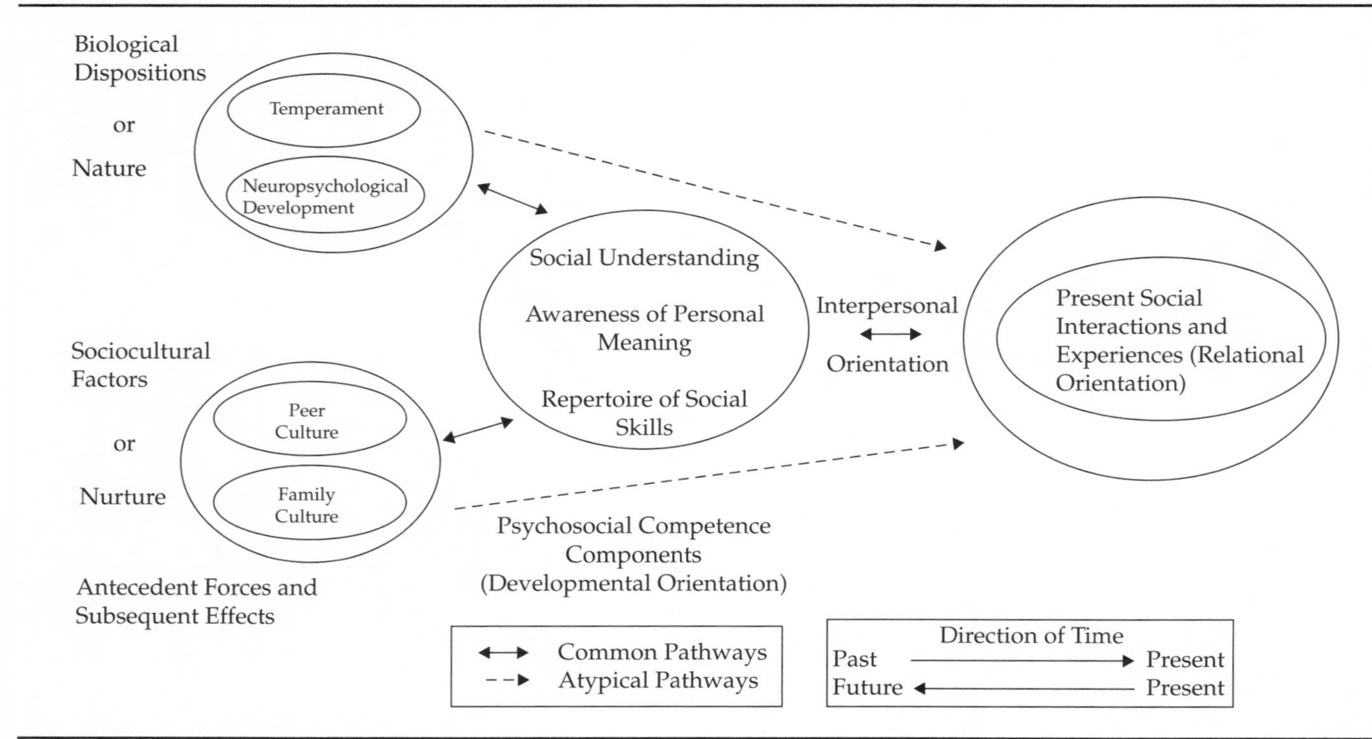

Source: Author's configuration.

first in thinking and writing about the rift between Felita and Gigi, then in using the conflict escalator to try to identify a point at which the two fictional friends might have been able to avoid the conflict between them. So far, so good. (It was Marisol who came up with a scenario in which the two girls protected their friendship by speaking to each other honestly about their rivalry for a starring part in the school play.) But when it came to taking the characters' points of view and trying the ABC method to figure out how to heal the breach once it had occurred, Marisol (as Gigi, who got the part that both girls wanted after concealing the fact that she planned to try out for it) and Rosario (as Felita, who broke off their friendship without expressing her anger) could not even agree on what the problem was, let alone brainstorm solutions or choose the best one.

They were stuck with the platitude "We need to talk it over" until Ms. Burgos pushed them a bit further, in front of the class, to actually *do* it—by improvisation (which is how much of life occurs), in the moment, and in a way that both repaired the fictional friendship and broke through the impasse that the two real girls had been wrestling with as learning partners.

Figure 12.3 represents the relatively simple idea that at each moment in time in the interaction between Marisol (Gigi) and Rosario (Felita), Marisol's interpersonal orientation toward Rosario, and Rosario's toward Marisol, involves an observable linkage between their current repertoires of psychosocial competencies and their observable interpersonal performance. But obviously, neither simply receives the other's communications. Each also responds, and the bidirectional arrows in this still rather clumsy picture represent the fact that this interaction influences each participant—strongly or inconsequentially, for better or for worse. (Sadly, we suppose that this diagram could also be used to represent negative influences as well as positive ones, even the breakdown of a relationship.)

The bidirectionality of the arrows in figure 12.3 portrays in pictures what we are trying to say in words. Growth in psychosocial competence for Marisol and Rosario occurs as a result of the positive interactions that occur in the space and time of partner learning. Lasting social development occurs over time as each member of the partnership practices her interpersonal skills and internalizes the personal meaning of her experience with her partner. Obviously, in the context of schools and children, the teacher helps a great deal to ensure that the interaction continues to head in a positive (developmentally forward) direction.

We think that Marisol and Rosario's role-playing interaction in front of the class resulted in both a solution to the fictional problem

Figure 12.3 The Risk and Relationship Social Interaction Model

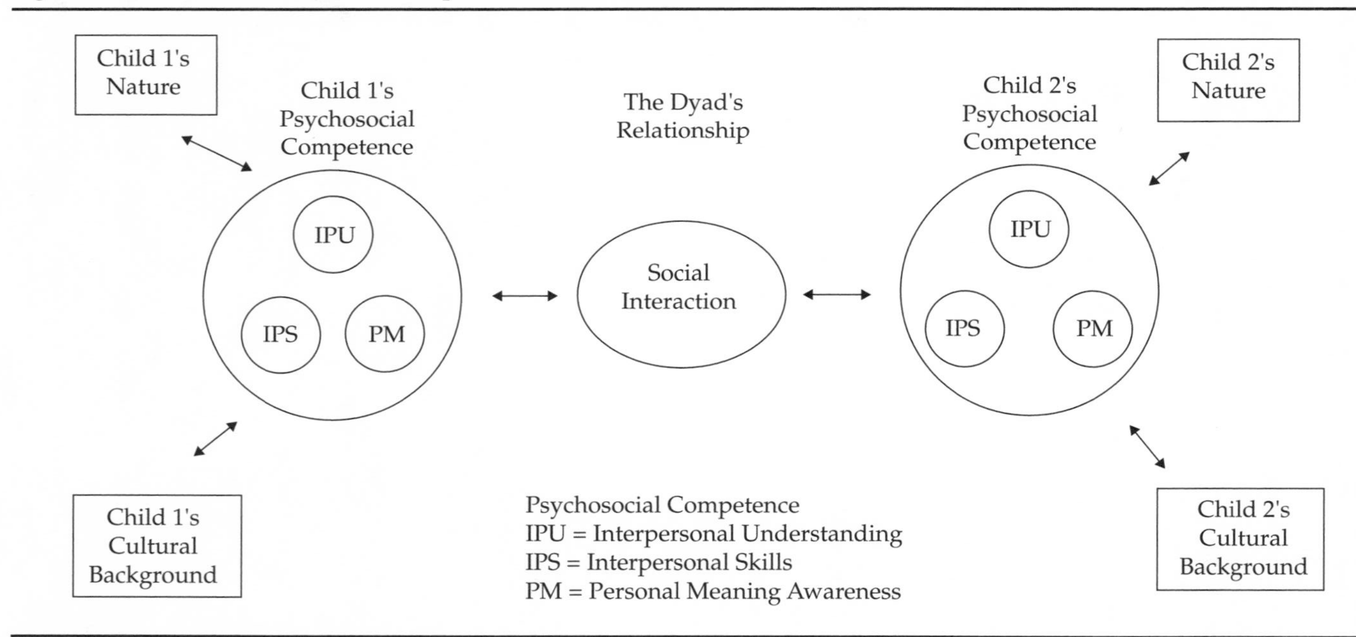

Source: Author's configuration.

and positive growth in each real girl's social awareness and competence. Before this exercise, they had been stuck, entrenched in their respective positions—"talking it over" had meant each telling the other what was wrong with her. Behind the safe screen of fictional roles, and guided by someone they trust, they could take the risk of articulating their thoughts and feelings directly. Engaged emotionally as well as intellectually, both were willing for the moment to listen and consider the perspective of the other. All of these elements—safety, trust, engagement, and openness—contributed to a step forward in *both* Marisol's and Rosario's ability to coordinate perspectives and (somewhat suddenly and evidently to the surprise of the two role-players) to resolve a conflict and repair an alliance. In our theoretical language, we would say that during that interaction this pair *together* moved, not permanently, but at least at that moment, from a lower level of social functioning and competence to a higher one.

One can imagine their developing awareness occurring in the role-play right before our eyes. Rosario, as Felita, moved from "I am aware that maybe I am angry (jealous) that Gigi went out for the part I wanted" (an easy level of awareness at which to arrive) to "I am aware that I am angry (hurt) that Gigi did not tell me she was going out for the part and kept it a secret from me" (a harder level of awareness to achieve).

But there is an even more difficult developmental step for Rosario to take: "I am aware that I am upset that my personality and behavior may have influenced Gigi to act the way she did." This is a very challenging level of awareness to hold on to. Not only may holding on to it take more experience than most fifth-graders have, but it is a level of awareness that challenges us even as adults.

Something like this might have happened spontaneously between these two girls over a dispute on the playground (or between negotiators deciding the fate of unions or corporations or nations around a conference table), but we think that the "scaffolding" provided by the VLF curriculum—and a committed and savvy teacher—played a major role in this case. Rosario and Marisol may know each other outside of class, but working together on assignments that require them to collaborate has helped them get to know each other in a new context. Furthermore, the atmosphere of tolerance of divergent opinions that Ms. Burgos has established in her classroom allows them to take the risk of speaking forthrightly.

We are just beginning this line of research, but we believe that finding ways to help children learn the ethics of relationship by practicing social skills in a setting that is both safe and emotionally engaging can help bridge the gap between thought and action, and that a capacity to coordinate different perspectives can lead to the kind of intellectual and emotional habits of mind that encourage mutuality. These skills would be beneficial, we think, not only in interpersonal relationships but also in efforts to negotiate resolutions to intergroup conflicts on a larger scale.

Chapter 13

"Push Them Back" Versus "Forget About It": Developmental and Cultural Attunement to Students' Strategies for Dealing with Prejudice and Discrimination

About 40 percent of the four hundred students who attend Russell Elementary live in the Allston-Brighton neighborhood and walk to school. The others come on buses from various other parts of the city of Boston. Eighty percent of Russell's students qualify to receive free or reduced-price lunches. Sixty percent have limited proficiency in English; 50 percent speak Spanish as their primary language at home.

In Angela Burgos's Spanish-English bilingual class there are students who are impressively articulate in both languages, some who are still in the process of becoming fluent in their second language, and a few students whose oral and reading and writing skills in English are minimal to nonexistent. Ms. Burgos conducts her lessons almost entirely in English, but occasionally she will translate a phrase or a sentence into Spanish right after she has said it in English to make sure that everyone understands an important point. Sometimes she asks students to translate for their peers. (In addition to helping ensure that no one is excluded or alienated from class discussions, this reinforces the idea that her students can learn from each other as well as from their teacher.)

Allston-Brighton, a community once populated largely by Irish Americans and more recently by immigrants from Southeast Asia and Latin and South America, is certainly an appropriate setting for discussing the larger social issues that the VLF curriculum and the novel *Felita* address. Significant demographic changes began here about twenty years ago as new immigrants, fleeing economic woes, political strife, or even military conflict, flooded into the Boston area. In fact, at one point in the past decade Allston-Brighton had one of the highest immigration rates in the United States.

The children in Ms. Burgos's class hail from various sections of Boston besides Allston-Brighton, but they are all children of this new wave of immigrants, and all have had some experience of the kind of prejudice and discrimination that Felita and her family encounter when they move to the new neighborhood. In fact, there is a significant amount of tension between Ms. Burgos's class and the other fifth-grade class at the Russell School. Ms. Burgos's students perceive the kids in this other, "English-speaking" class as "the Americans," the majority, the "normal" kids; they define themselves as the Latinos, the Spanish-speaking kids, the "bilinguals"—and they carry with them the sense that their accents and their limited English proficiency mark them as outsiders.

Felita: The New Neighborhood

As we continued to videotape Angela Burgos's class, they moved on to discuss chapter 2 of the novel *Felita* (Mohr 1979). Felita's family has finally moved to the new neighborhood. Felita faces the prospect of making new friends and attending a new school. Understandably, she is nervous, although some of the children she has met seem friendly at first.

> I stood on the stoop, watching the group of girls I had seen from my window. They had stopped playing rope and were now playing hopscotch. . . . Slowly I went down the steps to the sidewalk and leaned against the stoop railing. Then I walked toward them and stood only a few feet away. They were having a good time, using bottle caps and keys to toss on the chalked squares. Hopscotch was one game I was really good at.
>
> "Hi! Hey you!" a girl with short brown hair and glasses wearing blue jeans called out. "You wanna play with us?"

Felita accepts the invitation to join the game, but as it happens, not all of the adults in the neighborhood are willing to welcome a new, Spanish-speaking family, and they intervene, calling their children away.

> The other girls all huddled together with the grown-ups. They all spoke in low voices. I waited. Were they coming back to play? They all stared

silently at me. . . . Suddenly I felt frightened and all alone. I wanted to get home, upstairs, where I would be safe with Mami. . . . Now the adults and girls were standing in a group beside the stoop steps. As I approached my building, I lowered my eyes and quickened my pace. I figured I would walk around them and get up the steps as fast as I could.

Thelma quickly stepped in front of me, blocking my way. "Why did you move here?"

"Why don't you stay with your own kind?" Mary Beth stood next to Thelma.

"Yeah, there's none of your kind here and we don't want you." As I tried to get by them the other three girls ran up the stoop and formed a line across the building entrance.

I turned toward the grown-ups. Some were smiling. Others looked angry.

"She should stay in her own place, right, Mama?"

"Can't you answer? No speak the English no more?" The grown-ups laughed.

". . . So many colors in your family. What are you?"

"Her mother is black and her father is white."

"They ain't white . . . just trying to pass!"

"Niggers."

"Shh, don't say that."

"All right, spicks. God only knows what they are!"

"Go on back to your own country."

"Let me through!" I screamed.

"Nobody's stopping you." Mary Beth and Thelma stepped aside. I took a deep breath, tried not to cry, walked up the stoop, and began to push past the other three girls blocking the entrance.

"Watch it!" They pushed back, shoving me down a couple of steps.

"Mami!" I looked up at the window. No one was there. "Let me go by!" I shouted.

I pushed again. I felt a sharp punch in my back and a fist hit the side of my face. Then a wall of arms came crashing down. I began to cry hard.

"Mami . . . Mamita. . . ."

"Here now. That's enough!" a man said.

"Let her go," a woman shouted. "She knows now she's not wanted here. Girls, let her through."

As I ran past, someone pulled at my skirt and I heard it rip. I ran up three flights of stairs, crying until I was safe inside my apartment. I made sure the front door was bolted behind me. I ran right into Mami's arms.

Issues of prejudice and discrimination are difficult to deal with at any developmental level, but Ms. Burgos's students do not have the luxury of ignoring them. They know from direct experience that there are people who dislike them merely because they speak a different language or have darker skin. Even in venues and institutions where people agree to celebrate cultural diversity and work hard to ensure that racial, class, or ethnic differences are respected—as they do at the Russell School—these differences matter.

Luis is one of the students Ms. Burgos relies upon to help those of his classmates who are struggling with a new language. He is a perceptive and articulate ten-year-old, but he has a propensity to regress socially, to pout or act silly when tense. (His past includes a substantial amount of time in homeless shelters with his mother, and we can speculate that this has left its mark on his personality and his thinking.) But despite his occasional lapses in social skills, Luis is a major player in Ms. Burgos's class. Because of his intellect and his willingness to participate, she often relies upon him to initiate or sustain class discussions. She calls on Luis toward the end of the morning's language arts session to present to the class his homework lesson from the night before.

The particular worksheet Luis is reading from is Ms. Burgos's adaptation of a VLF "ABC independent"—an "ask-brainstorm-choose" exercise designed for each student to do individually. Poised and confident in a situation where he knows that the teacher's authority keeps the class in order, he reads his response to the first homework question, "What is the problem Felita is facing?"

"Felita is facing the problem of living in the new neighborhood and getting insulted by other people," Luis declares in his distinctive nasal voice. He pauses for a moment, scans the room, takes a deep breath, and reads the next question from the worksheet. "How would you advise your character to deal with and cope with the difficult situation?" He looks up at Ms. Burgos before continuing. "I would advise Felita to ignore everybody and get on with her life."

An awkward silence follows. Luis's grammar is almost impeccable. His sentences are clear. But his classmates exchange knowing smirks and slight eye rolls. Luis has offended the norms of the group, most of whom think Felita and her family need to do *something* in response to the discrimination they have experienced. Even among students who all feel like outsiders, there are majority and minority opinions, and Luis has uttered advice that relegates him to the social margins of the classroom.

What are some of the other children's responses to the same question—"How would you advise the character?" Watching the classroom conversation on the videotape of this morning's VLF session, we can distinguish four positions on the question of what Felita and her family should do in response to the hostility they face when they move to a neighborhood in which they are a minority. The students recommend:

- *Fight back:* If someone pushes you, push them back (Rosario, Felipe, Manuel, Jorge, and most of the other boys)
- *Organize:* Rally support to protest the injustice (Juanita alone)
- *Retreat:* Walk away and avoid such situations in the future (Flora, Alegria, and most of the other girls, students who advocate returning to the old neighborhood)
- *Ignore provocation:* Just let it be; forget about it (Luis alone)

Evidently Ms. Burgos thinks that although Luis's position has been met with scorn, it has merit; she assumes the task of attempting to expand on his viewpoint and connect it to those of his peers. "Interesting what Luis has shared," she says, and she points out that he and Flora agree that the situation Felita found herself in was a difficult one from which she may have had to withdraw, even though Flora's ultimate solution to the problem of discrimination was to return to the old neighborhood. "What do you mean, 'get on with her life'?"

After almost three months in her class, Ms. Burgos's students trust their teacher enough to say what is on their minds—what they really think, not just what they think she wants to hear. And although Luis is well aware that most of his peers do not agree with him, he maintains his position. He looks up at Ms. Burgos, tilts his head, shrugs his shoulders, and responds as if his previous answer should have been clear enough.

"Like, to ignore other people," he says, "and to just, like, try to do the things that she does, but not to get into any more problems and stuff like that. So the people will get used to them and stop bothering them. Something like that. So that she can live in peace."

On the one hand, Luis's answer may seem socially appropriate if not fully mature: we can see that refusing to respond to fairly strong provocation might be a better course of action than confronting the overwhelming force of the perpetrator. On the other hand, as a clinical psychologist who knows something about Luis's history, I might suspect that his exposure to life on the streets and in homeless shelters has led him to feel helpless in the face of difficult circumstances, and that he deals with conflict by simply ignoring it, which might not necessarily be the best strategy to follow in all social situations. And as we can see on the videotape, Luis's classmates, even those who would advise Felita and her family to move back to their old neighborhood, do not think much of his suggestion that she should just shrug off her feelings of anger and confusion.

The Importance of a Teacher's Guidance

Ms. Burgos has to judge how hard to push for a shared understanding of the different meanings the children in her classroom attach to the events described in the novel—and of the best strategies for dealing with prejudice and discrimination. She must also juggle the response of Luis's classmates to his opinion. Is responding to aggression with aggression the answer? Or, to avoid danger and the spiral of violence, should one allow oneself to be victimized by others? Perhaps there is no one answer. Perhaps one needs different strategies for different situations. And although Ms. Burgos is certainly no advocate of a passive response to life's challenges, she knows from her own experience that sometimes Luis's approach might be the wisest one for her students to take.

Ms. Burgos asks the class to consider Luis's response. "What type of action can Felita take? Luis says, 'Ignore it. Keep going. Do the things that you always do.'" She asks, "How many of you have ever been in a situation like Felita's? Have you ever been treated differently, or made fun at, or teased for being different? . . . Has anyone ever had that experience?" Several children raise their hand. "Yes? Where someone is rejecting you because you're from a different background?" Our video camera catches Rosario in profile with a slight smile and a short nod of agreement. "Or . . . ," Ms. Burgos pauses dramatically, "because you speak another language? Has that ever happened to you?" More students are nodding. "Outside or inside of school?" Heads are nodding even more vigorously. "Was there ever a time when you felt like you were in Felita's shoes? When you were treated differently?" Looking around for a volunteer, Ms. Burgos calls on Antonio.

ANTONIO: Yes. When I first moved to Huntington Avenue.

MS. BURGOS: Did you experience the same thing?

ANTONIO: Not really the same thing, but people were calling me names.

MS. BURGOS: They were calling you names? Names that hurt—because you were . . . ?

ANTONIO: Because I was from somewhere else.

MS. BURGOS: You were from somewhere else. And how did that make you feel?

ANTONIO: It made me feel sad because my family was still new and living in that building.

MS. BURGOS: Did you do anything about it? [*Antonio nods.*] What did you do about it?

ANTONIO: I went to the people that work in the building and told them that people were bothering me.

MS. BURGOS: And what—did they take action?

ANTONIO: They went to their house and told their mom about it.

MS. BURGOS: And did it stop? [*Antonio nods yes.*] And you were okay after that? [*Antonio nods again.*]

Throughout this dialogue the students' eyes have been riveted on Ms. Burgos. She has swept them along with her into territory few teachers explore in their classrooms. What makes her performance on this morning—and many others—so powerful? She is interested in the lives of her students. She goes into their world with the confidence that this is where she should be going, and she participates *with* them in making meaning of their experience.

"Well, I experienced that," she confides to her students. "I wasn't going to talk about it, but I think we need to talk about it a little bit because Luis brought up something important. . . . When I was about—I was in my twenties—I went to New York City to visit my mom, because that's where I was from. And I took a train—my mother and I were going somewhere—and we got on the train and we were sitting down, and our stop was coming, and we went to get up. . . . We were the only Hispanics on the train, [but] we didn't think anything of it—nothing. New York is very multicultural. And as we got to the door—I was holding on and my mother was standing behind me—this woman got up and came right directly to me and started saying terrible things, just like in *Felita*."

"A lady?!!" asks a slightly incredulous voice from the class.

"A lady," Ms. Burgos responds. "This woman came up and said, 'Go back to your country!' And I just stood there. And her face was so close to mine, and she said, 'Go back to your country. What do you think—because you dress nice? You're Spanish. . . .' She went on and on and on. I didn't know why it was happening because I hadn't said a word, but I think because my mother and I were the only Hispanics on the train—I don't know what it was, we still couldn't explain it. And the doors—I was protecting my mother because I didn't know—this woman just kept saying, 'Go back to your country. Who do you think you are?' And the train doors wouldn't open—well, the ones we thought—[at this station] they opened on the other side. So I had to go *another* train stop."

Ms. Burgos delivers the story with real feeling. Watching the videotape, you can hear the fear in her voice—and the anger. She pauses to look around the room.

"How many have ever been on a train?" she asks the class. "You know, it's the next stop, and you're like . . ." She makes a hurry-up gesture. "And no one else on the train did anything. Everybody just sat there, and I went through another stop because this woman kept going, 'Go back to your country,' and when we got off the train, I felt just like Felita. I was nervous and hurt and everything else. But we couldn't—there was nothing we could do. I could not take action. Felita felt angry—*I* felt angry because I had not done anything to [this woman]. I didn't understand. And my mother and I talked about it and said that—just as Felita's mother said—'Sometimes you do come across people like that [and] you cannot explain why it happened, but that shouldn't let us hate everybody.'

"And could I have taken action? Not the way you guys would like to." Ms. Burgos glances at some of the students who have advocated a tough stance. "And I don't think Felita could have taken action at that point. I don't know. To me, we resolved it the best way we could. We talked about it just like you suggested," she nods to Flora, "but sometimes you're going to encounter people like this and situations like that.

"But, as Luis says, you talk about it, you face it, and even if it's hard, you think about yourself and keep doing what you always do. And I knew I was going to encounter people like this, but I kept on. And to this day . . . it's in the back of my mind. I think about it, but I don't hate anyone as a result of it. So do you understand? Sometimes you cannot take action, no matter how badly you may want to." Ms. Burgos now invites a response from the class. "Yes, Rosario?"

"Why didn't you push her and tell her that 'You talk too much'?" Rosario suggests, eliciting laughter from several students. Ms. Burgos's response, however, takes Rosario's remark seriously.

"Well, you know, I couldn't. You know, I was in shock. I was—I didn't know what this woman was going to do—I didn't know if this woman had a knife on her and was going to hurt my mother, hurt me. . . . But would you have done that?"

Rosario nods her head yes, indicating she is sticking by what she's said earlier. Some students giggle.

"I think if you were in this situation," Ms. Burgos tells her, "where a person's in your face, yelling at you, saying all these things, I think you'd think about it twice before you even attempted to take action. Because you don't know—and when you're outnumbered—what can you do? Sometimes you have to find the strength—and that's what I did—as the book says, I found the strength within, because I couldn't handle it any other way."

"So what did you do to solve it?" Manuel asks.

"Well, I prayed," she says, laughing. "I did pray, you know, I said this has got to be something out of nature, or something out of the norm, and 'God, please let me get to the next stop.' And when the doors opened . . . we got out and I couldn't even move. My legs were like jelly because never in my life had I experienced something like that where someone was yelling at me because I was different.

"[And] no one in the train got up. And that's what I'm saying—*why* do you think? It's not because they didn't like me, it was because *they too were afraid*. So, anyway, I think Luis has a point. Sometimes you can't explain certain things that happen to you, but you have to deal with it, talk about it, but you have to move on."

As with Rosario and Marisol's role-playing interchange, described in chapter 12, Ms. Burgos's story has allowed at least some of the students in her class to go beyond their initial responses to the fictional situation depicted in *Felita*. By telling them about a parallel incident in her own life, Ms. Burgos has engaged them on a personal level. She has also persuaded some of the children who scoffed at Luis's position to consider it in a more complex way, and this is an important step for them developmentally.

It is possible that Luis's approach might someday keep them from harm by preventing a nasty situation from becoming a dangerous one: sometimes, as the saying goes, discretion is the better part of valor. By bringing her students into her own story, Ms. Burgos has made that point in a way that is compelling and immediate for them.

Interpreting the Children's Responses

In theoretical terms, we draw upon three primary analytic approaches—developmental, cultural, and biographical—to interpret the personal meaning that Luis, Rosario, and the other students make of Felita's actions and feelings when she is confronted by the hostility of her new neighbors. For instance, if we interpret Luis's solution to Felita's problem ("just forget about it") as unilateral (as compared to either impulsive or reciprocal), we are using a developmental analysis to frame the meaning and assess the complexity of his thoughts and actions. Similarly, Rosario's strategy to push back when pushed can also be interpreted as unilateral, even if it appears to be a polar opposite response.

If we were to interpret "forget about it" as a "typical Latino" (as compared to Anglo) thing to say, as some viewers of the documentary from that background have pointed out to us, we are using cultural categories to interpret Luis's response to Felita's situation. Gender also seems to be a powerful framing factor, as most of the boys seem compelled to avenge the attack or fight back somehow. (In either interpretation, however, how would we account for the "push them back" stance of Rosario, a Latina girl?) And if we say, "Luis is telling Felita to forget about it because he is a child with a personal history of abuse that he copes with by avoidance," we are bringing our knowledge of Luis's biography, his unique personal history and circumstances, to our analysis. If we knew that Rosario's family has taught her to never let an attack go unreciprocated (we do not know this), this too would be a relevant piece of biographical information.

Each kind of analysis or interpretation can shed light on how Luis and Rosario and the other students think about Felita's dilemma and the strategies they suggest to deal with the problem *as they see it*. We believe that teachers who work with powerful material like the novel *Felita* need to be aware of each of these ways of looking at and listening to children's responses. They also need to give thought to how culture, personal history, and a child's developmental status interact to influence the meaning students make of the material.

The majority of Ms. Burgos's male students do not subscribe to the idea that since "forget about it" will allow one to live and fight another day, it might be the best strategy for Felita to follow. They believe that provocation requires retaliation, wherever it occurs and whatever the consequences. This may not be what adults want to hear, but parents and educators must remember how important it is that children not feel the need to present themselves as "socially appropriate" so strongly that they cannot tell us what they really think and feel. Even if we criticize the students' idea that plotting revenge will solve the problem, we still can appreciate that they trust Ms. Burgos enough to tell her that is how they really feel. If we are to help them as they strive to understand themselves and the world, we must first earn their trust.

In Ms. Burgos's case, it helps that she shares a common cultural background with her students. Her own life history gives her a special sensitivity to their needs, and it strengthens her bond with the class that when she talks about her own early experiences she is talking about making her way as a Puerto Rican in New York City. But we would say that it is even more important that she treats her students with respect, acknowledges that adults too sometimes find it hard to choose the best way to deal with a difficult situation, and participates with them in looking for answers to complex problems.

Listening from a Cultural Perspective: Social Class, Ethnicity, and Race as Sources of Variation

Anthropologists and cultural psychologists look for the shared premises that underlie the social interactions and relationships between members of a given society, or of groups within a larger whole, and cultural analyses of this kind often focus on how those premises vary. In the United States we have become accustomed to speaking about cultural differences among our various ethnic and racial groups. Some readers might hear the responses of the students in Ms. Burgos's fifth-grade bilingual class as reflecting variations within the context of a Latino culture. However, the "push them back" philosophy might also be attributed to social class more than ethnic group. It may be that the "fight back" strategy advocated by the largest number of Ms. Burgos's students reflects their socioeconomic environment more than it does their specific ethnic or racial backgrounds (which are quite varied).

Are we claiming that the emphasis on retaliation we hear in the majority of these children's voices is a distinctly inner-city attitude? Of course not. Children growing up in economically disadvantaged circumstances in poor urban neighborhoods do not have a monopoly on the social strategy of retaliation when provoked, and certainly not on the feelings of anger that engender it. The tragic school killings that have occurred in more affluent settings and captured national headlines make this point painfully clear. In these cases, whatever psychopathology may be at work, the violence is often in reaction to powerful feelings of exclusion and ostracism. Retaliation, whether by individuals or by groups, is an almost universal human reaction. Tempering it requires perspective.

But as we emphasized earlier, interpretive frameworks—developmental, cultural, and biographical—are crucial to understanding both behavior and beliefs. I do think it is fair to speculate that the majority of middle-class children are protected, to a greater degree, from the kind of verbal and physical racial assault that happened to Felita, and that the Latino students at the Russell School know they must be prepared to manage such assaults. Children of the middle class usually live in physically safer and economically more secure environments. However annoying and painful the teasing and taunts of their peers may be, these behaviors do not usually threaten their physical safety or represent the kind of prejudice and discrimination that denies them equal social, political, and economic opportunities.

These remarks are simplified, but they serve to clarify what we mean by the phrase "listening culturally." For some of Ms. Burgos's students, of course, their call to "take action" may represent the kind of bravado expressed only within the confines of a safe classroom. These children might not act in accordance with what they are saying. Others may feel like Luis but are not willing to say so. The majority line up behind Felipe, Filomena, and the especially outspoken Rosario: if someone pushes you, push them back. Even Flora, who advocates a strategic retreat followed by organizing against her persecutors, says that if Felita does nothing to challenge the people who have tormented her, "I think they are still going to bother her, because they will tell her that she doesn't know how to fight," and "she has to go and defend herself." These deeply held beliefs are born of everyday experience. They are not theoretical.

Listening Developmentally

Even as we listen for cultural differences we must also focus on developmental themes and variations in students' thoughts and actions. A developmental analysis of children's social points of view cuts vertically across the horizontal dimension of cultural attitudes we hear in this classroom ("push them back" versus "forget about it"). When we use a developmental analysis of social viewpoints, we tend to ask two kinds of questions: First, what kind of approach would these students have taken at an earlier time in their lives—what perspective have they "moved beyond"? What perspective are they missing? What will come later if they mature in their point of view? Second, how do events and experiences, relationships and situations, pull kids back to lower levels of action or awareness?

Putting the first question slightly differently, when we use a developmental analysis, in what way are both strategies—fighting back or putting the matter aside—"typical" fifth-grade attitudes? Are there distinctly different attitudes we might hear at another developmental phase in these children's lives—in the second or third grade, or seventh or eighth grade? Is it likely that at a younger age children would more readily suggest that Felita seek help from an authority, while older children might use more complex strategies than those that either Luis or his classmates have suggested? Seeking an authority, like backing down, may be viewed by older children as another form of weakness, or they may not trust authorities. Complex strategies develop to solve complicated situations.

We know from our own developmental research that by the time they are old enough for fifth grade most children are able to take a second-person perspective on tough social situations but often have a hard time understanding a third-person viewpoint. Their negotiation strategies tend to range from unilateral to reciprocal. Their awareness of the personal meaning of these social situations to themselves is more likely to be "rule-based" (unreflective and arbitrary) than "need-based" or contextualized (characterized by an awareness of both self and others in the context of the particular incident).

Figure 13.1 The Classification of Methods That Students Suggest to Deal with Intergroup Conflict: Combining Developmental and Cultural Frameworks

The horizontal axis represents cultural variations in point of view

← - - - - -   - - - - - →

"Forget About It"	"Push Them Back"
Walk away to reflect on how to take future action to prevent this happening again	Tell them they have no right to treat you this way and you will deal with it later.
LUIS: Put them out of your life and your mind. Ignore them and get on with your life.	ROSARIO: Tell them that you will get them back, alone or with your friends. Show them you are not afraid.
Run away, or give in to them, and maybe they will leave you alone.	Charge into them and attack, no matter what the consequences.

The vertical axis represents developmental levels of conflict resolution strategies: from "lower" at the bottom to "higher" at the top

Source: Author's configuration.

But a developmental analysis is not just a function of age. For one thing, words that might sound on the surface like the same position or attitude may mean something different according to the child's level of psychosocial awareness at the moment. For example, "fighting back" could mean impulsively charging into the offenders, both fists flailing, or it could mean protesting by expressing the injustice and unkindness to which one has been exposed. As mentioned earlier, actions that appear opposite (fight and flight) may be based on the same level of organization. If so, how do we make these differential assessments? This kind of developmental listening has important implications for both effective pedagogy and the prevention of violence.

How, though, does all of this relate to the different approaches that Ms. Burgos's students have suggested for coping with the particularly difficult social problem of being singled out as different and subjected to hostility and discrimination? Figure 13.1 outlines the integration of our developmental analysis of these strategies with what might be either a cultural or biographical one. The horizontal axis represents the two primary alternative approaches proposed during the class discussion; the vertical axis puts students' responses in a maturational order based on our basic developmental framework (see table 4.2).

Bringing Difficult Material into the Classroom

Of course, for every child a unique combination of biological temperament, personal history, and social and cultural circumstances colors the way he or she copes with conflict. Focusing on personal or political issues in the classroom is a tricky business, and shifts, temporary or transformational, in children's social development, personal awareness, and culturally influenced attitudes do not occur overnight or in one class session. And just what does the phrase "fostering social development" really mean?

With good reason, many educational administrators and policymakers are skeptical that given current institutional resources and structures, teachers can, or even should, teach social awareness and conflict resolution skills effectively in the classroom. As practitioners on the front lines, teachers themselves often wonder whether programs like VLF will have any impact. At workshops and institutes where they can speak to us honestly (just as the children in Ms. Burgos's class trust her enough to voice unpopular opinions), we have heard comments and questions in response to viewing the video like the following:

> You can't teach kids these skills—they're already used to fighting.
>
> Kids feel like they need to fight to protect themselves.
>
> How do you know the kids will use the skills taught in the classroom in a real-life situation?
>
> How do you *deal* with parents who say, "If someone pushes you, just push back"?
>
> Should we open kids up to such powerful issues if we can't deal with their strong reactions?
>
> Who are we to say what's the right thing for kids to do?
>
> We would like to teach this way, but won't it take time away from academics?

These practitioners raise powerful, challenging, and legitimate concerns. Our goal here is to provide a framework within which to discuss them. We believe that collectively, as a nation, we must find ways to structure and support schools so that teachers *can* raise such important and sensitive issues of national concern as prejudice and discrimination and discuss them in a developmentally appropriate way with their students at all grade levels. And while we honor the primacy of the role of parents in passing on their values to their children, we believe that helping children become more socially aware by teaching them to listen to and consider the perspectives of others can only strengthen their moral, ethical, and intellectual development.

As we have said, we do not assume that everyone will approve of every aspect of Angela Burgos's pedagogical performance in scenes like the one we have described in these chapters. Some may think she talks too much, or that the story she tells her students from her own life is too personal for a classroom. Some may think it is not personal enough. Some may think material like this is too political, that it does not belong in public education at all; some may think it is not political enough. Others may see its relevance only if we can prove it has a positive effect on academic achievement or on actual behavior and conduct.

Our view is that although academic skills will be increasingly important as we move further into the age of information technology and communication, we will be doing our children and our society a disservice if as educators we ignore fundamental questions about practicing fairness and ethics in our personal relationships and about living up to our national ideals of justice and equality in the larger context of our multicultural society.

The novel *Felita* raises all of these issues in a powerful way, and the VLF curriculum offers teachers who use this book in their classrooms good practical and methodological support for addressing them. But there are two kinds of teaching practices, both embodied in Ms. Burgos's performance, that we see as essential to teaching this material in a culturally and developmentally appropriate way:

- Probing students' responses for their awareness of the personal meaning that underlies their own social strategies, rather than assuming that we (or they) already understand the reasons they offer for their own or others' moral conduct.
- Being willing to share personal experiences in a way that promotes students' awareness of the personal meaning of stories of social justice for them and for ourselves.

From a developmental perspective, the two strategies "forget about it" and "push them back" converge and become more and more integrated as children mature and learn to think about intergroup conflict in a more complex and flexible way. Looking back at figure 13.1, we can see that two of the children's responses, "Walk away to reflect on . . . future action" and "Tell them they have no right . . . [and] take action to deal with it later," prevent the escalation of conflict by allowing the children to extricate themselves from the immediate situation and make a commitment to address the source of the conflict in the future. Follow-through is, of course, another matter, and we would advocate including brainstorming about how to do so in any curriculum that addresses questions of ethics and fairness in a larger social context.

To state this suggestion in concrete terms, Ms. Burgos's job is to gently push her students to the next level, beyond either automatic tit-for-tat confrontation or simple avoidance of conflict. She does that by helping them expand their understanding in such a way that they can use their gifts—Luis's considerable intellect, for example, or Rosario's forcefulness and self-confidence—to find longer-term solutions to the problems they face. Fifth grade is not too early to start to learn that there are other ways to take action against a real or perceived injustice beyond reflexively fighting back or impulsively running away, and that there are other ways to avoid being injured by conflict besides forgetting about it.

The concerns raised in the novel *Felita,* from the personal to the societal, are not just "feel good" issues, nor are they relevant only in the realm of what some call identity politics. They are among the most basic issues that all of us face in our personal lives and as members of society; this is why we believe they must be addressed in our schools. However, to introduce these issues into classrooms, they must fit with the other core mission of education: the teaching of academic skills. Because reading, writing, and speaking—the language arts—are the tools of critical thought as well as self-expression and communication, they are central to academic achievement as well as to social development.

In part V, we take a closer look at ways to strengthen the connection, both practical and theoretical, between social and academic learning.

Part V

Deepening Social Awareness and Literacy Skills: Lessons from the Integration of Developmental Theory, Research, and Classroom Practice

Chapter 14

Bridging the Gap: Connecting Social Awareness to Literacy Practice

What is a neighborhood? How are Felita's old and new neighborhoods similar? How are they different? How did Felita feel about moving to a new neighborhood? Why?
—Angela Burgos, on the first day of teaching the novel *Felita*

THROUGHOUT the history of public education in this country, reading primers for the very young have often carried moral lessons, and the literature studied by older children, adolescents, and young adults has always been carefully chosen to transmit that particular body of knowledge that has been seen as crucial to the moral and cultural as well as practical education of the next generation. (For reprints of early reading primers and textbooks, see Svobodny 1985.) Community and national concerns and goals vary, and they change over time. We have seen many debates over the clash between traditional ways versus the assumptions of modernity, over "the Western (European) canon" versus a more multicultural vision of our heritage, over what constitutes "American values" (see Ravitch 2000). But as we are reminded periodically whenever there is another outcry over the presence of one book or another in the school library or on the reading list for English class, the interconnection between literacy and the teaching of moral and social values has been a constant (see Juel 2000).

In offering the expertise of our practice-based research to help design the original Voices of Love and Freedom program, we were able to bring our understanding of children's moral and social development and our experience with our own Risk and Prevention Program to the process of creating a literature-based curriculum aimed at increasing students' social and conflict resolution skills. We were on familiar ground in the early days when the guiding purpose of VLF was to combat the alarming rise in poor urban communities of youth violence and involvement in "risky" behavior such as alcohol and drug use, gang activity, and sexual promiscuity. But when VLF extended its reach and evolved into a more complete language arts program that incorporated exercises in reading comprehension, vocabulary, spelling, and writing skills along with social awareness and conflict resolution strategies, we entered the new pedagogical world of language and literacy. Our first task was to educate ourselves by reading the latest theory and research and speaking to experts in the field.[1]

Beyond the basics of learning to decode the marks on a page (in itself a complex process about which much has been written), good readers learn to follow an author's patterns of thought, make inferences, and, in reading fiction or fact-based narratives, analyze characters' motivations (see Oakhill and Yuill 1996; Vacca and Newton 1995; Walpole 1999). Being social developmentalists, it is the acquisition of the last skill that most intrigues us.[2] Of course, several of the literacy experts we consulted[3] have pointed out that many of the written materials that we and our children need to be able to comprehend have very little to do with moral values or social awareness: road signs, income tax returns, science texts, instruction manuals, treatises on all kinds of interesting subjects from how to make a pizza to auto mechanics to celestial navigation.[4] Fair enough.

Nevertheless, a great deal of what we read—and by extension, listen to or watch as "texts" presented through the media of radio, television, and films—comes to us from a particular social or political perspective, and so our comprehension must involve systems of values and social understanding as well as intellectual skills. All three processes come into play when we read the newspaper or listen to a radio or television news broadcast, when we see a film documentary or read a novel, or when we try to interpret the campaign promises of politicians, the exhortations of religious leaders, or even the remarks of the family and friends who surround us. It is within the intersection of social awareness, culture, and language that we feel a developmental approach such as ours can make a contribution to the practice of teaching literacy.

What a Social Developmental Approach Offers

As observers in Angela Burgos's class in Allston-Brighton, we saw a strong connection between the development of social awareness and literacy practices. We first noticed how powerfully the children engaged in the story, and how the teacher connected the novel to her students' personal lives. But we also realized that children interpreted the meaning of the story differently. More precisely, some children seemed to express deeper insight and social understanding than did others in the same class. Our observations led to the formulation of several research questions. What accounts for the variation we observed? How do we know that the understanding expressed is deeper and not just different? How might we validate our observations?

In our research, when we attempted to assess the quality of individual students' understanding of the story of *Felita,* we focused on the social relationships in the story and the ways in which the children understood them. We wanted to better understand how the life experiences, knowledge, and attitudes that the children brought to the meaning-making process affected their comprehension of the novel, and also how their capacity to coordinate social perspectives contributed to that comprehension. We asked: To what degree were social developmental processes contributing to their ability to interpret the text?

In this chapter, we explore that question by looking at the various ways in which students in Angela Burgos's class demonstrated their comprehension of the characters, plot, and concerns of *Felita.* We describe the context and our methodology and share some of our thoughts about what we found.

Reading Comprehension and Social Awareness

On the day she introduces *Felita,* Ms. Burgos encourages her students to consider the question: "What is a neighborhood?" She leads the class in a conversation about what it means to be part of a neighborhood and what it would feel like to move someplace new and unfamiliar. She asks the students to draw pictures of their own neighborhoods, which she pins up on the wall, and she tells them something about the history of Puerto Rican immigration to specific communities in the United States.

Over the next six weeks, in addition to taking part in class discussions, role-playing, and conflict resolution exercises, the students will answer reading-comprehension questions, both in class and as part of their homework assignments. We have chosen children's responses to two of those questions for analysis here.

The first of these questions has two parts: How are Felita's old and new neighborhoods similar? How are they different? Here are some representative student answers. Pedro, who is struggling with English grammar and spelling, wrote:

> The kitchen was almost alike. The bilden was desein [designed] like the other bilden. The street of the new neighborhood was clean.

Alegria, the shy girl paired with Juanita (see chapter 12), read her response in class:

> They are alike in the neighborhood because both the neighborhoods had a school and some stores. They are different in that in the old neighborhood she got friends and in the new neighborhood she doesn't.

Evita wrote on her worksheet:

> The things that the new and old neighborhood had in common were the stores, schools and building. The difference was the people's attitudes and how they treated other people.

The psychosocial model helped us to refine the pedagogical questions we asked to assess the development of the students' social awareness. For instance, we designed the question about the two neighborhoods specifically to capture the students' understanding of the link between social relationships and living conditions. Not all of the students made this connection, although each of the three student answers quoted here is accurate in regard to the text. In the novel, Felita's new neighborhood is described as cleaner, and her family wants to live in a more physically attractive part of the city. However, Pedro's response does not address an important part of the definition of the word "neighborhood" that the class had previously discussed—the quality of the social relationships among the people in it. He has focused on the physical descriptions in the story, without saying anything about the intergroup relationships that clearly differentiate the two neighborhoods in the novel. Does Pedro respond differently from Alegria and Evita because of his limited English reading and comprehension skills? Because of gender differences? Or is his response less complex and less differentiated than those of the girls because he is less socially mature? We would need to know more before accepting any of these conclusions, but all three may be valid.

Now let's compare the responses of Alegria and Evita. At first glance, they may appear to have the same level of comprehension—their responses are similar in complexity and content. However, from a developmental perspective, we can discern differences between them that may represent something important about the ways in which children understand and negotiate social relationships.

Alegria wrote that "in the old neighborhood she got friends and in the new neighborhood she doesn't." Alegria's response suggests that she understands that the quality of the relationships among the people in each neighborhood is a key difference between them. But we found it significant that she states this point from a self-referential perspective: other people are either my friends or they are not my friends. Now compare that part of Alegria's response to its parallel in Evita's: "The difference was the people's attitudes and how they treated other people." Evita's statement is more abstract, and it suggests a broader perspective—she can see that the reason the people in the new neighborhood treat Felita badly is not based on their reaction to her personally, as an individual, but a function of how they behave in general toward people who are different from them. Felita does not simply lack friends; she is part of a larger social group that is seen as different and unwelcome in the new neighborhood.

Two other students, Marisol and Luis, took their analyses of the new neighborhood one step further, into the realm of values and emotions. Marisol wrote:

> In the old neighborhood they have the hopscotch game. The houses are the same sides. [In the new neighborhood] kids don't respect adults. There is no respect for each other. There are selfish people.

Luis wrote:

> They are alike because they both are calm neighborhoods. They are both different because the people there [in the new neighborhood] have a hard heart and they make Spanish people miserable.

Although Marisol's and Luis's responses are not grammatically smooth (Ms. Burgos will help them work on this), from a social awareness perspective their reflections are sophisticated. Marisol and Luis look beyond actions and attitudes to consider important internal (and interpersonal) feelings—respect, selfishness, and "hard hearts."

Following our developmental framework, we organized a coding scheme for the analysis of the first reading-comprehension question (see table 14.1).

This research method attempts to use reading-comprehension exercises taken from a novel rich in interpersonal conflict to assess one aspect of students' social competence. Why do we consider this kind of analysis important? First, we believe it demonstrates that children's

Table 14.1 How Angela Burgos's Fifth-Grade Class Understands What Is Similar and Different About Felita's New Neighborhood

Profiles of Social Understanding	Descriptions of Neighborhood Characteristics	Forms (or Levels) of Social Experience
Concrete and particular: Manuel, Eduardo, Pedro	*Physical descriptions:* Buildings, streets, stores	*Asocial and unreflective:* Does not consider people's intentions at all.
Social and dichotomous: Felipe, Flora, Antonio, Juanita, Filomena	*Social descriptions:* Felita has friends in the old neighborhood, not this one. Good people versus bad people. Friendly versus dangerous.	*One-way reflective:* Considers people, but only sees them as friends or not friends, good or bad, friendly or dangerous. Does not describe more complex qualities of people.
Relational and societal: Marisol, Evita, Frederico, Rosario, Luis	*Active motivational descriptions:* They are selfish; they make Spanish people miserable; there is no respect for each other.	*Empathic:* Considers human qualities, social behaviors, and attitudes (respect, selfishness, racism) needed in friendship.

Source: Authors' compilation.

developing levels of social awareness can influence their comprehension of anything they read that involves values and relationships between people. (*Felita,* of course, was picked by VLF and Ms. Burgos precisely because it focuses on these concerns, but they are also central to the study of literature, history, philosophy—all of the subjects we call the humanities—and to our understanding of everything from a political speech to a newspaper article.)

For example, it is significant that Luis demonstrated that he comprehends that the attack on Felita is motivated by prejudice against anyone Spanish. Unlike Alegria, Luis's understanding of this incident—which is central to the difference between the two neighborhoods—goes beyond a one-person perspective to include an awareness of conflict between different groups in our society. Luis and Marisol show that they are thinking on a broader, more societal level, whereas Alegria is still thinking about the conflict in relation to Felita.

Second, this analysis is especially important because while many fifth-grade students, especially those who are bilingual, may not be sophisticated enough in their writing skills to use a word like "prejudice" or to describe it clearly, they probably know it when they experience it. It is therefore necessary to look beyond vocabulary, spelling, and sentence structure to try to listen to what the children *mean* to say. For instance, although Marisol's sentences are choppy and her lack of proficiency in spelling and syntax make her writing unclear, her level of social awareness is high—at least by our standards. When she writes, "Kids don't respect adults. There is no respect for each other. There are selfish people," we believe (although it can be argued differently) that she captures the essential meaning of prejudice: that people do not respect each other's differences.

Third, this type of analysis is essential because of what it may imply about fostering children's intellectual growth and their capacity to understand their own lives, and about the potential of increased literacy skills to improve levels of social awareness and competence. If Alegria, for instance, can see her peers only in terms of "friends" and "not friends," she may never understand why the girls of the new neighborhood harassed and assaulted Felita. She may be bewildered by what she perceives to be a personal and inexplicable attack, directed at Felita herself rather than toward the unwanted migration of Latinos into the neighborhood. There is a difference. In identifying both the cultural and personal characteristics—racism, selfishness—of the children and adults who initiated the conflict, Marisol and Luis place the responsibility for it where it belongs: it was not what Felita said or did that caused the problem, it was the fear and prejudice of others. In the novel itself, the experience is no less hurtful once Felita comes to realize this, but it is less confusing and less damaging to her sense of self. Moving children to this level of awareness is essential to our goals, and if we can demonstrate that this can happen within classrooms such as Angela Burgos's, aided by a literature-based curriculum such as VLF, even better.

Clearly the intergroup conflict in the novel can be understood on several levels, and it is important to be sensitive to cultural as well as developmental differences among the children's responses. For example, earlier we suggested that boys, for reasons that are not yet well understood, may approach these social awareness—reading-comprehension questions in ways that are systematically different from how girls approach them.[5] We do not wish to simply "box" responses into a theoretically driven coding rubric, be it developmental or cultural. Nevertheless, we believe that looking at students' responses in the context of a developmental framework is valuable because it gives us information about when children develop various social concepts, under what conditions they best can express them, and how they might use them to solve social problems.

For instance, in the novel, Felita's family eventually decides to move back to Spanish Harlem. Once her parents realize that the people of the new neighborhood are prejudiced against them as Puerto Ricans, their decision to avoid confrontation by returning to the old neighborhood is based on their belief in the irreversibility of this prejudice. While we, and many of the students in Ms. Burgos's class, might not agree that this is the only or best course of action, an understanding of the motivations and actions of other people is for all of us a key first step in deciding how to manage interpersonal and intergroup relationships. For these students, their study of the novel *Felita* has important implications for their ability to cope with racism in their own lives. This is one example of how literacy and social development, in our opinion, may be linked in the service of a comprehensive vision of education.

The Push Toward Standardization

As we read Ms. Burgos's fifth-grade students' written homework exercises from a social-developmental perspective, we began to wonder how the complexity of language and thought we observed in them would be understood and evaluated using traditional measures of literacy assessment. We decided to settle down for an extended stay in the land of literacy. Like any new kid on the block, we needed to explore the neighborhood.

We soon discovered that this field is one of the most closely watched and researched domains in education. Universal literacy has been one of the most important goals—if not *the* central goal—of public education in this country for most of the last two centuries (see, for example, Hill and Larsen 2000; Sarroub and Pearson 1998; MacGinitie and MacGinitie 1986; Snow, Burns, and Griffin 1998). Today, faced with one of the largest increases in immigration in the history of the United States and a widening gap between the wealthy and the very poor, politicians and publicly minded citizens are responding with a focus on academic achievement. Standards-based reform is a major focus of school districts across the country, and reading scores are one of the most commonly used measures of the overall effectiveness of a school's curriculum (Hill and Larsen 2000; MacGinitie and MacGinitie 1986).[6] In our increasingly multiethnic and multilingual country, hope remains that universal access to good public education may be a force for reducing injustice and social inequality (Berliner and Biddle 1996; Bartolemé 1994).

For all of these reasons, the current ongoing debate about literacy methods and practices is sometimes a fierce one. As we read studies and consulted experts, we found that research is quickly and sometimes inappropriately adopted by one ideological camp or the other to hold children and schools accountable for a specific set of outcomes rather than to further knowledge in the field (Sarroub and Pearson 1998; Allington and Woodside-Jiron 1999; Snow, Burns, and Griffin 1998). All too often, literacy education, like the teaching of other academic subjects, is no longer seen as a process but is driven by the need to achieve expected results quickly (Finn 1990).

At the center of the way literacy is assessed today is a widespread reliance on standardized tests of reading comprehension (Finn 1990), and accountability seems to have become synonymous with improved student scores on standardized tests. Reform efforts that sought to incorporate cultural and social knowledge into the assessment process have largely failed, and with the widespread acceptance of standardized testing, school districts will try almost any method to increase their students' scores (Berliner and Biddle 1996).

The Massachusetts Comprehensive Assessment System, known as the MCAS, offers one example of outcome-oriented tests becoming the first and sometimes the only measure of acquired literacy skills—and of the consequences of this policy (Massachusetts Department of Education 2000a). In the Commonwealth of Massachusetts, as in many states, the educational establishment has focused much of its considerable energy and funding on improving academic achievement by raising literacy standards. Today MCAS exams in English language arts are used almost exclusively to identify areas in need of improvement and to direct attention toward individual students, teachers, schools, and districts. Tenth-grade MCAS results in English and mathematics are used as a graduation requirement. Across the state, teachers, principals, and superintendents work hard to prepare students for each year's MCAS exams. "Teaching to the test" has become an everyday phrase, and not only do teachers at all grade levels admit to structuring curriculum and classes according to what the MCAS tests for, but they are in fact expected to do so. A single test has become a very high-stakes measure indeed for students, parents, and school professionals.

The Massachusetts curriculum framework in language arts presents a thorough set of literacy goals for grades kindergarten through twelfth. Language, literature, composition, and use of media—each topic has its own extensive set of learning standards, set by the Massachusetts Department of Education in 1997. In the conventional scoring system for all state assessment tests, evaluators code—or watch for—certain elements in a written response to a question. Students are expected to recognize English vocabulary, learn to understand meaning through word relationships, identify the basic facts and essential ideas in what they have read, and correctly identify and describe the structure of the English language conventions (Massachusetts Department of Education 1997).

Beyond Massachusetts, the Stanford achievement test series, a widely used national assessment measure upon which many other tests like the MCAS are modeled, appears to have a more ambitious agenda (Harcourt Brace Educational Measurement 1996). The assessment protocol asks scorers to consider how well the student understands the story as a whole; connects relationships among ideas in the selection and to the real world; considers why and for whom the story was written and comprehends character traits, motivations, and relationships; understands setting and plot; and demonstrates an understanding of the underlying meaning of the selection and of the techniques the author used to convey the message. This is a sophisticated and extensive set of considerations, yet most often the reading-comprehension questions themselves, such as the one presented in figure 14.1, do not probe textual content very deeply, nor does the coding rubric provide any firm theoretical markers to identify levels of competence comparable across raters or responses.

In the example we present in figure 14.1, the Stanford Nine for grade 5 tries to determine whether the student's response indicates an understanding of the meaning of a "figurative phrase" as well as the expression "run faster than the wind."

Reading comprehension involves being able to both negotiate text and understand structural devices such as figurative phrases, but it also means being able to make inferences and connections from the deeper "referential" meanings found in texts (Spires and Donley 1998; Roller 1990; Sarroub and Pearson 1998). We applaud instruction that is guided toward developing children's capacity to understand and use literary devices, yet we feel that something is missing from the scoring rubric here: any consideration of the underlying theme of the reading selection, which in this case involves the values that Peter and his family hold and the question of what constitutes achievement.

This points to another important difference between the Stanford Nine or the MCAS reading-comprehension standards and what we would consider a good test of social literacy: the meaningfulness of both the materials students are asked to read and the questions they are asked about them. From our perspective, one problem with the Stanford Nine and the MCAS assessments is that although the analyses are thorough (if one defines comprehension rather narrowly), the selections students are asked to interpret are often somewhat insipid. If we want to assess how well children understand what they read, it is important not only to choose materials that are interesting and relevant to their lives both thematically and culturally but also to include reading-comprehension questions that address social as well as literal meaning.

Figure 14.1 Analysis of a Short-Answer Reading-Comprehension Coding Rubric

Reading Selection

Somewhere near you lives a boy like Peter. Peter is in the fourth grade. It takes him a long time to do his work at school, and often he needs help with it. . . . But Peter always does his best. His family taught him that.

Every afternoon when school is over, Peter runs to his house. . . . Peter likes to run. He feels good when he runs, because his legs do what he wants them to do. His arms and feet do too. The wind hits his face and blows his hair. When he runs, Peter feels as if he is flying. . . .

One day, Peter's big brother told Peter that he should try out for the school track team. His brother said the team needed fast and steady runners. . . . All that day, Peter thought about it. . . . The next day, Peter ran over to the track field to try out for the team.

Some things are different for Peter. . . . Peter gets home from school late now, but his family doesn't mind. They're proud of Peter, who may be slow at doing some things, but is faster than the wind when he runs.

—*Faster Than the Wind* by Lois Grambling

Comprehension Questions

Peter's family says that he is faster than the wind. What does that mean?

How do you know that?

Responses as Coded by Stanford 9 Rubric, from Low to High Levels

"It means that he runs fast because he runs everywhere and he runs on the track team Peter likes to run. Because I read the story and that's what it says Peter runs fast also because he like to run and has good practice at it."

"Peter can run very fast. It is a comparison."

"Faster than the wind means he runs very very fast. Because he runs and so if he runs fast his parents use that expression to say he is a fast runner."

"That means in figurative language it means that he can run very fast. I know that because it would be impossible for a human to run faster than the wind."

Source: Authors' compilation based on Stanford Achievement Test, 9th ed., intermediate 2 scoring guide (Harcourt Brace 1996).

Note: Responses include our corrected spelling and are arranged from low levels at the top to high levels at the bottom of the list.

"Thought and language are essential tools for learning and communicating" reads one paragraph in the introduction of the report outlining the statewide curriculum for Massachusetts. "We use thought and language when we listen, make observations, and remember experiences. We use language when we think critically and creatively and when we convey our ideas and feelings to others. All discourse is dependent on thought and language working together" (Massachusetts Department of Education 1997).

But what does "thought" and "discourse" really mean? In our opinion, one of the most powerful kinds of thought, at any age but especially for preteens and adolescents, is thought about social relationships. Certainly we know that there are some students (some people) who care more about how carburetors work than about how social interactions work—and we all need to be able to read for that kind of knowledge—but we would argue that children (all of us) must also learn the logic and ethics of social and societal relationships if they (we) are to function well within our families and communities and as citizens of a democracy. Furthermore, we all use language (discourse) to function as part of a culture and group (Gee 1991, 3). Developmentally speaking, fifth grade is an important time for this kind of learning.

Every day the students in Ms. Burgos's class experience conflicts with each other, with students in other classes, with friends and relatives, and sometimes with people they do not even know. It is inevitable that such experiences absorb a good deal of their energy and attention as learners. As educators, we cannot ignore this part of their lives—at this age children are thinking social thoughts and their social awareness and competence affects their academic learning as well as their behavior. Instead of avoiding socially charged themes like fairness, prejudice, and justice, as many educators, policymakers, and test designers might have us do, we embrace them. We would never endorse a test for "correct" opinions on these issues, but we think social concerns need to be part of education and therefore part of learning assessment.

Thought (Reflection) and Personal Meaning

In observing Ms. Burgos's class, we had the opportunity to study the power of peers to help each other gain intellectual and social competence—as when students were paired for role-play and discussion, for example, or for working on their reading-comprehension and writing skills. Especially when guided by a teacher like Ms. Burgos, who is experienced in this area, the VLF curriculum works well to help students use their own personal experience as a platform upon which to develop their reading, writing, and social skills simultaneously. To test this view, let's go back to the text of *Felita* (Mohr 1979, 59) and take a look at the responses that Ms. Burgos's students gave to a second reading-comprehension question we designed for the teacher's guide, one that we think is especially challenging.

Several weeks after moving back to her old neighborhood, Felita talks with her grandmother about the conflict with the neighborhood girls. Remember that she is the narrator.

> "Abuelita, I don't want Mami or anybody else to know that I . . . I feel like this."
>
> "Like how, Felita?"
>
> "Bad . . . and like I can't stand up for myself."
>
> "Well, then I promise you, nobody will know but us, yes?" She smiled and hugged me real tight.
>
> "It's about when I lived in that new neighborhood and what happened to me." I told Abuelita the whole story, just like it happened. "Probably Mami told you already, but I don't think she really knows how I feel."
>
> "Now what makes you say that?"
>
> "Abuelita, I never said anything to those girls. Never. It was as if they were right, because I just walked away, you know?"[7]

As reflected in this dialogue, Felita has not achieved the complex task of finding personal meaning for herself in the incident. The reading-comprehension question begins with her last statement and focuses on what Felita means by it: Felita says to her Abuelita, "I never said anything to those girls. Never. It was as if they were right, because I just walked away, you know?" What does Felita mean?

This question asks the students to do more than reference a passage in the story. It probes for the levels of understanding that children have not only about the fictional characters but also about the social world around them. Within a developmental framework, although a student may not answer this or any other reading-comprehension question fully, his or her response nevertheless offers insight into how he or she is thinking about relationships generally. As we considered the students' written responses to this question (our data), three distinct patterns of interpretation seemed to emerge.

Some students were primarily concerned with Felita's innocence. They interpreted the passage to mean that the other girls, not Felita, caused the problem:

ANTONIO: I think Felita meant that she didn't start the fight but that they did.

MANUEL: Felita means that she didn't do anything to those girls, and also she didn't start the trouble with those girls.

PEDRO: That means that she not did nothing and she never said a bad word to them.

LUIS: Felita means that she's innocent and that she didn't do anything to provoke them to beat her up.

FREDERICO: She says that because she wanted to be friends with them and have a wonderful life.

This group of students seemed to believe that Felita's intention is to tell Abuelita that the attack was not her fault. They responded to the first part of what Felita says to her grandmother: "I never said anything to those girls. Never." They seemed concerned that Abuelita should know that Felita did not start the fight.

An alternative pattern or theme emerged among a second group of students.

MARISOL: What she means is it's that she was trying to avoid trouble but the girls wanted to fight her.

ALEGRIA: Felita means that she didn't fight back, she just walked away because she don't want to get [hurt].

EVITA: Felita means that she didn't do anything to the girls and that she just walked away from the girls.

FLORA: She wanted to say that she [ignored] them and [passed them] over.

FELIPE: She means that they thought she was a chicken. Because she walked away and didn't fight them back.

These students focused on the fact that Felita walks away to stop the conflict situation from becoming even more violent. They were not primarily concerned with assigning blame or trying to figure out who caused the conflict, but instead try to explain why Felita acts the way she does—that she leaves to avoid fighting or getting hurt.

In terms of how reading comprehension relates to social awareness and development, what is interesting here is that each student in these two groups seemed to consider only part of the quoted passage, perhaps the part they related to most immediately in terms of its meaning to them. The first group, when they read the question, focused only on the fact that Felita did not provoke the confrontation; the second group answered the question as if it asked only why she ran away.

A third group of student responses centered on yet another interpretive theme—that Felita did not "say anything" to the girls. Once again, we see a developmental difference between merely stating the facts and considering what they mean.

> EDUARDO: She means she didn't talk back to the girls [so they thought they were right].
> ROSARIO: Felita means that she did not do anything she just walked away. Also she means that she did not talk or say anything [even though she should have].
> JUANITA: Felita means when she says, [it] is as if they were right because I just walked away "you know." She means that they had the reason why to beat her up because she walked away and didn't say anything while she was leaving.

With the student responses grouped according to the similarities in interpretation that emerged from their writing, we move to a second level of analysis—looking at the three thematic patterns in relation to the level of social awareness they seem to reflect.

The first group of students, Antonio and his peers, seemed to be concerned with concrete knowledge—they sought to understand what happened and who is to blame. "Felita means she is innocent and didn't do anything to provoke them to beat her up," said Luis. Although Luis was aware of the role of the other girls, he seemed only to attend to Felita's view of herself.

The next group of students focused instead on the problem of strategy—how to deal with conflict between Felita and her attackers. "What she means is it's that she was trying to avoid trouble but the girls wanted to fight her," Marisol wrote. Unlike the students who were concerned only with having Felita prove her innocence, Marisol knew that Felita did nothing to provoke the attack, so she concentrated on Felita's response to it. Similarly, Felipe believed that Felita is afraid to be seen as a coward: "She means that they thought she was a chicken. Because she walked away." Although the resolution strategies that Marisol and Felipe were grappling with by implication—either walk away or strike back—seem to be opposites, we would say that these two students share a similar level of understanding in that each saw that part of what most upsets Felita is what the other kids thought about her.

Only a few students implied that there is an even deeper meaning to Felita's words. Juanita wrote: "Felita means . . . [it] is as if they were right because I just walked away. She means that they had the reason why to beat her up because she walked away and didn't say anything while she was leaving." Juanita's sentence can be confusing at first, but we believe that she caught something most of the other children missed—that Felita could have made some effort, no matter how small, to talk to the girls and try to change their perception of her and defuse the conflict. Juanita also realized that Felita thinks that because she walked away she has implicitly validated her attackers' view of their ugly, discriminative behavior. Juanita's understanding requires a sophisticated level of social awareness, one that, developmentally speaking, we would expect to be out of the range of most fifth-graders.

As a child matures, he or she learns to view an interpersonal situation from different angles—to step into the shoes of others, so to speak, and think about how another person's perspective relates to his or her own. Looking at social perspective coordination levels in students' written responses to reading-comprehension exercises is a way to connect thematic concerns and developmental analyses.

Going back to the text, we would say that Felita is not just concerned with what caused the conflict (her factual knowledge) or upset that she walked away from a challenge instead of fighting (her risk management strategy). She is concerned about what her actions mean personally, to herself and to her tormentors, and worried that her reaction might have legitimated their actions in their own eyes. To Felita, walking away has a deep personal meaning. She is aware that the actions of the girls in the new neighborhood were wrong, and although she was afraid of being hurt, Felita wonders whether, by not challenging them, she has implicitly agreed with their belief that she does not belong in their neighborhood.

Essentially, the reading-comprehension question "What did Felita mean?" explores whether the students who study this novel can grasp the complexity of the social situation the author has described in chapter 3. In particular, it asks whether they can identify the existence of an interplay between perspectives: what Felita thinks, what the girls in the new neighborhood think, what Felita understands the girls to be thinking about her, and so on.

Table 14.2 lays out our combined thematic and developmental analysis of students' responses to this second reading-comprehension question.

Understandably, this social labyrinth was hard for the fifth-grade students in Angela Burgos's class to negotiate. It would be difficult for many adults. The VLF reading-comprehension questions ask students to read the story closely, understand the personal and societal aspects of conflict, and consider and evaluate strategies for dealing with it. The questions tap into literacy skills, students' ability to think logically, and their capacity to coordinate multiple social perspectives as a way to make meaning of social experience.

Table 14.2 Social Perspective in Reading Comprehension: Analysis of Levels of Interpretation in Angela Burgos's Fifth-Grade Class of (1) "It Was as If They Were Right" and (2) What "Running Away" Means Personally to Felita

Profiles of Social Perspectives: Who Is Taken into Account	Degree of Coordination of Viewpoints	Theme Expressed and Strategy Suggested
First person: Frederico thinks Felita wants to be friends with the girls and have a wonderful life.	Only sees Felita's point of view—she wanted to be friends—and what she can do to achieve it.	Feels sad and powerless and proclaims, "I'm innocent."
Second person uncoordinated: Marisol and Luis think Felita thinks the girls want to fight her but she wants to avoid trouble so she decides to leave.	Takes the other girls' view into consideration but does not coordinate it with Felita's view; also decides Felita acted just to avoid trouble.	Believes that she cannot change others' point of view, so choices are to fight back to defend self or to walk away to protect self.
Second person coordinated: Felipe believes Felita means the girls think she is a coward.	Considers what Felita thinks the other girls think *about her* when she walks away.	Believes that one's own actions will influence how others will treat you. Fights back or walks away.
Third person coordinated: Juanita thinks Felita feels the girls think they are justified (right) in their discrimination because Felita just walks away without protesting.	Takes the other girls' view *of themselves* into consideration, based on the coordination of their view with Felita's view of them and herself.	Fights, walks away, or tries to talk, but transforms opinions of antagonists or persecutors. Is concerned for future implications of actions.

Source: Authors' compilation.

To fully address the question "What does Felita mean?" when she talks to her grandmother about her reaction to being the target of harassment and discrimination requires stepping into the shoes of both Felita and her antagonists. It requires taking more than a first-person perspective (Felita proclaims her innocence) or a second-person perspective (Felita's concern about how "they" see her action). Only a third-person point of view can open the door to a fuller understanding of the conflict for Felita (and Ms. Burgos's students), and perhaps to a social strategy that goes beyond fight or flight as a way of resolving conflict. This is tough stuff.

Bridging the Gap

While tests such as those included in the MCAS or the Stanford assessment programs may give educators important information about how well students comprehend some aspects of the texts they read, we argue that a developmental approach, grounded in the validation of clearly identified levels of social understanding, may have much to contribute to the assessment of literacy in a broader sense.

We further hypothesize that to the extent that children are naturally embedded in social and cultural contexts, their understanding of reading matter with any kind of social content is based in part on connections to their own context and what they make of it. We believe that instead of avoiding conflict-laden subject matter in language arts and English classes, educators should include it in a carefully designed curriculum as a way to promote the kind of intellectual understanding and social awareness that can operate under conditions that are highly meaningful personally—because it is under just such real-life conditions that perspective is often lost.

Even if an association between literacy and the development of social awareness can be proven to exist in Ms. Burgos's classroom, the causality—an explanation of the connection and how it works—remains empirically unclear. Do the children who display a deeper level of social understanding of the text of *Felita* have better reading skills through which they are better able to capture the story? In this class complicated by bilingualism, is it a question of language mediating a display of social awareness? Does a deeper social understanding—an ability to take different characters' points of view and think deeply about their actions—contribute to a student's ability to understand a text intellectually? We are not sure, but clearly these are important issues for further research.

Regardless of what that research shows, important policy questions remain. Literacy practice, we have learned, is often politically controversial, and it has always reflected the values and concerns of the day (Snow, Burns, and Griffin 1998; Svobodny 1985). But those who have recently been advocating that educators concern themselves with academic achievement alone—that there is no room in the curriculum of our public schools for a program like VLF and it is not the business of schools to teach values, social awareness, or conflict resolution—have forgotten two important facts of life.

First, learning cannot occur without motivation. We all know from our own experience how hard it is to memorize a set of boring facts, and how quickly we pick up information that is interesting to us. Second, children are inherently social; they are interested in their own social lives and the social lives of others. It seems obvious to us that a child who is engaged in the content of a text—in this case, a book like *Felita*—because it has direct meaning to him or her will also be engaged in the process of learning to read it. We, of course, believe that it *is* important to foster social awareness and social competence in our schools. And we are persuaded that when students can connect the themes of books to their own lives, under the guidance of an experienced teacher who is not afraid to take risks and discuss topics such as discrimination and prejudice, positive change (development) occurs both intellectually and socially.

However, while we are impressed by what an intensive study of *Felita* has meant to students in one class in Allston-Brighton, would such a program fly in an upper-middle-class Massachusetts town such as nearby Brookline? We think so. The issue of how to deal with direct, flagrant prejudice may not be as urgent for the children of that community (although eliminating such injustice should be of concern to us all), but they too must cope with incidents of peer ostracism, intimidation, and harassment. A book like *Felita* is universal as well as particular.

In the course of our observations and analysis we found that the responses of the students in Ms. Burgos's class to reading-comprehension questions did indeed reflect developmental differences in social thought. We believe that experienced teachers can "scaffold" these sequences, as Ms. Burgos does, to help their students reach new levels of understanding. Here, one more quote from *Felita* seems appropriate.

In their conversation at the end of chapter 3, while Felita is still trying to come to terms with the incident, her grandmother says to her:

> "Felita, you will always meet some mean people and bullies in this world. . . . All right then, let's figure this out. I don't think that hurting them is going to make anything better or really count right now. After all, what happened is over. You are far away from there. But maybe you could be prepared for the future. When you come across people like this, you could let them know how ignorant they are. Yes?"

Abuelita is attempting to bring Felita to another level of understanding—and action. In pointing out that another option in such a situation would be to speak up for oneself and try to change the other person's perspective, Abuelita is voicing an understanding that arises from her own lifelong experience. She joins the crucial ingredient of the passage of time to the construction of meaning as a way to gain perspective. The process of sharing one's own understanding with others is an essential component of interpersonal development. When people listen carefully to the perspectives of others they trust and honestly share their own—as Felita and her grandmother have done in this scene—they educate and learn from each other. The ability to understand the points of view of others is a core competence we could all afford to cultivate and refine—teachers, students, and researchers alike.

This chapter was cowritten by Robert L. Selman and Amy J. Dray.

Chapter 15

The Power of Persuasion: Who Is the Audience and Where Does It Stand?

Dear Principal,
Did you know that there is a conflict between Spanish speaking and English speaking students in the school. During recess teim [time] there is a conflict between the other class and my class wit [with] the playground. They allways get the playground and we get the hard part to run. I would like to have a conversation with the other class so we could take turns and have fun.
Sincerely,
Filomena

BY EARLY December, Angela Burgos's class had completed many of the social skills exercises recommended in the Literacy and Values teacher's guide for the first four chapters of *Felita*. The students had worked on their own, as well as in small groups and in whole-class discussions, to write and talk about the feelings and motives of the characters in the novel. They had also practiced, in pairs, role-playing exercises designed to try out different strategies for resolving conflicts between individuals and groups.

Now, in an activity that came under the "To Express" and "To Participate" components of the curriculum, the students were invited to become socially active—to make a connection between the broader issues introduced in *Felita* and their own experience. The activity told them to "Speak Out!"

> Write a letter about a conflict or problem in your school or community. You can write your letter to the editor of the school or the local newspaper. In your letter, describe the conflict or problem. . . . How does it

affect you and the other people who live in the community? Then make an argument about what you think should be done about this problem or conflict. Be persuasive!

Similar to the reading-comprehension—social-awareness exercises in chapter 14, the letter-writing activity was designed with two goals in mind. First, "Speak Out" was created to help students take the social skills they had learned in class and apply them to a real-life problem. In the curriculum exercises as well in as the stories, themes of social justice prevail. It is not enough for children simply to read novels such as *Felita.* They should also connect the themes to their own lives; by understanding the social strategies used by fictional characters in the novel, they can compare them with the strategies they may use to deal with their own real-life situations.

But at the same time the exercise was created to teach important literacy skills; it provides an opportunity for students to write about a specific topic, for a particular reason and audience. Most literacy researchers would agree that the more practice students have writing the better (New Standards Primary Literacy Committee 1999). Furthermore, this particular assignment, a persuasive essay, is frequently found on national and state assessments.[1] Policymakers and educators often feel that students must learn how to form an opinion and to create and evaluate an argument (Crammond 1998). Persuasive argumentation is part of the process by which students develop critical thinking skills, and in a certain sense persuasive writing has its roots in the values of our Western culture. It is woven into the fabric of our democratic society that a student must learn to argue about a topic and persuade others to support or change an opinion.[2] (Once you dig deep enough, you realize how pervasive "values" are, even in supposedly value-neutral statewide assessments.)

As in chapter 14, our analysis of the data follows a dual method, using at first the lens of a social developmentalist. We examine, for example, the types of problems in the school the children select to write about—that is, to complain about. What do they see as the causes of these problems, and what are the strategies they suggest for resolving them? We use our psychosocial framework to gauge the social awareness that the students demonstrate in the writing samples.

Second, we also consider the responses through the eyes of a literacy researcher who may be concerned about how the students will manage the literacy demands of our society, as well as the challenges of the standardized assessments within the school system. How can children learn the literacy skills that they need and that our culture values? What makes for a "persuasive" letter? How would raters guided by statewide tests (such as the MCAS) assess the students' letters? And can a deeper understanding of children's social awareness help teachers and curriculum developers strengthen the teaching of children's persuasive writing?[3]

These are tricky questions to answer. For Ms. Burgos and the other teachers, it is a challenge just as complicated as it is in research to bridge the worlds of literacy and social development in practice. Yet, as we argue throughout this last section of the book, we believe it is through the integration of literacy and social awareness that growth in both fields can develop in mutually supportive ways. We attempt to illuminate this point further through the discussion and preliminary analysis of the children's writing in this chapter. Let's begin by returning to the classroom, where Angela Burgos has just introduced the "Speak Out" exercise.

Letters to the Principal: Expressing One's Own Point of View

As she has done throughout the semester, Ms. Burgos keeps this assignment close to home. She asks her students to write their letters to the elementary school principal about a problem they see within the school community. The students respond enthusiastically. Given the content of the novel *Felita* and the discussions they have had in class so far, it is not surprising that the issues the students choose to address involve fairness, and, in many cases, what they perceive as prejudice and discrimination. Here is what some of the students have to say.[4]

> Dear Russell School,
>
> The problem in this school is that there are people in this school that are really being treated like animals and that there is to many fights in the schoolyard. (Antonio)

> Dear Principal,
>
> I want to change the lunch mother because sometimes our lunch mother doesn't let us play in the park. (Pedro)

> Dear Principal,
>
> Some people from the Russell School fight in the bathroom. (Manuel)

Dear Russell School,
I think the main problem is that the kids from the other room are always being mean with us because we are spanish. They are always pushing us around and making fun of us. (Luis)

Dear Principal,
I would like to change racism or prejudice in my school. I think the way to stop this is by putting a spanish teacher to teach voices of freedom that way they learn. (Juanita)

Dear Anthony DiCarlo,
I would like you to take some of your time to talk how Spanish people feel for that English students dont acept us like somebody of their group. I would also like people in the school to treated us the same. I think the solution is to put poster of shaking hand and maby that will change them. (Flora)

For the first time in this book, we hear the students describe their own lives, and what they say is powerful. Their letters describe a school with fighting, anger, and perceived injustice. Intergroup conflict of some kind (perhaps several kinds at once) plays a role in the lives of these students, not only during school but outside the confines of the classroom as well. And our collective experience—from our own memories to the grim lessons of history and the latest headlines—tells us that this is a serious matter.

As researchers, however, we also need to be carefully critical about what we hear and how we interpret the students' letters. For instance, we can begin by asking: To what extent has the focus on prejudice and discrimination been influenced by the students' discussion of *Felita*? Has the book's strong focus on intergroup conflict, or Ms. Burgos's influence, pushed the students toward these ideas? Or have the novel and Ms. Burgos only helped the students find the words to express feelings they have held all along? How much of a problem is racism at the Russell School, or in these children's lives generally?

Additionally, we are faced again with a challenge in interpreting their responses: How much do the children's letters reflect their ability to write in English? How much are they using social awareness in the exercise? And how can their social awareness be analyzed? We return to the psychosocial framework of understanding, strategy, and personal meaning to illuminate the students' essays. We begin by identifying the children's understanding of the kinds of social problems they perceive to exist within the Russell School.

Goal 1: To Understand Their World—What Problem Do Students See?

Dear Anthony DiCarlo,

What is happening in the school between bilingual and regular class? Is that they are prejudice. They don't like to play with us because we're Latin. What I think that the regular class should spend a day in our shoes so that they could know how it feels. If they don't like when we do the same to them they should not do it to us.

Thank you.

Sincerely, Marisol

Dear Teachers,

The problem is some teachers are racist. They do not like black people and Spanish people and that is a big problem in this school. Also I want to fix this problem and fast before it gets bigger. You know how to solve this problem is to talk with all of the teachers and say you should treted the kids the same and it doesn't matter if they are black or spanish or wite. (Rosario)

All of the essays share a common concern for fairness and justice. The students have no problem telling us their point of view and describing a problem in their school. We start by sorting the children's descriptions of the problems into four categories.

- Fighting (Antonio, Frederico, Manuel)
- Arguing with the lunch mothers (Pedro, Eduardo)
- Problems on the playground (Filomena, Evita)
- Racism and prejudice (Flora, Luis, Evita, Juanita, Marisol, Rosario)

In some cases our categories overlap—for instance, Filomena's description of a conflict between the bilingual and monolingual ("regular") classes over the use of the playground, or Pedro's letter complaining that the lunch mother will not allow the class to play in the park. But as a first grouping, these categories will do.

Reading the students' letters, we are sure of two things. First, there is fighting among students in the school—for instance, in the bathroom and over the use of the playground. Second, conflict often occurs between members of the two fifth-grade classes, one of which is bilingual; many of Ms. Burgos's students frame the problem in terms of relations between identity groups (Spanish- or English-speaking). Clearly their collective perception is that many of the conflicts they encounter at school are driven by cultural or group differences.

From our perspective, it seems that the children are using their capacities for social awareness to identify—be able to "see"—a problem. It is possible, for instance, that the fighting in the bathroom that Manuel describes is a racial incident, but he does not perceive it as such. On the other hand, Rosario is convinced that all the teachers are racist. Is this true, or is Rosario seeing race issues where they do not exist? And Pedro does not even seem to see a large social problem—he is mainly arguing that the class should use the playground at lunch or during recess.

As both researchers and practitioners, we are torn between wanting to validate children's feelings and knowing that we need to teach them to question their first assumptions—to not assume that their point of view is always correct, any more than someone else is always right. We may be uncomfortable with questioning a child's perception of an incident as involving racial or cultural discrimination. Similarly, we may be reluctant to point out that fighting in the bathroom could be caused by prejudice, especially if we suspect that the child in the case (Manuel) might be the victim.

However, while we cannot solve the cultural and social problems faced by the children in the Russell School, we nevertheless believe that it is necessary to begin to do the type of research that will shed light on the way children make sense of their social world, even if that world is far from perfect. We hope to promote their capacity to better handle, if not solve, the inevitable challenges they will face. We also wish to develop the type of teaching methods and learning environments that support this type of positive growth. In our opinion, fifth grade is not too early to begin to learn ways to resolve problems between groups of people. But to determine what growth is possible, we must start by looking at where the students are located in their awareness currently, and we must develop replicable methods of coding that capture their development over time.

We believe the letters written by Ms. Burgos's fifth-graders represent a range of levels of social awareness, similar in form to the levels we identified in earlier chapters. The nature of the problem that the students have been asked to identify—their understanding of a problem existing in their school or community—lends itself to a variation on the developmental analysis described in chapter 14.

Some of the students, for instance, seem to "locate" or identify the problems within the school solely in the behaviors and attitudes of "the other," regardless of the connection of the other to the self. Pedro, for example, wrote: "My problem is the lunch mothers . . . if like I ask them for a spoon they scream in our ears." Pedro's problem is narrowly focused on his immediate needs. Furthermore, his interpretation reflects only his own point of view: the lunch mothers are the problem. His letter does not reflect any sense that the problem might also be located in how he treats the lunch mothers—it is independent of any of his own actions or attitudes. In other words, the problem has a "they" but no "we."

A second way in which students identify a set of problems can best be described as "we versus they," or "them and us." Marisol said: "*They* don't like to play with us because *we're* Latin." Flora wrote: "English students don't accept *us* like somebody of *their* group." These students demonstrate a sense that the cause of the problem resides in differences in perspective between two groups, their own class and the other class, instead of seeing the problem as based in the inexplicable and arbitrary bad behavior of others. Nevertheless, it is still the perceptions and behaviors of the other group that are viewed as fundamentally misinformed and misguided. In other words, "It's *their* problem, not *mine.*"

The third—and to our mind most sophisticated—way of describing the problem locates it as much in the atmosphere of the institution as in one or another of the factions within the institution. Juanita wrote: "I would like to change the racism and prejudice that's in the school." Describing the issue this way reduces, even if it does not eliminate, the finger-pointing so prominent in the first two kinds of problem identification. Understandably, very few students see things this way, which is difficult for adults as well.

Race and culture are not comfortable topics to address or to consider deeply. As adults, we may avoid being honest about our own tendencies and be reluctant to face our own biases—not only the inclination to overlook racism but also the tendency to see it in every social interaction. In fifth grade the task is even more challenging: How, as children or even as adults, do we develop not only our point of view but also the capacity to think critically about it?

A Variation on the Relationship Between Social Thought and Action: How to Persuade

We can try to fit the content of these letters into the developmental frameworks we have worked hard to construct across past chapters, but doing so is by no means the end of the bridge building between social awareness and literacy. If, for instance, we step back for a minute and think about the role of a persuasive essay, it is implicit in the idea of the "Speak Out" exercise that the student is writing about a problem in order to persuade the principal to take social action, for example, either to change his mind about an issue or to be sufficiently persuaded that an issue is important enough to warrant his immediate attention. In other words, the students are expected to encourage the principal to solve a problem. In fact, students are asked to think about how the problem affects them and the people in their community, and make an argument about what they think should be done about this problem.

The creation of a good persuasive letter or essay in the world of politics and civics depends heavily on a child's understanding of the social and societal problems at stake, in combination with his or her understanding of the current view of the audience (in this exercise, the principal) toward these issues. It takes a high level of perspective coordination—the ability to coordinate viewpoints—for a student to persuade someone else to think or act differently about a topic.

We are far from the first to recognize the important role that audience plays in writing. In fact, understanding audience has been proven to be an important component of the writing process. Good writers both draft and revise writing pieces with their audience in mind, and overall it has been shown that expert writers have a better sense of their audience. However, college-level instructors know more about audience awareness; in general, research on audience awareness has not filtered down to practice or research in elementary school writing development. This may be due to a belief that children lack the social cognition capacity to consider their audience, or a general feeling that audience awareness is too complicated a task for children who are developing basic writing skills. Here a social developmental perspective might shed light on the field of literacy (see Frank 1992; Wollman-Bonilla 2001).

What seems to separate the students in our sample from one another is their degree of understanding of what the audience—in this case, the principal—will care about in his own mind. Some of the students, for instance, do not seem to have the depth of understanding to consider whether the principal automatically shares their opinion about the social problem in the school, and if not, why. Others do seem to have this awareness but do not seem to consider what evidence might influence his point of view.

Therefore, our analysis also suggests a way to look more closely at the "audience" for the persuasive letters in this exercise—the principal. Having identified the students' understanding, we now turn first to analyzing their strategies for *solving* the school problem they chose to write about, and then to considering the *persuasive quality* of their letters by studying their ability to coordinate their perspective on the problem with that of their audience.

There is a subtle difference here from what we have done previously. When we think about these letters from a literacy perspective, it strikes us that they are not necessarily convincing. As we stated earlier, we do not want to ignore Rosario's striking claim that the teachers are racist. But she offered no facts (no "data") to back up her claim. In fact, her letter was written entirely from her own perspective. Although it was about an important social topic, the letter seemed to assume the audience would automatically share her opinion. Would the principal believe all of his teachers are racist, simply because Rosario says so? This seems doubtful.

How, then, can we incorporate the concept of "audience awareness" into our coding? How can audience awareness be analyzed and assessed? Once again we return to our theory of perspective coordination. Once more we search for a "levels analysis" that might help to capture the competencies of the students as writers in the class.

Arguments, or persuasive essays, are coded as "persuasive" within a literacy framework if they contain particular elements, often referred to as "claims" and "data" (Crammond 1998). Claims are statements about the problem, and a persuasive essay or letter needs to have a strong statement about the problem to be addressed. "Some people are being treated like animals," written by Antonio, is not particularly strong because it is not very clear. The audience is left wondering what Antonio means. On the other hand, Rosario's claim that "the problem is that some teachers are racist" is very strong.

However, a strong claim by itself is not enough to be convincing. A persuasive essay needs some facts to back up the claim. Filomena offers some data. "During recess time there is a conflict . . . with the playground." This illuminates the problem specifically—there is a problem between the Spanish and English classes over the playground.

Why does this dissection of the children's essays matter? Consider the MCAS assignment for the spring of 2001.[5] Eighth-grade students were asked to do the following:

> Write a persuasive essay stating whether children under the age of 16 should be required to wear helmets while biking, scooting. . . . Remember you must argue in such a convincing manner that others will agree with you. The outcome of the state legislature's vote on helmets could be decided by your essay.

The assignment, part of their written composition assessment, was coded using a rubric that asked for "logical" language and "strong details." Yet this type of persuasive argument is not intuitive. Teachers need to understand the genre of persuasion in order to teach its elements effectively. But persuasive writing also depends on both the students' capacity to coordinate perspectives and their ability to use their literacy skills to craft a convincing essay. A social developmental lens offers a crucial insight into how students' capacity may be influenced by their understanding of relationships and others' points of view. In our opinion, it is not just logical argumentation and strong detail that make an essay persuasive. It is the writer's understanding of how the other views the logic of the world in general as well as the issue at hand in particular. This understanding, as the research in this book demonstrates, changes with the development of social awareness.

Goal 2: How to Solve the Problem: Knowing Their Audience

How does one persuade another person to act? One way is by offering a suggestion. The students in Angela Burgos's class were asked to suggest ways to solve the social problem in the school they had identified. Their suggestions for the principal are connected to both their understanding of the social problem itself (their point of view) and how well they are able to coordinate it with the point of view or role of the principal (the audience's perspective).

As expected from children of this age, many of the students want a higher authority to solve the problem for them. For example, they asked the principal to put a monitor in the bathroom or on the playground and to ensure that the same standards of fairness apply to all people. Antonio, for instance, recommended that "the people who [were] not treated right should not handle this themselves but to tell the teacher or the principal about it."

The strategies suggested by these students are reasonable in a developmental sense and feasible for a principal to solve, even if a specific strategy, such as bathroom monitors, is not the way the principal will go. Schools are places where rules and order are important, and most adults would agree that it is the principal's responsibility to ensure that students are treated fairly and not physically hurt on school property.

However, when the problems become more abstract and less clearcut, the solutions are not so easy. In follow-up to her belief that all teachers are racist, Rosario suggested that an authority figure (she does not say who, but we assume she means the principal) "talk with all the teachers and say you should [treat] the kids the same." Sometimes there is a mismatch between the children's understanding of the problem and the strategy they use to solve it. Evita's strong letter, for instance, argues that the use of the playground should be reevaluated: "It should be made clear to all the students as to who, and when the playground should be [used]." But her letter ends with an action plan that reveals the possible Achilles' heel of this strategy: "I appreciate if you would take the time to talk with us whenever it is convenient for you."

What happens if the audience to whom Rosario and Evita have appealed—in this case, the principal—dismisses Rosario's complaint as unwarranted or does not have the time or interest in enforcing Evita's idea of fairness on the playground? Similarly, Marisol's statement—"I think the regular class should spend a day in our shoes so that they could know how [prejudice] feels"—is not really a workable strategy either.

Flora took up the same theme, albeit as part of an appeal to the principal. "Put poster of shaking hand and maby that will change them." But like Luis's statement ("I think you should help convince *them* to be friends with us so that we can get along"), Flora's solution is idealistic. Unfortunately, both students suggested simple solutions that would most likely have little effect as single actions. Posters are not going to solve deep-seated social problems. Racism and prejudice cannot be swept away so easily. But our skeptical, adult-oriented critique aside, the comments and suggestions of these students reveal why communication is an important part of the difficult task of resolving conflicts and creating harmony between groups of people who see themselves as different from each other.

So, for example, when writing to the principal, some of the students may have viewed him as having the absolute power to control the hearts and minds of all the citizens of the school, from the teachers on down: "You should talk with all the teachers . . . and say you should treat the kids the same." Others may have realized that he does not have all that much power, and so they wrote, "You should help convince them to be friends with us." In other words, it takes a sophisticated awareness of social relations and conception of the other (that is, of character), intersecting with a strong logic of argumentation, to generate a first-class persuasive letter. In a letter or essay such as the "Speak Out" activity assigned by Ms. Burgos, the development of both sides of the literacy–social-awareness dialectic must be understood, both in theory and in practice.

Understanding the Need to Coordinate and Learning How

One of the acknowledged challenges of written communication is that, unlike oral communication, the audience is not immediately present to respond to the writer (Kantor and Rubin 1981). Students need to learn how to imagine their audience and write with it in mind, but as we have seen, even face-to-face communication is extraordinarily difficult.

In chapter 12, we described how Marisol and Rosario stood in front of the class and role-played Felita and her best friend Gigi as they tried to resolve a conflict over the school play. Marisol and Rosario had tried to "to talk it over" but basically ended up with each telling the other what she had done wrong. Ms. Burgos pushed them to try it again in front of the class. At first neither girl received the other's communication. Eventually, however, they learned to listen to each other and to see the problem in a new way.

In this chapter, we have attempted to demonstrate a way of coding literacy exercises from a social developmental perspective. Our methods are evolving, but we hope that they demonstrate an important point—that literacy practices and pedagogical exercises need to be embedded in real attempts to communicate and get along with others. Understanding one's own point of view and others' points of view is a social skill. But coordinating these perspectives is mediated by language and literacy in the real-life challenges of the world of social emotions. It is through communication, both oral and written, that one learns about "the other." And it is the desire to communicate that may drive our need to master the literacy and language skills that make it happen.

The VLF exercises were designed to improve students' social awareness. We believe practice role-playing, brainstorming, and working in partners and with peers may also improve language and literacy skills. We are also convinced that it takes strong teaching to accomplish these dual goals. We return to Angela Burgos's classroom for a final example.

Week 5, Day 3: The Students Discuss What They Have Written

Perhaps without realizing it, Ms. Burgos lays the groundwork for tackling the important questions we have raised about persuasive writing. She herself is not necessarily convinced about the problems the students have brought up. For instance, she does not automatically assume that the other teachers are racist, as Rosario suggested, but she does not shy away from having tough conversations around the topic. Instead, she asks her students to discuss their letters, and as can be seen in the following classroom conversation, she helps them to think critically about their own feelings, reactions, and proposals. In this exercise, knowingly or not, she demonstrates the power of teaching social skills and literacy simultaneously. By expanding the students' understanding of the problems they see in the school, she equips them with a skill that may help them write a more persuasive letter next time.

"Everyone take out your letters," Ms. Burgos begins. "Who can identify the problems in the school that you came up with yesterday?"

As the students volunteer their restatements of the issues they discussed the day before, Ms. Burgos writes the entries on the board. Ultimately there are four.

- Fighting
- Conduct (behavior in the cafeteria)
- Respect for teachers and students
- Relationship between bilingual and monolingual students

Throughout the discussion, Ms. Burgos does not blindly accept the students' points of view, especially the idea that the teachers (or the "lunch mothers") are prejudiced. Furthermore, when she writes on the board "respect for teachers and students," she is in fact carefully rephrasing Rosario's "we-they" statement—"teachers are racist"—as a problem located not in "we" or "they" alone but within the school atmosphere. It implies a search for respect that involves all parties, indirectly pointing out that respect is a two-way street—if we expect to receive it, we must be willing to grant it to others. The class seems to accept this idea.

When it comes to interactions with their non-Hispanic peers, however, Ms. Burgos's students stick to their we-they guns. "They don't respect us," Flora says. "They don't feel like we feel inside. They don't realize that they make us feel bad," Juanita adds. "They hurt people. They call Spanish people names."

Ms. Burgos pushes the class to think deeply about this problem and their reactions to it. "When that happens, do you tell your own teacher or the teacher in charge?" she asks at one point. She tries to enlarge their perspective by asking them to consider what might motivate hurtful behavior, even whether it is intended to be hurtful. "I think what Juanita is saying—are they doing it intentionally? Sometimes it's fear." Fear is often rooted in ignorance, she explains, and she invites her class to consider the possibility that, for example, the monolingual students may feel that the Spanish-speakers are using their language to keep secrets and talk about them behind their backs.

At one point Flora has a hard time explaining what she thinks is going on between the two fifth-grade classes. Ms. Burgos lets her continue for a while, then steps in to frame the issue once more as a "problem in the relationship within the school as community." Again, she does not assume that prejudice is the issue, nor does she make any assumptions about the intentions of the students from the other class. This is important. While conflicts between the two fifth grades do exist—they fight, and the Latino students feel that the lunch and playground monitors favor the other class—Ms. Burgos wants her students to think about each incident separately and in a more complex and critical way.

Ms. Burgos's teaching style is to promote her students' interaction in solving problems, and although she sometimes states her viewpoint energetically, she does not force it on them. After the general discussion, she has them break into small groups to consider the solutions they have written about in their letters. This further discussion reinforces the lesson that this is an exercise not only in literacy but in social action.

During the exercise Ms. Burgos walks around the room, observing, listening, and sometimes making a comment or asking a question. At the beginning she sits down at the table with Juanita, Anita, and Flora. Juanita starts the discussion by saying that a "Spanish teacher" should do the VLF curriculum with all the kids in the school so that they will understand how the Hispanic kids feel. Flora thinks this is a good idea.

Anita, though, is concerned that the younger kids are learning bad habits from the older children. In Spanish, with Flora and Juanita translating into English for her,[6] Anita proposes moving the younger kids to a different school so that they will have no direct contact with the older students. Ms. Burgos questions whether this would solve the problem or simply circumvent it. After a little thought and discussion, the girls agree that sheltering the younger children from bad influences will not teach them anything and that it might be better to address the problem with the older kids. By working with the children closely and carefully, Ms. Burgos is able to bring Anita to the point where she realizes the flaw in what is essentially a strategy of avoidance.

When the children reassemble to end the lesson with another whole-class discussion, they begin with more complaints. Antonio tells everyone: "The other class takes things from us—like pencils." Juanita adds that a kid stole something from her and the teacher paid no attention. Ms. Burgos listens for a while and then brings the discussion back to the topic of solutions. "We're not able to solve these things in one day," she says, "like putting a Band-Aid on a cut. But what are some solutions—how can we make it better? Empowering you to make it better—what do you recommend?"

Flora says that she wants all the kids to treat each other the same. Juanita calls for action: "Maybe we can have a party—put up posters." Ms. Burgos nods. "Create a movement in the school. Go ahead—plan it!" She goes on to say that it does not have to be done by only the Hispanic kids. Planning something with the other fifth-grade class, she suggests, might go a long way toward breaking down some of the barriers and bad feelings.

"How do you gain trust?" she asks. "Something to think about!"

Personal Meaning and Real-World Connections

Good classroom instruction helps children make connections between the subject matter they are studying and the real world. We believe that effective schooling in conflict resolution and the ethics of relationships can lead to the kind of interpersonal-intergroup understanding that can be applied to real-life situations. We have discussed the necessity of using a child-centered pedagogical approach; we need to consider the child's level of social awareness and emotional maturity in order to understand how he or she deals with important positive social issues like trust and mutuality, and difficult ones like prejudice and discrimination. And we have made the point that this kind of curriculum requires that the teacher play a strong role.

We also think it is important to consider the personal meaning that children bring to events and relationships and to look at their actions through the lenses of social context, culture, and biographical history. For us, it is not enough merely to measure levels of skill or performance, be it in math or literacy or social competence. If we want to promote learning in any arena, we need to understand meaning and motivation so that we can design and refine effective curricula and teaching methods and practices.

By our standards, it is not enough for students simply to read the novel *Felita* and be able to discuss its plot and analyze its characters. We want them to be able to go a step further. In the same way that they bring lessons learned from their own personal lives into the classroom, we hope that the process can work in reverse—that they can use what they have learned from the book, from each other, and from their teachers in the wider world. For this to happen, the content of what is being taught must be meaningful to students, and teaching methods must engage them at a level that goes beyond memorization or a desire to do well on a test. It needs to move to a level where point of view is paramount.

The concept of point of view, which has long been central to the study and teaching of literary genres from essays and autobiography to fiction and poetry, encompasses the awareness that each of us evaluates and responds to a situation according in part to our cultural and personal experiences, both past and present. What we, as social developmentalists, mean by the constructs "perspective taking" and "social perspective coordination" is closely related to what literacy theorists mean by point of view—but the terms are not synonymous. The former refers to an activity or operation, and the latter to an idea or a stance.

It is not necessary, pedagogically speaking, to wait for this operative ability to develop before we can expect to teach students to write persuasive essays. Just the opposite. We can strengthen the connection between perspective coordination and point of view by inviting children to engage in activities that require them to move from one point of view to another. Thinking, discussion, and writing about fictional characters and situations involve a reciprocal transformation of both stance and activity. These traditional elements of the teaching of literacy enhance the development of perspective coordination as a well-practiced operation, just as the evolution of this operative ability contributes to the acquisition of the language and skills that constitute literacy.

This chapter was coauthored by Amy J. Dray and Robert L. Selman.

Chapter 16

Thinking Like a Developmentalist: Understanding Social Awareness Through Its Promotion and Assessment

Many things we need, can wait.
The child cannot.
Now is the time his bones are being formed,
His blood is being made,
His mind is being developed.
To him we cannot say tomorrow.
His name is today.
—Gabriela Mistral

THROUGHOUT this book I have reported the collaborative work of our group. Now I want to share with you what I have come to believe through this work about practices and policies associated with the social and ethical development of children in schools. My belief centers on the following questions: What should children learn about the ethics of social relations in schools? How can we, as adults, help them figure out how to learn it? And how are we to teach it?

When I describe the work reported here either to colleagues or to friends, they often react to our use of books like *Felita* in the language arts curriculum with remarks such as, "Why do you have to deal with that kind of stuff in schools? We never had those kinds of conversations when we went to school. Is that what school is supposed to be about?" Speaking personally, I too was never introduced to this kind of material in school, and the schools I went to certainly had many of the same problems as the Boston schools in which we studied.

Still, I think the answer is, yes, it is what schools are supposed to be about. As adults, even if our circumstances have been relatively comfortable, most of us can look back and see ways in which we could have managed certain social situations or relationships differently. We may wish that we had had the social competence to deal better with tough situations, to say what we felt, to not feel so frightened, or angry, that we could hardly think, let alone speak or act. Certainly, the vicissitudes of life—being treated unfairly, being left out or let down, having to compete for love and respect—are virtually universal. They are an inevitable part of growing up social, and often we learn more about the management of our social relations from our past mistakes than from our early successes. This is one reason for finding a place for the inclusion of this discipline and the promotion of these skills in the school.

But there is another. A large percentage of children, because of circumstances they can do little or nothing about—their ethnicity, race, social class, or family situation—face additional challenges trying to get along. For these children, it is even harder to understand, deal with, and make meaning of social conflicts. This is because the source of the conflict is not simply personal, or social, but societal. And given that we all live in a globally multicultural world—where intergroup conflict sometimes seems more common than cooperation between people of different backgrounds and cultures—if we do not teach this material when children are young, then when will we? And if children are not taught to deal with these issues in schools, then where will they learn?

For these reasons, I believe that programs designed to teach social awareness and the interpersonal skills that go with it should be part of the fundamental education of all of our children in the elementary grades. Furthermore, these programs need to be fully integrated into the curriculum, not inserted into the school day here and there as add-ons. Otherwise, they do not have a chance.

These programs should include consideration of issues of fairness and social justice and the teaching of conflict resolution skills and cooperative strategies. That is what VLF has tried to do.[1] There are, however, serious roadblocks to the implementation of this recommendation. Some are obvious, for example, concerns about the need to find enough time, effort, and resources for teaching fundamental academic skills, let alone social ones. But other barriers are subtle, less obvious, and more philosophical.

Because it has been so central to the work we have described in this book, I first consider these barriers through an example drawn from classroom practice, once again drawing upon Sarah Shmitt's field notes, which describe the participation of the teacher and her aide in the attempt to promote social awareness. I then turn my attention to analysis of the philosophical barriers from the perspective of developmental theory.

Practice and the Promotion of Social Awareness: The Challenge to Teachers

LEER ES PODER. Reading is power. These words hang from Ms. Hernandez's classroom door at the Russell School. Inside the room there are equally powerful messages on the walls, including a large sign over the chalkboard quoting the nineteenth-century Cuban independence leader José Marti: LOS NINOS SON LA ESPERANZA DEL MUNDO. The children are the hope of the world. Another large sign at the front of the classroom exhorts students to TREAT OTHERS AS YOU WANT OTHERS TO TREAT YOU.

Ms. Hernandez and her paraprofessional, Ms. Guerrero, have worked together for nearly thirteen years at the Russell School in Allston-Brighton. Ms. Hernandez, a native New Yorker, is an energetic, strict, and caring second-grade teacher who expects her students to excel. As a lead teacher, she serves on the student support services team at the Russell, and she is also the ELA (English Language Arts) standards coordinator for the entire school. Ms. Guerrero, originally from Ecuador, is a creative and dedicated assistant who often takes on major responsibilities for teaching, contacting parents, and attending school and districtwide meetings on behalf of bilingual students. Both are respected and well liked by the students, as well as by the students' parents, who often visit the classroom.

During VLF time, which is always after lunch, half of the students from the monolingual second-grade class taught by Ms. Chin file into Ms. Hernandez's classroom and half of Ms. Hernandez's students go next door to Ms. Chin's. Each student is paired with a child from the other classroom for all VLF activities. This arrangement was deliberately designed to alleviate the tensions between the two classes that both second-grade teachers had noticed on the playground: kids calling each other names, getting into fights, making fun of each other's differences. After using VLF intensively for two years, Ms. Hernandez, Ms. Chin, and Ms. Guerrero say with confidence that using VLF and mixing up the students from the two classrooms has significantly reduced the number and intensity of fights on the playground and given rise to several friendships between Ms. Chin's and Ms. Hernandez's students.

Consider the following field notes during two social awareness lessons in Ms. Hernandez's room.

Observation: Second Grade, Ms. Hernandez's Class, April 9: Ms. Hernandez is out of the classroom today, so Ms. Guerrero is in charge. When I come in, she is running a reading group with students who have difficulties with reading, and the rest of the children are working quietly and independently. Ms. Guerrero comes over to me and explains that they will be doing VLF since I had made a special trip to see it, even though Ms. Hernandez has been called away. She then notifies Ms. Chin's class of the plans to continue with the originally planned VLF activity.

As students from Ms. Chin's class file into Ms. Hernandez's room, Ms. Hernandez's students immediately say, "It's VLF time!" and the designated group leaves for Ms. Chin's room. One African American girl from Ms. Chin's class, Leanora, sits next to Yesenia [a troubled Guatemalan girl who has few friends] for the VLF activities. Yesenia holds Leanora's hand and turns to look at me. "This is my friend," she says to me, smiling.

Ms. Guerrero begins the lesson on *Stellaluna* [Cannon 1993][2] by talking about how people are sometimes different and yet similar at the same time. She asks the students, "How are Ms. Hernandez and I the same? How are we different?" Some of their responses are: "You have long hair, Ms. Hernandez has short hair"; "You wear lots of rings, Ms. Hernandez doesn't"; "Ms. Hernandez is short and she's black, and you're taller and you're not black"; "Ms. Hernandez wears glasses and you don't." There is a male student teacher in the room today . . . and the students begin to compare him with Ms. Guerrero as well: "He can't be a substitute for you because he's a man," says one student. "You wear perfume and he doesn't," says another.

Ms. Guerrero then asks the students to think about a friend who they either have a lot in common with or from whom they are very different. She instructs the students to close their eyes and think for a few minutes about this, and then, she says, she will tell them a story about a friend of hers. For two or three minutes the class sits quietly, some with eyes closed, others looking around the room at nothing in particular. Then, quietly, Ms. Guerrero begins to tell her story to the class:

"When I was younger, almost your age, I had a friend that I saw all the time. We did everything together. We would play house and pretend to be able to cook. We used to play hide-and-seek, ride bicycles together—but not roller-skate, because she would push me." As Ms. Guerrero tells about her friendship, students raise their hands with their own friendship stories, many of which are about their dogs or cats. Celia, one of Ms. Hernandez's students, tells a story about her friend Katie, who wears the same earrings she does. Steven tells about his friend Brian. He describes how they always play cops and robbers, Twister, hockey, and Star Wars; moreover, he wants to stay at his friend's house and live there forever. He wants Brian to be his brother.

What is the point of Ms. Guerrero's question about individual differences among people? What is she trying to accomplish with her story about her own friendship? Is this conversation, the questions she asks, the responses she gives to the students, at an "appropriate" developmental level for children at this grade level? In *Stellaluna*, it seems so easy: if bats and birds can get along, why can't English- and Spanish-speaking kids? Is this all we wish the students to consider from the story of *Stellaluna*? Or should we push them to understand the reasons why it is so hard sometimes to get along with kids from other backgrounds?

These children are second-graders. We need to have a better sense of what kind of social awareness we can expect of them, both developmentally and culturally, and we should not leave it up to each individual teacher to judge what he or she believes are socially appropriate responses for eight-, nine-, or ten-year-olds. Pursuing practice, theory, and research simultaneously, we can help to decide whether to recommend that Ms. Guerrero push her students harder, toward a deeper understanding of what constitutes significant differences among bats and birds or boys and girls, or wait a few years until a time when they are more likely to understand what it means to get along with birds who are not of the same feather.

The systematic analysis of the kinds of conversations we hear in classrooms, through practice-based research, can provide some answers to what are actually deeply theoretical questions. But research that appears only in a peer-reviewed article in a scientific journal, in the blind hope that somewhere down the line it may be picked up by a practitioner or two, is unlikely to have much impact. Instead, research attitudes and activities need to be instilled in the heart of practice, locally and regularly. Otherwise, the responsibility for social growth sits too much on the shoulders of individual teachers, who are neither trained in the discipline of social development nor provided with solid guidelines for its assessment. For instance, when Ms. Hernandez picks up the baton the next day, the issues discussed seem more charged, and more complex. Here, again, are Sarah's field notes:

Observation: April 10: Ms. Hernandez announces that it's time for VLF. The students from Ms. Chin's class come into the room and immediately sit next to their partners. They begin to work on their half-completed partner worksheets from *Stellaluna.* Francisco does not under-

> stand the instructions for the worksheet. Ms. Hernandez goes over to William and Francisco to assist them. She asks about their differences. Francisco says, "He is black, I am white." "You are white?" the teacher asks him. "Are you sure about that?" There is a long silence. Francisco looks very confused. "You are not white, Francisco. You are Hispanic." Francisco remains silent.

What does Ms. Hernandez hope to accomplish by challenging Francisco's assertion that he is white? Is it necessary or possible for a second-grader to make a differentiation between ethnic background and skin pigmentation? What might happen if Francisco goes home and tells his parents that his teacher told him he is not white when all along that is what they have been telling him? Is this an opportunity for learning, or is it an event that could lead to misunderstanding between student and teacher, misgivings between teachers and parents, confusion between students and their parents? Is this good practice, good pedagogical method? It strikes me that these are tough questions without easy answers.

Research into the connection between developmental aspects of children's understanding and their cultural identity can provide some tentative answers, some indications of the value of the approach these two teachers are taking, both in this particular instance and in general terms (see, for example, Bigler and Liben 1993; Hirschfeld 1995, 1996). But certainly not in all instances. Because, after all, some of these questions are concerns about the values and beliefs of adults, both parents and professionals, not simply questions about the developmental level of children's social awareness.

What Do Teachers Value?

We found it interesting, but not surprising, that in our study sample it was primarily the bilingual teachers and students who showed the most interest in VLF's multicultural reading program.[3] Obviously, the fact that VLF has made an effort to find quality children's literature that depicts not only the European American and African American experiences but also the lives of people from the Dominican Republic, Puerto Rico, Vietnam, and Japan made the curriculum particularly valuable for those teachers who are committed to engaging their students in more than a tourist's understanding of other cultures. However, we realized that it is often the bilingual teachers—whatever language they are proficient in besides English, and whether they teach in Boston or elsewhere—who must be able to connect with the lives of children who are trying to find a firm footing in a new culture. I believe that programs such as VLF can serve as a doorway for these children into the safe atmosphere of a well-run classroom in which they can begin to share their stories and enrich the lives of their classmates while learning to read and write in English.

Even more interestingly, VLF's appeal to the bilingual teachers in our study seemed to go beyond the specifics of its reading list. The English-Spanish bilingual teachers we met in the Boston public school system had either immigrated from somewhere other than the mainland United States or grown up in the barrios of New York and Los Angeles, where they learned many hard lessons about being "different" in the United States. Some of these teachers were motivated to use VLF to help prepare their students for life in this country as they themselves wished they had been prepared. To these teachers, the VLF approach was personally meaningful.

For instance, Angela Burgos recognized the need for her fifth-grade students to examine issues of discrimination and racism, to assess critically the nature and quality of their education, and to feel confident enough to take on the challenges of succeeding in the dominant culture while maintaining their own set of values and cultural practices. In fact, she went far beyond the questions and activities suggested in the VLF teacher's guides. She augmented VLF's lessons with her own ideas—for example, her class wrote a play about an issue relevant to their lives and performed it for the entire school in order to encourage dialogue among the whole student body. Ms. Burgos encouraged her students to write critical autobiographies and staged class "talk shows" during which the "host" asked his or her "guests" questions about the difficult issues raised by the books they were studying.

Ms. Burgos motivated her students to think about their own bilingualism, first in journal activities in relation to the novel *Felita,* next in essays that were presented to the principal, and finally in letters to the state board of education. This process could have taken a bad turn at any point—the discussion of racism in the school could easily have resulted in destructive finger-pointing rather than a constructive analysis of power differentials. But under Ms. Burgos's direction, it did not. Instead, Ms. Burgos pushed her students to look closely at their own perceptions of racism and how they might even perpetuate it themselves.

Teachers' Integration of Professional, Political, and Personal Goals

Although personal commitment on the part of teachers is a key component of successful implementation of approaches that integrate social and ethical awareness into the literacy program, I do not therefore conclude that bilingual teachers or teachers from immigrant backgrounds are better equipped to teach this approach because their personal and political struggles have somehow automatically conferred on them a measure of sensitivity and awareness to the program's themes that other teachers lack. For instance, not all of the bilingual teachers we observed could be considered effective or competent by our standards. Furthermore, we witnessed teachers, such as Karen Lewis, whose personal histories did not include experiences of discrimination or "difference" but who did an outstanding job with the curriculum.

However, the basic questions of individual outlook and motivation remain: What determines whether a teacher's view of the profession includes fostering interpersonal development and social awareness as fundamental components of his or her students' growth? What allows teachers to be open to change and innovation in this domain? How do we find out? Part III of this book, the work started in Iceland and imported to Boston, reflects our approach, the research, and, ultimately, the evolving theory that allows us to study a question that, once again, is as much a question of value as a question of fact or of conceptual analysis.

Integrating our values and our theory, we conclude that competent, motivated, and self-aware teachers like Ms. Lewis, Ms. Hernandez, and Ms. Burgos found in VLF the academic, intellectual, and ethical challenges they were hungry for. These teachers often went beyond what the curriculum guides suggested. They connected the VLF units to other subject matter, especially social studies and art, in meaningful ways; they often had students create a final, public product, such as a mural or a play, that required all of them to work together cooperatively toward a common objective; and they worked carefully and patiently with students individually, devoting many hours to making sure each student understood the task, was included, and did the work.

On the other hand, teachers like Ms. McDougan seemed too overwhelmed by all the other changes and demands they faced to effectively put VLF into practice. Others, like Ms. Kelly and Ms. Gibbs, found VLF irrelevant or off-putting, maybe even vaguely threatening. Lacking a personal or professional connection to the program—that is, a basic commitment to teaching interpersonal skills, a personal belief in the need to teach students to think critically, or a belief in the value of a multicultural curriculum—this group of teachers seemed unable to grasp the purpose of VLF exercises even after it had been explained to them. Moreover, they were often unwilling or unable to get their students to work effectively as partners. Why?

It is true that some teachers occasionally failed to read the guides carefully or listen to the guidelines of the researchers. The work they turned in was often improperly done, done at the wrong time, or not done at all. When presenting VLF material to the class, sometimes these teachers established a negative environment in which students did not feel safe enough to share their stories, or they conveyed a distorted picture of the context of the lesson. For instance, to prepare her class for the book *A Day's Work,* Ms. Kelly told her students that immigrants to the United States had taken jobs away from people in her own family, who were implicitly Americans. In the end, what we saw during the Carnegie study challenged the belief that any teacher could become a "good" VLF teacher after some basic instruction in the program's aims and methods.

Our classroom observations suggested that, given the complexity and sophistication of the VLF program, we had to entertain the possibility that, although when in good hands it is a powerful and positive tool, in the hands of teachers who do not understand it well, do not have the skills to implement it, or are not in sympathy with its pedagogical methods and philosophy, it may be ineffective, perhaps even harmful. Teachers who are ill prepared to deal with matters of discrimination, difference, and cultural bias may find that the VLF approach takes them into stormy and uncharted territory where they are likely to stumble or be unable to prevent their students from being bruised.

In other words, it is difficult to teach social awareness in schools for many reasons. First, the content or discipline is challenging and does not fit into most educators' notions of what constitutes the core disciplines of instruction in schools. Second, it requires teachers to have sophisticated interpersonal skills, including both communication and listening abilities. And third, the teacher must be motivated and find the enterprise personally meaningful.

Beyond the challenges posed by these difficulties embedded in the art and science of teaching social awareness, I think there is another factor, a more subtle but nevertheless powerful reason, that makes this such a challenging issue in education, an already challenged profession.

Theory and Practice: The Debate Within the Character Education Movement

Beyond the depth of understanding, the skills, and the commitment necessary to teach social awareness, a subtle but nevertheless major obstacle to its acceptance in schools actually is philosophical and theoretical. This resistance is based on fundamental differences in the way we think about the relationship between language and thought, and between thought and action in the social and ethical domain. These differences speak directly to some of the heated arguments that are taking place *within* the "character education" movement, which has taken on the mantle of professional development in this field (see Molnar 1997).

The conservative branch of the movement, for instance, thinks that the primary goal of character education is to raise children with a particular set of values and virtues, based on the ethos of the society within which the children live. The best method for achieving this goal, they believe, is to teach firm societal rules that can be internalized, provide positive role models who exemplify these societal values, use the power of extrinsic rewards and punishments to shape behavior toward those values, and inculcate "top down" the core traditions, norms, and beliefs of the society. (For an interesting analysis of this issue from the conservative perspective, see Hunter 2000.) "Shape behavior and thought will follow" might not be an unfair characterization of this frame of mind.

In other words, the conservative side of the character education movement seems to focus on the relation of thought and action, and to prioritize culturally defined norms of behavior over social and self-awareness. To this way of thinking, action is the measurable standard and awareness by itself is an unreliable predictor of conduct, especially when people are under duress or in conflict over what is the right thing to do.

The liberal branch of the character education movement probably focuses less on the connection of thought and action and more on the connection of thought to language, or to "voice" (see Kohn, 1998a). To them, action without reflection and discussion holds the potentially greater danger. It is very important to the liberal branch to recognize and acknowledge that cultural experiences influence the construction of awareness, and hence can lead to different actions. On this side of the debate, there is a belief that each of us can have a different awareness, a different understanding of social situations. Therefore, the pedagogical method of choice might best be characterized as "bottom up," learning to voice one's concerns clearly; the preference is for open discussion in which wisdom is constructed anew by individuals as they come to know these differing points of view, rather than having a point of view passed down to them without choice.

To the extent that each side is wary of the other, the conservative side equates the liberal emphasis on reflection with the anathema (to them) of ethical relativity, and the liberal branch equates the conservative emphasis on loyalty and patriotism with the anathema (to them) of absolutism and blind obedience.

As this debate smolders,[4] today's schools face extraordinary challenges. They are becoming increasingly accountable in the search for higher academic standards. At the same time they must struggle with issues of the management of social behavior in the classroom and school. The oppositional nature of the debate within the character education movement has done many schools a disservice by forcing them to choose approaches as if the menu is "either-or"—either awareness or behavior, either role models or reflection, either "love" of country or "freedom" to voice choices. A "which-when" approach would be a pedagogically sounder strategy. Both are important and each needs the other as a counterbalance.

Ambivalence Over What Should Be Assessed: The Deep Resistances to the Promotion of Social Awareness

Connected to these concerns are reasons for the resistance to a developmental approach such as ours that integrates the promotion of children's awareness of social and societal issues through the language arts curriculum, and aims for the improvement of social as well as academic literacy. To a large extent the resistance lies within what all people—professionals, parents, and partisans—fundamentally and implicitly believe is the relationship among language, social awareness, and social behavior, and these beliefs can cause a deep-seated distrust of the work we have described here, even among sympathizers and advocates. This resistance does not show up in the research, but it starkly shows itself when the discussion turns to education, assessment, and evaluation.

To explain what I mean, let's review the implications of our analyses of the findings in chapters 14 and 15. In those chapters, the assessment of fundamental "literacy practices," which asked the students to do reading-comprehension and persuasive-writing assignments, also served as a method to assess their social awareness. Specifically, in chapter 14, Amy Dray and I reported some pilot work on what might be called the researcher's version of an "authentic assessment."[5] We designed a pilot study to embed a method to assess social and ethical awareness directly into the fabric of a homework assignment to understand how students in one fifth-grade class responded to the following reading-comprehension question:

> What did Felita mean when she said, "I never said nothing to those girls, so they thought they were right"?

As a question about a character in a novel, it asks readers to put themselves in Felita's shoes and think about her perspective toward both herself and the other girls. Driven by a theory that emphasizes the importance of promoting social perspective coordination, we treated the question as one about social awareness and constructed a simple developmental rubric that, by now, should be familiar to the reader: first-person, second-person, and third-person coordination of perspectives for the students' written responses that focused on levels of social awareness.

In chapter 15, we used a similar strategy to design a measure of social persuasion and a rubric for its assessment with the same theoretical origins to classify the letters written by the Spanish-speaking students to their principal to protest their treatment by the English-speaking kids. Specifically, we were looking to see whether we could fathom the degree to which students took the principal's point of view into account as they lobbied for him to address their own concerns. There we showed that the sophistication of their argumentation was related to the depth of their understanding of their social concerns and their ability to coordinate perspectives.

Here is the paradox. On the practice side, I suspect that many educators would advocate that their students be encouraged to better understand the views of others, even the views and motivations of others who antagonize them. Similarly, very few would deny the importance of being self-reflective, even if what one reflects upon is painful as it was for Felita when she wondered why she did not defend herself. Certainly they would tend to advocate that Felita, and their own students, strive to achieve the kind of social and self-awareness classified at the higher levels in this simple rubric. Furthermore, I believe that very few researchers would disagree on where students' responses would fall in these classification systems.

However, I suspect that many practitioners would object to the use of this approach as the sole basis for assessment of the social awareness of any particular student. They would object, I believe, on one or both of two grounds. First, some would be concerned about the accuracy of the assessment in the "diagnosis" of individual students. In particular, they would be concerned that it might *underestimate* the capacity of students to voice their social awareness. I call this the "liberal's concern." Second, even if they are so able, some would be concerned that the assessment does not tell us how students who express an awareness at each level will *act* in their own lives when faced with similar situations. Here, the concern is that the approach *overestimates* how students will behave. I call this the "conservative's concern." Both these concerns have merit, and I need to clarify my point of view on each. But they should not be confused in our own minds.

With respect to the liberal's concern, the reluctance to use the rubric as the basis of an assessment to diagnose the social or ethical competence of individual students, I want to point out that in chapters 14 and 15, our goal was not to assess the competencies of any particular individual reader or writer. It is always dangerous in any kind of assessment to use only one instrument to determine the competencies and skills of a particular child. However, we must start somewhere, and we start from a point where people at least can agree some forms of awareness are more adequate, deeper, and more complete than others.

With respect to the conservative concern, when I have shown educators the developmental rubric for coding the students' interpretation of what *Felita* means, they often respond with "That's interesting," or, "Sure, that makes sense." However, as soon as I recommend the application of this analysis in the large-scale assessments of "ethical awareness" standards, for example, as part of standardized testing in the same spirit as the need for assessment in language arts or social studies, they say, "Whoa, you can't do that." Their concern is not so much the liberal concern with the accuracy of an assessment of an individual's best social awareness. Their concern is whether any assessment of awareness can tell us what children will actually do in their own lives. It is this connection of awareness to action that is the most slippery, and where the conservatives have strong reservations. To them I say the road to mature ethical action must eventually go through the ability to express one's thoughts.

The conservative branch looks at developmental qualities—the sequence of levels that are the emphasis of our approach, and especially the emphasis on giving credit to the student who develops the capacity to express both sides of a debate and sees it as too wishy-washy and relativistic. These critics insist that in our emphasis on considering all points of view, we do not emphasize enough the very absolutism of virtues and values, good and evil, that the liberal critics abhor and think is emphasized too much. The liberals, on the other hand, may think a developmental approach favors a hierarchy, but they mistake higher levels of awareness for a form of absolutism, or worse, universalism, they find distasteful, and believe is favored by the conservatives. We need to get out of the crossfire. Each of these views is incorrect. A way to help to figure out what our analysis actually suggests is to ask: How does a developmentalist really think about these matters?

What It Means to Think Like a "Developmentalist"

How then can thinking like a developmentalist help integrate assessments and educational approaches such as ours into the heart of the language and literacy curriculum, as well as get the opposing Character Education parties to vote together on a strategy to do so?

First, we must be clear that thinking like a developmentalist does not simply mean knowing what a typical student at a particular age, for example in elementary, middle, or high school, is like. For instance, in the previous two chapters, we reported the comparative analysis of individual children, of course, but in reality we were trying to analyze the range of responses the whole class provided to a difficult social question—that is the actual performance of a limited sample of fifth-grade students (maybe not representative of fifth-graders in general). The analysis examined the breadth of the themes of the responses (for example, "Felita wanted those kids to like her," or, "Felita doesn't want those kids to think she's chicken"). It also studied the level of social awareness that the reader (whether a fifth-grader, or third-grader, or seventh-grader) took into account—Felita's, the other girls', "society's"—in response to the prompt.

There we claimed that Juanita's interpretation—that Felita was upset because she felt her running away from those girls sent a message to her tormenters that their actions were justified—was more adequate (and accurate) than the interpretations of the other students in the class. However, we need to reemphasize that the interpretations of the other students are not necessarily wrong. It is quite likely that Felita actually both *did* want to make friends and, at the same time, *did not* want to be thought of as a coward, a chicken. That is exactly what makes Juanita's interpretation more sophisticated, more socially aware than the other students' responses. Juanita suggests Felita's comment to her grandmother actually integrates the opposing tension between confronting and maintaining social connection with the other kids. By talking with her grandmother she realizes how hard it is to both stand up for herself and keep the other girls' friendship, but at least she is newly aware of a way to act that may keep their respect. And perhaps even more important, her own.

Second, a developmental approach does not simply mean coding responses in terms of levels, as if levels were people or fixed traits. *It means seeing (or listening for) social awareness as change across periods of time and examining that change, be it forward or backward, through a devel-*

opmental framework. Psychologically speaking, one can think like a developmentalist about change in awareness over any amount of time, not just months or years. Developmental analyses can be applied to the growth of social and ethical awareness that spanned the six minutes in which Marisol and Rosario, role-playing Felita and Gigi, resolved their feelings of ambition and betrayal in their friendship (chapter 12); to the six-week period in which Ms. Burgos's class studied *Felita* and developed a deeper awareness of the conflicts inherent in intergroup relationships, as well as strategies to resolve them (chapter 13); to the years from six to sixteen when individuals improve and transform their social perspective coordination abilities to achieve the capacity for awareness of mutuality (chapters 2 to 4), to the ways students' social awareness at any age applies to their social and literacy skills (chapters 11 through 15), and even to teachers (chapters 8 and 10) who reflect on why it is essential to teach the promotion of social awareness in their classrooms.

In Conclusion

Our brand of developmentalism then has two fundamental characteristics that make it useful for the study and promotion of social awareness. First, its core emphasis is on the growth of social perspective coordination capacity; it carefully analyses what that growth can and cannot imply for expressing oneself and for taking action. Second, it is fundamentally meaning-oriented. I think the first characteristic is self-evident, at least at this point in the book. But what about the second characteristic—our approach's orientation toward meaning? What are the implications of a meaning-centered view for practice, especially in the debate within the character education movement?

Beyond awareness, teachers and other youth practitioners are naturally concerned with the behavior—the moral and social action—of the child on a day-to-day basis. But behavior is often viewed as occurring in the moment, the moment of action. It is often thought of as occurring at a single point in time, or as a specific kind of action (for example, whether or not to rob a store, throw a rock, or fight back). Awareness, on the other hand, evolves over time. Felita made meaning of her actions in one way in the past—that is, at the moment she faced the girls who taunted her. With the help of her grandmother several months after the incident occurred, she was able to make a different meaning of the traumatic confrontation she had with the kids in the new neighborhood. Perhaps she will make new meaning in the future if she faces similar situations. As a developmentalist, that's how I (and my colleagues) look at things. Our story is one of growth and change in the process of making meaning over time.

As for the children in this book, we have caught all the students at a particular moment in time, one that is long gone. By now Ms. Burgos's students are well into high school. Their present lives as well as their futures are of great interest to us. That, too, is what it means to think like a developmentalist. The students' responses on our rubrics no longer matter in the moment. But the child is now, and the child is the future, both at the same time. It is this understanding that keeps many of us in practice-based research hoping to see the future by examining its connection to the past and present—rather than examining awareness and action only in the moment.

Notes

Chapter 1

1. The other participating faculty members—all leading researchers or theoreticians in the field at the time—included Bernard Kaplan, Clark University; Zella Luria, Tufts University; Freda Rebelsky, Boston University; Herb Saltstein, MIT; and Sheldon White, Harvard University. The dean of the Harvard Graduate School of Education had offered Kohlberg a permanent position, and although this was a trial year for Kohlberg, he probably had already decided to move from the Committee on Human Development at the University of Chicago, whose focus was primarily research, to a professional school with an emphasis on bridging research to practice.
2. During those years it was called the Judge Baker Guidance Center. The name was changed in the mid-1980s when the institution shifted its focus from the treatment of mental illness to its prevention and the promotion of mental health. I say more about this evolution later in the book.
3. In 1992 we took the step of establishing a formal institutional entity associated with our interests, but not driven by them, by founding the interdisciplinary research and training program we call the Risk and Prevention Program, within the Human Development and Psychology Area of Harvard's Graduate School of Education. This institutional program is still evolving. Currently the Risk and Prevention Program is a one-year master's degree program that trains graduate students to help children and adolescents whose difficult life circumstances place them at risk for a range of academic and social difficulties. Usually, but not always, these circumstances are exacerbated by the limited financial resources of their families or communities. Many of the projects and programs that Risk and Prevention faculty are involved in are located in or connected to schools, from preschools to high schools. Many, but not all, of these practices target the promotion of resilience to adversity in individuals; some focus on the promotion of resilience in local institutions and in even larger systems.
4. The idea that the academic and social skills of schoolchildren are inextricably linked has been a focus of our thinking and research for several

decades. At the level of practice, the Developmental Studies Center (DSC) in California has designed important programs and generated many writings on this subject and related issues, including school reform, schools as communities, cooperative learning, substance abuse and violence prevention, and teacher education and professional development. These have influenced our thinking, as well as our partnership with VLF. See, for example, Battistich et al. (1991) for an early evaluation of the program. See also Solomon et al. (2000) for the most recent evaluation of the school reform work of DSC.

Chapter 2

1. John Flavell was one of the first translators of Jean Piaget's theory of human mental development for American psychologists. His initial interpretation was offered in the classic volume *The Developmental Psychology of Jean Piaget* (1963); later he integrated it into a broadly read text, *Cognitive Development* (1993). Flavell describes a developmental (or "structuralist-organismic") approach that had its origins in the work of not only Piaget but other European theorists, such as Heinz Werner (see, for example, Werner 1980 [1948]). The branch of cognitive development within which Kohlberg worked at the time was called social cognition—the understanding of the social world (see Flavell and Miller 1998). While current trends in theories of social cognition have moved beyond Piaget and Kohlberg, no overarching reformulation has dominated the field.

2. For a particularly clear explanation of Piagetian theory, see Beilin (1989). Piaget (1983) is also a good reference.

3. The most well-known and widely employed hypothetical dilemma that Kohlberg used to measure moral development is the "Heinz dilemma," an ambiguous problem about stealing that was designed to study the development of moral reasoning. The dilemma is presented as follows:

    > In Europe, a woman was near death from a very bad disease, a special kind of cancer. There was one drug that the doctors thought might save her. It was a form of radium that a druggist in the same town had recently discovered. The drug was expensive to make, but the druggist was charging ten times what the drug cost him to make. He paid $200 for the radium and charged $2,000 for a small dose of the drug. The sick woman's husband, Heinz, went to everyone he knew to borrow the money, but he could get together only about $1,000, which was half of what it cost. He told the druggist that his wife was dying and asked him to sell it cheaper or let him pay later. But the druggist said, "No, I discovered the drug and I'm going to make money from it." Heinz got desperate and broke into the man's store to steal the drug for his wife.

Some of the questions that researchers asked to probe interviewees' responses to the Heinz dilemma included: Should the husband have done that? Was it right or wrong? What if Heinz did not love his wife? If it is right for Heinz to steal for his wife, would it be right for him to steal for a stranger? If he steals the drug and is caught, should he be punished? What would be a fair punishment?

These questions could be answered by children as young as six. Other questions focused on older individuals and were meant to clarify the differences among the more complex stages. Is your decision that it is right (or wrong) objectively right, is it morally universal, or is it your personal opinion? If you think it is morally right to steal the drug, you must face the fact that it is legally wrong. What is the basis of your view that it is morally right, then, more than your personal opinion? Is it anything that can be agreed on? Can one take anything but a relativist position on the question?

The responses to this thorough questioning were scored with a very involved six-stage coding system. After years of research this method was summarized in Colby et al. (1987).

4. Elliot Turiel (1998) provides an excellent review of these academic battles. This paper includes an extensive review of the field of moral development; a report on the work of Turiel and his colleagues on the various domains of social awareness; and an explanation of how research on the distinctions in how individuals make judgments can be understood in part as a function of whether the judgment is seen as personal, social conventional, or moral.

5. See Colby et al. (1987) and Kohlberg (1964, 1971) for a review of the psychological research behind the practice. The notion that a higher-stage environment stimulates moral development was derived earlier from experimental findings by Turiel (1983) and Rest (1979) that adolescents tend to assimilate moral reasoning from the next stage above their own, while they reject reasoning below their own stage.

6. A pediatrician by profession, Richmond had previously been a medical school dean; he had also served as the first director of Head Start (in 1965) and as president of the Society for Research in Child Development (in 1968). In addition to being the director of the third-oldest child guidance center in the United States, which had an international reputation for training mental health professionals, Richmond chaired the Child Psychiatry Service at Boston Children's Hospital, and he was a professor at Harvard Medical School.

7. Fortunately, in 1973 a grant came through from the newly founded Spencer Foundation to fund our proposal for research on the growth of interpersonal understanding in both well-adjusted and troubled children between the ages of six and sixteen. It was this project that led to the founding of the Group for the Study of Interpersonal Development and its commitment to keeping open the connections between theory, re-

search, and practice. The founding and early members of GSID who worked with me on developing the interpersonal understanding interview methodology and research included Steven Brion-Meisels, Elizabeth Bruss-Saunders, Diane Byrne, Ellen Ward Cooney, David Forbes, Carmel Gurucharri, Daniel Jaquette, Gregory Jurkovic, Debra Lavin, and Carolyn Stone. The focus of this early research was the idea that children's understanding of social relationships—particularly their often intense interactions with parents and the intricacies of friendship and other relations with peers—is based in large part on their perspective-taking abilities. These ideas, supported by empirical data, are reported in my first book (Selman 1980).

8. Kohlberg, Richmond, and I were not the only researchers and theorists to make the connection between social and moral development. Turiel (1998) offers a thorough explanation of the relationship.

9. In 1971 the company, called Guidance Associates, produced the filmstrip series *First Things: Values* along with a discussion guide, *A Strategy for Teaching Values*. Holly's dilemma was part of the curriculum focused on promises ("You Promised . . ."). Other *First Things: Values* topics included honesty ("The Trouble with Truth"), rules ("What Do You Do About Rules?"), and property rights ("But It Isn't Yours"). The following year we developed dilemmas focused on social relationships at the elementary-grade level (*First Things: Social Reasoning*), and in 1974 we produced materials (*Relationships and Values*) for use in middle schools and junior high schools. Later Guidance Associates became the Center for Humanities, and today it produces a wide range of educational and training videos for schools, colleges, and corporations.

10. This team included many of the individuals mentioned in note 7, especially Diane Byrne.

11. Piaget first espoused the idea that development occurs when problems arise that challenge children's existing understandings, and that insights can be gained from observing children's reactions to the unfamiliar. For more on this topic, see Kuhn and Siegler (1998); see also Siegler (1998).

    Similarly, in moral development, cognitive-developmental theory stresses that development is promoted by another factor in addition to role-taking opportunities and the perceived moral level provided by an institution: cognitive-moral conflict. Structural theory stresses that movement to the next stage occurs through reflective reorganization, arising from sensed contradictions in an individual's current stage structure. Experiences of cognitive conflict can occur through exposure to decision situations that arouse internal contradictions in the individual's moral reasoning structure or through exposure to the moral reasoning of significant others that is discrepant in content or structure from the individual's own reasoning. This principle is central to the initial moral discussion program that Kohlberg and his colleagues implemented in schools (Blatt and Kohlberg 1975). Thus, research supports the notion that peer-group moral discussion of dilemmas leads to moral stage change through exposure to the next stage of reasoning. Other evidence suggests that discussion without such exposure can also lead to moral change: Colby (1978) found, for example, that a program of moral discussion led to some development of postconventional (stage 5) thinking on a post-test in a group of conventional-level students who had shown no postconventional reasoning in the pre-test.

The researchers working in the Kohlbergian framework also thought that the concept of exposure to a higher stage was not limited to stages of moral reasoning but might also be applied to exposure to moral action and moral institutions. Moral atmosphere studies show that "individuals respond to a composite of moral reasoning, moral action, and institutionalized rules as a relatively unified whole in relation to their own moral stage" (Kohlberg 1984, 202). These researchers claimed that the program led to an upward change in moral reasoning and to later changes in lifestyle and behavior (presumably moral behavior).

Ultimately this would evolve into the "just community" movement, which advocated democratic self-government through community decisions and small-group moral discussion. Lawrence Kohlberg and his colleagues Joseph Hickey and Peter Scharf (1980) first developed a just community in a women's prison; the primary institutional focus of just-community approaches, however, was primary and secondary schools. For more historical information on the approach of Kohlberg and his colleagues to moral education, see a fascinating book by Clark Powers, Ann Higgins, and Lawrence Kohlberg (1989) on the just-community approach, published two years after Kohlberg's death, as well as Marvin Berkowitz and Fritz Oser (1985) and Dawn Schrader (1990).

12. Piaget developed his "methode clinique," or clinical method, when he was a young Swiss biologist working in a school for boys in Paris. Theodore Simon, known for the IQ tests he authored with Alfred Binet, suggested to Piaget that he develop a French version of Cyril Burt's tests of reasoning in his laboratory (left vacant by his departure after the death of Binet). Instead of administering the tests in a standardized way, Piaget interviewed the children at length. He did not simply note their answers to the test questions but probed their responses to illuminate their thinking as they formulated and solved problems (Gruber and Voneche 1995). At the same time Piaget was studying (adult) logic formally, he used this new clinical method to work out the developing logic of children's thinking (Piaget 1965 [1932]). Trained as a clinician, I found many similarities to the way we were taught to conduct our practice. One difference was that clinicians do not systematically collect data for research purposes.

13. This was how one did clinical research within the framework of an "academic medical model." Researchers could take advantage—in the best sense of that phrase—of the cooperation of students, parents, and public school teachers and officials, and of the accessibility of the client-patients

in the clinic or hospital with which they were affiliated in order to gather data to generate, explore, or confirm their theoretical formulations—not only in the service of their own careers, of course, but more importantly, for the benefit of the children.

14. Later we were able to do longitudinal studies, going back in subsequent years to ask the same children to share their thoughts about Holly's problem as they got older, in order to see whether, and how, their reasoning had changed.

15. Interviewing also led us to further research on the question of the relationship between children's verbal responses to hypothetical situations and their observable behavior with their peers. This is why careful interviewing, the "methode clinique," has always been so important to our approach: it allows us better access to children's developing beliefs about the nature of friendships and peer-group relationships.

16. The interpersonal understanding manual was the first in a series of scoring manuals authored by the GSID (see Selman 1979). Other GSID manuals include Schultz, Yeates, and Selman (1989), which grounds the work in chapter 3 of this text, and Levitt and Selman (1993), which organizes the work in chapter 4. Without such manuals, scientific work to test the legitimacy of the theoretical framework cannot proceed with validity.

17. In the time since we began our work, a great deal of research has been done in the field of social cognition to demonstrate the perspective-taking competencies of younger and younger children. This work, sometimes described as children's theories of minds (their own and others), uses methods that do not rely as heavily on reflective verbalized thought. Our own work uses social perspective-taking levels less as real levels located inside a child's developing mind and more as a theoretical tool to organize the way we see and interpret social thought, behavior, and interaction. This orientation, which will become clearer throughout the course of this book, explains why we do not emphasize the particular age at which we might expect to see the application of a level, as exemplified by the omission of ages in table 2.2.

18. Jerome Kagan (1998), for instance, argues that a child's temperament plays a major role in social decisionmaking.

19. At the time some critics of cognitive-developmental approaches to social or moral research saw little relation between the development of thought and real-world action. Thus, they viewed the development of interpersonal understanding (Selman 1980) and moral reasoning (Colby et al. 1987) as inconsequential and therefore not worthwhile. See Ashton (1978) for points and counterpoints on these issues. This was a compilation of articles published during the 1970s in the *Harvard Educational Review.* Contributors included Deanna Kuhn, Roger Landrum, Patricia Teague Ashton, John C. Gibbs, Carol Gilligan, David Elkind, Eleanor Duckwork, Lawrence Kohlberg, Rochelle Mayer, D. C. Phillips, Marvis

E. Kelly, and myself. In 1986 Modgil and Modgil (1986) edited a major volume that offered chapters authored by both supporters and critics of cognitive-developmental theories to further the debate about the value and pitfalls of this approach to socio-moral development, with a particular focus on the work of Kohlberg. The book aimed to evaluate the theory from the perspectives of a range of areas of knowledge: philosophy, psychology, education, research methodology, cross-cultural research, curriculum studies, religious education and theology epistemology, and social and political studies. Proponents of this theoretical tradition (those who were primarily positive though still critical) who contributed to this volume included Dwight R. Boyd, Robert Kegan, Robert Enright, James Rest, Helen Weinreich-Haste, and Carolyn Pope Edwards. Contributors who predominantly, but not entirely, disagreed with the theory included Jane Loevinger, John M. Broughton, Roger Straughan, and Edmund V. Sullivan. Kohlberg provided a concluding chapter.

Chapter 3

1. Autonomy, in this example, means that Kathy cannot always do what others want her to do. Instead, she must learn to balance what she needs with the needs of others. For a more detailed explanation, see Selman and Schultz (1990).

2. Harry Stack Sullivan was a psychiatrist who made an important contribution to the field of developmental psychology, even though he was trained as a medical doctor (see, for example, Sullivan 1953a). He described stages of human development that emphasized the importance of chumship in preadolescence, a concept that is central in our work with pair therapy. Sullivan writes that "if you will look very closely at one of your children when he finally finds a chum—somewhere between eight-and-a-half and ten—you will discover something very different in the relationship—namely, that your child begins to develop a real sensitivity to what matters to another person. And this is not in the sense of 'what should I do to get what I want,' but instead 'what should I do to contribute to the happiness or to support the prestige and feeling of worthwhileness of my chum'" (245–46). His biography by Helen Swick Perry (1982) charts not just the development of Sullivan's theory of interpersonal relations but the importance to his professional work and theory building of his own childhood, which was spent largely as a lonely, shy, and socially awkward youth.

3. A thorough summary of the work we did on pair therapy at the Manville School can be found in Selman and Schultz (1990), which describes in depth both a practice focused on the treatment of children with serious emotional and psychiatric problems and the practice-based theory we summarize in this chapter. A later book (Selman, Watts, and Schultz 1997) focuses on our research in the context of pairing children for the

prevention of psychosocial disorders and speaks to many of the questions I address in chapters 4 and 5.

4. For a fuller description and more detailed theoretical information about our formulations about intimacy and shared experience within a developmental framework, see chapters 2 to 4 of Selman and Schultz (1990).

5. For an alternative psychological framework within which to understand the complementarity between the development of self and relatedness, see the recent work of Joseph Allan (Allan et al. 1994). For an analysis of this dichotomy at the cultural level, see Markus and Kitayama (1991), as well as Miller et al. (1997).

6. The empirical work we undertook to validate this second phase of our research has been presented in a number of articles. Some focus on our observations of normative populations using the framework; see, for example, Selman et al. (1983) and Stone and Selman (1982).

7. The social development of infants, including the earliest form of "shared experience," is well documented in the classic book by Daniel Stern, *The Interpersonal World of the Infant* (1985). For an eloquent description of how pair therapy can promote the social interaction of toddlers and preschoolers and how this work can lead to the description of social interaction skills in these young children, see Kane, Raya, and Ayoub (1997).

8. In the mid-1980s we collaborated with William Beardslee, a child psychiatrist who has done extensive work on the prevention of depression in children from families with a history of clinical depression. Before designing his family-based intervention with children at risk for depression, eloquently described in his recent book (Beardslee 2002), Beardslee conducted a longitudinal epidemiological study of the psychosocial development of children whose profiles indicated they were members of a population at high risk for developing a psychiatric diagnosis of depression. We interviewed these children using the interpersonal negotiation strategies method for assessment and found that the children who showed the capacity for mature communication with others—for example, who exhibited compromise and collaborative strategies, skills, and styles (using our framework)—were more likely to be protected from negative life outcomes than those who demonstrated only impulsive and unilateral forms of relating to others. For details of the use of this sample to validate the theoretical model, see Selman et al. (1986). For the application of the model to risk and prevention research, see Beardslee, Schultz, and Selman (1987).

9. Such differentiation and integration are in keeping with a fundamental principle of a psychology that uses a developmental analysis (see Werner 1980 [1948]).

10. The primary levels of interpersonal understanding, as laid out in our first main work (Selman 1980), were subsequently translated into levels of interpersonal negotiation strategies and shared experience (Selman

and Schultz 1990). In practice, when scoring children's responses to our interview dilemmas, we scored half-levels when one level was evident in a rudimentary way but not in a consolidated way (see Yeates and Selman 1989; Selman, Yeates, and Schultz 1991; Yeates, Schultz, and Selman 1991).

Our colleague Maria LaRusso has formalized the scoring of partial levels of social perspective coordination in her work with the GSID. Recently, in examining the interpersonal negotiation strategies suggested by youngsters to hypothetical dilemmas, Maria found that she could reliably identify four sublevels within the transitions from one level to the next (see LaRusso 2001). This "subatomic" analysis holds great promise for further understanding of the connection between social thought and social action, especially when used to evaluate intervention programs designed to promote social competence.

Chapter 4

1. For the influence of Lawrence Kohlberg on this initiative, see Kohlberg (1966) and Kohlberg and Mayer (1972).
2. This thinking also developed from research on psychological risk and "resilience," a term used to describe the positive ways in which individuals respond to stress and adversity and the understanding of the protective factors that may ameliorate the effects of being born into a high-risk population. For reviews of the research in this field, see Rutter (1990), Masten (1994), Gordon and Song (1994), and Werner (1990).
3. In particular, see an extensive review by Weissberg and Greenberg (1998). For a thorough review of current programs, I suggest a recently published review by Solomon, Watson, and Battistich (2001), who look at a number of school-based character development and psychosocial prevention approaches that emerged in the last twenty years. Another good source is Molnar (1997). Other significant work in this area can be found in Berkowitz and Grych (2000); Elias and Tobias (1990); Johnson and Johnson (1996); and Oser (1986).
4. Much of the work during this period was done in collaboration with Keith Yeates and Lynn Hickey Schultz; see Yeates and Selman (1989); Selman, Yeates, and Schultz (1991); Schultz and Selman (1989); Yeates, Schultz, and Selman (1990); Yeates, Schultz, and Selman (1991).
5. In the late 1980s we surveyed attempts at moral education and psychosocial prevention in light of our own work. Mira Zamansky Levitt, who was the clinical director of the Manville School in 1988, joined our research team and led us to the insight from which we constructed personal meaning as the third component of our framework; she contributed a great deal to the analysis that followed as well. Our critique of prior psychosocial prevention efforts can be found in Levitt, Selman, and Richmond (1991). Our initial application of this model to pair counsel-

ing, with its focus on the personal meaning of fighting, can be found in Selman et al. (1992), from which the material on Clarisa and Callie is drawn.

6. The interdisciplinary Human Development and Psychology area (most of its faculty are trained in developmental psychology or cultural anthropology) focuses on the application of research and theory to educational practice. HDP also hosts a doctoral-level training program with a strong emphasis on research. I directed the Risk and Prevention Program from its inception through 1999. Other faculty who have played important roles in its implementation include Catherine Ayoub, Michael Nakkula, and, in its early years, Gil Noam. See, for example, Ayoub, Raya, and Geismer (1996); Nakkula and Ravitch (1997); and Noam et al. (1996).

7. To a great degree, the impetus for the establishment and evolution of Risk and Prevention came from the graduate students themselves. In the late 1980s the new doctoral candidates entering the counseling psychology program were well aware that children growing up in poor, urban, and minority communities faced dangers and difficulties beyond those that could be attributed simply to individual or family dynamics. These men and women came to us for their professional training already highly committed to providing services for this underserved population. They did not think of the kids they wanted to work with as necessarily "disordered" or needing to be "cured." Instead, they thought of them as having been "placed at risk"—as needing some support growing up in communities plagued by poverty, drugs, and violence and in a society where they face the risk of discrimination because they are members of racial or ethnic minorities or simply because they are poor. This is the "prevention" part of the project.

   During their first year the doctoral students worked at the Manville School in "tertiary prevention." As interns who provided therapeutic services, they provided psychological treatment for children with severe psychiatric disorders as part of their training, and they learned to do pair therapy as a treatment regimen. The following year they worked in selected schools within the Boston Public School District to provide psychological services for targeted children who had been identified by their teachers as being at high risk for developing psychosocial problems (secondary prevention). This work ranged from individual psychological counseling for a child unable to do his academic work because he was worried about family difficulties at home to interventions like pair counseling for children who had major difficulties in getting along with their peers. Senior staff clinicians at the Judge Baker, supported through public funds and private foundation grants, provided ongoing support and supervision for the work done at both the clinic and the public school sites.

   Most of these doctoral candidates focused their dissertation research on the risks to psychosocial development that affect poor and minority children from urban settings. Most went on to become practitioners—

direct providers of mental health services—but some continued to do practice-based research in academic settings or to design prevention-oriented demonstration projects in urban public schools. That smaller group joined forces with me and other faculty to design Risk and Prevention as a way of extending our reach beyond the treatment of children who were already suffering from serious psychosocial disorders.

We had come to understand that prevention on a wider scale required, among other things, that we provide cost-effective services to a much larger number of children. We realized that we needed to design prevention approaches that could be implemented by people whose training was not so intensive and narrowly focused. That is why we designed our curriculum for practicing psychosocial prevention specialists at the master's level.

Over a period of several years we transformed a counseling psychology doctoral program—originally designed to train practitioners to treat the psychological disorders of (most often) middle-class children and adults—into a program to train master's degree students in the prevention of largely socially based disorders in children from poor, urban neighborhoods, most often children from very different backgrounds, with a wide range of cultural norms that would challenge our existing theories.

8. Dr. Caroline Watts, who had graduated from our doctoral program several years earlier, played a leading role in the design of this practicum and was, along with me, the lead conceptualizer and founding director of the Pyramid of Prevention Program at the public school where Kesia was placed.

9. For her work in this service-oriented program, Kesia received a modest stipend from an endowment established at the Judge Baker in 1993 by Claire and Jeff Stern, in memory of their daughter Ellen, and augmented with additional funds raised over the preceding ten years. This endowment was designed to serve two purposes: to promote the social competence of children placed at risk at least in part owing to economic disadvantage; and to help young practitioners get a head start in a professional career working with such children. This money was matched by federal work-study funds, available through the university, at a rate of two dollars for each dollar provided by the Judge Baker, bringing Kesia's stipend to about $4,000 for the year. Since 1993, when it was first established, the Ellen Stern Memorial Fund has supported more than fifty master's-level interns in this and other practicum experiences oriented toward promoting social competence.

10. The aphorism attributed to Lewin is, "There is nothing so practical as a good theory." Kurt Lewin was a well-known social scientist who immigrated to the United States to escape persecution in pre–World War II Germany. During the 1930s and 1940s Lewin undertook much practice-oriented research. In one of his most well-known studies (Lewin, Lippitt,

and White 1939), he demonstrated significant differences in the social behavior of late-elementary-grade boys asked to function under "theoretically different" socially structured settings. For example, when the researchers manipulated boys' groups to be structured as "democratic," "autocratic," and "laissez-faire" in boys' clubs and summer camps, they found that boys in the democratically structured groups behaved more cooperatively and less aggressively during club meetings. See also Lippitt and White (1952).

11. For a review of the literature on aggressive behavior within the context of research in child development, see Coie and Dodge (1998).

12. For our initial attempt to describe the developmental taxonomy of personal meaning, based on perspective coordination theory, see Levitt and Selman (1996).

13. Our model can examine any domain of risky activity in the context of the quality of any of an individual's specific interpersonal relationships. In our brief analysis in this chapter on Mark and Lance, we focus on their relationships with their peers—and with their pair therapist. The list of meaningful social relationships that connect to risks is not limited to just these two categories. It could easily expand to include grandparents, siblings, other kin, teachers, coaches, mentors, as well as, obviously, parents and primary caretakers. Deciding which social relationships we study depends on which are important to the individual in the context of the risks in question. For a more thorough explanation of this theoretical approach, see Selman and Adalbjarnardottir (2000).

14. Of course, any given individual's life course is susceptible to many unpredictable influences beyond his or her patterns of relationship maturity or psychosocial competence. Case studies, such as the one presented here, make a start at generating some hypotheses about the power of personal meaning grounded in the capacity to coordinate points of view. To test them, we need longitudinal quantitative research designs that use samples and methods that can do the work of the study of life histories on a larger scale.

15. A recent empirical study by Sigrun Adalbjarnardottir (2002) provides some of the support we are looking for. In that study, in a sample of more than one thousand tenth-grade students in Reykjavík, Iceland, adolescents who demonstrated greater awareness of the personal meaning of drinking were less likely to drink heavily than those who showed less maturity in this competence.

Chapter 5

1. According to Dryfoos (1990), by the early 1990s one in four children of the 28 million in the United States were considered to be at risk for problem behaviors (school dropout, substance abuse, and so on).

2. It has been said by some that findings from developmental psychology "die in Japan," meaning that the U.S. and Japanese cultures are so different that American-born psychological theories do not apply to the Japanese psyche. If true, this conclusion certainly would apply to the area of moral development. True or not, this comment has both theoretical and practical implications. Theoretically speaking, for example, following the introduction of Kohlberg's work (see Kohlberg 1971), researchers attempted to discover whether his theory of moral stages and his method of posing hypothetical moral dilemmas would hold up in other countries. Testing across the world is common in the field of child development, since researchers are seeking to fully understand what is universal, what is culturally specific, and what is individually based. Turiel (1998) in particular offers a more complete review of the key cross-cultural moral development studies. Even today, however, the question remains: Do universal moral norms exist, or is morality localized and specific to cultures?

   Japanese issues of moral education in both practice and policy are not unfamiliar to educators in the United States (see, for example, Schoppa 1991; Terasaki 1992). As in the United States, some Japanese educators and politicians argue that moral education should teach "traditional" Japanese values—flag, anthem, a "sympathetic heart." Others, like Yayoi Watanabe, a colleague of mine, take a developmental point of view. Yayoi, for instance, has used Voices of Love and Freedom, the practice we describe in this chapter, with great success, so perhaps it is no longer true that a developmental approach cannot be translated or adapted to the Japanese educational system (see Watanabe 2001a, 2001b). See also Lewis (1995).

3. At the time the Boston public schools were divided into four zones, each of which had an administrative leader titled the zone superintendent. Currently the district has one superintendent and twelve cluster leaders.

4. For a taste of the two very different sides of the character education debate, see, for example, Benninga and Wynne (1998) and Kohn (1998b).

5. An idea that is not always welcome; see, for example, Ravitch (2000).

6. In any curriculum, terms such as "values" and "literacy" need to be examined closely. In the original VLF model the social development components (the "values") were viewed as steps in a pedagogical scope and sequence. Currently there is much less emphasis on the steps, but the components do provide a useful framework for activities. Over time the term "literacy" has also changed in response to policy, as discussed later in the book.

7. For an early description of the program, see Schaps, Solomon, and Watson (1986); for an early evaluation, see Battistich et al. (1991); for the most recent evaluation of the school reform work of DSC, see Solomon et al. (2000); for an overview of the field, see Solomon, Watson, and Battistich (2001).

8. Its work takes several forms, including developing school-based programs, after-school and parent involvement programs, and professional development services, as well as the production and dissemination of educational materials. CDP now includes collaborative classroom learning, problem-solving-oriented classroom management, and "literature-based reading and language arts, which integrate social and ethical lessons into the academic curriculum." "Reading, Thinking, and Caring" (grades kindergarten through third) and "Reading for Real" (grades fourth through eighth) provide teacher's guides for 250 carefully selected books that help teach reading skills and stimulate writing and discussion about issues that are on the minds of young students. These include getting along with others, coping with bullies, dealing with being different, and making tough choices.

9. For this reason, both organizations are worried about national policies. In consequence, the pedagogical philosophies and practical activities of both organizations are continually evolving. In fact, both organizations have found it necessary to their survival these days to focus ever more on reading, writing, spelling, oral language skills, vocabulary, and phonics. Even as I write about the research we have done using the third generation of the VLF curriculum, for instance, VLF itself has moved on to a fourth generation with an even stronger focus on literacy.

10. *Amazing Grace* was chosen as an American Library Association Notable Children's Book and a Reading Rainbow feature selection; it was also listed as a *Booklist* "Editors' Choice," *American Bookseller* "Pick of the List," *Horn Book* "Fanfare Choice," and one of *School Library Journal*'s "Best Books."

11. Some teachers were steadfastly committed to the Collins Writing Portfolio approach to reading, writing, and student assessment, while others were less interested in process and more interested in traditional methods of teaching and assessing language arts, such as memorization and mechanics. Similarly, some schools leaned heavily toward the whole-language approach to reading, while others blended whole language and phonics, and still others stressed phonics over context. In addition, bilingual schools presented their own issues. VLF needed to be bilingual; because a large proportion of the students it was trying to reach came from Spanish-speaking households, the program's designers had to be sure that everything they wrote in English worked for bilingual students in Spanish as well. But they also knew that their guides had to be usable and useful for all teachers, regardless of their preference for a particular reading or writing program or the languages in which they taught. We were caught in a bit of a paradox: VLF's guides could not rely on any one approach to language arts, and yet VLF was billing itself as a comprehensive *literacy*, character education, and prevention program.

12. Once the series was in print, our work changed from theory and research helping practice to practice informing research. As our graduate

student teacher-researchers worked with us in supervision, we began to think about how the guides (and our theory) were used in real-life inner-city classrooms. Chapter 7 introduces some of the challenges that our theory and practice posed for Boston teachers, while part IV of the book explores how the children's classroom-based activities posed interesting challenges for our theory.

13. There were also many intense discussions about what constitutes a distinct cultural group in the United States and how to talk about people of various backgrounds. Should blacks be categorized as African American, Afro-Caribbean, and African? Or just "black"? Where are the boundaries of Asia? Who should be considered Asian and who Central Asian? Is the Middle East part of Asia or Africa, or is it its own region? Are we talking about language groups, literary styles, or religious traditions? How do we refer to indigenous peoples, including Native Americans? Do we use the word "Indian"? How many groups and subgroups should be on the list per grade? What if we want to "go national"? Do we need to be able to show that we are prepared for teaching in any region of the country, regardless of its ethnic constituencies? And then there was the question of authenticity: Do all the books on the VLF list need to be written by a card-carrying member of the group its main character or characters represents? Does it matter that the author of *Amazing Grace* is a white Englishwoman? Violet Harris (1997), a noted scholar of multicultural education, notes that *Amazing Grace* has received criticism for its stereotypical portrayal of Native Americans, in pictures and text, more than for its characterization of Afro-Caribbeans.

14. Surprisingly little research has been done on this topic. For a thorough recent review of what systematic study has been undertaken, see Van Ausdale and Feagin (2001).

Chapter 6

1. I think it is important to point out that neither I nor any members of the GSID received any royalties from sales for our work in the creation of the VLF guides. We sometimes received support from grants for the time we put into the consultation, and especially for the research we subsequently implemented. There is nothing inherently wrong about getting compensation in the form of royalties, but such income would both hamper and make a bit more suspect any judgment we made about the quality of the curriculum. As academic researchers, our primary goal was to see our work expand into the classroom and to have the freedom to work both independently and collaboratively with practice.

2. Over the years the VLF curriculum has evolved in response to the changing educational marketplace and the need for schools and teachers to be accountable, especially in the area of literacy. In 1997 the guides were very balanced between social skill and literacy skill development. Recently VLF has moved toward a more literacy-focused comprehensive language arts approach, which is discussed later.

3. The observations of the two classroom teachers are based on the field notes of our research staff, especially Sarah Shmitt, as well as videotapes of teachers and children using VLF materials that I have condensed and edited.
4. In an earlier version of this guide, the final writing exercise asks students to write about a time when someone lied to them or to someone they cared about. But following our research on how teachers used this guide in the classroom, the program's developers changed this "To Express" assignment to the following: "Write an essay about why you think it's important to tell the truth."

Chapter 7

1. The half-dozen field observers who participated in the Carnegie Research Study—and whose observations enrich this narrative—were master's and doctoral-level students at the Harvard Graduate School of Education, and one was a Harvard undergraduate.
2. The second-grade books were *Grandfather's Rock* and *Stellaluna.* The third-grade books for the following year were *Angel Child/Dragon Child* and *Irene and the Big Fat Nickel.* The fifth-grade books were *Felita* and *Mayfield Crossing.*
3. Later in this chapter, I draw upon the extensive observations of Sarah Shmitt, who managed the team of observers in the schools.
4. In addition, we had designed our own independent or "home-grown" measures of social competence specifically for use in studies such as this one. We call these collectively the GSID Relationship Questionnaires, or "Rel-Q" for short. Rel-Q questionnaires use our theoretical framework (focusing on levels of perspective coordination) as an assessment tool when it is important to a research project that data be gathered from large numbers of subjects in a cost-effective way.
5. This all-day event was held at the Hynes Convention Center in downtown Boston, the only venue in the city capable of accommodating 2,300 teachers in one room, and it gave VLF the opportunity to present its recommended multicultural literature list and its five-component pedagogical framework, unveiled as a "multicultural literacy, ethics, and prevention program." The curriculum was tacitly endorsed by the keynote speakers, Thomas Menino, the mayor of Boston, and Thomas Payzant, the city's new superintendent of schools.
6. In particular, we were told, in some parts of the Boston public school system Harvard has a reputation for producing callow interns who do little work in the classroom beyond what is required for them to earn a passing grade as student teachers. On sighting the research project manager in the hallway, one veteran teacher used to yell from the door of her room, "Here comes Harvard! Run for your lives!"

Chapter 8

1. The three chapters in part III describe a collaborative effort that draws on the work of Adalbjarnardottir in Iceland and Selman in the United States. This chapter and chapter 9 describe work based upon the Icelandic Teacher Professional Development Project, part of a larger social education initiative under Adalbjarnardottir's design and direction (hereafter called the "Icelandic Project"). Chapter 10 builds on that work with data collected as part of the Carnegie Research Study of VLF in Boston. Carolina Buitrago joins Selman and Adalbjarnardottir in the authorship of chapter 10.

2. In 930, Althingi (Parliament) was established at Thingvellir, about forty kilometers east of Reykjavík. Christianity was adopted in Iceland at Althingi in the year 1000. The Icelandic Commonwealth, a form of republic, lasted until 1262, when Iceland came under the rule of the Norwegian crown. After the collapse of the Icelandic Commonwealth, conditions in Iceland deteriorated, owing in part to harsher climate and natural disasters and also to disruptions in trade. In 1383 both Norway and Iceland came under the rule of the Danish crown. In 1874 Iceland received its own constitution and control of its finances. In 1904 Iceland won home rule, and in 1918 it gained its independence, although the king of Denmark remained as sovereign. The Republic of Iceland was formally proclaimed at Thingvellir on June 17, 1944.

3. This saga also recounts the arrival of Christianity in Iceland, and it suggests that the only end to the cycle of violence will involve replacing the pagan virtues of heroism and pride with the Christian virtues of self-sacrifice and humility. In this sense, the saga explains the country's loss of freedom and specifies what is needed (Christian love) to restore it.

4. In 1983 I visited Iceland for the first time, at Edelstein's invitation, to give a workshop on our work to Icelandic educators who were developing the social studies curriculum.

5. As an elementary grade teacher in the 1970s, Sigrun Adalbjarnardottir was a part of the social studies curriculum reform movement for ten years. Upon receiving her doctorate in 1988 in human development and psychology from the Harvard Graduate School of Education, she began the Icelandic Project in partnership with the public elementary schools of Reykjavík.

6. In "The Process and Product of Reflective Activity: Psychological Process and Logical Form," written in 1933, John Dewey laid out the process of thinking in much the same terms adopted by developmental psychologists in the 1980s (see Archambault 1964, 242–59).

7. On the work of our project using this intermediate model in our evolving framework, see Selman et al. (1986); Schultz, Yeates, and Selman (1989); Adalbjarnardottir and Selman (1989); Adalbjarnardottir and Wil-

lett (1991); Yeates, Schultz, and Selman (1991); and Selman, Yeates, and Schultz (1991).

8. We discuss a three-step version of this pedagogical practice used by VLF in chapter 12. In VLF's "ABC" approach to conflict resolution, A stands for "Ask what the problem is," B is for "Brainstorm ways to solve it," and C stands for "Choose the best way." There is nothing "sacred" about five steps or three steps when research is translated into practice. Neither "steps" nor "levels" are carved into some absolute theoretical truth. In Dewey's sense, what counts is how functional the model is.

9. Based on what we had already learned, for example, we expected that when it came to defining the problem embodied in a dilemma, the teachers would find that the responses of the children in their elementary school classrooms would range from a focus on the effects of the problem on only one party (level 1 in terms of the developmental framework outlined in tables 2.1, 3.1, and 3.2) to the beginnings of mutuality (level 3).

10. A good source for research on the importance of reflection for teachers in the areas of moral, social, and character education is the *Journal of Moral Education*. See also Christensen et al. (2001); Johnston (2001); Oser and Althof (1993); Oser, Dick, and Patry (1992); Powers, Higgins, and Kohlberg (1989); Silva and Gimbert (2001); Smith (1996); Welker (1992).

Chapter 9

1. The comments from Icelandic teachers in the first two sections of this chapter are adapted from Adalbjarnardottir (1994); see also Adalbjarnardottir (1992).

2. In the next section, we draw very heavily from Adalbjarnardottir and Selman (1997).

3. Researchers who have studied teacher development in general (see, for example, Huberman 1992, 1995) and how it can be facilitated (Bartlett 1990; Leithwood 1992; McGregor and Gunter 2001; Sawyer 2001) suggest that programs designed to promote an increase in reflective teaching can achieve their goal (see, for example, Bullough 1989; Hollingsworth, Dybdahl, and Minarik 1993; Johnston 1997). It is not clear, however, from these studies whether changes in complexity of reflection relate to transformations in beliefs or practice (see Oser and Althof 1993). In one positive example, using in-depth analyses with a small sample of teachers, Johnston and her collaborative teachers (Johnston 1994; Cryns and Johnston 1993; Hunsaker and Johnston 1992) found that teachers who participated in projects designed to promote reflection did obtain a more complex view of beliefs and teaching practices, but it was not possible to predict the direction of change of beliefs or the connection between changes in beliefs and changes in teaching practices. Particularly relevant to our analysis, however, Cryns—the teacher—did broaden her

view from a singular focus on classroom issues to concerns with the connection between classroom issues and broader historical and sociopolitical contexts (Cryns and Johnston 1993). How to clarify whether or when such expanded visions are simply changes in beliefs or focus or reflect a significant change in a teacher's level of professional development (that is, greater differentiation and integration of thought and action, theory and practice) is a key issue we address in our analysis.

Chapter 10

1. For the last decade, studies have focused on how teachers' views of their own childhood, their parents' upbringing styles (Butt et al. 1992), their schooling both in youth and adulthood (Aitken and Mildon 1992), and various experiences in both their personal and professional lives (Connelly and Clandinin 1990; Goodson and Walker 1991; Kelchtermans 1993; Kelchtermans 1994; Kelchtermans and Vandenberghe 1994) play an important role in their professional competence and relate to the way they work with students. Kelchtermans and Vandenberghe (1994) claim that teachers' professional vision cannot be understood without connecting it to their life story and that studying teachers' lives deepens our understanding of why teachers act as they do (see also Goodson 1992; Goodson and Walker 1991).

Chapter 11

1. The focus in this and the following chapters is on one classroom and one teacher, but these chapters exemplify the kinds of data we collected in nineteen other classrooms as well. (Remember that our research had multiple goals.) Our approach in the Carnegie study was "qualitative," in that it focused on small samples and was oriented toward interpretive analyses. In addition to classroom observations, our data included teacher and student interviews as well as samples of worksheets completed by students in class and homework assignments.

   We also used the opportunity provided by this project to validate a questionnaire derived from our Risk and Relationship Framework; we expect that questionnaire to be useful to ourselves and others interested in further investigating the relationship between social competence and practice (see Schultz, Barr, and Selman 2001).

2. Notice that Ms. Burgos does not refer explicitly here to instructional competence. She seems directed instead toward the ultimate aim of all education—to enable students to take their place in society, to contribute to it, to be "empowered." Her endpoint for her students extends beyond the next standardized test. This focus is different from what one would expect to hear in a high-stakes testing environment, where teachers cannot help but aim toward the latest benchmark. This apparent disconnect, or tension, is why research on the connection between social competence and content areas, especially literacy, is so important.

3. Selected as an NCSS-CBC Notable Children's Trade Book in the field of social studies, *Felita* is also used by the Developmental Studies Center (see chapter 5) and Educators for Social Responsibility, two innovative organizations whose mission is to make teaching social responsibility a core practice in education.
4. *The King's Equal* (1992) by Katherine Paterson is a novel the students read earlier in the year.

Chapter 12

1. One approach that has a kinship with partner learning is cooperative learning, an approach made popular by both Robert Slavin and the Johnson brothers, David and Roger. For two classic works on this topic, see Slavin (1990) and Johnson and Johnson (1989).
2. We found the videotape material upon which we have built this chapter so compelling that we made a documentary to capture it. The documentary film goes by the same name as this chapter (*The Power of Peers*) and was produced by Cindy McKeown and myself. We use it as part of the training for graduate students working in the Risk and Prevention Program and as part of our professional development programs for teachers. To obtain a copy of the video, please write to Robert L. Selman, 609 Larsen Hall, Harvard Graduate School of Education, Cambridge, Mass. 02138.
3. To keep our discussion focused on the theme of children's developing understanding of personal relationships, we have jumped ahead to *Felita*'s chapter 5, in terms of both the chronology of the novel and our real-time observations in the classroom. In chapter 13, we will take a step back in order to pick up on a different developmental thread and consider two other research questions.
4. Some of the Icelandic teachers (see chapter 9) referred to a five-step conflict resolution process, taught by Sigrun Adalbjarnardottir and her colleagues, that is a close cousin to ABC. Many such problem-solving protocols have been developed by various developmentally oriented groups and individuals for use in schools here and abroad. (And the debate as to the right number of steps, and their proper order, sometimes becomes quite heated.) Research has shown that elementary school students and teachers find ABC and other structured processes for analyzing social conflict to be both compelling and useful. For a thorough review of the research basis for social problem-solving approaches for children and youth, see Weissberg and Greenberg (1998); see also Shure and Spivak (1982).
5. We call the developmental analysis of the process we have just observed "microgenetic" because it describes development—that is, the performance of higher levels of social competence—in the moment of the interaction itself. Using our framework, Rosario and Marisol's dyadic in-

teraction changes from level 1 (unilateral) to level 2 (reciprocal); in other words, it shifts from each partner thinking the problem is what the other did—or felt—to understanding and acknowledging their own roles in the conflict as well as the relationship between them.

Chapter 14

1. Catherine Snow, the author, coauthor, and editor of many articles and texts in the area of language and literacy, was one expert we consulted. Additionally, in 1999, Rand Education, at the request of the Department of Education's Office of Educational Research, asked a group of experts in language and literacy to provide an overview of the current research in the area of reading comprehension. The Rand study group includes Catherine Snow, Donna Alvermann, Janice Dole, Jack Fletcher, Georgia Earnest Garcia, Irene Gaskins, Arthur Graesser, John Guthrie, Michael Kamil, William Nagy, Annemarie Sullivan Palinscar, Dorothy Strickland, Frank Vellutino, and Joanna Williams. Draft versions of their report to the Office of Educational Research (Rand Study Group 2001) are available on a public website, *www.rand.org/multi/achievementforall*, for discussion purposes only.
2. The relationship between social thought and literacy is of increasing interest to researchers; for an interesting article on the connection between discourse, literacy, and culture, see Gee (1991); see also the work of our colleague Colette Daiute (1993) and Bruner (1996).
3. Including Catherine Snow, whose review of this chapter helped us to refine our thinking.
4. One of the most frequently cited sources on the importance of non-narrative texts as literacy tools is Snow, Burns, and Griffin (1998); see also Spires and Donley (1998).
5. Just as we think it is useful to distinguish between developmental differences (for example, pinpointing the age at which certain negotiation strategies are likely to appear in a child's repertoire) and a developmental framework (using a "levels" analysis to organize data such as we present in this book), it is also useful to differentiate between gender differences and a "gendered" analysis, which looks at data from the perspective of theories about or from gender. To use interpersonal negotiation strategies as an example, in our own research (see, for example, Adalbjarnardottir and Selman 1989) we have found consistent empirical differences in level of negotiation when children deal with peers (higher) as compared with adults (lower). We also have found that, all other things being equal, girls perform at higher levels on our scales of social awareness and skills than boys, starting at about the second grade (see Selman et al. 1986). It is not uncommon to find this gender difference in developmental capacities in the comparison of boys and girls, but the findings are not always as obviously interpretable—or clear-cut—as

they may first appear. For a fuller analysis of gender differences across a range of psychological variables, functions, aptitudes, traits, and so forth, see Maccoby (1998).

6. For a review of policies on the new standards, see Finn (1990), Berliner and Biddle (1996), and Marzano and Kendall (1998). Bronfenbrenner (1996) offers a sociological review of the demographic changes we are facing as a nation.

Chapter 15

1. Especially in Massachusetts, but in effect in all other states as well. See the 2001 Massachusetts eighth-grade language arts composition assignment at: *www.doe.mass.edu/mcas/student/2001/g8comp.html.*
2. Crammond (1998) strongly argues the connection between persuasive writing and democracy. In Massachusetts this link is similarly obvious. See the 2001 Massachusetts writing assignment cited in note 1, which asks students to "imagine that Massachusetts is considering [a law on bicycle helmets]. Your class has been assigned to write an essay for the state legislature. Your essay will be sent to lawmakers who will then decide whether to draft the new law and put it to a vote. . . . The outcome of the state legislature's vote on [bicycle] helmets could be decided by your essay."
3. Our interest in the application of the risk and relationship framework to students' writing was initially stimulated by the work of our colleague, Colette Daiute (for example, Daiute 1993 and Daiute and Griffin 1993). More recently, Daiute has gone on to develop her own theoretical analysis of "social relational knowing" in the context of writing development (for example, Daiute 2002).
4. We use the children's original spelling, punctuation, grammar, and case in the letters we exhibit in this chapter.
5. See note 1.
6. As mentioned before, Ms. Burgos is completely bilingual, and she sometimes speaks to her students in Spanish to make a point clear to all. But it is important, especially for Anita but also for the other girls, that this discussion takes place in English. Hearing what she has said repeated in English helps Juanita learn the language; translating for her (with Ms. Burgos as backup) helps Flora and Guadalupe refine their skills in both languages. Being fluent in both Spanish and English and in translating between the two languages is both useful in the daily lives of these children and a potentially marketable skill.

Chapter 16

1. I do not want to suggest that this is a new idea. A number of initiatives, including the work of Tom Roderick and Maxine Phillips of the Educa-

tors for Social Responsibility, are working to implement ideas and practices such as this one (see Roderick and Phillips 2001). I have already mentioned the work of the Developmental Studies Center's programs, such as "Character Development and Academic Competence Through Literature" ("Reading, Thinking, and Caring" for grades kindergarten through three, and "Reading for Real" for grades four through eight). The Yale University School Development Program designed by James Comer does not specifically infuse social awareness into the literacy program, but it does put such a strong emphasis on social competence that it has a strong influence on all aspects of the curriculum. See also the work of the Collaborative for Academic Social and Emotional Learning at the University of Illinois, Chicago Circle.

2. *Stellaluna* tells the story of a baby bat that is dropped by her mother into a bird's nest as the mother evades the attack of a night owl. The baby bat becomes fast friends with the birds despite their many "behavioral" differences (food preferences, sleeping patterns, and so forth).

3. The material in this section is a revision of a report that Sarah Shmitt and I prepared for the Carnegie Corporation of New York.

4. The debate within the character education movement is not unlike many debates within the field of education—over vouchers, charter schools, whole language, phonics. Indeed, the parallels are fascinating, including the sense that dichotomization oversimplifies all the complexities of the views within each camp.

5. "Authentic assessment" in the context of assessment of students' skills and knowledge means that students do something other than the traditional norm-referenced or criterion-referenced standardized measurement to demonstrate that they have obtained the requisite knowledge and skills. For a concise look at key aspects of authentic assessment and the strategies necessary for its implementation, see Fischer and King (1995). We are suggesting a way in which teachers could develop their own rubrics for assessment of social and ethical awareness that would give them a sense of the general understanding of their own students, as it relates directly to material they are reading and about which they are writing.

References

Adalbjarnardottir, Sigrun. 1992. "Fostering Children's Social Conflict Resolutions in the Classroom: A Developmental Approach." In *Effective and Responsible Teaching: The New Synthesis,* edited by Fritz Oser, Andreas Dick, and Jean-Luc Patry. San Francisco: Jossey-Bass.

———. 1993. "Promoting Children's Social Growth in the Schools: An Intervention Study." *Journal of Applied Developmental Psychology* 14(4): 461–84.

———. 1994. "Understanding Children and Ourselves: Teachers' Reflections on Social Development in the Classroom." *Teaching and Teacher Education* 10(4): 409–21.

———. 2002. "Adolescent Psychosocial Maturity and Alcohol Use: Quantitative and Qualitative Analyses of Longitudinal Data." *Adolescence* 37(145): 409–21.

Adalbjarnardottir, Sigrun, and A. Eliasdottir. 1992a. *Samvera-Verum vinir* (Being Together—Let's Be Friends). Reykjavík: Namsgagnastofnun.

———. 1992b. *Samvera-Verum saman: Í fríminútum* (Being Together—Let's Play Together: During Recess). Reykjavík: Namsgagnastofnun.

———. 1992c. *Samvera-Vinnum saman* (Being Together—Let's Work Together: Within the Classroom). Reykjavík: Namsgagnastofnun.

———. 1992d. *Samvera-Ræðum saman: Heima* (Being Together—Let's Discuss: At Home). Reykjavík: Namsgagnastofnun.

———. 1992e. *Samvera-Handbók fyrir kennara* (Being Together—Teachers' Guides). Reykjavík: Namsgagnastofnun.

———. 1992f. *Samvera-Ræðum saman: Heima-Handbók fyrir foreldra* (Being Together—Let's Discuss: At Home—Parents' and Teachers' Guides). Reykjavík: Namsgagnastofnun.

Adalbjarnardottir, Sigrun, and Robert L. Selman. 1989. "How Children Propose to Deal with the Criticism Of Their Teachers and Classmates: Developmental and Stylistic Variation." *Child Development* 60(3): 539–50.

———. 1997. "'I Feel I Have Received a New Vision': A Developmental Analysis of Teachers' Professional Awareness of Their Work with Children on Interpersonal Issues." *Teaching and Teacher Education* 13(4): 409–28.

Adalbjarnardottir, Sigrun, and John B. Willett. 1991. "Children's Perspective on Conflicts Between Student and Teacher: Developmental and Situational Variations." Part 3. *British Journal of Developmental Psychology* 9(September): 177–91.

Aitken, J. L., and D. A. Mildon. 1992. "Teacher Education and the Developing Teacher: The Role of Personal Knowledge." In *Teacher Development and Educational Change,* edited by Michael Fullan and Andrew Hargraves. London: Falmer Press.

Allan, J. P., S. T. Hauser, K. L. Bell, and T. G. O'Connor. 1994. "Longitudinal Assessment of Autonomy and Relatedness in Adolescent Ego Development and Self-esteem." *Child Development* 65: 179–94.

Allington, Richard, and Haley Woodside-Jiron. 1999. "The Politics of Literacy Teaching: How 'Research' Shaped Educational Policy." *Educational Researcher* 28: 4–13.

Archambault, R. D., ed. 1964. *John Dewey on Education: Selected Writings.* New York: Modern Library.

Ashton, P. T. 1978. *Stage Theories of Cognitive and Moral Development: Criticisms and Applications.* Reprint 13. Cambridge, Mass.: *Harvard Educational Review.*

Ayoub, Catherine, Pamela Raya, and Kathryn Geismer. 1996. "Pair Play: A Relational Intervention System for Building Friendships in Young Children." *Journal of Child and Youth Care Work* 11: 105–18.

Bartlett, Leo. 1990. "Teacher Development Through Reflective Teaching." In *Second Language Teacher Education,* edited by Jack C. Richards and David Nunan. Cambridge: Cambridge University Press.

Bartolemé, Lilia. 1994. "Beyond the Methods Fetish: Toward a Humanizing Pedagogy." *Harvard Educational Review* 64(2): 173–94.

Battistich, Victor, Marilyn Watson, Daniel Solomon, Eric Schaps, and J. Solomon. 1991. "The Child Development Project: A Comprehensive Program for the Development of Prosocial Character." In *Handbook of Moral Behavior and Development,* vol. 3, *Application,* edited by W. M. Kurtines and J. L. Gewirtz. Hillsdale, N.J.: Lawrence Erlbaum.

Battistich, Victor, Daniel Solomon, Marilyn Watson, and Eric Schaps. 1997. "Caring School Communities." *Educational Psychologist* 32: 137–51.

Beardslee, William R. 2002. *Out of the Darkened Room.* Boston: Little, Brown.

Beardslee, William R., L. H. Schultz, and Robert L. Selman. 1987. "Level of Social Cognitive Development, Adaptive Functioning, and *DSM-III* Diagnoses in Adolescent Offspring of Parents with Affective Disorders: Implications of the Development of the Capacity for Mutuality." *Developmental Psychology* 23(6): 807–15.

Beilin, Harry. 1989. "Piagetian Theory." *Annals of Child Development* 6: 85–132.

Benninga, Jacques, and Edward Wynne. 1998. "Keeping in Character." *Phi Delta Kappan* 78: 439–48.

Berkowitz, Marvin, and J. Grych. 2000. "Early Character Development and Education." *Early Education and Development* 11(1): 55–72.

Berkowitz, M., and F. Oser, eds. 1985. *Moral Education: Theory and Application.* Hillsdale, N.J.: Lawrence Erlbaum.

Berliner, D. C., and B. J. Biddle. 1996. "Standards Amidst Uncertainty and Inequality." *The School Administrator* 53: 42–47.

Bigler, R. S., and L. S. Liben. 1993. "A Cognitive-Developmental Approach to Racial Stereotyping and Reconstructive Memory in Euro-American Children." *Child Development* 64: 1507–18.

Blatt, M. M., and Lawrence Kohlberg. 1975. "The Effects of Classroom Moral

Discussion upon Children's Level of Moral Judgment." *Journal of Moral Education* 4: 129–61.

Bronfenbrenner, Urie, ed. 1996. *The State of Americans: This Generation and the Next.* New York: Free Press.

Brookfield, S. D. 1995. *Becoming a Critically Reflective Teacher.* San Francisco: Jossey-Bass.

Bruner, Jerome. 1996. *The Culture of Education.* Cambridge, Mass.: Harvard University Press.

Bullough, R. V. 1989. "Teacher Education and Teacher Reflectivity." *Journal of Teacher Education* 40: 15–20.

Bunting, Eve, and Ronald Himler. 1994. *A Day's Work.* New York: Clarion Books.

Butt, R., G. McCue, D. Raymond, and L. Yamagishi. 1992. "Collaborative Autobiography and the Teacher's Voice." In *Studying Teachers' Lives,* edited by Ivor F. Goodson. London: Routledge.

Calderhead, James, and Peter Gates. 1993. *Conceptualizing Reflection in Teacher Development.* Philadelphia: Falmer Press.

Cannon, Janell. 1993. *Stellaluna.* New York: Harcourt Brace Jovanovich.

Christensen, L. M., E. K. Wilson, S. K. Anders, M. B. Dennis, L. Kirkland, M. Beacham, and E. P. Warren. 2001. "Teachers' Reflections on Their Practice of Social Studies." *The Social Studies* 92: 205–8.

Coie, J. D., and K. A. Dodge. 1998. "Aggression and Antisocial Behavior." In *Handbook of Child Psychology,* 5th ed. Vol. 3, *Social, Emotional, and Personality Development,* series edited by William Damon, volume edited by Nancy Eisenberg. New York: Wiley.

Colby, Anne. 1978. "The Evolution of a Moral Development Theory." In *Moral Development: New Directions for Child Development,* edited by William Damon. San Francisco: Jossey-Bass.

Colby, Anne, Lawrence Kohlberg, Betsy Spelcher, Alexandra Hewer, Daniel Candee, John Gibbs, and Clark Power. 1987. *The Measurement of Moral Judgment.* New York: Cambridge University Press.

Connelly, F. M., and D. J. Clandinin. 1990. "Stories of Experience and Narrative Inquiry." *Educational Researcher* 19: 2–14.

Crammond, J. G. 1998. "The Uses and Complexity of Argument Structures in Expert and Student Persuasive Writing." *Written Communication* 15(2): 230–68.

Cryns, T., and Marilyn Johnston. 1993. "A Collaborative Case Study of Teacher Change: From a Personal to Professional Perspective." *Teacher and Teacher Education* 9(2): 147–58.

Daiute, Colette. 1993. "Youth Genres and Literacy: Links Between Sociocultural and Developmental Theories." *Language Arts* 70: 402–16.

———. 2002. "Social Relational Knowing in Writing Development." In *Language, Literacy, and Cognitive Development: The Development and Consequences of Symbolic Communication,* edited by Eric Amsel and James P. Byrne. Mahwah, N.J.: Lawrence Erlbaum.

Daiute, Colette, and Terri Griffin. 1993. "The Social Construction of Written Narrative." In *The Development of Literacy Through Social Interaction,* edited by Colette Daiute. San Francisco: Jossey-Bass.

Damon, William. 1998. *Handbook of Child Psychology,* 5th ed. New York: Wiley.

Dodge, K. A., G. S. Pettit, C. L. McClaskey, and M. M. Brown. 1986. "Social Competence in Children." *Monograph of the Society for Research in Child Development* 51(213): 2.

Dryfoos, Joy. 1990. *Adolescents-at-Risk: Prevalence and Prevention*. New York: Oxford University Press.

Edelstein, Wolfgang. 1983. "Cultural Constraints on Development and the Vicissitudes of Progress." In *The Child and Other Cultural Inventions*, edited by F. S. Kessel and A. W. Siegel. New York: Praeger.

Elias, M. J., and S. E. Tobias. 1990. *Problem Solving/Decision Making for Social and Academic Success*. Washington, D.C.: National Education Association.

Finn, C. E. 1990. "The Biggest Reform of All: Defining Education as a Product Rather Than Process." *Phi Delta Kappan* 78: 584–92.

Fischer, C. F., and R. M. King. 1995. *Authentic Assessment: A Guide to Implementation*. Thousand Oaks, Calif.: Corwin Press.

Flavell, John. 1963. *The Developmental Psychology of Jean Piaget*. New York: Van Nostrand Reinhold.

———. 1993. *Cognitive Development*. Englewood Cliffs, N.J.: Prentice-Hall.

Flavell, John, and P. H. Miller. 1998. "Social Cognition." In *Handbook of Child Psychology*, 5th ed. Vol. 2, *Cognition, Perception, and Language*, series edited by W. Damon, volume edited by D. Kuhn and R. Siegler. New York: Wiley.

Frank, L. A. 1992. "Writing to Be Read: Young Writers' Ability to Demonstrate Audience Awareness When Evaluated by Their Readers." *Research in the Teaching of English* 26: 277–98.

Freire, Paolo. 1998. *Teachers as Cultural Workers*. Boulder, Colo.: Westview Press.

Fullan, Michael, and Andrew Hargraves. 1992. "Teacher Development and Educational Change." In *Teacher Development and Educational Change*, edited by Michael Fullan and Andrew Hargraves. London: Falmer Press.

Gee, James. 1991. "What Is Literacy?" In *Rewriting Literacy: Culture and the Discourse of the Other*, edited by Candace Mitchell and Kathleen Weiler. New York: Bergin and Garvey.

Good, T. L., and J. E. Brophy. 1997. *Looking in Classrooms*. New York: Longman.

Goodson, Ivor, ed. 1992. *Studying Teachers' Lives*. London: Routledge.

Goodson, Ivor, and Rob Walker. 1991. *Biography, Identity, and Schooling*. London: Falmer Press.

Gordon, Edmund W., and L. Song. 1994. "Variations in the Experience of Resilience." In *Educational Resilience in Inner-City America: Challenges and Prospects*, edited by Margaret C. Wang and E. Gordon. Hillsdale, N.J.: Lawrence Erlbaum.

Gruber, H. E., and Jacques Voneche, eds. 1995. *The Essential Piaget: An Interpretive Reference and Guide*. Northvale, N.J.: Jason Aronson.

Harcourt Brace Educational Measurement. 1996. "Open-ended Scoring Guide." In *Stanford Achievement Test*, 9th ed. San Antonio, Tex.: Harcourt Brace.

Harris, V. J. 1997. "Children's Literature Depicting Blacks." In *Using Multiethnic Literature in the K–8 Classroom*, edited by V. Harris. Norwood, Mass.: Christopher Gordon.

Haste, Helen. 1993. "Morality, Self, and Sociohistorical Context: The Role of Lay Social Theory." In *The Moral Self*, edited by Gil Noam and Thomas Wren. Cambridge, Mass.: M.I.T. Press.

Hickey, Joseph E., and Peter E. Scharf. 1980. *Toward a Just Correctional System: Experiments in Implementing Democracy in Prisons.* San Francisco: Jossey-Bass.

Hill, Clifford, and Eric Larsen. 2000. *Children and Reading Tests.* Stamford, Conn.: Ablex.

Hirschfeld, Lawrence. 1995. "Do Children Have a Theory of Race?" *Cognition* 54: 209–52.

———. 1996. *Race in the Making.* Cambridge, Mass.: M.I.T. Press.

Hoffman, Mary. 1991. *Amazing Grace.* Illustrated by Caroline Binch. New York: Dial Books for Young Readers.

Hollingsworth, Sandra, Mary Dybdahl, and Leslie T. Minarik. 1993. "By Chart and Chance and Passion: The Importance of Relational Knowing in Learning to Teach." *Curriculum Inquiry* 23(1): 5–35.

Hoyle, Eric, and Peter John. 1995. *Professional Knowledge and Professional Practice.* Vol. 1, *The Idea of a Profession.* London: Cassell.

Huberman, Michael. 1992. "Teacher Development and Instructional Mastery." In *Understanding Teacher Development*, edited by Andrew Hargraves and Michael Fullan. New York: Teachers College Press.

———. 1995. "Professional Careers and Professional Development: Some Intersections." In *Professional Development in Education: New Paradigm and Practice*, edited by Thomas Guskey and Michael Huberman. New York: Teachers College Press.

Hunsaker, Linda, and Marilyn Johnston. 1992. "Teacher Under Construction: A Collaborative Case Study of Teacher Change." *American Educational Research Journal* 29(2): 350–72.

Hunter, J. D. 2000. *The Death of Character: Moral Education in an Age Without Good or Evil.* New York: Basic Books.

Jessor, R., and S. Jessor. 1977. *Problem Behavior and Psychosocial Development: A Longitudinal Study of Youth.* New York: Academic Press.

Johnson, D. W., and R. T. Johnson. 1989. *Cooperation and Competition: Theory and Research.* Edina, Minn.: Interaction Book Co.

———. 1994. "Contrasts and Similarities in Case Studies of Teacher Reflection and Change." *Curriculum Inquiry* 24: 9–26.

———. 1996. "Conflict Resolution and Peer Mediation Programs in Elementary and Secondary Schools: A Review of the Research." *Review of Educational Research* 66(4): 459–506.

———. 1997. *Contradictions in Collaboration: New Thinking on School/University Partnerships.* New York: Teachers College Press.

Johnston, Marilyn. 1989. "Moral Reasoning and Teachers' Understanding of Individualized Instruction." *Journal of Moral Education* 18: 45–59.

———. 1994. "Contrasts and Similarities in Case Studies of Teacher Reflection and Change." *Curriculum Inquiry* 24: 9–26.

———. 1997. *Contradictions in Collaboration: New Thinking on School/University Partnerships.* New York: Teachers College Press.

Juel, C. 2000. "Literacy Problems and Solutions." Lecture on Early Reading

Instruction and Reading Texts, Proseminar on Human Development and Psychology. Cambridge, Mass.: Harvard Graduate School of Education.

Kagan, J. 1998. *Three Seductive Ideas.* Cambridge, Mass.: Harvard University Press.

Kandel, D. B., J. G. Johnson, H. R. Bird, G. Canino, S. H. Goodman, B. B. Lahey, D. A. Regier, and M. Schwab-Stone. 1997. "Psychiatric Disorders Associated with Substance Use among Children and Adolescents: Findings from the Methods for the Epidemiology of Child and Adolescent Mental Disorders (MECA)." *Journal of Abnormal Child Psychology* 25: 121–32.

Kane, Steven, Pamela Raya, and Catherine Ayoub. 1997. "Pair Play Therapy with Toddlers and Preschoolers." In *Fostering Friendship: Pair Therapy for Treatment and Prevention,* edited by Robert L. Selman, Caroline L. Watts, and Lynn H. Schultz. New York: Aldine de Gruyter.

Kantor, K. J., and D. L. Rubin. 1981. "Between Speaking and Writing: Processes of Differentiation." In *Exploring Speaking-Writing Relationships: Connections and Contrasts,* edited by B. M. Kroll and R. J. Vann. Urbana, Ill.: National Council of Teachers of English.

Kelchtermans, Geert. 1993. "Getting the Story, Understanding the Lives: From Career Stories to Teachers' Professional Development." *Teaching and Teacher Education* 9: 443–56.

———. 1994. "Biographical Methods in the Study of Teachers' Knowledge." In *Teachers' Minds and Actions: Research on Teachers' Thinking,* edited by Ingrid Carlgren, Gunnar Handal, and Sveinung Vaage. London: Falmer Press.

Kelchtermans, Geert, and Roland Vandenberghe. 1994. "Teachers' Professional Development: A Biographic Perspective." *Journal of Curriculum Studies* 26: 45–62.

Kohlberg, Lawrence. 1964. "Development of Moral Character and Moral Ideology." In *Review of Child Development Research,* vol. 1, edited by Martin L. Hoffman and Lois W. Hoffman. New York: Russell Sage Foundation.

———. 1966. "Moral Development in the Schools: A Developmental View." *School Review* 74(1): 1–30.

———. 1968. "The Child as a Moral Philosopher." *Psychology Today* 2: 25–30.

———. 1971. "From Is to Ought: How to Commit the Naturalistic Fallacy and Get Away with It in the Study of Moral Development." In *Psychology and Genetic Epistemology,* edited by T. Mischel. New York: Academic Press.

———. 1984. *The Psychology of Moral Development: The Validity of Moral Stages.* San Francisco: Harper & Row.

Kohlberg, Lawrence, and Rochelle Mayer. 1972. "Development as the Aim of Education." *Harvard Educational Review* 42(4): 449–96.

Kohn, Alfie. 1992. *No Contest: The Case Against Competition.* Boston: Houghton Mifflin.

———. 1998a. *What to Look for in a Classroom and Other Essays.* San Francisco: Jossey-Bass.

———. 1998b. "How Not to Teach Values: A Critical Look at Character Education." *Phi Delta Kappan* 78(6): 428–39.

Korthagen, F. A. J. 1993. "The Role of Reflection in Teachers' Professional Development." In *Teacher Professional Development: A Multiple Perspective Ap-*

proach, edited by L. Kremer-Hayon, H. C. Vonk, and R. Fessler. Amsterdam/Lisse: Swets and Zeitlinger B.V.

Kreidler, W. J. 1994. *Teaching Conflict Resolution Through Children's Literature.* New York: Scholastic Professional Books.

Kreidler, W. J., and Educators for Social Responsibility. 1991. *Elementary Perspectives 1: Teaching Concepts of Peace and Conflict Resolution,* 2d ed. Cambridge, Mass.: Educators for Social Responsibility.

Kuhn, Damon, and Robert Siegler, eds. 1998. *Handbook of Child Psychology,* 5th ed. Vol. 2, *Cognition, Perception, and Language,* series edited by William Damon. New York: Wiley.

LaRusso, M. 2001. "From Fighting to Fairness: The Reliability and Validity of an Expanded Measure of Social Development." Qualifying paper, Harvard University Graduate School of Education.

Leithwood, K. A. 1992. "The Principal's Role in Teacher Development." In *Teacher Development and Educational Change,* edited by M. Fullan and A. Hargraves. London: Falmer Press.

Levitt, M. Z., and Robert L. Selman. 1993. "A Manual for the Assessment of Personal Meaning." Unpublished paper, Harvard University, Cambridge, Mass.

———. 1996. "The Personal Meaning of Risky Behavior: A Developmental Perspective on Friendship and Fighting." In *Development and Vulnerability,* edited by K. Fischer and G. Noam. Hillsdale, N.J.: Lawrence Erlbaum.

Levitt, M. Z., Robert L. Selman, and J. B. Richmond. 1991. "The Psychosocial Foundations of Early Adolescents' High Risk Behavior: Implications for Research and Practice." *Journal of Research on Adolescence* 1(4): 349–78.

Lewin, K., R. Lippitt, and R. White. 1939. "Patterns of Aggressive Behavior in Experimentally Created Social Climates." *Journal of Social Psychology* 10: 271–99.

Lewis, C. C. 1995. *Educating Hearts and Minds: Reflections on Japanese Preschool and Elementary Education.* New York: Cambridge University Press.

Lippitt, Robert, and Ralph White. 1952. "An Experimental Study of Leadership and Group Life." In *Readings in Social Psychology,* rev. ed., edited by G. E. Swanson, T. M. Newcomb, and E. L. Hartley. New York: Henry Holt.

Literacy and Values Teacher's Resource: A Day's Work. 1999. Newton, Mass.: Perfection Learning Corporation and Voices of Love and Freedom, Inc.

Literacy and Values Teacher's Resource: Amazing Grace. 1999. Newton, Mass.: Perfection Learning Corporation and Voices of Love and Freedom, Inc.

Literacy and Values Teacher's Resource: Felita. 1999. Newton, Mass.: Perfection Learning Corporation and Voices of Love and Freedom, Inc.

Louden, William. 1991. *Understanding Teaching: Continuity and Change in Teachers' Knowledge.* New York: Teachers College Press.

Maccoby, Eleanor. 1998. *The Two Sexes: Growing up Apart, Coming Together.* Cambridge, Mass.: Belknap Press of Harvard University Press.

MacGinitie, Walter, and Ruth MacGinitie. 1986. "Teaching Students Not to Read." In *Literacy, Society, and Schooling: A Reader,* edited by S. de Castell, A. Luke, and K. Egan. Cambridge: Cambridge University Press.

Magnusson, Magnus, and Hermann Palsson. 1960. *Njal's Saga.* New York: Penguin.

Markus, H. R., and S. Kitayama. 1991. "Culture and the Self: Implications for Cognition, Emotion, and Motivation." *Psychological Review* 98(3): 224–53.

Marzano, Robert, and John Kendall. 1998. *Implementing Standards-Based Education.* Washington, D.C.: National Education Association.

Massachusetts Department of Education. 1997. *English Language Arts Curriculum Framework.* Malden, Mass.: Massachusetts Department of Education.

———. 2000a. *The Massachusetts Comprehensive Assessment System: Release of Spring 1999 Test Items.* Malden, Mass.: Massachusetts Department of Education.

———. 2000b. "Massachusetts Eighth-Grade Language Arts Composition Assignment." Malden, Mass.: Massachusetts Department of Education. Available at: *www.doe.mass.edu/mcas/student/2001/g8comp.html.*

Masten, Ann S. 1994. "Resilience in Individual Development: Successful Adaptation Despite Risk and Adversity." In *Educational Resilience in Inner-City America: Challenges and Prospects,* edited by Margaret Wang and Edmund Gordon. Hillsdale, N.J.: Lawrence Erlbaum.

McGregor, Debbie, and Barry Gunter. 2001. "Changing Pedagogy of Secondary Science Teachers: The Impact of Two-Year Professional Development Program." *Teacher Development* 5(1): 59–74.

Miller, P. J., A. R. Wiley, H. Fung, and C. H. Liang. 1997. "Personal Storytelling as a Medium of Socialization in Chinese and American Families." *Child Development* 68(3): 557–68.

Modgil, Sohan, and C. Modgil, eds. 1986. *Lawrence Kohlberg: Consensus and Controversy.* Philadelphia: Falmer Press.

Mohr, Nicholasa. 1979. *Felita.* New York: Bantam Doubleday Dell.

Molnar, A. 1997. *The Construction of Children's Character.* Chicago: University of Chicago Press.

Nakkula, Michael, and Sharon Ravitch. 1997. *Matters of Interpretation: Reciprocal Transformation in Therapeutic and Developmental Relationships with Youth.* San Francisco: Jossey-Bass.

New Standards Primary Literacy Committee. 1999. *Reading and Writing Grade by Grade: Primary Literacy Standards for Kindergarten Through Third Grade.* Pittsburgh: National Center on Education and the Economy/University of Pittsburgh.

Noam, G., K. Winner, A. Rhein, and B. Molad. 1996. "The Harvard RALLY Program and the Prevention Practitioner: Comprehensive, School-Based Intervention to Support Resiliency in At-Risk Adolescents." *Journal of Child and Youth Care Work* 11: 32–48.

Oakhill, Jane, and Nicola Yuill. 1996. "Higher Order Factors in Comprehension Disability: Processes and Remediation." In *Reading Comprehension Difficulties: Processes and Intervention,* edited by Cesare Cornolid and Jane Oakhill. Hillsdale, N.J.: Lawrence Erlbaum.

Olweus, Dan. 1993. *Bullying at School.* Oxford: Blackwell.

Oser, F. K. 1986. "Moral Education and Values Education: The Discourse Perspective." In *Handbook of Research on Teaching,* 3d ed., edited by M. C. Wittrock. New York: Macmillan.

Oser, F. K., and W. Althof. 1993. "Trust in Advance: On the Professional Morality of Teachers." *Journal of Moral Education* 22(3): 253–75.

Oser, F. K., A. Dick, and J. Patry, eds. 1992. *Effective and Responsible Teaching: The New Synthesis.* San Francisco: Jossey-Bass.

Paterson, Katherine. 1992. *The King's Equal.* New York: HarperCollins Children's Books.

Perry, H. S. 1982. *Psychiatrist of America: The Life of Harry Stack Sullivan.* Cambridge, Mass.: Belknap Press of Harvard University Press.

Piaget, Jean. 1965 [1932]. *The Moral Judgment of the Child.* London: Routledge and Kegan Paul.

———. 1983. "Piaget's Theory." In *Handbook of Child Psychology,* 4th ed. Vol. 1, *History, Theory, and Methods* series edited by P. Mussen, volume edited by W. Kessen. New York: John Wiley.

Powers, F. C., A. Higgins, and Lawrence Kohlberg. 1989. *Lawrence Kohlberg's Approach to Moral Education.* New York: Columbia University Press.

Rand Study Group, C. Snow, chair. 2001. "Reading for Understanding: Towards an R&D Program in Reading Comprehension." Prepared for the Office of Educational Research and Improvement (January). Available at: *www.rand.org/multi/achievementforall* (March 21, 2002).

Ravitch, Diane. 2000. *Left Back: A Century of Failed School Reforms.* New York: Simon & Schuster.

Rest, James. 1979. *Development in Judging Moral Issues.* Minneapolis: University of Minnesota Press.

Richardson, Virginia. 1994. "Conducting Research on Practice." *Educational Researcher* 23: 5–10.

Roderick, T., and M. Phillips. 2001. *The 4Rs: Reading, Writing, Respect, and Resolution.* New York: Educators for Social Responsibility Metropolitan Area.

Roller, C. 1990. "The Interaction of Knowledge and Structure Variables in the Processing of Expository Prose." *Reading Research Quarterly* 25: 79–89.

Rubin, K. H., W. Bukowski, and J. G. Parker. 1998. "Peer Interactions, Relationships, and Groups." In *Handbook of Child Psychology,* 5th ed. Vol. 3, *Social, Emotional, and Personality Development,* series edited by W. Damon, volume edited by N. Eisenberg. New York: Wiley.

Russell, Tom, and Hugh Munby, eds. 1992. *Teachers and Teaching: From Classroom to Reflection.* London: Falmer Press.

Rutter, Michael. 1990. "Psychological Resilience and Protective Mechanisms." In *Risk and Protective Factors in the Development of Psychopathology,* edited by Jon E. Rolf, Ann S. Masten, Dante Cicchetti, Keith H. Nüchterlein, and Sheldon Weintraub. New York: Cambridge University Press.

Sarroub, Loukia, and P. D. Pearson. 1998. "Two Steps Forward, Three Steps Back: The Stormy History of Reading Comprehension Assessment." *Clearing House* 72: 97–105.

Sawyer, R. D. 2001. "Teacher Decisionmaking as a Fulcrum for Teacher Development: Exploring Structures of Growth." *Teacher Development* 5(1): 39–58.

Schaps, E., E. F. Schaeffer, and S. McDonnell. 2001. "What's Right and What's Wrong in Character Education Today." *Education Week* 21(2): 40, 44.

Schaps, E., D. Solomon, and M. Watson. 1986. "A Program That Combines Character Development and Academic Achievement." *Educational Leadership* 43: 32–35.

Schön, D. A. 1987. *Educating the Reflective Practitioner: Toward a New Design for Teaching and Learning in the Professions.* San Francisco: Jossey-Bass.

Schoppa, L. J. 1991. *Education Reform in Japan: A Case of Immobilist Politics.* London: Routledge.

Schrader, Dawn, ed. 1990. *The Legacy of Lawrence Kohlberg.* San Francisco: Jossey-Bass.

Schultz, L. H., D. Barr, and Robert L. Selman. 2001. "The Value of a Developmental Approach to Evaluating Character Education Programs: An Outcome Study of Facing History and Ourselves." *Journal of Moral Education* 30(1): 3–27.

Schultz, L. H., and R. L. Selman. 1989. "Bridging the Gap Between Interpersonal Thought and Action in Early Adolescence: The Role of Psychodynamic Processes." *Development and Psychopathology* 1(2): 133–55.

Schultz, L. H., K. O. Yeates, and R. L. Selman. 1989. "The Interpersonal Negotiation Strategies Interview Manual." Unpublished manuscript, Harvard University, Cambridge, Mass.

Selman, Robert L. 1979. "Assessing Interpersonal Understanding: An Interview and Scoring Manual in Five Parts." Unpublished manuscript, Harvard University, Cambridge, Mass.

———. 1980. *The Growth of Interpersonal Understanding: Developmental and Clinical Analyses.* Orlando, Fla.: Academic Press.

———. 1984. "Interpersonal Negotiations: Toward a Developmental Analysis." In *Social Interaction and Social Understanding,* edited by W. Edelstein and J. Habermas. Frankfurt, Germany: Suhrkamp Verlag.

Selman, Robert L., and Sigrun Adalbjarnardottir. 2000. "A Developmental Method to Analyze the Personal Meaning Adolescents Make of Risk and Relationship: The Case of 'Drinking.'" *Applied Developmental Science* 4(1): 47–65.

Selman, Robert L., W. R. Beardslee, L. H. Schultz, M. Krupa, and D. Podorefsky. 1986. "Assessing Adolescent Interpersonal Negotiation Strategies: Toward the Integration of Structural and Functional Models." *Developmental Psychology* 22(4): 450–59.

Selman, Robert L., and A. Demorest. 1984. "Observing Troubled Children's Interpersonal Negotiation Strategies: Implications of and for a Developmental Model." *Child Development* 55: 288–304.

Selman, Robert L., and M. Lieberman. 1975. "Moral Education in the Primary Grades: An Evaluation of a Developmental Curriculum." *Journal of Educational Psychology* 67(5): 712–16.

Selman, Robert L., M. Schorin, C. Stone, and E. Phelps. 1983. "A Naturalistic Study of Children's Social Understanding." *Developmental Psychology* 19(1): 82–102.

Selman, Robert L., and L. H. Schultz. 1990. *Making a Friend in Youth: Developmental Theory and Pair Therapy.* Chicago: University of Chicago Press.

Selman, Robert L., L. H. Schultz, Michael Nakkula, D. Barr, C. L. Watts, and J. B. Richmond. 1992. "Friendship and Fighting: A Developmental Approach to the Study of Risk and Prevention of Violence." *Development and Psychopathology* 4(4): 529–58.

Selman, Robert L., C. L. Watts, and L. H. Schultz. 1997. *Fostering Friendship: Pair Therapy for Treatment and Prevention.* New York: Aldine de Gruyter.

Selman, Robert L., K. O. Yeates, and L. H. Schultz. 1991. "Interpersonal Thought and Action: A Developmental and Psychopathology Perspective on Research and Prevention." In *Rochester Symposium on Development and Psychopathology,* vol. 3, *Models and Integrations,* edited by D. Cicchetti and S. Toth. Rochester, N.Y.: University of Rochester Press.

Shulman, L. S. 1987. "Knowledge and Teaching: Foundations of the New Reforms." *Harvard Educational Review* 57: 1–22.

Shure, M., and G. Spivak. 1982. "Interpersonal Problem Solving and Prevention in Young Children: A Cognitive Approach to Prevention." *American Journal of Community Psychology* 10: 341–56.

Siegler, Robert. 1998. *Children's Thinking,* 3d ed. Upper Saddle River, N.J.: Prentice-Hall.

Silva, D. Y., and B. G. Gimbert. 2001. "Character Education and Teacher Inquiry: A Promising Partnership for Enhancing Children's Classrooms." *International Journal of Social Education* 16: 18–33.

Sizer, T., and N. Faust Sizer. 1999. *The Students Are Watching: Schools and the Moral Contract.* Boston: Beacon Press.

Slavin, R. E. 1990. *Cooperative Learning: Theory, Research, and Practice.* Englewood Cliffs, N.J.: Prentice-Hall.

Smith, R. A. 1996. "Reflecting on the Ethics and Values of Our Practice." *New Directions for Teaching and Learning* 66: 79–88.

Snow, Catherine, M. Susan Burns, and Peg Griffin. 1998. *Preventing Reading Difficulties in Young Children.* Washington, D.C.: National Academy Press.

Solomon, Daniel, Victor Battistich, Marilyn Watson, Eric Schaps, and Catherine Lewis. 2000. "A Six-District Study of Educational Change: Direct and Mediated Effects of the Child Development Project." *Social Psychology of Education* 4: 3–51.

Solomon, Daniel, Marilyn Watson, and Victor Battistich. 2001. "Teaching and Schooling Effects on Moral/Prosocial Development." In *Handbook of Research on Teaching,* edited by Virginia Richardson. Washington, D.C.: American Educational Research Association.

Spires, H. A., and J. Donley. 1998. "Prior Knowledge Activation: Inducing Engagement with Informational Texts." *Journal of Educational Psychology* 90: 249–60.

Stern, Daniel. 1985. *The Interpersonal World of the Infant: A View from Psychoanalysis and Developmental Psychology.* New York: Basic Books.

Stone, C., and Robert L. Selman. 1982. "Social Negotiation Strategies: Their Development and Use." In *The Development of Social Skills and Peer Relations,* edited by K. Rubin and H. Ross. New York: Springer-Verlag.

Sullivan, H. S. 1953a. *The Interpersonal Theory of Psychiatry.* New York: W. W. Norton.

———. 1953b. *Conceptions of Modern Psychiatry,* with a foreword by the author and a critical appraisal of the theory by Patrick Mullahy. New York: W. W. Norton.

Svobodny, Dolly. 1985. *Early American Textbooks 1775–1900.* Manhasset, N.Y.: Alvina Trust Burrows Institute and the U.S. Department of Education Office of Educational Research and Improvement.

Terasaki, Masao. 1992. "Moral Education in Japanese Schools: Points of Issue and Difficulties." In *Moral Education II,* edited by J. H. Rosenthal. New York: Carnegie Council on Ethics and International Affairs.

Turiel, Elliot. 1983. *The Development of Social Knowledge: Morality and Convention.* New York: Cambridge University Press.

———. 1998. "The Development of Morality." In *Handbook of Child Psychology,* 5th ed. Vol. 3, *Social, Emotional, and Personality Development,* series edited by William Damon, volume edited by N. Eisenberg. New York: Wiley.

Vacca, R., and E. Newton. 1995. "Responding to Literary Texts." In *Thinking and Literacy: The Mind at Work,* edited by Carolyn Hadley, Patricia Antonacci, and Mitchell Rabinowitz. Hillsdale, N.J.: Lawrence Erlbaum.

Van Ausdale, D., and J. R. Feagin. 2001. *The First R: How Children Learn Race and Racism.* Lanham, Md.: Rowman & Littlefield.

Walpole, Sharon. 1999. "Changing Text, Changing Thinking: Comprehension Demands of New Science Textbooks." *The Reading Teacher* 52(4): 358–69.

Watanabe, Y. 2001a. *An Introduction to Voices of Love and Freedom: A Program for the Promotion of Empathy* (in Japanese). Tokyo: Tosyobunka.

———. 2001b. "A New Educational Program for Promoting Empathy." In *The Forefront of Clinical and Developmental Psychology* (in Japanese), edited by K. Sugihara. Tokyo: Kyouikushuppan.

Weissberg, R. P., and M. T. Greenberg. 1998. "School and Community Competence-Enhancement and Prevention Programs." In *Handbook of Child Psychology,* 5th ed. Vol. 4, *Psychology in Practice,* series edited by William Damon, volume edited by I. E. Sigel and K. A. Renninger. New York: Wiley.

Welker, Robert. 1992. *The Teacher as Expert.* Albany: State University of New York Press.

Werner, Emmy. 1990. "Protective Factors and Individual Resilience." In *Handbook of Early Childhood Intervention,* edited by Samuel Meisels and Jack S. Shonkoff. New York: Cambridge University Press.

Werner, Heinz. 1980 [1948]. *The Comparative Psychology of Mental Development.* New York: International Universities Press.

Wolke, Dieter, and Katherine Stanford. 1999. "Bullying in School Children." In *Exploring Developmental Psychology: From Infancy to Adolescence,* edited by David Messer and Stuart Millar. New York: Oxford University Press.

Wollman-Bonilla, Julia. 2001. "Can First-Grade Writers Demonstrate Audience Awareness?" *Reading Research Quarterly* 36: 184–201.

Yeates, K. O., L. H. Schultz, and Robert L. Selman. 1990. "Bridging the Gaps in Child-Clinical Assessment: Toward the Application of Social-Cognitive Developmental Theory." *Clinical Psychology Review* 10(5): 567–88.

———. 1991. "The Development of Interpersonal Negotiation Strategies in Thought and Action: A Social-Cognitive Link to Behavioral Adjustment and Social Status." *Merrill-Palmer Quarterly* 37: 369–405.

Yeates, K. O., and Robert L. Selman. 1989. "Social Competence in the Schools: Toward an Integrative Developmental Model for Intervention." *Developmental Review* 9: 64–100.

Zeichner, K. M. 1994. "Research on Teacher Thinking and Different Views of Reflective Practice in Teaching and Teacher Education." In *Teachers' Minds and Actions: Research on Teachers' Thinking,* edited by G. Carlgren, G. Handal, and S. Vaage. London: Falmer Press.

Zeichner, Kenneth M., and Daniel Liston. 1996. *Culture and Teaching.* Mahwah, N.J.: Lawrence Erlbaum.

Index

Numbers in boldface refer to figures and tables.